The Politics of Nuclear Non-Proliferation

T0418168

This book examines the puzzle of why some states acquire nuclear weapons, whereas others refrain from trying to do so – or even renounce them.

Based on the predominant theoretical thinking in International Relations it is often assumed that nuclear proliferation is inevitable, given the anarchic nature of the international system. Proliferation is thus often explained by vague references to states' insecurity in an anarchic environment. Yet, elusive generalisations and grand, abstract theories inhibit a more profound and detailed knowledge of the very political processes that lead towards nuclearisation or its reversal.

Drawing upon the philosophical and social-theoretical insights of American pragmatism, *The Politics of Nuclear Non-Proliferation* provides a theoretically innovative and practically useful framework for the analysis of states' nuclear proliferation policies. Rather than recounting a parsimonious, lean account of proliferation, the framework allows for the incorporation of multiple paradigms in order to depict the complex political contestation underlying states' proliferation decisions. This pragmatist framework of analysis offers ways of overcoming long-standing metatheoretical gridlocks in the IR discipline and encourages scholars to reorient their efforts towards imminent "real-world" challenges.

This book will be of much interest to students of nuclear proliferation, international security and IR theory.

Ursula Jasper is a Senior Researcher at the Center for Security Studies (CSS), Swiss Institute of Technology (ETH), Zurich. She holds a PhD in Political Science from the University of St Gallen, Switzerland.

CSS Studies in Security and International Relations

Series Editor: Andreas Wenger

Center for Security Studies, Swiss Federal Institute of Technology (ETH), Zurich

The *CSS Studies in Security and International Relations* series examines historical and contemporary aspects of security and conflict. The series provides a forum for new research based upon an expanded conception of security and will include monographs by the Center's research staff and associated academic partners.

War Plans and Alliances in the Cold War
Threat perceptions in the East and West
Edited by Vojtech Mastny, Sven Holtsmark and Andreas Wenger

Transforming NATO in the Cold War
Challenges beyond deterrence in the 1960s
Edited by Andreas Wenger, Christian Nuenlist and Anna Locher

US Foreign Policy and the War on Drugs
Displacing the cocaine and heroin industry
Cornelius Friesendorf

Cyber-Security and Threat Politics
US efforts to secure the Information Age
Myriam Dunn Cavelty

Securing 'the Homeland'
Critical infrastructure, risk and (in)security
Edited by Myriam Dunn Cavelty and Kristian Søby Kristensen

Origins of the European Security System
The Helsinki Process revisited
Edited by Andreas Wenger, Vojtech Mastny and Christian Nuenlist

Russian Energy Power and Foreign Relations
Edited by Jeronim Perovic, Robert W. Orttung and Andreas Wenger

European–American Relations and the Middle East
From Suez to Iraq
Edited by Daniel Möckli and Victor Mauer

EU Foreign Policymaking and the Middle East Conflict
The Europeanization of national foreign policy
Patrick Müller

The Politics of Nuclear Non-Proliferation
A pragmatist framework for analysis
Ursula Jasper

Regional Organisations and Security
Conceptions and practices
Edited by Stephen Aris and Andreas Wenger

The Politics of Nuclear Non-Proliferation

A pragmatist framework for analysis

Ursula Jasper

Routledge
Taylor & Francis Group

LONDON AND NEW YORK

First published 2014
by Routledge
2 Park Square, Milton Park, Abingdon, Oxfordshire OX14 4RN

and by Routledge
711 Third Avenue, New York, NY 10017

First issued in paperback 2015

Routledge is an imprint of the Taylor & Francis Group, an informa business

British Library Cataloguing in Publication Data
A catalogue record for this book is available from the British Library

Library of Congress Cataloging-in-Publication Data
Jasper, Ursula.
 The politics of nuclear non-proliferation : a pragmatist framework for
 analysis / Ursula Jasper.
 pages cm. – (CSS studies in security and international relations)
 Includes bibliographical references and index.
 1. Nuclear nonproliferation. 2. International relations. I. Title.
 JZ5675.J37 2013
 327.1'747–dc23
                                                          2013012178

ISBN13: 978-1-138-93371-2 (pbk)
ISBN13: 978-0-415-82139-1 (hbk)

Typeset in Times
by Wearset Ltd, Boldon, Tyne and Wear

Contents

Acknowledgments

This book would not have been written without the magnificent support and encouragement that I have received along the way.

At the institutional level I am greatly indebted to the Institute of Political Science at the University of St. Gallen; the Belfer Center for Science and International Affairs at Harvard University; and the Center for Security Studies at ETH Zürich. I also gratefully acknowledge the funding that was provided by the Swiss National Science Foundation (SNF). This allowed me to spend ten months as a pre-doctoral researcher at Harvard University and to enjoy this outstanding academic environment.

Moreover, the project has benefited immensely from the scholarly advice, constructive criticism and intellectual insights of the following colleagues: The fabulous "IPW-RWA4-group"; my teachers and co-fellows of the 2009/2010 cohort at Harvard's MTA and ISP program; Andreas Wenger and my colleagues at CSS, in particular Roland Popp and Liviu Horovitz. My supervisors James W. Davis and Heiner Hänggi not only allowed me to pursue my research independently, but also helped me to find my way out of dead-ends and pointless detours by providing useful critique.

I am moreover particularly grateful to Ulrich Roos, Målfrid Braut-Hegghammer, Ralph Weber, Martin Beckstein, Emma Belcher, Kaspar Schiltz, Bernd Bucher and above all Ulrich Franke for critically reading various or even all parts of the manuscript at different stages. Their help was immense; any mistakes that remain are of course my responsibility. Special thanks also go to two anonymous reviewers, Andrew Humphrys and Annabelle Harris of Routledge as well as Lorraine Traynor who have patiently helped me to turn the "PhD beast" into a readable and much improved book manuscript.

Finally, my deepest gratitude goes to my friends and family for all the support, love, encouragement, and companionship. You mean so much more to me than you could possibly know. This book is dedicated to you.

1 Introduction

Why have some states acquired nuclear weapons whereas others have abandoned their nuclear aspirations – although they possess the technical and economic capabilities needed to weaponize?[1] Even today, six decades into the military application of nuclear technology, this question remains one of the central puzzles for the discipline of International Relations (IR). Based on the predominant theoretical thinking which is largely shaped by (neo-)realist conjectures, many IR scholars and policymakers alike tend to assume that nuclear proliferation is inevitable, given the anarchic nature of the international system. Nuclear proliferation is thus traced back to "a fallen humanity's raw quest for power" or is explained by "vague references to security dilemmas and the capacity for evil that lurks within all of us," as Hymans has put it so vividly.[2] However, this reading obscures the fact that there are a large number of nuclear-capable states pitted against a still relatively small number of de-facto nuclear-weapon states. Without lapsing into naive nuclear optimism, it should in fact be acknowledged that of the approximately 50 states that are capable of building nuclear weapons at the beginning of the twenty-first century, fewer than ten currently command a nuclear force. Arguably, this figure still represents a grave danger to international peace and security; yet it also suggests that the picture of nuclear proliferation is more complex and less clear-cut than is often assumed.

At the same time, traditional theoretical approaches to international security fail to offer a convincing explanation for this nebulous picture. While both realist and non-realist scholars alike have successfully interpreted some of the broader trends and generalized developments, their accounts often remain vague and underspecified – or fail to deal with important exceptions in crucial cases. Above all, neither the realist focus on security rationales, nor the non-realist focus on prestige, domestic-bureaucratic pressures and economic imperatives successfully explain why some states not only refrain from nuclear weapons acquisition, but even roll back programs they had previously started. All too often, hazy generalizations and grand, abstract theories inhibit a more profound and detailed knowledge of the very political processes that lead towards nuclearization or nuclear reversal. The absence of pandemic nuclearization or at least widespread proliferation is a puzzle that has hardly been solved by contemporary approaches to IR. Consequently, the aim of this study is to elaborate a theoretically innovative and practically useful framework that eclectically draws on different IR approaches and thereby allows us to deepen and supplement our understanding of the "causes" – motives, reasons, objectives or purposes – behind nuclear restraint.

It is argued that to realize this aim we must not rely on an analysis of external threats that are allegedly givens, or objectively measurable security dynamics or predetermined interests. Instead, we need to open the "black box" of the state and try to understand how – in a deeply political process – narratives and frames regarding its identity, threat perception, preferences or position in the international system emerge and shift.[3] These narratives embody the cognitive-ideational basis for state action. They offer, in other words, a coherent template for the understanding of a certain event and provide orientation for further action in a complex societal situation. Analyzing the dominant frames and narratives thus allows us to comprehend how actors perceive themselves and their environment and how they sketch possible courses of action. Accordingly, the underlying analytical question is which interpretations of the self, of others, of the security environment or of the "value" of nuclear weapons constrain and enable states to pursue or abandon nuclear weapons programs?

Rather than treating the state as a discrete given entity that acts according to a clear set of (externally given) national interests and needs, the study thus pays attention to the multiple ways in which a state's "place in the world" is discursively constructed. It is these very social-psychological representations that shape "who" and "what" states are, how actors perceive their environments and counterparts, and which policies are to be pursued in order to confront a challenging situation. The study is thus based on an understanding of international security that regards neither states' nor individuals' threat perceptions as given, but instead investigates the interpretive processes that both construe these very actors and make certain actions or practices possible in the first place. With respect to nuclear weapons, this implies that the search for "apparent" material or systemic causes of proliferation and nuclear armament is – if only temporarily! – suspended; the analysis of beliefs and narratives gains center stage. We need to investigate the way in which armament decisions are based on a political "story" that gives meaning to actors and objects – be they conventionally treated as either material (the international environment or system) or ideational (a state's identity). After all, intersubjectively shared notions of self and others as well as ideas of the international environment enable and legitimize a state's policies. This study does not, therefore, primarily seek to falsify and supplant existing theoretical explanations of nuclear proliferation and nuclear reversal. Rather, it aspires to supplement the conventional "toolbox" by adding an alternative analytical "instrument" to enable us to better understand *how* political beliefs or narratives emerge and how they constitute policies. To do so, I seek to bridge paradigmatic chasms and to draw upon and synthesize different existing approaches.[4]

The theoretical starting point for this study is a rereading of the rich yet partially buried sociological and social-psychological contributions made by American pragmatists. Their work helps us comprehend the underlying dynamics that bring about the intersubjective establishment of shared meanings and identities. Unlike customary, predominantly cognitive approaches to international politics, which often consider rationally acting individuals to be the unquestioned core of their research, a pragmatist-inspired analysis provides a broader perspective on social phenomena. It transcends the idea that human beings merely act rationally on external stimuli. Rather, pragmatist scholars claim that human action is better understood as a process of continuous interaction between human actors and their environment – and as a permanent practice of interpretation, in which human beings give meaning to the components of their environment. With concrete reference to the proliferation puzzle, a pragmatist notion of political action leads us to assume that a state's proliferation policy does not depend on purportedly given objective threats or on the given conditions of the international system. Rather, from a pragmatist point of view we should depict a state's (non-) proliferation moves as the result of an ongoing process in which the state's identity, its role and position in the environment are discursively established and in which potential courses of action are construed. Consequently, if it is correct to claim that a state's armament policy is enabled by prevailing narratives of the state's interests and preferences, its position in the world, by its attitude toward significant others and by its constructed identity, then we need to excavate these narratives in order to better appreciate a state's policy decision. In other words, the key to understanding why states pursue or abandon nuclear weapons programs lies in understanding the key underlying beliefs that are evident in the national "nuclear discourses."[5] To corroborate this claim, the study focuses on a discourse analysis of two cases of nuclear "non-proliferation" or reversal – Switzerland and Libya.

The study proceeds as follows. In a first step (Chapter 2) the study is situated in relation to the existing body of literature on nuclear proliferation and international security. It is argued that even supposedly non-theoretical, policy-focused studies are based on certain (often covert, implicit) theoretical assumptions that fundamentally shape the research outcome. I then describe how these theoretical assumptions define what is taken for granted in the study of nuclear (non-)proliferation. Over the course of several decades these rules of research have contributed to the consolidation of a realist orthodoxy in security studies that has left little room for alternative approaches. Mainstream presuppositions such as pre-defined interests, objectively identifiable threats or the presumably given anarchical condition of the international system, together with the positivist desire to find causal laws and objectively proven regularities within the social world, have shaped – and narrowed – our thinking about international security issues. Even many research projects that – at first sight – seem to follow a broader research agenda by paying attention to non-materialist aspects such as beliefs, ideas, identity or culture ultimately remain dedicated to a rationalist logic. As a consequence, they lack a sufficiently comprehensive understanding of the intersubjective processes that constitute social action. Moreover, the common adherence to a natural science-inspired model of cause finding sets strict boundaries for possible routes of enquiry and necessarily disregards the broad array of social facts and intersubjective, shared meanings that enable or preclude a specific course of action and that constitute the reality in which further policymaking takes place. It is this gap that needs to be addressed if we are to gain a better and more substantial understanding of states' nuclear policies. At the same time, a "pragmatist turn" enables us to bridge the gap that has emerged between metatheorizing on the one hand and problem-solving on the other. "Pragmatism starts with action,"[6] as Kratochwil reminds us. It explicitly calls for more attention to "real-world" problems and concrete political challenges – but in a theoretically reflexive, conscious way.

A review of the literature indicates that although a pragmatist-interactionist approach is innovative for security studies, it can nevertheless build upon and connect with many ideas and reflections already inherent in contemporary (IR theory) writings. Accordingly, the literature synopsis has two objectives within the overall structure of the study. On the one hand it explores shortcomings in the existing body of literature on nuclear proliferation in order to show that a pragmatist understanding of state action can fill a significant theoretical void and can supplement current approaches in the realm of foreign and security studies. On the other hand, it aims to highlight given links and junctions between some existing works and the suggested pragmatist-inspired approach.

In Chapter 3 I outline the social-theoretical mainstays of a pragmatist-interactionist framework of analysis and its methodological implications. Drawing on the writings of authors such as George H. Mead, Herbert Blumer and Friedrich Kratochwil, I claim that the discursive practices of making sense of and interpreting the world act as the source and starting point for human action: they give both material and non-material objects of our environment an "identity," i.e., a distinctiveness or meaningfulness to which we refer when we construe potential courses of action. A pragmatist understanding of the social world thus replaces the realist notion of a given, fixed reality; it presupposes instead that even core realist concepts such as "threats," "national interests" or "security" need to be understood as socially created. Taking this presupposition seriously allows for an emphasis on the contingency and language dependency of meaning, and brings political agency – the creative, mindful behavior of social/political actors – back into our analysis. Moreover, it helps us to discern how state action – and a state's security and nuclear policies – is shaped by socially shared political, historical and cultural imaginaries and narratives.

In the second part of the chapter the methodological implications that accompany a pragmatist approach are illustrated. The two basic methodological steps on which each case study is based are outlined. The first step consists of a "historiographic reconstruction" of the events; it provides a process-tracing account of the historical undercurrents and of the political circumstances that underlie the specific procurement decision in question. This reconstruction is designed to increase familiarity with the case and to outline the broader socio-political and cultural environment in which the nuclear discourse is embedded. It also helps to discern the discursive realm, i.e., it identifies key participants and their major contributions to the debate. The concrete analysis of the documents – step two of each case study – is based on a discourse analysis of publicly available government publications as well as non-governmental contributions to the debate. Hence, in order to grasp more fully the heterogeneous and multi-linear process of meaning-making, the analysis not only covers documents issued by state representatives or state agencies, but also includes articles, leaflets and other printed material published by societal groups and non-governmental actors. The underlying assumption is that basic policy beliefs and narratives are not merely imposed by one actor but evolve through a socially shared, intersubjective process. With regard to the practical terms of research, the analysis of each case does not start with a given, testable hypothesis but shifts repeatedly between data collection, analysis and concept formation or theory building. As a result, the procedure does not seek to verify or falsify pre-established theories. Its goal is rather the collection and continuous refinement of data that only eventually leads to the generation of new concepts, contingent generalizations and possibly theories of medium range.

Chapters 4 and 5, the empirical core of the study, then put these theoretical and methodological considerations into practice. Chapter 4 contains an analysis of the "rise and fall" of Switzerland's interest in nuclear weapons during the 1950s and 1960s. The analysis reveals that the decision-making process concerning the (non-)acquisition of nuclear weapons took place in a multi-layered and non-linear manner that cannot be reduced to a security rationale. Consequently, it is argued that it was not the emergence (and later disappearance) of an objectively given, concrete external threat or a threat perception which "caused" the Swiss interest in (and later dismissal of) a military nuclear capability. Rather, instead of merely reacting to objectively given exogenous impulses or inputs, the decision to abandon the program followed from a fundamentally political exchange of perceptions and views and an ongoing renegotiation of key narratives and frames. More precisely, the study suggests that during the course of the debate there was a significant shift in the central underlying narratives of the country's self-perception as a neutral state and on its role in the world, as well as the socially shared characterization of nuclear weapons. These narrative shifts ultimately precluded the acquisition of nuclear weapons.

The analysis of the Libyan case which follows in Chapter 5 also calls for increased attention to be paid to underlying narratives and frames. On the grounds of both historiographical reconstruction and discourse analysis it appears misleading to reduce the emergence and abandonment of Libya's nuclear program to security considerations. The study reveals that even fundamental political categories such as "threat," "enemy," "ally" and "security" were not fixed and settled concepts but exhibited oddities, inconsistencies and apertures for the renegotiation of meaning. As a consequence, the security narrative was not powerful and was thus not convincing enough to spur far-reaching, wholesale and sustained efforts to acquire nuclear weapons. An examination of socially prevalent beliefs reveals, on the other hand, that Libya's initial interest in nuclear weapons was spurred by a deeply engrained desire for regional and global status and equality. At the same time, the case is striking for its clear lack of explicit references to the nation state and the absence of a narrative of Libyan statehood or Libyan modernity. The idea of the Libyan nation remains vague and disembodied. Arguably, this lack of a state narrative contributed significantly to the eventual failure of Libya's nuclear ventures: there was no compelling national frame to spur broad-based national efforts and to provide sufficient momentum in order to maintain a fully fledged research program over several decades. In other words, without a convincing and coherent narrative of "what Libya is," all the efforts to establish a Libyan nuclear weapons program eventually suffered from insufficient political momentum.

The final chapter (Conclusion) offers a summary of both the theoretical and empirical parts of this study. In addition, it outlines implications for the further theory development in IR as well as for our practical political dealings with the issue of nuclear (non-)proliferation. In theoretical terms the study has two major implications. First, a pragmatist approach to IR and international security calls for "theoretical modesty" and for the abandonment of large-scale, universal causal theories. We are urged to pay tribute to human agency, reflexivity and historical contingency, rather than parsimony, causality and universality. Consequently, instead of achieving systematic simplification and generalization, our research should attempt a better grasp of the complexities and intricacies of social phenomena. It appears necessary, therefore, to limit our efforts in explanation and theory building to the development of contingent generalizations and middle-range theories, such as are always preliminary and revisable. Second, pragmatism might hold the potential to overcome the long-standing dispute between meta-theoretically inclined IR scholars and advocates of more policy-oriented research. Pragmatists advocate a "multi-perspective" research strategy that suspends unsolvable meta-theoretical contestations and instead calls for cross-paradigmatic dialogue and cooperation in IR. Yet they do so without relinquishing theoretically sound and stringent knowledge production and without promoting theoretical arbitrariness. Rather, pragmatism provides the chance to put on hold meta-theoretical quarrels and concentrate instead on eminent political challenges and "real-world" problems. At the same time, it encourages us to eclectically synthesize different analytic insights in order to develop more comprehensive, multifaceted explanatory accounts.

In practical and empirical (i.e., proliferation-related) terms the study suggests that a pragmatist-inspired framework of analysis can deepen our understanding of the "nuclear trajectories" of both Switzerland and Libya. It directs our attention away from allegedly given motifs and causes and instead elucidates the role of narratives and beliefs in shaping both the origin and termination of each program. This has significant consequences for the further elaboration of global efforts to curb or even roll back nuclear proliferation. Instead of merely reducing the nuclear dynamic to a given security rationale, we need to increase our understanding of the political processes and the domestic nuclear discourses of potential "nuclear weaponizers." If we accept that the nuclear decision-making of states follows from the intersubjectively shared beliefs and narratives regarding the country's identity, its self-perception or its position vis-à-vis significant others, then the international community should increase its efforts to intervene politically in these discursive processes. The case studies illustrate that even fundamental frames and concepts such as "enemy," "ally" and "threat" are not fixed, but alterable and open for renegotiation: they are amenable to political discourse and "de-securitization" moves. In a similar vein, it is conceivable that a global "nuclear weapons convention," while it would most likely not trigger immediate disarmament steps or nuclear reversal by states of concern, could, however, lead to a strengthened anti-nuclear weapons discourse and to an increased opposition to nuclear weapons. In the longer run, a (codified) condemnation of the possession and use of nuclear weapons might contribute to a negative framing of nuclear weapons and in turn reinforce the political obligation to act in accordance with the norm. While such instruments are not likely to trigger the immediate renunciation of the weapons ambitions of certain states of concern, they provide a fruitful side avenue for the strengthening of global non-proliferation efforts.

In sum, this study aims to make three distinct contributions. First, it seeks to broaden our abstract understanding of the "causes" of state action in general and of states' nuclear (non-)proliferation policies in particular. It does so by introducing a pragmatist-interactionist lens of analysis that helps us better understand the intersubjective discursive processes of meaning-making and interpretation which – it is argued – build the basis for ensuing political action. Second, by offering a fresh look at the cases of nuclear reversal in Switzerland and Libya, the study contributes to our concrete knowledge of nuclear proliferation and, above all, reversal. It reveals that an analysis of underlying "nuclear-related" narratives and beliefs provides crucial insights that have hitherto been neglected. Third, the study shows that a pragmatist framework of analysis offers an opportunity to overcome long-standing gridlocks in IR discipline and instead encourages IR scholars to reorient their efforts toward imminent "real-world" challenges.

Notes

1 I will use the terms "to weaponize" and "to nuclearize" interchangeably. Both are meant to describe the process by which a state acquires a nuclear weapons capability. For a detailed discussion of the difficulties in defining concepts such as "nuclearization," "weaponization" or "hedging," see: Gabrielle Hecht, "A Cosmogram for Nuclear Things," *Isis* 98, no. 1 (2007); Jacques E. C. Hymans, "When Does State Become a 'Nuclear Weapons State'? An Exercise in Measurement Validation," in *Forecasting Nuclear Proliferation in the 21st Century*, ed. William C. Potter and Gaukhar Mukhatzhanova (Stanford, CA: Stanford University Press, 2010).

2 *The Psychology of Nuclear Proliferation. Identity, Emotions and Foreign Policy* (Cambridge: Cambridge University Press, 2006), 1.

3 According to Gavin, "a focus on weapons and postures, and not the underlying politics" still dominates contemporary research on the causes and implications of nuclear proliferation – see Francis J. Gavin, "Politics, History and the Ivory Tower–Policy Gap in the Nuclear Proliferation Debate," *Journal of Strategic Studies* 35, no. 4 (2012): 583.

4 Cf. Peter J. Katzenstein and Rudra Sil, "Eclectic Theorizing in the Study and Practice of International Relations," in *The Oxford Handbook of International Relations*, ed. Christian Reus-Smit and Duncan Snidal (Oxford; New York: Oxford University Press, 2008).
5 In this study the term "nuclear discourse" refers to the set of domestic debates that broadly revolves around the nuclear weapons issue in the country under consideration. "Nuclear decision-making" refers to the more specific set of decisions and choices that leads toward the acquisition of nuclear weapons or to the abandonment of a nuclear weapons research program.
6 Friedrich Kratochwil, "Ten points to ponder about pragmatism. Some critical reflections on knowledge generation in the social sciences," in *Pragmatism in International Relations*, ed. Harry Bauer and Elisabetta Brighi (London; New York: Routledge, 2009), 14.

2   Debating (non-)proliferation

In this chapter I will outline how the proposed pragmatist framework relates to the existing literature on nuclear proliferation and how it also fits into the broader realms of IR theory. It should be recalled that this study attempts not only to extend our knowledge of two particular cases of nuclear reversal. It aims equally to bridge the gap between literature in security and strategic studies on the one hand and political theory and IR on the other. It will be shown how an approach that considers the intersubjective negotiation of beliefs and frames to be fundamental to political action, deviates both from the prevalent positivist focus on variables and stark causal mechanisms and from (middleground) constructivist concepts. At the same time, it will become clear that there are many links and points of contact between some existing works and a pragmatist-based approach which allow for theoretical synthesis or complementation.

Positivist orthodoxy

One of the major characteristics of most analyses of nuclear (non-)proliferation is that they proceed from – implicit or explicit – positivist assumptions. Accordingly, most authors maintain that the state system is inhabited by a multitude of like-units ceaselessly competing for survival in a hostile environment that is characterized above all by anarchic uncertainty. In order to maximize their own security, all state actors – while being fearful of the intentions of other states – act rationally according to a clear set of objectively given (national) interests, needs or preferences. Accepting such auxiliary premises helps us to produce highly parsimonious, lean and generalizable accounts. However, achieving parsimony runs the risk of yielding results that may be grand, but are also intangible and ethereal. Bernstein *et al.* even maintain that

> five decades of well-funded efforts to develop theories of international relations have produced precious little in the way of useful, high confidence results. Theories abound, but few meet the most relaxed 'scientific' tests of validity. Even the most robust generalizations or laws we can state – war is

more likely between neighboring states, weaker states are less likely to attack stronger states – are close to trivial, have important exceptions, and for the most part stand outside any consistent body of theory.[1]

Moreover, much of the recent work in security studies and – a fortiori – in studies on nuclear proliferation is based on particular social-theoretical and philosophical provisions which are rarely explicated. This disregard for meta-theoretical questions solidifies a positivist research orthodoxy that complicates the development and emergence of new approaches and findings.[2] "From the beginning of the academic study of international politics," Ken Booth writes, "the concept of security has focused on sovereign states, military power, and the preservation of international order. Security studies therefore derived from a combination of Anglo-American, statist, militarized, masculinized, 'top-down' methodologically positivist and philosophically realist thinking."[3]

Since the end of the Cold War, the field – in line with IR in general – has undergone a major review and reframing of its main assumptions and principal tenets.[4] This has led to a reconceptualization, widening and deepening of the security concept and to the emergence of new – often sociology based – theoretical approaches. Traditional security studies' focus on strategic studies has receded and made room not only for new security referents, but also for new understandings of the – discursive, performative – processes of "security making."[5] However, these disciplinary developments have been received very differently in the American and European academic context. Not only that, but they have also affected the subdisciplines quite differently. In the subfield that addresses issues related to nuclear proliferation, the positivist framework remains the benchmark of most studies.[6] Even research projects that inquire into non-realist and non-materialist aspects of the social world, such as beliefs, ideas, norms, identity or culture, often remain dedicated to a rationalist-positivist logic and to a (rather narrow) ideal of cause-finding and abstract, large-scale theory-building. The downside is that such a research paradigm deprives us of the ability to promote a richer understanding of the intersubjective processes that are constitutive of states' decisions.

For this reason, my contribution seeks to call attention to alternative modes of reasoning and knowledge generation, which complement and enrich existing approaches and which enhance our thinking about the wider "causes" of nuclear proliferation. I argue that we need to open the "black box of the state" and try to examine how its identity, role, culture, threat perception and so on emerge through an intersubjective, linguistically mediated and fundamentally *political process* of "meaning-making." To do so, I suggest that we abandon our search for deterministic "causes" and universal, non-contingent, law-like regularities of (non-)proliferation and instead focus our attention on understanding the inter-subjective, social constitution of meaning, which gives rise to and enables human action in the first place.[7] Rather than adhering to the goal of reductionism and parsimony, the suggested approach cherishes a form of causality that "by advancing causal pluralism and by rejecting the metatheoretical persuasiveness of the causal vs. constitutive theory divide, holds open the possibility for new kinds of integrative and holistic theoretical engagements with world political processes."[8]

Theories of nuclear (non-)proliferation – the state of the art

Subsequent pages are devoted to a review of major studies on the causes of nuclear proliferation and reversal. It seeks to summarize main contributions to the field and to outline the potential for cross-paradigmatic connections.

Systemic pressures and self-help

The debate concerning the causes of nuclear proliferation has traditionally been dominated by the (neo-)realist school of thought.[9] Although they show certain variations, realist accounts of proliferation are generally based on the assumption that states acquire nuclear weapons due to the insecurity inherent in the international system. Hence, proliferation is traced back to external, systemic pressures: under conditions of anarchy and self-help all states are eventually tempted to acquire the "ultimate weapon" in order to guarantee their survival. The quest for nuclear weapons is consequently regarded as a rational and almost mechanically occurring behavior on the part of the main units in the system.[10] Often, this argument is further fortified by reference to a perceived "proliferation automatism" inherent in the technology itself.[11] According to this reading (and drawing on the applied biologistic metaphor of proliferation), technology is considered a socially and culturally neutral and objective achievement.[12] Its further dissemination occurs naturally; hence it is difficult to inhibit. Once a country is scientifically capable of using civilian nuclear technology, it is likely to explore the nuclear weapons option.[13]

"Observe a nuclear weapons decision and then work backwards"

Despite the neatness and parsimony of this theoretical explanation, it is often challenged on several grounds.[14] First, references to "anarchy," "insecurity" or "self-help" remain underspecified and vague, so that realism's persuasive force is difficult to assess. As Sagan has said, "an all too common intellectual strategy in the literature is to observe a nuclear weapons decision and then work backwards, attempting to find the national security threat that 'must' have caused the decision."[15] Second, realist accounts of proliferation face opposition on empirical grounds. If the pursuit of nuclear weapons is indeed the ultimate choice for any state, then we should expect to see an intensive proliferation dynamic. Yet, contrary to frequently voiced prophecies, the number of nuclear armed states has stabilized at a fairly low level over the past few decades. We neither live in "a nuclear-armed crowd";[16] nor are we surrounded by several dozen nuclear states, as John F. Kennedy predicted in 1963.[17] This assessment becomes even weightier if one considers the fact that the number of nuclear-*capable* states has risen enormously over the past decades. Of the approximately 50 states that today have the technological and economic wherewithal to acquire this kind of weapon, fewer than ten have so far done so, as Figure 2.1 underlines.[18] And, perhaps even more astonishingly from a realist point of view: not only have many nuclear-capable countries refrained from building their own nuclear weapons, but several dozen have even reversed nuclear programs that they had initially started.[19]

Ariel E. Levite provides a convincing explanation of why some states decide not to acquire nuclear weapons even though they have the technical and financial capabilities to produce them. Arguing that many cases of nuclear restraint in fact merely mirror a hedging policy that could easily be turned into a comprehensive weapons program, Levite maintains that

> [n]uclear hedging appears to have played a critical role in facilitating nuclear reversal in practically every case under examination.... The appeal of nuclear hedging goes well beyond the nuclear weapons option that it facilitates politically as well as technically. Its greatest appeal is the "latent" or "virtual" deterrence posture it generates toward nuclear weapons aspirants or potential aggressors, and the leverage it provides in reinforcing a state's coercive diplomacy strategy, particularly against the United States.[20]

Nonetheless, the overall figures on non-proliferation and reversal have cast doubt on the explanatory power of realism, and they have forced realists to reconsider and make some adjustments to several of their assumed intervening variables in order to cover these theoretical "anomalies." The more recent realist literature on the causes of proliferation therefore emphasizes the role of alliances,

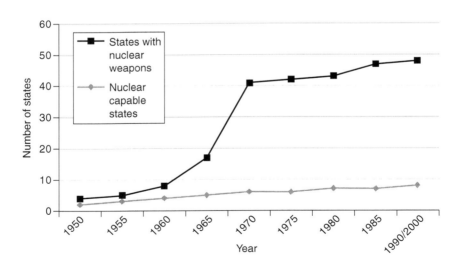

Figure 2.1 Nuclear capabilities and nuclear proliferation.

extended deterrence and security guarantees in shaping states' nuclear traject-ories.[21] It argues moreover that even under the conditions of anarchy states do not proliferate automatically, but carefully weigh their security options as well as the implications of going nuclear.[22] Analytically this is an important move, since it helps to explain why states might decide not to acquire their own nuclear deterrent. What remains problematic, however, is that the argumentation is still often based on somewhat fuzzy references to analytically crucial terms such as threat, security environment or survival.

Security cooperation: institutions and regimes

A neoliberal/neoinstitutionalist reading helps to develop a more comprehensive explanation of non-proliferation and of the circumstances which lead states to refrain from going nuclear. Neoliberal institutionalism's strength lies in its pro-vision of a neat account of why states might come to regard cooperation as pos-sible and why they might consequently decide to abandon the pursuit of their own weapons capability. In following a functionalist logic, neoinstitutionalists argue that institutions can indeed play a significant role in the achievement of security by reducing transaction costs, creating stable expectations and facilit-ating package deals and inter-issue bargaining. Hence, instead of acquiring the "ultimate weapon," states might enter into a security cooperation or security arrangement in order to satisfy their security needs. If institutionalized coopera-tion is expected to be less costly than the independent pursuit of national security measures, states are prepared to join forces.[23] However, as Roger Smith writes,

> regimes are more difficult to establish in the security area than in the eco-nomic realm because of the inherently competitive cast of security concerns, the unforgiving nature of the problems, and the difficulty in determining how much security the state has or needs.[24]

Despite this concern, several authors argue that the NPT "has discouraged the proliferation of nuclear weapons capability" – "albeit imperfectly," as Nye writes.[25]

Domestic and economic politics

Drawing on a classically liberal approach, Solingen, however, questions the neatness of the regime perspective. Referring to her in-depth case studies of pro-liferators and non-proliferators, she concludes that there is only partial corrobo-ration for the argument that the NPT had a significant influence on states' decision-making processes.[26] Instead, she identifies the preferred "survival strategy" of state leaders as the crucial variable for the explanation of prolifera-tion. States that are integrated into the global economy refrain from acquiring nuclear weapons, because they consider the political costs too high. Instead, they "seek refuge" in economic growth and prosperity. Countries which, on the other hand, are opposed to free trade and an open economic system, tend to favor the pursuit of their own nuclear capabilities.

Scholars working in the liberal tradition thus hold that:

> state–society relations – the relationship of states to the domestic and transnational social context in which they are embedded – have a fundamental impact on state behavior in world politics. Societal ideas, interests and institutions influence state behavior by shaping state preferences, that is, the fundamental social purposes underlying the strategic calculations of governments. For liberals, the configuration of state preferences matters most in world politics – not, as realists argue, the configuration of capabilities.[27]

Proliferation can then only be understood if we manage to decipher long-term domestic decision-making processes and fractional interests which shape the often inconsistent and non-linear processes of (military) nuclearization. Rebutting references to technological imperatives or security automatisms, liberal authors focus on the domestic processes that lead to proliferation. Nuclear weapons "do not generate spontaneously from stockpiles of fissile material."[28]

Yet while his argument helps us to sharpen our understanding of domestic decision-making and to gain a better understanding of the non-unitary actorness of states, it has at least two problematic aspects. First, it remains attached to a rational choice framework, which makes it unable to discover the symbolic or non-rational characteristics of nuclear procurement; second, it does not sufficiently delineate how exactly the processes of domestic bargaining take place and how certain factions or interest groups win out over others at a given point in time, i.e., how interests and preferences emerge and how they are established.

Explaining nuclear reversal

Both Jim Walsh and Mitchell B. Reiss address this gap and focus on the domestic processes of proliferation.[29] Starting from the claim that "the most striking feature of the nuclear age is that there are so few nuclear states," Walsh argues that "the dominant theory of nuclear behavior – one based on external threats and technical capability – is unsupported by the facts." Nor, he argues, can nuclear outcomes be attributed to international norms. Instead, the results of his inquiry suggest that the "influence of institutions and the internal politics of decision-making are consistently more important than power, resources, or ideas in explaining nuclear behavior, and in particular, in explaining the puzzle of limited proliferation."[30] Reiss similarly claims that most studies on nuclear proliferation fail to take into account the broader framework of a country's domestic political situation. He directs our attention toward those countries that have not (yet) acquired nuclear weapons, even though they have the technological capacity to do so. In this way he elaborates an approach that takes more account of the processes of domestic bargaining and (foreign) policymaking.[31] More generally, Reiss identifies four sources of nuclear restraint – "international nonproliferation arrangements," "domestic pressures," "bilateral incentives," and a "general consensus against nuclear weapons." He concludes that the domestic struggle among a broad range of diverse interest groups and players in these four domains often prevents a country's pursuit of nuclear weapons.

Constructivist explanations: norms, culture and identity

More recently, several constructivist authors have further examined how the causes and consequences of nuclear politics could be conceptualized. Essentially, there are two types of constructivist (in the broadest sense) accounts. The first deals with the role of norms in constraining the behavior of states; the second focuses on the role of identity and culture in the realm of security politics.

Explaining the non-use of nuclear weapons since the attacks on Hiroshima and Nagasaki in 1945, Nina Tannenwald shows that nuclear non-use can only be understood if we also consider the effect of a global norm of non-deployment. Delegitimizing and stigmatizing nuclear weapons as inhumane and unacceptable, this norm has brought about a universal normative (albeit non-codified) prohibition of nuclear use.[32] Hence, states have not refrained from nuclear warfare for rational cost-benefit reasons such as the fear of unwanted and unbearable retaliation, as realism would suggest, but rather for moral reasons: they came to consider the use of nuclear weapons inappropriate for a civilized state. In other words, the abstention from nuclear warfare is a constitutive criterion for the identity of civilized nations. According to Tannenwald, the taboo has "become part of a broader discourse – a set of practices – of international law and diplomacy of the society of states, which defines what it means to be a 'civilized' member of the international community."[33]

Likewise, Maria Rost Rublee maintains that:

> the international social environment, supported by first an emergent and then a full-fledged nuclear nonproliferation regime, has helped to provide that systemic impetus toward nuclear nonproliferation. The emerging anti-nuclear norm led to the development of the nuclear nonproliferation regime, which set forth a clear injunctive norm against nuclear proliferation; and then as states acceded to the treaty, the expanding regime established a descriptive norm against nuclear proliferation as well. The negotiations to create the regime, and the regime itself, communicated that a nuclear weapons program was a violation of international norms, instead of an act of national pride.[34]

Hymans, on the other hand, links states' proliferation decisions to prevalent national identities held by individuals.[35] He argues that the decision in favor of or against the acquisition of nuclear weapons is neither determined by the constraints of the international system, nor by universal norms, regimes or domestic bureaucratic interests. Instead, the proliferation of nuclear weapons is dependent on "the hearts of state leaders," i.e., their national identity conceptions (NIC).[36]

These conceptions, in Hymans' terms, are "an individual's understanding of the nation's identity – his or her sense of *what the nation naturally stands for* and of *how high it naturally stands*, in comparison to others in the international arena."[37] Without problematizing their intersubjective establishment, Hymans distinguishes four possible identity conceptions: sportsmanlike subaltern, sportsmanlike nationalist, oppositional subaltern, and oppositional nationalist. Each of these identities is linked with particular emotions – either fear or pride. While a nationalist attitude generates pride, an oppositional mindset leads to fear when facing the opponent. In sum, Hymans holds that:

> leaders' choices on the bomb are the result of NIC-driven emotions that shape their information sets, their action tendencies, and indeed their willingness to act at all on the nuclear issue.... Beyond the critical question of going or not going nuclear, the leader's NIC type also proved to be a good predictor of his or her preferences on ancillary nuclear issues – the desire for nuclear technological autonomy; the willingness to join the non-proliferation regime, and the pursuit of a superpower guarantee against potential existential threats.[38]

The contingent process of technology construction

In addition, a range of sociologically inspired works analyze the link between an actor's identity and his proliferation behavior. Eyre and Suchman, for example, argue that (developing) countries acquire certain types of (conventional) weapons in order to mimic what they perceive to be rituals of modern statehood. This means that weapons procurement does not simply follow rationally established strategic needs and unambiguous security considerations, but is instead embedded in a wider vision of statehood, modernity and autonomy:

> [W]eapons spread not because of a match between their technical capabilities and national security needs but because of the highly symbolic, normative nature of militaries and their weaponry. Weapons have proliferated because of the socially constructed meanings that have become associated with them.[39]

Weapons thus come to be regarded as precious and desirable for their inherent politico-symbolic nature, since a state "tends to assert and authenticate its sovereign status with the ultimate symbol of nationhood, a military."[40] Authors like Abraham, MacKenzie and Flank, moreover, emphasize that the very development or acquisition of weapons technologies rarely follows a straightforward, palpable path.[41] Rather, weapons procurement has to be perceived as an incremental, heterogeneous and contingent process, involving a multitude of actors and players and progressing in ways that are anything but linear. Thus, procurement processes deviate significantly from the determinism upheld by rationalist, materialist approaches.[42]

More generally, when thinking about the relation between identity and policy, it is important not to fall prey to a monocausal and rather reductionist and static notion of both identity and culture, but rather to apply a conceptualization that allows us to understand the emergence, constitution and shifting of identities and cultures over time. (National) identities need to be grasped as non-permanent, alterable "artifacts" of political and socio-cultural interactions.[43] Identity is thus not a static social phenomenon but the product *and* constituent of political and cultural *processes*.[44] What needs to be analytically covered, therefore, is the very discursive process under which identities shift and change.[45] A pragmatist-interactionist approach in particular would emphasize that identities are not static, but are time and again reworked, rearticulated and revised.[46] Such an approach embraces "the idea that cultures and identities are emergent and constructed (rather than fixed and natural), contested and polymorphic (rather than unitary and singular), and interactive and process-like (rather than static and essence-like)." It discards the "categorical, essentialist, and unitary understandings of these concepts."[47]

The linguistic turn in security studies

The alternative approach suggested here builds on the recent linguistic turn in security studies. Since the mid-1990s, a number of publications have broadened our understanding of the role of language and discourse in co-generating actors and their identities as well as their interests and foreign and security policies.[48] Two principal assumptions appear key to a language-based approach to foreign and security policy analysis. First, language is not a transparent, referential medium that merely reproduces or represents an already-given, objective outer reality, but rather a "fragile," socially conventionalized system of meaning. Hence it is only through language and the linguistic, intersubjective establishment of meaning that the world is structured. Neither subjects nor objects of knowledge have meaning in themselves – meaning is a contingent result of an ongoing social process of negotiation, a result that is never completely fixed.[49]

Second, interpretive political analysis discards the "cheap talk" argument of mainstream IR, according to which language is nothing but a rhetorical instrument strategically applied in order to influence, convince, persuade or deceive opponents and followers.[50] Interpretivists claim instead that if we want to understand "why" states act the way they do, we need to turn toward approaches that enable us to grasp how the world in which actors act is endowed with meaning in the first place. Hence, interpretive foreign policy analysis is based on the conjecture that discursive representations provide the very basis upon which foreign policies are situated.[51] Discourses, in other words, constitute the issues and actors of foreign policy. They ascribe meaning to the situation, demarcate friends and enemies, construct the national interest, delineate a realm of possible and intelligible policies and actions, and constitute an actor's subjectivity.[52]

Summary and outlook

The foregoing remarks have indicated that traditionally prevalent "rules of doing research" have significantly shaped intellectual endeavors and research outcomes in security studies, and have contributed to realist orthodoxy in the field. Even those research projects that focus on non-realist and non-materialist aspects of the social world, such as beliefs, ideas, identity or culture, are often dedicated to a rationalist logic and disregard intersubjective discursive processes that are constitutive of social action. The review of the large body of literature on the sources of nuclear proliferation has furthermore highlighted the fact that there is rarely a parsimonious, monocausal explanation of why states opt for or against the acquisition of nuclear weapons. Indeed, hardly any case of proliferation or restraint seems to fit easily under the explanatory umbrella provided by one single existing account. Rather, it appears that we need to draw upon different explanatory logics if we want to arrive at a satisfying picture.

Taken together, therefore, it seems that there is both a demand as well as a significant potential for cross-paradigmatic communication and cross-fertilization between different paradigmatic explanations and reasonings. Turning toward the literature of American pragmatism would allow us to build upon and complement existing accounts and to apply an alternative framework to the issue of nuclear proliferation. As will be described in more detail in the following chapter, such a pragmatist framework would help us overcome the methodologically individualist focus and instead enable us to grasp nuclear proliferation as the result of an intersubjective, social process – a process in which certain interpretations of reality become dominant, and eventually prepare the ground for subsequent armaments decisions. It would help us to take into account the fact that "both the 'national interest' and the various derivative practices of statecraft are social constructions that derive their meanings out of the intersubjective and culturally established representations through which foreign policy officials make sense of the world."[53]

At the same time, the eclecticist, pragmatist approach advocated here does not privilege a certain explanatory mechanism or IR paradigm, nor does it aim to merge different theoretical strands into a "super-paradigm." On the contrary, like a mosaic it seeks to bring together different parts without amalgamating the components.[54] It creates space for multiple explanatory strands within one narrative: drawing simultaneously on different IR paradigms, it allows for a combination of explanations. Within the boundaries of a post-positivist research logic it examines the way in which not only a state's identity, role, culture, but also its threat and security perception as well as its interests emerge through an intersubjective, linguistically mediated and fundamentally political process. It is the mundane, everyday phase of politics where preferences, threat perceptions, normative constraints, identities and the like evolve and develop and ultimately provide the ground for states' foreign and security policy.[55] Hence, it lives up to Booth's call to go beyond merely technical and strategic analyses:

Without deepening in the sense of drilling down to uncover the political theory from which security attitudes and behavior derive, security studies remains a largely technical matter, the military/strategic problem-solving dimension of realism ... security studies must go beyond the technical and strategic, and open up fundamental questions about politics.[56]

This has two implications. First, we should refrain from subsuming our "puzzles" under pre-established categories or "favorite variables" (whether norms, threats or preferences) and allow for more complex explanations. Second, we should abandon our positivist search for deterministic "causes" and universal, non-contingent, law-like regularities of (non-)proliferation and instead pay more attention to understanding the intersubjective, social constitution of meaning – even though critics are likely to object that this is too broad an approach to nuclear proliferation and that we should merely focus our attention on the immediate steps leading toward the acquisition (or abandonment) of nuclear weapons. In the next chapter I will show what such an alternative account might look like.

Notes

1 Steven Bernstein *et al.*, "God Gave Physics the Easy Problems: Adapting Social Science to an Unpredictable World," *European Journal of International Relations* 6, no. 1 (2000): 44.
2 Hugh Gusterson, "Missing the End of the Cold War in International Security," in *Cultures of insecurity: states, communities, and the production of danger*, ed. Jutta Weldes, Mark Laffey, and Raymond Duvall (Minneapolis: University of Minnesota Press, 1999), 320–321.
3 Ken Booth, *Theory of world security* (Cambridge: Cambridge University Press, 2007), 28.
4 For an overview of the historical evolution of modern security studies see Stephen Walt, "The Renaissance of Security Studies," *International Studies Quarterly* 35, no. 2 (1991); Joseph S. Nye, Jr. and Sean M. Lynn-Jones, "International Security Studies: A Report of a Conference on the State of the Field," *International Security* 12, no. 4 (1988); For a critical evaluation see Simon Dalby, "Contesting an Essential Concept: Reading the Dilemmas in Contemporary Security Discourse," in *Critical security studies concepts and cases*, ed. Keith Krause and Michael C. Williams (London: Routledge, 1997). Referring to new developments in security studies, Krause and Williams claim moreover:

> A result of this disciplinary turmoil is that reconceptualizing security has often come to resemble a grab bag of different issue areas, lacking a cohesive framework for analyzing the complementary and contradictory themes at work. Simply articulating a broad range of newly emerging threats to human survival or well-being will not in itself move security studies away from its traditional concerns.
> (Keith Krause and Michael C. Williams, "From Strategy to Security: Foundations of Critical Security Studies," in *Critical security studies concepts and cases*, ed. Keith Krause and Michael C. Williams (London: Routledge, 1997), 35)

5 Barry Buzan and Lene Hansen, *The Evolution of International Security Studies* (Cambridge: Cambridge University Press, 2009). For a critique see Steven E. Miller,

"The Hegemonic Illusion? Traditional Strategic Studies in Context," *Security Dialogue* 41, no. 6 (2010).

6 Wæver, for example, complains: "In security studies neorealism actually is hegemonic (in contrast to general IR, where numerous articles are legitimized as critiques of the allegedly hegemonic neorealism, and critiques far out-number the purported hegemon." Ole Wæver, "The Sociology of a Not So International Discipline: American and European Developments in International Relations," *International Organization* 52, no. 4 (1998): 724.

7 This means that human behavior is not strictly and mechanically determined by any objects, rules or norms. Instead, in the course of action the human individual interprets a situation and gives meaning to it. This neither denies the existence of material facts external to human thought, nor does it imply that all post-positivist approaches are inherently "cause-free." On the contrary, social causes ("reasons") provoke agents to act according to a certain set of rules, norms or beliefs – which provide guidance and an inducement for appropriate behavior. Cf. Donald Davidson, "Actions, Reasons, and Causes – Symposium," *Journal of Philosophy* 60, no. 23 (1963); Milja Kurki, "Causes of a Divided Discipline: Rethinking the Concept of Cause in International Relations Theory," *Review of International Studies* 32, no. 2 (2006).

8 "Causes of a Divided Discipline: Rethinking the Concept of Cause in International Relations Theory," 214.

9 Other overviews on the state of the literature: Scott D. Sagan, "The Causes of Nuclear Weapons Proliferation," *Annual Review of Political Science* 14, no. 1 (2011); Jacques E.C. Hymans, "Theories of Nuclear Proliferation," *The Nonproliferation Review* 13, no. 3 (2006); Tanya Ogilvie-White, "Is There a Theory of Nuclear Proliferation? An Analysis of the Contemporary Debate," *The Nonproliferation Review* 4, no. 1 (1996); William C. Potter and Gaukhar Mukhatzhanova, eds, *Forecasting nuclear proliferation in the 21st century. The Role of Theory*, vol. I (Stanford, CA: Stanford University Press, 2010).

10 Kenneth N. Waltz, *The spread of nuclear weapons: more may be better*, Adelphi papers (London: International Institute for Strategic Studies, 1981); "Nuclear Myths and Political Realities," *The American Political Science Review* 84, no. 3 (1990); John J. Mearsheimer, "Back to the Future: Instability in Europe after the Cold War," *International Security* 15, no. 1 (1990); Charles L. Glaser, "The Causes and Consequences of Arms Races," *Annual Review of Political Science* 3 (2000). See also Zanvyl Krieger and Ariel Ilan Roth, "Nuclear Weapons in Neo-Realist Theory," *International Studies Review* 9, no. 3 (2007). For a discussion see Geoffrey L. Herrera, *Technology and International Transformation: The Railroad, the Atom Bomb, and the Politics of Technological Change* (New York: State University of New York Press, 2006), 15–18.

11 Frank Barnaby, *How nuclear weapons spread: nuclear-weapon proliferation in the 1990s* (London: Routledge, 1993).

12 Mutimer argues that the "proliferation metaphor" conceals "the reasons for which states produce, transfer, and acquire arms." The image:

> hides the fact that to be a state in the contemporary world means having certain military assets; moreover to be a leading state means, among other things, having access to a wide range of highly advanced military technologies. Indeed, and ironically, the "proliferation" image tends to hide weapons themselves in its focus on the technological underpinnings of those weapons.
>
> (David Mutimer, *The weapons state: proliferation and the framing of security* (Boulder, CO: Lynne Rienner, 2000), 156)

See also: Hugh Gusterson, "Nuclear weapons and the other in the western imagination," *Cultural Anthropology* 14, no. 1 (1999); Benoît Pelopidas, "The Oracles of Proliferation," *The Nonproliferation Review* 18, no. 1 (2011).

13 Barry R. Schneider, "Nuclear Proliferation and Counter-Proliferation: Policy Issues and Debates," *Mershon International Studies Review* 38, no. 2 (1994); Matthew Fuhrmann, "Spreading Temptation: Proliferation and Peaceful Nuclear Cooperation Agreements," *International Security* 34, no. 1 (2009); Matthew Kroenig, "Exporting the Bomb: Why States Provide Sensitive Nuclear Assistance," *American Political Science Review* 103, no. 1 (2009); "Importing the Bomb: Sensitive Nuclear Assistance and Nuclear Proliferation," *Journal of Conflict Resolution* 53, no. 2 (2009). For a review and critique of some of these new quantitative studies on proliferation see Alexander H. Montgomery and Scott D. Sagan, "The Perils of Predicting Proliferation," *Journal of Conflict Resolution* 53, no. 2 (2009).

14 Scott D. Sagan, "Why Do States Build Nuclear Weapons? Three Models in Search of a Bomb," *International Security* 21, no. 3 (1996).

15 "Why Do States Build Nuclear Weapons? Three Models in Search of a Bomb," 63.

16 Albert J. Wohlstetter, *Moving Toward Life in a Nuclear Armed Crowd? Final Report Prepared for U.S. Arms Control and Disarmament Agency* (Pan Heuristics, 1976).

17 Quoted in Moeed Yusuf, "Predicting Proliferation: The History of the Future of Nuclear Weapons," *Policy Paper* 11(2009).

18 Source: Sagan, "The Causes of Nuclear Weapons Proliferation," C-2. The exact numbers obviously depend on the definitions one applies. For valuable discussions see: "Nuclear Latency and Nuclear Proliferation," in *Forecasting nuclear proliferation in the 21st century*, ed. William C. Potter and Gaukhar Mukhatzhanova (Stanford, CA: Stanford University Press, 2010); Hymans, "When Does State Become a 'Nuclear Weapons State'? An Exercise in Measurement Validation."

19 For an overview see Harald Müller and Andreas Schmidt, "The Little Known Story of Deproliferation. Why States Give Up Nuclear Weapons Activities," in *Forecasting nuclear proliferation in the 21st century*, ed. William C. Potter and Gaukhar Mukhatzhanova (Stanford, CA: Stanford University Press, 2010).

20 Ariel E. Levite, "Never Say Never Again: Nuclear Reversal Revisited," *International Security* 27, no. 3 (2002): 72. In plain conceptual terms, Levite's work furthermore points to another problem. It reminds us of the difficulties in reaching agreement even on the most basic questions – namely: How do we code the "nuclear behavior" of certain states? Is country A exploring a nuclear weapons option? Or is it even pursuing it? Is it "hedging"? Is Japan a typical case of non-weaponization, as Etel Solingen puts it, or rather a typical "nuclear hedger," given its mastery of the complete fuel cycle and its large plutonium stockpile? Not only does this categorization largely depend on the way we define each category, but any clear-cut codification also conceals the fact that many nuclear weapons programs develop in a much more incremental, ambiguous fashion. It appears that the beginning of a nuclear weapon program is often not embodied in a "big decision" taken by the government, but stems from small-scale, tentative, gradual and somewhat stubborn experiments and research projects undertaken by certain arms of the military, the defense community or the scientific community. This problem is then aggravated by the fact that, even within governments, we have multiple players and actors that influence and shape the development or structure of a project. Hence, the crucial point is that "going nuclear" or "moving toward nuclear weapons acquisition" is often not based on one clear discernible step or a leadership's "big decision," but is more often based on the non-linear interplay of several actors. This further complicates any efforts to code and operationalize states' proliferation efforts. Abraham's work underlines these considerations: Itty Abraham, "The Ambivalence of Nuclear Histories," *Osiris* 21, no. 1 (2006).

21 Kenneth N. Waltz, "The Emerging Structure of International Politics," *International Security* 18, no. 2 (1993); Benjamin Frankel, "The Brooding Shadow: Systemic Incentives and Nuclear Weapons Proliferation," *Security Studies* 2, nos 3–4 (1993); John J. Mearsheimer, "Nuclear Weapons and Deterrence in Europe," *International Security* 9, no. 3 (1984). But see also Lawrence Freedman, *The evolution of nuclear*

strategy (Basingstoke: Palgrave Macmillan, 2003), 404–406; Edward Rhodes, "Nuclear Weapons and Credibility: Deterrence Theory Beyond Rationality," *Review of International Studies* 14, no. 1 (1988).

22 T.V. Paul, *Power versus prudence: why nations forgo nuclear weapons* (Montreal: McGill-Queen's University Press, 2000); Zachary S. Davis, "The Realist Nuclear Regime," *Security Studies* 2, nos 3–4 (1993).

23 Harald Müller, "Security Cooperation," in *Handbook of international relations*, ed. Walter Carlsnaes, Thomas Risse-Kappen, and Beth A. Simmons (London; Thousand Oaks, CA: Sage, 2002).

24 Roger K. Smith, "Explaining the Non-Proliferation Regime: Anomalies for Contemporary International Relations Theory," *International Organization* 41, no. 2 (1987): 253. See also Robert Jervis, "Security Regimes," *International Organization* 36, no. 2 (1982).

25 Joseph S. Nye, "Maintaining a Nonproliferation Regime," *International Organization* 35, no. 1 (1981): 36. See also Trevor McMorris Tate, "Regime-Building in the Non-Proliferation System," *Journal of Peace Research* 27, no. 4 (1990). For a critical assessment of the independent influence of institutions see John J. Mearsheimer, "The False Promise of International Institutions," *International Security* 19, no. 3 (1994): 13–14. Realists thus argue that the regime has only been a means applied by the existing nuclear powers to prevent further proliferation – yet it has not changed the member states' genuine interests.

26 Etel Solingen, *Nuclear logics: contrasting paths in East Asia and the Middle East* (Princeton, NJ: Princeton University Press, 2007), 14–15. Hymans arrives at a similar conclusion, since "if the regime were indeed the key to containing proliferation, then proliferation should have been rampant before the regime became a real factor in states' calculations, in the mid-1970s" (Hymans, *Psychology*, 6).

27 Andrew Moravcsik, "Taking Preferences Seriously: A Liberal Theory of International Politics," *International Organization* 51, no. 4 (1997): 513.

28 Stephen M. Meyer, *The dynamics of nuclear proliferation* (Chicago, IL: University of Chicago Press, 1984), 6.

29 Jim Walsh, "Bombs Unbuilt: Power, Ideas and Institutions in International Politics" (dissertation manuscript, Massachusetts Institute of Technology, 2001); Mitchell Reiss, *Without the bomb: the politics of nuclear nonproliferation* (New York: Columbia University Press, 1988); Kurt M. Campbell, Robert J. Einhorn, and Mitchell Reiss, eds, *The nuclear tipping point: why states reconsider their nuclear choices* (Washington, DC: Brookings Institution Press, 2004).

30 Walsh, "Bombs Unbuilt," 1 (ch. 1).

31 He nevertheless holds that the search for a general theory (and strategy) of proliferation and non-proliferation is wrong-headed, since each case was idiosyncratic in nature.

32 Nina Tannenwald, *The nuclear taboo: the United States and the non-use of nuclear weapons since 1945* (Cambridge: Cambridge University Press, 2007).

33 *The nuclear taboo*, 46.

34 Maria Rost Rublee, *Nonproliferation norms. Why states choose nuclear restraint* (Athens: University of Georgia Press, 2009), 202. Arguably, Rost Rublee employs a fairly positivist notion of constructivism which leads her to conceptualize norms and ideas as intervening variables rather than as co-constitutive "forces." For a general distinction of different post-positivist – i.e., "reflectivist," "poststructuralist," "thick constructivist" and "middle-ground constructivists" – explanations, see Walter Carlsnaes, "Foreign Policy," in *Handbook of international relations*, ed. Walter Carlsnaes, Thomas Risse-Kappen, and Beth A. Simmons (London; Thousand Oaks, CA: Sage, 2002).

35 Hymans, *Psychology*. See also Thomas U. Berger, "Norms, Identity, and National Security in Germany and Japan," in *The culture of national security: norms and*

identity in world politics, ed. Peter J. Katzenstein, *New directions in world politics* (New York: Columbia University Press, 1996). Brubaker and Cooper caution, however, that an "operationalization" of identity within an explanation of policymaking needs to avoid an overstretch of the concept itself: "Conceptualizing all affinities and all affiliations, all forms of belonging, all experiences of commonality, connectedness, and cohesion, all self-understandings and self-identifications in the idiom of 'identity' saddles us with a blunt, flat, undifferentiated vocabulary" (Rogers Brubaker and Frederick Cooper, "Beyond 'Identity'," *Theory and Society* 29, no. 1 (2000): 2. For a general discussion of the identity–foreign policy link in poststructuralist IR see also Gearóid Ó Tuathail, "Review Essay: Dissident IR and the Identity Politics Narrative: A Sympathetically Skeptical Perspective," *Political Geography* 15, nos 6–7 (1996).

36 Hymans, *Psychology*, 7.
37 Ibid., 18.
38 Ibid., 206.
39 Dana P. Eyre and Mark C. Suchman, "Status, Norms, and the Proliferation of Conventional Weapons. An Institutional Theory Approach," in *The culture of national security: norms and identity in world politics*, ed. Peter J. Katzenstein (New York: Columbia University Press, 1996), 86.
40 "Status, Norms, and the Proliferation of Conventional Weapons," 113.
41 Steven Flank, "Exploding the Black Box: The Historical Sociology of Nuclear Proliferation," *Security Studies* 3, no. 2 (1993); Donald MacKenzie, "Missile Accuracy: A Case Study in the Social Processes of Technological Change," in *The social construction of technological systems: new directions in the sociology and history of technology*, ed. Wiebe E. Bijker, Thomas Parke Hughes, and T.J. Pinch (Cambridge, MA: MIT Press, 1989); Wiebe Bijker and John Law, "General Introduction," in *Shaping technology, building society: studies in sociotechnical change*, ed. Wiebe E. Bijker and John Law (Cambridge, MA: MIT Press, 1992); Abraham, "The Ambivalence of Nuclear Histories."
42 Both the analysis of the Swiss as well as of the Libyan case strongly supports this view. In neither of the two countries was nuclearization instigated (or ended) by one clearly discernible "big decision"; and neither proceeded in a linear and straightforward fashion.
43 Bruno J. Strasser, "The Coproduction of Neutral Science and Neutral State in Cold War Europe: Switzerland and International Scientific Cooperation, 1951–69," *Osiris* 24, no. 1 (2009): 167.
44 See, for example, the debate about continuity and change in Germany's foreign policy which is depicted in Gunther Hellmann *et al.*, "'Selbstbewusst' und 'stolz'. Das außenpolitische Vokabular der Berliner Republik als Fährte einer Neuorientierung," *Politische Vierteljahresschrift* 48, no. 4 (2007).
45 See, for example: Jeffrey T. Checkel, *Ideas and international political change: Soviet/ Russian behavior and the end of the Cold War* (New Haven, CT: Yale University Press, 1997); Martha Finnemore, *National interests in international society*, Cornell studies in political economy (Ithaca, NY: Cornell University Press, 1996); Tannenwald, *The nuclear taboo*.
46 Hellmann *et al.*, "'Selbstbewusst' und 'stolz'," 653–654.
47 Yosef Lapid, "Culture's Ship: Returns and Departures in International Relations Theory," in *The return of culture and identity in IR theory*, ed. Yosef Lapid and Friedrich Kratochwil (Boulder, CO: Lynne Rienner, 1996); Paul Kowert and Jeffrey Legro, "Norms, Identity, and their Limits: A Theoretical Reprise," in *The culture of national security: norms and identity in world politics*, ed. Peter J. Katzenstein, *New directions in world politics* (New York: Columbia University Press, 1996).
48 Cf. Jim George, *Discourses of global politics. A critical (re)introduction to international relations*, Critical perspectives on world politics (Boulder, CO: Lynne

Rienner, 1994); Roxanne Lynn Doty, "Foreign Policy as Social Construction: A Post-Positivist Analysis of U.S. Counterinsurgency Policy in the Philippines," *International Studies Quarterly* 37, no. 3 (1993); Ole Wæver, "Securitization and Desecuritization," in *On security*, ed. Ronnie D. Lipschutz (New York: Columbia University Press, 1995); David Campbell, *Writing security: United States foreign policy and the politics of identity* (Minneapolis: University of Minnesota Press, 1998); Henrik Larsen, *Foreign policy and discourse analysis: France, Britain, and Europe* (London; New York: Routledge, 1997); Lene Hansen, *Security as practice: discourse analysis and the Bosnian war* (New York: Routledge, 2006); Jutta Weldes *et al.*, eds, *Cultures of insecurity: states, communities, and the production of danger* (Minneapolis: University of Minnesota Press, 1999); Barry Buzan, Ole Wæver, and Jaap De Wilde, *Security: a new framework for analysis* (Boulder, CO: Lynne Rienner, 1998).

49 Ernesto Laclau and Chantal Mouffe, *Hegemony and socialist strategy: towards a radical democratic politics* (London: Verso, 1985), 105.

50 Rodger A. Payne, "Neorealists as Critical Theorists: The Purpose of Foreign Policy Debate," *Perspectives on Politics* 5, no. 3 (2007).

51 Doty, "Foreign Policy as Social Construction: A Post-Positivist Analysis of U.S. Counterinsurgency Policy in the Philippines," 303.

52 Mark Laffey, "Locating Identity: Performativity, Foreign Policy and State Action," *Review of International Studies* 26, no. 3 (2000): 431.

53 Andrew Latham, "Constructing National Security: Culture and Identity in Indian Arms Control and Disarmament Practice," *Contemporary Security Policy* 19, no. 1 (1998): 129.

54 Katzenstein and Sil, "Eclectic Theorizing in the Study and Practice of International Relations," 118–119.

55 For a similar call to grasp the political dimension of proliferation see Jim Walsh, "Learning from Past Success: The NPT and the Future of Non-Proliferation," ed. Weapons of Mass Destruction Commission (Stockholm, 2005).

56 Booth, *Theory of world security*, 157–158. Elsewhere, Booth criticizes the "compartmentalisation" of our thinking about defense and security issues and calls for a comprehensive analysis of nuclear matters: "Nuclearism, Human Rights and Constructions of Security (Part 1)," *The International Journal of Human Rights* 3, no. 2 (1999); "Nuclearism, Human Rights and Constructions of Security (Part 2)," *The International Journal of Human Rights* 3, no. 3 (1999).

3 A pragmatist framework of analysis

In the previous chapter I argued that the mainstream positivist approach in the realm of security studies proceeds from a particular set of rather narrow (and often implicit) metatheoretical assumptions.[1] Given the devotion to an empiricist epistemology, positivist social science entraps itself within the limits of what Taylor calls "brute data identification,"[2] i.e., the search for facts which are purely observable, objectively given and non-interpretable. Due to its adherence to a natural science-inspired model of cause-finding and verification/falsification, it sets strict boundaries for any possible inquiry. Moreover, many ontological fixations and deep-seated metatheoretical stipulations that are inherent in the prevalent paradigms result in a theoretical stand-off, with approaches becoming mutually incommensurable and incapable of dialogue. It seems promising to put these debates on hold and tackle the issue of proliferation from a different – eclecticist – angle rather than to keep arguing endlessly over whether systemic threats *or* hostile identities *or* universal norms *or* economic considerations tipped the scales in favor of or against the acquisition of nuclear weapons. The goal is to elaborate for each case a multiperspectival, pluralist explanation which sheds light on the deeply political negotiation processes underlying states' nuclear trajectories.

Pragmatism as an alternative research agenda

What, then, might a different approach look like and what would we gain from it? Drawing upon the broad and diverse array of literature that is often summed up under the label "American pragmatism" provides a fruitful starting point for new thinking in IR and security studies.[3] However, pragmatism does not function as a "grand theory" that explains all the facets and phenomena of the social world – it is not supposed to be the one "super-theory" that seeks primacy over and replaces all others. Rather, it is a "theoretical toolkit" for doing social research:

> *Theories thus become instruments, not answers to enigmas, in which we can rest.* We don't lie back upon them, we move forward, and, on occasion, make nature over again by their aid. Pragmatism unstiffens all our theories, limbers them up and sets each one at work.
>
> (italics in the original)[4]

Hence, we should regard pragmatism not as a new dogmatic, law-like theory, but rather emphasize its preliminary, contingent and provisional character.[5]

Despite the lack of a strictly canonical body of writings on American pragmatism, there are several metatheoretical and empirical convictions upon which most pragmatist scholars commonly draw and which shape how research is being conducted. In the first step on metatheoretical premises I show that pragmatists put primacy on action, and not on, for example, social order; that they usually question foundational assumptions about knowledge and doubt a linear-accumulative notion of scientific progress; and that they favor contingent observations and preliminary theories over large-scale, transhistorical causal laws. A pragmatist approach to proliferation thus encourages us primarily to seek "orientation" in a given proliferation case rather than establish grand theories and abstract generalizations of generally applicable causes of proliferation.

Metatheoretical assumptions

Pragmatism is a theory of action. At its center is not, as, for example, in Talcott Parsons' or Niklas Luhmann's work, the question of how social order can be explained and maintained, but rather how humans act and how action can be understood. Human practice thus becomes the central concern of pragmatist inquiries.

> Pragmatism is attuned to the "practice turn" in social ontology. From a pragmatist standpoint, there is reason to hope that social practices will be a particularly rewarding object of study.[6]

Pragmatists thereby deviate not only from system theory approaches and their prime focus on social order, but also from the basic premises of Cartesian philosophy (which considers fundamental doubt to be the principal trait of human existence). They urge us to focus our attention on the explanation of action, rather than on static objects or given "matter."[7] At the same time, practice theories deviate from both the norm-based and the utilitarian logic of IR. Rather, they seek to explain

> actions by reconstructing the symbolic structures of knowledge which enable and constrain the agents to interpret the world according to certain forms, and to behave in corresponding ways. Social order, then, does not appear as a product of the compliance of mutual normative expectations, but embedded in collective cognitive and symbolic structures, in a "shared knowledge" which enables a socially-shared way of ascribing meaning to the world.[8]

The pragmatist focus on practices thus encourages us to inquire what makes agents believe that the world is ordered in a particular way and why they have to act the way they do under these circumstances.[9]

Such an inquiry into practices will most likely reveal that most of the time human activity is guided by relatively stable beliefs and a significant degree of "orderliness" which is only interrupted in times of crises (see below).[10] The implications of these considerations are twofold. (1) Of central importance to a pragmatist research endeavor is the focus on how a set of beliefs or narratives limits and facilitates a specific course of action. To put it differently: instead of examining how, for example, a stable social order is produced or maintained, pragmatists would rather ask which set of beliefs underlies and guides an actor's actions. Which beliefs and ideas about the world and of the world's subjects and objects are held by an actor, and how do these beliefs enable or constrain that actor's actions? Which beliefs provide the underlying framework of knowledge that an actor draws upon in order to outline and envision his own course of action? (2) The question of "what is" should recede into the background: something is perceived to be "real" if people act upon it. "If men define situations as real, they are real in their consequences."[11] Hence, if human actors base their actions on the belief that there is an international system, then this justifies our taking this system into account. Instead of continuing an endless quarrel about the ontological qualities of the world, we can "remain agnostic about what society is really made of."[12] Pragmatism thus "liberates us from unnecessary headaches," as we no longer have to run after "delusional projects" on our search for "the thing in itself," but start with an examination of how people act.[13]

A second metatheoretical principle of pragmatism refers to its anti-foundationalist character. As has already been established at the beginning of this chapter, one of the key assumptions of positivist theorizing consists of its firm belief in the existence of a true reality or certainty "out there" that can be grasped by a strict and rigorous application of our scientifically generated concepts. This, however, presupposes the accessibility of an "Archimedean" point of view that is an "objective," disentangled and disinterested standpoint from which a "judge" can decide freely on the rightness and truthfulness of any claim.

> [P]recisely because social facts are not natural but have to be reproduced through the actions of agents, any attempt to treat them like "brute" facts becomes doubly problematic. For one, even "natural" facts are not simply "there," they are interpretations based on our theories. Second, different from the observation of natural facts, in which perceptions address a "thing" through a conceptually mediated form, social reality is entirely "artificial" in the sense that it is dependent on the beliefs and practices of the actors themselves.[14]

If there is no "Archimedean" point from which to review and assess the truthfulness of any claim, then there is equally no way of estimating if one claim is any closer to the truth than another and if human beings are approximating the ideal of perfect knowledge.[15] In other words, we simply lack an objective, transhistorical and transcontextual ground from which to decide about the truth or rightfulness of any (scientific) argument.[16]

This also takes into account that we as scientists are not detached or impartial observers who simply discover "the world out there"; rather, we apply our own socially constructed concepts to make sense of our "impressions." Unlike positivists, who presuppose that we as researchers command a linguistic toolkit which we can apply in order to firmly apprehend and mirror reality, pragmatists maintain that language is not a neutral transmission medium that lets us grasp "reality as it is" and that matches our concepts with some existing phenomena. Scientific findings are therefore theory-laden, even though this does not imply that they are determined by our theoretical assumptions.

> [A]s Wittgenstein's language theory was showing, our concepts do not function as simple matches of the objects "out there," making their "essence" transparent to us. The nature of objects is not simply recorded by a neutral observational language, but is largely constituted by it.[17]

Instead of perceiving scientific progress in a linear fashion like a ladder that ultimately leads ever closer to "the truth," we should therefore conceptualize growing knowledge as a net that becomes ever more densely knotted. This allows us to construe more compelling, comprehensive readings of the phenomenon under scrutiny – that is, to elaborate and acquire – in Rorty's words – a "vocabulary" that enables us to better deal with the challenges we experience. Rejecting a correspondence theory of language, Rorty encourages us to "think of *vocabularies* as tools for coping rather than media for copying."[18] Accordingly, the yardstick is not the pretended approximation of objective truth, but rather the question: "Useful vocabulary or relatively useless vocabulary?"[19]

In a similar vein, stressing the idea of science as a social practice, Kratochwil emphasizes that this understanding of truth by no means amounts to an "anything goes" attitude:

> [P]ragmatism recognizes that science is social practice, which is determined by rules and in which scientists not only are constitutive for the definitions of problems (rather than simply lifting the veil from nature), but they also debate seemingly "undecidable" questions and weigh the evidence.... Instead of applying free-standing epistemological standards, each science provides its own court, judging the appropriateness of its methods and practices.... "[T]ruth" has not been abolished or supplanted by an "anything goes" attitude. Rather, it has become a procedural notion of rule-following according to community practices.[20]

Pragmatists are thus not ignorant with respect to truth; yet they share a belief in the *undecidability* of truth claims. The lack of pre-given, objective criteria for the evaluation of truth claims means that we can evaluate the results of our inquiries only in our practical encounters with the world. In other words, the benchmark for assessing our work should not be some deceptive, abstract idea of "coming closer to the truth." Instead, the community of scientists acts as a court which evaluates whether our findings are plausible and compelling and whether they contribute to a tightening explanatory net.[21]

Ultimately, these metatheoretical considerations lead to the dismissal of rigorous causal inference, of alleged universal and transhistorical laws and of grand theory-building. Instead of elaborating large-scale, comprehensive causal theories, pragmatist research favors the elaboration of preliminary and fairly tentative understandings of the phenomenon under investigation. The elaboration of causal theories "is not the gold standard of scientific success. Given the contingent nature of the social world, the best we can hope for in social science is contingent generalizations," Friedrichs and Kratochwil write. "Orientation in a relevant field is more important than causal theorizing."[22] Pragmatism's emphasizing of contingency thus pays tribute to the language dependency of our observations and of our truth and knowledge claims. It obliges the researcher to reflect upon her own stance, to revise and reformulate her theoretical descriptions of the world and to "invent new vocabularies" where needed.[23]

At the same time, the underlining of contingency also pays tribute to the fundamental openness of social action. Accordingly, social action is principally indeterminate; it always takes place under the possibility of openness and non-decidedness; it is situated within historically specific contexts; and for most of the time an actor can choose from more than one path of further action. Norms, for example, do not determine a particular course of action, but merely provide a more or less compelling background of possibilities of action.[24] A certain course of action is enabled and enacted against a background of several possibilities. This is where the pragmatist appraisal of mindful action comes back into the equation. The very focus on human action and on the potential for creativity in crisis situations allows and leads pragmatists to apply a strong actor-centric, non-determinist focus in their approach to understanding the social world. As a result, this appreciation of creative agency requires the researcher to accentuate contingency and context-dependency.

These concerns delineate pragmatism in metatheoretical terms from concurrent paradigmatic approaches to IR. In the following pages I will show that pragmatism also encourages us to proceed according to particular empirical assumptions, since it points our attention at issues which might otherwise remain unaccounted for.

Empirical assumptions

I will focus on (and address in turn) five empirical aspects which I deem seminal to a pragmatist analysis in IR: the strong process orientation; the role of meaning-making, interpretation and language; intersubjectivity and sociality; recovery of human agency; and a more sophisticated, multi-layered notion of actorness and identity.

Processual evolution and emergence

At the center of any pragmatist-interactionist empirical investigation are the two notions of processual evolution and emergence, since these two notions are intrinsically tied into the pragmatist framework. In an analogy with the natural world, human life and the social world are conceptualized as being non-static, in flux and changing. This does not necessarily imply that change does occur all the time. On the contrary, habits, shared cultural experiences and institutions provide continuity and stability. Nonetheless, pragmatism seeks to realign continuity and change by providing an account of development and adaption. This explains why Dewey explicitly draws on Darwin and the metaphor of evolution to illustrate the social philosophy's idea of fluidity and change:

> The conception that had reigned in the philosophy of nature and knowledge for two thousand years, the conceptions that had become familiar furniture of the mind, rested on the assumption of the superiority of the fixed and final; they rested upon treating change and origin as signs of defect and unreality. In laying hands upon the sacred ark of absolute permanency, in treating the forms that had been regarded as types of fixity and perfection as originating and passing away, the "Origin of Species" introduced a mode of thinking that in the end was bound to transform the logic of knowledge, and hence the treatment of morals, politics, and religion.[25]

Indeed, the evolution image seems valuable for several reasons. Not least, it allows us to understand any human behavior as an adaptation to the actor's environment: an actor does not simply act on the basis of a given substantialist drive, but – just as much or even more so – on the basis of an exchange with his or her surroundings. Further, the social world is regarded as an always dynamic "moving target." This means that neither agents and their qualities nor their deeds can be stripped down to an essentialist, intrinsic core for an explanation of social action. Social life is consequently depicted as an ongoing interactive – and mutually constitutive process – between the environment (be it social or natural) and human agents.[26] This processual, co-constitutive understanding of human actors and their social as well as natural environment provides the basis for a relational understanding of social actors.[27] Likewise, their rules of action emerge, shift and change – i.e., they become adapted – through interaction with the actor's social and non-social environment.

Language and interpretation

This processual understanding of the social world also impacts on the conceptualization of meaning-making and interpretation. Accordingly, we should not consider human beings as autonomous, singular entities that react merely "quasi-compulsorily" to objectively existing subjects of the outer world. Instead, pragmatists and interactionists stress that human action must be understood as an ongoing practice of interpretation, in which the human being gives meaning to the components surrounding him or her: the process of semiosis. Blumer specifies three presumptions which he deems central to this pragmatist idea and to the interpretation–action nexus:

> The first premise is that human beings act toward things on the basis of the meanings that the things have for them. Such things include everything that the human being may note in his world – physical objects, such as trees or chairs; other human beings, such as a mother or a store clerk.... The second premise is that the meaning of such things is derived from, or arises out of, the social interaction that one has with one's fellows. The third premise is that these meanings are handled in, and modified through, an interpretative process used by the person in dealing with the things he encounters.[28]

What Blumer seems to emphasize, furthermore, is that if one focuses solely on how certain psychological "stimuli" or inputs trigger specific behavior, or if one simply traces behavior back to sociological concepts such as "class" or "role," then meaning is not sufficiently problematized. Instead, it is subsumed as given under these very triggers or inputs. From a pragmatist-interactionist perspective, in contrast, meaning evolves from "the process of interaction between people. The meaning of a thing for a person grows out of the ways in which other persons act toward the person with regard to the thing. Their actions operate to define the thing for the person."[29] The establishment of meaning is thus not an individual finding or realization.

In addition, Blumer underscores the processual and, above all, the interpretive mode in which this takes place:

> While the meaning of things is formed in the context of social interaction and is derived by the person from that interaction, it is a mistake to think that the use of the meaning by a person is but an application of the meaning so derived.... [T]he use of the meaning by a person in his action involves an interpretative process.[30]

Hence, meaning is reinterpreted over and over again. This conceptualization allows symbolic interactionism to explicitly highlight two facets: first, meaning is never permanent and settled but is always open to change – it needs to be socially defined and "consolidated"[31]; second, human action, too, is always processual and in flux, since actors adapt to their revised interpretations.[32] States therefore do not simply and permanently act out a distinct, given role, but rather reinterpret their environment, their relations vis-à-vis significant others as well as their self-conception, and adapt their course of action accordingly.

Consequently, this pragmatist take on the role of language and meaning differs from the more standard conceptualizations of communication in IR, political psychology or foreign policy analysis, which conceptualize linguistic representations merely as neutral, analogous and static pictures of the objects that inhabit "the world out there." They thereby disregard the ongoing processes during which actors actually (intersubjectively) negotiate and define meanings (of other actors, objects, events, norms and so forth).

Intersubjectivity

Moreover, pragmatism emphasizes that the definition or attribution of meaning does not happen solipsistically or merely as an outcome of particular psychical or neurological processes within an individual's brain. On the contrary, it is the result of an "intersubjective," social process. This assumption highlights the key role that society plays in pragmatism. Unlike methodologically individualist accounts that ultimately reduce the analysis of social phenomena to the traits, deeds and cost–benefit considerations of individuals, pragmatism holds that

> the whole (society) is prior to the part (the individual), not the part to the whole; and the part is explained in terms of the whole, not the whole in terms of the part or parts. The social act is not explained by building it up out of stimulus plus response; it must be taken as a dynamic whole – as something going on – no part of which can be considered or understood by itself.[33]

Action is thus not the simple outcome of individualist choices couched in a solipsist understanding of the world, or the result of purely individual cognitive-psychological decision-making processes. Instead, the individual, and with it any social action, is densely and co-constitutively tied into the sociality that surrounds the actor. On the basis of a constant, ongoing interplay between human actors and their social and natural environments, actors become capable of "making sense" of the world and (as we will see below) of themselves. At the same time, their own suggested lines of interpretation, meaning-making and action reflect back on their counterparts:

> [S]ocial interaction is a process that forms human conduct instead of being merely a means or a setting for the expression or release of human conduct. Put simply, human beings in interacting with one another have to take account of what each other is doing or is about to do.... One has to fit one's own line of activity in some manner to the actions of others.[34]

Intersubjectivity, then, represents a pattern of communicative action between social actors that is not only constantly shaping and delineating objects and their meanings, as well as possible courses of action, but which also represents the ongoing co-constitution of the actors (i.e., of their their subjectivities and identities) themselves. This in turn urges us to pay closer attention to the very political processes during which these "negotiations" take place.

Recovering human agency

Furthermore, by rejecting a deterministic outlook on action and interaction, pragmatism helps us to gain a more comprehensive understanding of "human agency," as it frees the actor from a plain stimulus-response behavior and instead endows him with a capacity and potential for innovation, creativity and non-routine, "deviant" actions.[35] In other words, the individual does not merely react to a given stimulus, but first selects, negotiates and interprets it before acting upon it:

> The influence that stimuli have upon human behaviour is shaped by the context of symbolic meanings within which human behaviour occurs. These meanings emerge from the shared interaction of individuals in human society.... Human behaviour is not a unilinear unfolding toward a predetermined end, but an active constructing process whereby humans endeavor to "make sense" of their social and physical environments.[36]

Hence, a stimulus (whether a norm, a rule, a threat or anything else) does not determine a (re-)action, but needs to be interpreted by the actor in the light of his or her ongoing activity. Likewise, human action does not take place on the basis of pre-established needs. This consequently leads to an activist, voluntaristic notion of the human actor and opens up a much broader conceptualization of agency and actorness than we see in behaviorist accounts of human action, for example.[37]

However, it has to be emphasized that, from a pragmatist perspective, action does not always occur in an unstructured, problematic and emergent way. The actor does not have to permanently select and interpret stimuli and constantly delineate new courses of action. Rather, most action occurs in the form of ritualized habits:

> Habits thrive where occasions for reflection are few, where normative challenges are unlikely to be made, and where competing discourses and voices from the margins or liminars are most likely absent. Time pressures that preclude conscious deliberation that might override habits are favorable sites for the logic of habit to operate. In terms of world politics, we should suspect the logic of habit to be at work where we see any durable relationships of enmity and amity between and among states, or any patterns of enduring practices between and among them.[38]

Action, then, takes place largely on the basis of internalized rules or behavioral patterns. Culture and traditions, for example, provide stable webs of meaning that actors can draw upon in their day-to-day routines and dealings.[39] Only if these habits and routines are disrupted by doubt – i.e., crisis situations and challenges – does the actor have to re-evaluate and redefine the situation in order to develop new beliefs and rules of action.[40]

For our analysis and for the study of International Relations in general, the pragmatist notion of habit and routine entails two important aspects: on the one hand, there is arguably a certain degree of stability and customary pattern to states' behavior – not every activity has to be developed "de novo" or takes place in an utterly fluid environment. On the other hand, situations that are problematic or critical provide space for "creativity" and new, voluntary courses of action. The role of agency is thus recovered and strengthened: action is conceptualized as more than a simple "re-action" toward external stimuli or predetermined needs. Pragmatism thereby provides a compelling theorization of both continuity and change.[41]

In addition, it differs from the narrow notion of action and interaction that is dominant in foreign policy analysis. While most analyses of states' foreign policy do attest to the significant, influential and consequential impact that one actor has on another, this impact or impulse is conceptualized as occurring in an automatic, "quasi-compulsive" way.[42] The underlying idea of agency is rather weak and "behaviorist," conceptualizing action in accordance with a "stimulus-response model." It presupposes that signals sent by unit A have only to be perceived (and are from time to time misperceived) by unit B in order to initiate new (re)actions (or what game theorists would call a new "set of moves"). Moreover, along with this understanding of interaction as impact and effect comes a tendency to consider action in discrete micro-pieces.[43] From a pragmatist point of view, on the other hand, actor A's decision/action cannot be cut off and analyzed independently of a larger and broader process of deliberation and political action. The decision to go nuclear, for example, cannot simply be disentangled from a state's historical experiences of vulnerability and fear or domination and humiliation.

Identity as a multi-layered process

Finally, the central characteristics of a pragmatist social theory lead to and are supplemented by more complex, multi-layered notions of actorness, self and identity. An actor's identity is assumed not to be fixed, but processually constructed. As we have already seen, this anti-essentialist assumption is very much in line with the broader pragmatist understanding of the intersubjective negotiation of meaning: both an object's meaning as well as "a person's meaning" (i.e., an actor's identity) emerge on the basis of social practice.

This conceptualization has several implications. First of all, an actor's identity is apprehended as a social object and hence not only as the result of but also a stimulus for a societal, intersubjective process. An actor's identity is not only stimulated through interaction with other actors, but also functions as a stimulus for other social objects – a process that also reflects back on the actor, as Mead shows. First, this provides the cornerstone for a notion of (self-) reflexivity: actors are not always driven by external stimuli or by their own role conception, but can reflect (and eventually act) both upon others as well as on their own self-understanding. Hence, the web of social relations in which an actor is embedded provides the basis for the emergence of a conception of the self.[44] Second, if we conceptualize identity (as well as meaning-making) as an intersubjective process between several actors, then this calls into question any methodologically individualist notion of the self and of social actors in general. Instead, individual and collective identities have to be considered as dialectically and above all co-constitutively interwoven:

> Ego's ideas about Alter, right or wrong, are not merely passive perceptions of something that exists independent of Ego, but actively and on-goingly constitutive of Alter's role vis-à-vis Ego.[45]

This implies that identity is not static, predetermined or essentially given, but open to change. Rather than a stable structure it is a process that has to be constantly reworked and regenerated.[46] It has to be "achieved" in interplay with and under consideration of other actors.[47] An interactionist framework of analysis thus calls for a relational understanding of the dynamic interplay between actors and their social and material environment, instead of conceptualizing identity as merely another fixed causal variable.[48]

In sum, a pragmatist framework of analysis replaces the realist notion of a given, fixed reality, and presupposes instead that threats, identities, actions or interests are understood as socially constructed and created in fundamentally political processes of deliberation and negotiation. In this way, the approach allows an emphasis on the contingency and language dependency of meaning, and brings political agency – that is, the creative, mindful behavior of social/political actors – back into our analysis of politics in general and nuclear proliferation in particular. It concurs with Walsh's demand that an understanding of states' proliferation decision requires a better understanding of preceding political processes "which have consistently been ignored":

> A political model does not imply that security threats or capability or alliances are irrelevant or unimportant. Instead, it suggests that these factors are mediated by politics and the policy process – that self-interested individuals and organizations understand, react to, and attempt to use context and events to their own advantage based on pre-existing attitudes about the desirability or legitimacy of these weapons.[49]

Moreover, the approach helps us to discern how states' security and nuclear policies are shaped by intersubjectively established rules of action, i.e., by political, historical and cultural imaginaries and narratives. Obviously, an analysis of these narratives will not shed light on the concrete and meticulous day-to-day steps of nuclear decision-making; but it will provide us with a better understanding of how socially shared public narratives provide the ground for nuclear decision-making.

A pragmatist-interactionist methodology

If we agree that a pragmatist-inspired analysis of states' nuclear decision-making grants valuable insights, we need to establish *where* this communicative and intersubjective exchange regarding the question of nuclear proliferation takes place. We also need to establish *how* it happens. Roos, for example, writes that the rules of action prevalent in the foreign (and security) policy realm do not emerge *ex nihilo* or by themselves. Rather, they evolve through a permanent, intersubjective discussion process in which a diverse set of actors – from leading figures of the executive to clerks in the ministry – take part. The rules underlying foreign policymaking are thus not the product of solitary decision-makers' solipsistic reasoning, but instead are anchored in socially shared and negotiated interpretations of a state's political and security environment.[50]

Interpreting public nuclear discourses

This is the reason why the publicly available documents – for example, those issued by states in order to announce or justify a certain decision and/or action, or the ones issued by opposition parties – become critical: they embody the political process and enable us to grasp how a common meaning is reached and how this ultimately makes a particular policy decision intelligible and justified. Moreover, if we take into account the discursive hegemony that governments maintain, especially in the field of foreign and security policy (because of their authoritative position and their perceived advantage in access to information, etc.), these public documents are even more important for any analysis of security discourses. Official statements shape and direct the structures and boundaries of political discourses and of broader societal debates; at the same time they arouse opposition and dissent.

However, in order to grasp more fully the heterogeneous process of meaning-making, the analysis should not be restricted to government documents. It should also include – if available – documents issued by powerful societal groups and actors, as well as influential media contributions, and it should study the structures of signification which these "inject" into the debate. These non-official, societal sources such as newspaper articles or statements by influential pressure groups and even pop-cultural representations also contribute to and shape the larger discourse by making particular modes of thinking and acting intelligible.[51] A broader analytical approach of this kind will not only help to situate public documents within a wider, "intertextual" discursive web, but will also bring about a more profound comprehension of how certain readings gain hold or are challenged (for example, by non-government actors), how they are changed and ultimately perhaps even repudiated.[52] Obviously, this procedure requires an intimate reading and interpretation of each source. Moreover, the results will be more elaborate and profound if the analyst can rely on primary sources in their original language. Even an exact translation might lead to a reduction of linguistic complexity and therefore distort or "abrade" some of the more subtle meanings. Surely, some of the original conscious or unconscious meaning of language is lost. The reader should bear this in mind when reading the case study on Libya, since the interpretation is mostly based on documents that were translated from Arabic into English.

At the same time, the study is deliberately not based on interviews. While an interview-based research design, too, grants valuable insights, the research focus would be different.[53] For the reasons outlined in previous chapters, this study is less interested in the specific and subtle processes of decision-making and in the views and beliefs of individuals, whether individual decision-makers, involved politicians or enlisted scientists. Rather, it seeks to uncover the underlying socially shared narratives and beliefs that led to (and were possibly influenced by) the evolution and later dissolution of the nuclear program – i.e., the broader *politics of proliferation*. It focuses therefore on a reconstruction of the political contestation, rather than on an analysis of individuals' (decision-makers, scientists, etc.) positions and decisions.

Meaning-making vs. "cheap talk"

The objection that the chosen procedure is likely to encounter, is, of course, that public documents in particular are "nothing but rhetoric" and that governments more often than not ignore even their own declarations once these have been issued, ultimately acting in accordance with various material needs rather than with discursively established beliefs. This objection cannot very well be sustained from a philosophy of language angle, however. From this perspective, one has to argue that all kinds of public declarations do have an impact – even lying and deception (which are in any case fairly ordinary features of language use and communication[54]). Cortell and Davis as well as Risse and Sikkink have argued, for example, that even those normative statements which were originally intended to be purely instrumental eventually "become part of the society's legitimating discourse, establish intersubjective understandings and expectations at both the domestic and international levels, and constrain policy options. The original embrace of an international norm may be purely instrumental, indeed cynical, yet still lead to salience."[55] Therefore, even if we tend to consider a certain statement a "lie" or "cheap talk," this does not imply that the statement or its analysis is in itself useless. No matter whether a statement is true, or "sincere" as Austin and Searle call it, it produces intelligibility of the phenomena it describes – it makes thoughts and social practices thinkable and at the same time discredits others; it lends authority to a certain set of speakers (whether governmental, academic or other) deemed to be in a position to make meaningful and "authoritative" assertions; it justifies political policies; and it creates a "reality."[56]

This holds true regardless of the political system or regime type of the government in question: every government – whether an authoritarian dictatorship, a military junta or a democratic polyarchy – has to gain support and legitimization for its policies. The objection that non-democratic regimes merely rule by the use (or threat of use) of force and thus do not need consent is untenable. On the contrary. Even "coercion requires arguments that are persuasive enough to convince those who will operate the mechanisms of coercion that coercion is necessary and that they must participate," as Crawford argues.[57] This implies that we can find examples of argumentative contestation in all political contexts – even in non-democratic ones – albeit with different audiences and for different purposes. While in (ideal-type) democracies the argumentative exchange serves the goal of facilitating public deliberation and eventually majority decision-making, in authoritarian regimes the process more resembles a form of "autocommunication." Instead of facilitating genuine deliberation and persuasion among the constituents, discursive practices in authoritarian regimes are primarily aimed at bolstering the existing order or disciplining the public. Even authoritarian regimes "require people to participate in the 'ritual of conformity'."[58] Thus, for autocommunication to work its effects, the audience does not have to be the general public or the eligible masses; the audience can be merely the power elite, members of the ruling party or a small circle of regime officials.

Between "operational codes," "syntagms" and "beliefs"

These qualifications notwithstanding, both the quest for legitimization and the submission to authority are essential attributes of all political entities – and both are inextricably linked to discursive processes of argumentation and justification. The aim of this analysis, therefore, is to uncover certain patterns or regularities within these discursive processes of argumentation and justification in the case of Switzerland and Libya respectively. What are the rules of action that provide the ideational ground for ensuing political decisions? How is the acquisition or non-acquisition of nuclear weapons justified in those two countries? What are the arguments in favor of or against the particular policy initiative? And how does the debate relate to broader narratives of identity, security and role perception? As Chilton writes:

> In all the texts that surround the nuclear phenomena are there systematic regularities? And if so, how do we describe and explain them?... One method, by which governments legitimate themselves and their policies is to create, through language and also through other semiotic means, a compatibility between policies and relatively stable stereotypes and narrative syntagms already present (probably with an existing ideological function) in traditional and popular culture.[59]

These narrative syntagms or structures of interpretation contain the rules of action that help us understand why actors follow a particular political path.[60] They are socially construed, historically situated, stable "interpretation devices" that emerge when actors have to make sense of a complex condition and to structure a certain course of action. Hence, they differ from more methodologically individualist, ephemeral concepts such as attitude, opinion, idea or interest.[61]

At the same time, this study does not try to understand foreign policy decisions "from the standpoint of the decision-makers by reconstructing their reasons" – unlike, for example, the operational code or frame literature.[62] Instead, it goes beyond cognitive-individualist approaches, "breaks apart the monolithic view of nation-states as unitary actors"[63] and examines socially shared narratives underlying governments' decision-making. Hence, this discourse-based approach should be:

> distinguished from cognitive approaches, which analyze what people perceive and think. If cognitive approaches sometimes use public texts, these serve as indicators for perceptions, thoughts, and beliefs, raising all kinds of problems regarding the validity of discourse as a source of knowledge about people's minds. Discourse analysis focuses attention on discourse as interesting in itself. It is not an indicator for something else and thus questions about whether "they really mean what they say" are irrelevant. A discourse analysis tries to find the structures and patterns in public statements that regulate political debate so that certain things can be said while other things will be meaningless or less powerful or reasonable.[64]

The focus of our analysis is therefore on narratives and intersubjectively shared interpretations, since these make certain events intelligible and offer actors orientation regarding further action in a historically complex, societal situation.[65]

The central task for the case studies then becomes to identify these interpretational structures with particular relevance to the issue of nuclear acquisition and to ask: Which interpretations of the self, of others, of the security environment or of the "value" of nuclear weapons were prevalent and how did they induce state actors to pursue or abandon nuclear weapons programs? In order to avoid the flaws that Sagan points out – namely that we simply observe a nuclear weapons decision and then work backwards, attempting to find the national security threat that "must" have caused the decision – it is important to enable an open analysis of the texts.[66] Therefore, we should not merely look for references to – existential – security threats that may have caused the decision, but instead attempt to gain a broader understanding of the self-conception, the ideological currents and worldviews on which the government's decision-making is based.

Research design: historiographic reconstruction and Grounded Theory

How can we infer the way in which people "see the world," if meanings cannot be observed directly but only through the interpretation of their artifactual representations, i.e., through discursive protocols?[67] The chosen research design of this study basically consists of two steps that are applied to each case. The first step encompasses a "thick description"[68] or "historiographic reconstruction" of the case: it provides a thorough account – or what George and Bennett call "process-tracing"[69] – of the historical undercurrents and circumstances that shape the specific procurement decision in question. It thereby aims to "make sense" of the broader socio-political and cultural environment in which the decisions take place. In addition, and more specifically, the historiographical description of the case grants the necessary insights regarding central actors, discursive nodal points and the historical sequel of the debate. We can then identify which publications and contributions are to be analyzed in step two – the Grounded Theory-based discourse analysis.[70]

Grounded Theory analysis

The method applied in step two of each case is a discourse analysis according to the principles of Grounded Theory (GT).[71] It is based on the assumption that "discourses operate as background capacities for persons to differentiate and identify things, giving them taken-for-granted qualities and attributes, and relating them to other objects."[72]

What is characteristic of a "Grounded Theory"-based research process is the constant interplay between data collection, analysis and concept formation or theory building. All these steps stand in a reciprocal relationship to each other. One does not begin with a theory and then prove it; rather, one begins with a "puzzle" or intriguing question and allows possible explanations or potentially relevant answers to emerge. The aim is thus not necessarily the establishment and verification/falsification of pre-established theoretical concepts and theories, but rather the inductive collection and continuous refinement of data that only eventually leads to the generation of new concepts and new "vocabularies" to describe a particular case.[73]

The actual discourse interpretation then proceeds in three steps. In the first phase of the analysis, that is, during the so-called open coding of the documents, a first, rather large set of preliminary codes are "read out" of the material. On the basis of a close (line-by-line) and systematic reading of a relevant text, the researcher identifies initial descriptive categories of significant phenomena and their respective characteristics. The aim of this first analytical dimension is to allow the researcher to come up with a range of provisional, perhaps even speculative interpretations of the material in order to gain a broad but not necessarily highly coherent understanding of the material.

Creating a first "grid of coherence" among the provisional categories is the aim of the second dimension, in which the "axial coding" is conducted. Here, the preliminary codes discovered during the open coding are scrutinized one at a time and then put into relation with each other. At the same time the initial descriptive categories are constantly re-examined and compared in order to find textual links, similarities or differences.[74] The questions that are asked are: What are a phenomenon's specific characteristics and properties; what conditions it; what are its effects? According to this scheme, researchers should not only examine the characteristic of the phenomenon under scrutiny, but also establish the reasons that led to it.[75]

In the third coding stage (i.e., during selective coding), the researcher then focuses on those categories which have emerged more frequently, which have proven to figure more prominently and significantly in the present text and which are likely to be central to the development of theoretical generalizations. The goal of this phase is to delineate those core concepts, as well as their properties and interconnections, that are critical for making more abstract and conceptual statements on the social phenomena under scrutiny.[76]

> The analyst should consciously look for a core variable when coding data. While constantly comparing incidents and concepts, he or she will generate many codes, being alert to the one or two that might be the core. The analyst constantly looks for the "main theme," for what appears to be the main concern of or problem for the people in the setting, for what sums up in a pattern of behavior the substance of what is going on in the data, for what is the essence of relevance reflected in the data.[77]

It is during this third coding dimension that the researcher draws theoretically meaningful conclusions. This is also the phase in which GT's eclecticist potential comes to the fore: the process of linking and combining core categories clearly resembles analytical eclecticism's idea of producing complex causal narratives that draw on and make use of different analytical traditions in IR.

Again, it should be kept in mind that Grounded Theory-based research projects do not necessarily aim to uncover a phenomenon in its full statistical range or to quantify all incidents or cases in which an identified category works its effect. Instead, the aim is to elaborate the conceptual categories necessary to better understand a particular case. Theoretical saturation therefore primarily means increasing our understanding with regard to a single case or perhaps our orientation within a given field, rather than providing a large-scale generalization that covers a large number of cases.[78]

Heuristic framework of analysis

The actual analysis has to strike a fine balance between merely testing pre-established analytical categories on the one hand and writing completely idiosyncratic case "descriptions" on the other. It is therefore built upon a heuristic framework which guides the interpretation without "forcing" the texts into congruence with predetermined explanations. Drawing on the works of Roos, as well as Ruggie and Wæver, a three-layered framework of analysis is applied to each document.[79]

Level 1 – Statements regarding the (ideational) self-perception of the state: How do participants in the debate see or characterize the state? What is "the state's vision of itself"? What is the underlying "idea" of the state? To what attributes do the state representatives and participants in the discourse subscribe? This level may also include references to shared cultural and historical myths, or to prevalent religious beliefs or economic and political principles if these are constitutive for the country's "selfhood."

Level 2 – Statements regarding the state's role toward other actors: How do they describe the state's role within the international system? Is their outlook on the state's external relations an antagonistic and hostile one or is it, rather, friendly and cooperative? In more abstract terms: What is the envisioned relational position vis-à-vis the country's "significant others"? Do we find evidence of a significant threat perception? Can we discern a threatening posture vis-à-vis other actors?

Level 3 – Statements regarding the nuclear issue: Which references are made regarding the nuclear issue? Do the actors who partake in the debate call for nuclear weapons or do they oppose the acquisition of nuclear weapons? How do they explain and justify their attitude? What are the attributes they use to describe nuclear weapons? How is the "nuclear frame" related to other frames – legal, prestige, security, cultural, religious, economic or normative?

The underlying heuristic is flexible and amorphous enough to possibly yield new insights and to promote the emergence of previously unaccounted-for explanations. At the same time, these questions provide an analytical matrix for the interpretation of each document and guarantee that the two cases, as well as the interpreted material, are amenable to a "structured, focused comparison."[80] The method thus integrates "configurative-idiographic" elements as well as "disciplined-configurative" components: it accounts for the many particulars of the cases while allowing for cross-case comparison.[81]

Case selection: nuclear reversal

The first step in the case selection consists of establishing the "universe of cases." For a study on nuclear reversal the universe of cases comprises all states which have at some point in time tried to acquire nuclear weapons technology but which eventually gave up their efforts. Following Levite, we can define nuclear reversal as "the phenomenon in which states embark on a path leading to nuclear weapons acquisition but subsequently reverse course, though not necessarily abandoning altogether their nuclear ambitions."[82]

While this definition is shared by many academics and nuclear experts in the field, it is not unproblematic – as Levite acknowledges. In his classification, "nuclear hedgers" (i.e., countries such as Japan, Germany or probably also South Korea and Taiwan),[83] which possess all the necessary technological components to go nuclear within a very short time, are also considered "reversers":

> Nuclear hedging refers to a national strategy of maintaining, or at least appearing to maintain, a viable option for the relatively rapid acquisition of nuclear weapons, based on an indigenous technical capacity to produce them within a relatively short time frame ranging from several weeks to a few years.... Indeed, some of the cases that have been assumed to involve nuclear reversal may on closer examination be cases of nuclear hedging.[84]

Arguably, this distorts the clear-cut definition and the resulting clustering, as one might well claim that a country which retains all crucial elements of the nuclear fuel cycle as well as all the elements necessary for weaponization has not fore-closed future weapons acquisition. This problem is further aggravated because we have multiple players and actors even within governments that influence and shape the development or structure of a project. The decision to "go nuclear" is based on the non-linear interplay of several actors, as research in sociological technology studies illustrates: the development of new technologies rarely happens in a straightforward, linear fashion, but rather develops back and forth. With regard to the selection of cases this implies that we face tremendous dif-ficulties in determining the status of a state's nuclear weapons program.[85] More generally, cases are not naturally given, but depend on our theory-laden defining and clustering. As Davis writes:

> Cases then are not empirical entities but rather social conventions: they are linguistic constructions that enjoy intersubjective validity.... Properly understood, the process of identifying cases is a matter of concept extension and not of identifying real or natural empirical borders.[86]

Bearing these qualifications in mind, we can generate an overview of the nuclear activities of states since 1945 (Table 3.1).[87]

As has been argued before, the current body of theoretical accounts of pro-liferation is starkly biased toward the relatively few cases of actual prolifera-tion. The majority of studies that have been published thus far examine causes of actual proliferation. Only comparatively few publications address the ques-tion of why many more countries either abandoned their nuclear weapons research programs at some point or never even started such programs in the

Table 3.1 An overview of the nuclear activities of states since 1945

Reversed nuclear program[88,89]		Ongoing attempts[90]	Successful acquisition of nuclear weapons	No nuclear ambitions
Algeria	Libya	Iran	China	All (?) others
Argentina	Netherlands	North Korea	France	
Australia	Nigeria		India	
Belarus	Norway		Israel[91]	
Brazil	Romania		Pakistan	
Canada	S. Africa		United Kingdom	
Chile	South Korea		USA	
Egypt	Spain		Soviet Union	
Germany	Sweden			
Indonesia	Switzerland			
Iraq	Taiwan			
Italy	Ukraine			
Japan	Yugoslavia			
Kazakhstan				

first place.[92] It seems both theoretically and politically worthwhile, therefore, to pay closer attention to those approximately 30 or so countries that have abandoned their nuclear ambitions. Consequently, the central part of this study comprises two detailed case studies of countries that commenced nuclear weapons research at some point, but eventually abandoned their efforts – Switzerland, which began to undertake nuclear weapons-related research soon after the end of World War II and eventually gave up its ambitions in the 1960s; and Libya, which commenced a military nuclear program in the 1970s and ultimately abandoned its ambitions in 2003.

Why are these two – maximally contrasting – cases chosen?[93] The two cases are selected on the basis of five criteria that reflect common assumptions regarding the causes of state action – time, geographical location, political system, economic system and cultural background. First, the selected cases cover the complete "nuclear age," i.e., the era ranging from the invention of nuclear weapons in the 1940s up until the present. The choice also ensures that the presumed political watershed of the "end of the Cold War" is taken into account, since Switzerland's decision to give up its nuclear program falls into the Cold War era, while Libya's reversal took place in the post-Cold War years. Second, the two states are located in geographically different regions of the world. This guarantees that we do not fall prey to a Eurocentric or transatlantic bias. Third, the two countries have strikingly different political systems and political traditions: the *Eidgenossenschaft* is frequently described as one of the oldest democracies and a prime example of direct democracy, which even held referenda on the nuclear question; Libya, on the other hand, is – during the period under consideration – at the opposite end of most democracy indices and is considered authoritarian, non-democratic and not free.[94] Fourth, in economic terms Switzerland presents a diversified, globally integrated free market economy, while Libya's economy is highly controlled by the state, with key industries being state owned. The economy is little diversified, with oil exports providing the crucial source of income. Fifth, the two cases differ in terms of the cultural traditions they exhibit: Switzerland's cultural traits are rooted in the ideas of Western Christianity and enlightenment, whereas Libya is deeply embedded in Bedouin culture and history as well as in Islamic traditions. Against the background of these criteria, it may be claimed that the two cases are sufficiently dissimilar to allow for a diverse set of insights and to illustrate the benefits of a pragmatist approach.[95] Moreover, the Swiss case in particular has not received much attention beyond Swiss academic circles. There are, in fact, hardly any non-German language publications about the case; none of the major international journals has paid attention to Switzerland's nuclear program. In addition, previous examinations of the case have been primarily from a military-history perspective; theoretical analyses of Switzerland's nuclear program remain fairly rare. Including the country in the sample of the current analysis seems therefore justified.

However, as explained earlier, the study does not merely aim to provide new insights into the nuclear activities of these two countries. Instead, the goal of the overall project is twofold. On the one hand, it encompasses the elaboration of a new – eclecticist – theoretical perspective and its introduction into the realm of security studies. On the other hand, the application of this pragmatist theoretical framework is meant to shed new light on possible mechanisms of nuclear reversal by allowing for theoretical synthesis and "complex causal stories."[96]

Summary and outlook

Pragmatism urges us to denaturalize often-times unquestioned IR concepts such as identity, threat or interest and instead encourages us to examine how socially shared narratives or beliefs enable or constrain political action. To do so, we should examine the fundamentally political processes in which actors interpret and determine their environment and delineate further courses of action. For, rather than merely acting out given roles or identities or acting upon certain external triggers, state action is based on intersubjectively shared narratives which function as a template for decision-making. Hence, from a pragmatist perspective, states' proliferation policies do not depend on given objective threats, essentialist identities or the given conditions of the international system. Rather, the decision to go nuclear or to reverse a nuclear program should be understood as the result of an ongoing, fundamentally political process in which the state's position in the security environment, its identity, role and interests are discursively established and in which potential courses of action are construed.

In disciplinary terms, a pragmatist-inspired approach to issues of international security not only broadens our social-theoretical understanding of state action. It also helps us to increase the practical applicability of today's IR scholarship – and to bridge the gap between practitioners and theorists. Pragmatism in fact enables us be aware of social theoretical theoretical caveats and be policy-relevant. It allows us to put on hold unsolvable metatheoretical quarrels and encourages us to tackle problems of political relevance instead. It emboldens us to neglect the pursuit of ontological and epistemological certainties and to pay increased attention to the problems that society encounters in its daily life – and yet it does so without promoting theoretical arbitrariness or superficiality.

> [P]ragmatism can remind IR of its forgotten political, ethical and normative vocation. Just as pragmatists saw knowledge as being oriented to the idea of "betterment," reconstruction and emancipation, IR, too, must rise to the challenges of responsibility and public engagement in a turbulent and increasingly global society. Pragmatism can thus provide a salient caution with which to anchor IR in a community of inquirers and actors, thereby bridging the gap between the worlds of IR intellectuals and the global political community.[97]

The following two chapters will provide two contrasting cases in order to illustrate the empirical and theoretical benefits of a pragmatist analysis of nuclear proliferation and reversal.

Notes

1 Smith writes: "Political science ... is dominated both by the lack of an explicit acknowledgement of an epistemological position and by the implicit acceptance of one such position, positivism" (Steve Smith, "The Discipline of International Relations: Still an American Social Science?," *The British Journal of Politics & International Relations* 2, no. 3 (2000): 375).

2 Charles Taylor, *Philosophy and the human sciences*. Philosophical papers (Cambridge: Cambridge University Press, 1985), 15–57. See also Dvora Yanow, "Thinking Interpretively: Philosophical Presuppositions and the Human Sciences," in *Interpretation and method: empirical research methods and the interpretive turn*, ed. Dvora Yanow and Peregrine Schwartz-Shea (Armonk, NY: M.E. Sharpe, 2006).

3 For examples of recent pragmatist writings in IR see: Harry Bauer and Elisabetta Brighi, eds, *Pragmatism in international relations*, The new international relations (London; New York: Routledge, 2009); Gunther Hellmann, "Pragmatismus," in *Handbuch der Internationalen Politik*, ed. Carlo Masala, Frank Sauer, and Andreas Wilhelm (VS Verlag für Sozialwissenschaften, 2010); Gunther Hellmann et al., "Beliefs as Rules for Action: Pragmatism as a Theory of Thought and Action," *International Studies Review* 11, no. 3 (2009); Friedrich Kratochwil, "Of False Promises and Good Bets: A Plea for a Pragmatic Approach to Theory Building (the Tartu Lecture)," *Journal of International Relations and Development* 10, no. 1 (2007); Ulrich Roos, *Deutsche Außenpolitik: Eine Rekonstruktion der grundlegenden Handlungsregeln* (Wiesbaden: VS, 2010); Martha Finnemore, *The purpose of intervention: changing beliefs about the use of force* (Ithaca, NY: Cornell University Press, 2003). For an analysis of pragmatism's intellectual roots see: Hans Joas, *Praktische Intersubjektivität. Die Entwicklung des Werkes von George Herbert Mead* (Frankfurt am Main: Suhrkamp, 1989); *Pragmatismus und Gesellschaftstheorie* (Frankfurt am Main: Suhrkamp, 1999); Robert Prus, "Ancient Forerunners," in *Handbook of symbolic interactionism*, ed. Larry T. Reynolds and Nancy J. Herman-Kinney (Lanham, MD: Rowman & Littlefield, 2003); Dimitri N. Shalin, "The Pragmatic Origins of Symbolic Interactionism and the Crisis of Classical Science," *Studies in Symbolic Interaction* 12, no. 12 (1991). Pragmatism's re-emergence in philosophy and sociology is reflected in: Richard J. Bernstein, "The Resurgence of Pragmatism," *Social Research* 59, no. 4 (1992); Richard Rorty, *Consequences of pragmatism: essays 1972–1980* (Minneapolis: University of Minnesota Press, 1982); Mike Sandbothe, *Die Renaissance des Pragmatismus: aktuelle Verflechtungen zwischen analytischer und kontinentaler Philosophie*, 1. Aufl. ed. (Weilerswist: Velbrück Wissenschaft, 2000).

4 William James and Bruce Kuklick, eds, *Writings, 1902–1910* (New York: Viking, 1987), 509–510. See also Ulrich Franke and Ralph Weber, "At the Papini Hotel: On Pragmatism in the Study of International Relations," *European Journal of International Relations* 18, no. 4 (2012).

5 To put it into Robert Cox's words: "Theory is always for someone and for some purpose.... There is, accordingly, no such thing as theory in itself, divorced from a standpoint in time and space" (Robert W. Cox, "Social Forces, States and World Orders: Beyond International Relations Theory," *Millennium – Journal of International Studies* 10, no. 2 (1981): 128).

6 Jörg Friedrichs and Friedrich Kratochwil, "On Acting and Knowing: How Pragmatism Can Advance International Relations Research and Methodology," *International Organization* 63, no. 4 (2009): 713.

7 Vincent Pouliot, "The Logic of Practicality: A Theory of Practice of Security Communities," *International Organization* 62, no. 2 (2008); Kratochwil, "Ten Points to Ponder about Pragmatism. Some Critical Reflections on Knowledge Generation in the Social Sciences"; Charles S. Peirce, "Some Consequences of Four Incapacities," *The Journal of Speculative Philosophy* 2, no. 3 (1868).

8 Andreas Reckwitz, "Toward a Theory of Social Practices: A Development in Culturalist Theorizing," *European Journal of Social Theory* 5, no. 2 (2002): 245–246.

9 Christian Büger and Frank Gadinger, "Culture, Terror and Practice in International Relations: An Invitation to Practice Theory," in *The (Re-)turn to Practice: Thinking Practices in International Relations and Security Studies* (Florence: European University Institute, 2007).

10 Ted Hopf, "The Logic of Habit in International Relations," *European Journal of International Relations* 16, no. 4 (2010).The emphasis on creativity does not imply that the pragmatist/interactionist school regards agents as unconstrained in their behavior. At least, as Stryker has elaborated, this does not have to be the case – symbolic interactionism and social structure are by no means mutually exclusive. Sheldon Stryker, *Symbolic interactionism. A social structural version* (Menlo Park, CA: Benjamin/Cummings, 1980).

11 William Isaac Thomas and Dorothy Swaine Thomas, *The child in America: behavior problems and programs* (New York: Johnson, 1970). Years later this maxim became known as the "Thomas Theorem."

12 James Fearon and Alexander Wendt, "Rationalism v. Constructivism: A Skeptical View," in *Handbook of international relations*, ed. Walter Carlsnaes, Thomas Risse-Kappen, and Beth A. Simmons (London; Thousand Oaks, CA: Sage, 2002), 53.

13 Friedrichs and Kratochwil, "On Acting and Knowing," 711.

14 Kratochwil, "Ten Points to Ponder about Pragmatism. Some Critical Reflections on Knowledge Generation in the Social Sciences," 17.

15 "Constructing a New Orthodoxy? Wendt's 'Social Theory of International Politics' and the Constructivist Challenge," *Millennium – Journal of International Studies* 29, no. 1 (2000): 98; "The Monologue of 'Science'," *International Studies Review* 5, no. 1 (2003).

16 John G. Gunnell, "Relativism – the Return of the Repressed," *Political Theory* 21, no. 4 (1993): 564–565.

17 Jörg Friedrichs and Friedrichs Kratochwil, "On Acting and Knowing," *Working Papers* MWP 2007/35(2007): 8.

18 Richard Rorty, "Response to Robert Brandom," in *Rorty and his critics*, ed. Robert B. Brandom (Malden, MA: Blackwell, 2000), 185 (emphasis added); Hellmann, "Pragmatismus," 151–153.

19 Rorty, "Response to Robert Brandom," 186.

20 Kratochwil, "Ten Points to Ponder about Pragmatism. Some Critical Reflections on Knowledge Generation in the Social Sciences," 22.

21 We subscribe to the consensus theory of knowledge, but not without a caveat. Consensus is a necessary prerequisite for social scientific knowledge, but not any kind of consensus is sufficient. Social scientific knowledge is necessarily committed to substantive and methodological standards shared by a community of scholars. But this is not sufficient. To avoid the risk of academic self-encapsulation, social scientific knowledge also needs to be externally evaluated. It should resonate with other academic disciplines, with the human "objects" of study, and with society at large. The more scholarly consensus is meaningful to such multiple constituencies, the more it warrants the exacting predicate of knowledge.

(Friedrichs and Kratochwil, "On Acting and Knowing," 706)

See also Richard Ned Lebow, "Social Science as an Ethical Practice," *Journal of International Relations and Development* 10, no. 1 (2007).

22 Friedrichs and Kratochwil, "On Acting and Knowing," 716.

23 Hellmann, "Pragmatismus."

24 Antje Wiener, "Enacting Meaning-in-Use: Qualitative Research on Norms and International Relations," *Review of International Studies* 35, no. 1 (2009): 178.

25 John Dewey, *The influence of Darwin on philosophy, and other essays in contemporary thought* (Bloomington: Indiana University Press, 1965), 1–2. See also Charles W. Morris, "Introduction: George H. Mead as a Social Psychologist and Social Philosopher," in *Mind, Self & Society from the Standpoint of a Social Behaviorist*, ed. George H. Mead and Charles W. Morris (Chicago, IL: University of Chicago Press, 1934).

26 Joas shows that this idea of adaptation has attracted much criticism from opponents of pragmatism, who considered it emblematic of what they describe as a cynical ideology of conformity with capitalist constraints. Joas, "Praktische Intersubjektivität," 40–41.

27 Mustafa Emirbayer, "Manifesto for a Relational Sociology," *American Journal of Sociology* 103, no. 2 (1997): 308–309.

28 Herbert Blumer, *Symbolic interactionism. Perspective and method* (Englewood Cliffs, NJ: Prentice-Hall, 1969), 2.

29 *Symbolic interactionism. Perspective and method*, 4.

30 Ibid., 5 (see also 78–79).

31 John P. Hewitt, "Symbols, Objects, and Meanings," in *Handbook of symbolic interactionism*, ed. Larry T. Reynolds and Nancy J. Herman-Kinney (Lanham, MD: Rowman & Littlefield, 2003), 308. See also Larry T. Reynolds, "Intellectual Precursors," in *Handbook of symbolic interactionism*, ed. Larry T. Reynolds and Nancy J. Herman-Kinney (Lanham, MD: Rowman & Littlefield, 2003). What remains underspecified in Blumer's account, however, is his conceptualization of the very processes of meaning-making. From the rather broad picture that he provides, one might assume that he regards the establishment of meaning as the result of a merely verbal negotiation process among a group of individuals. Mead, on the other hand, ascertains the importance of the material world and emphasizes that the establishment of meaning cannot be conceived without recognizing the actual practical handling of the object. The establishment of meaning in Mead's understanding is not arbitrary or merely the result of a definitional act, but follows from an intensive – even physical – engagement with the matter as such. An object's meaning, in other words, is thoroughly grounded in social praxis – that is, in the way people act toward this object. For further discussions see Joas, "Praktische Intersubjektivität," 163; Jörg Strübing, *Pragmatische Wissenschafts- und Technikforschung. Theorie und Methode* (Frankfurt: Campus Verlag, 2005), 144–149.

32 We will see later that this must not be interpreted as an utter lack of stability, order and establishment within the social world. Yet these traits are themselves a product of negotiation (a "negotiated order") and they, too, are not immutable.

33 George H. Mead, "The Point of View of Social Behaviorism," in *Mind, Self & Society from the Standpoint of a Social Behaviorist*, ed. George H. Mead and Charles W. Morris (Chicago, IL: University of Chicago Press, 1934), 7. See also Anselm L. Strauss, *Mirrors & masks: the search for identity* (New Brunswick, NJ: Transaction Publishers, 1997), 63.

34 Blumer, *Symbolic interactionism. Perspective and method*, 8.

35 Following the work of Franke and Roos I conceptualize the actor (i.e., "the state") not as a person (as Wendt does), but as a "structure of corporate practice." Accordingly,

> states are neither real persons nor actors but structures of corporate practice, which are more than the sum of the interactions of its members. Irreducible to their parts, structures of corporate practice are held to have neither actively causal powers nor intentions. Due to their corporeality, reflexivity, and aptitude for abduction, human beings are the sole actors in our model of the social world instead.
>
> (p. 1058)

Thus, in order to successfully address emerging problems, individuals jointly create social strategies – structures of corporate practice such as the state, an NGO and the like – for coping with the challenge. Such a depiction allows us to maintain human agency while at the same time acknowledging the *sui generis* characteristics and functions of "corporate social actors" such as states. Ulrich Franke and Ulrich Roos, "Actor, Structure, Process: Transcending the State Personhood Debate by Means of a Pragmatist Ontological Model for International Relations Theory," *Review of International Studies* 36, no. 4 (2010).

36 Quoted in Gil R. Musolf, "The Chicago School," in *Handbook of symbolic interactionism*, ed. Larry T. Reynolds and Nancy J. Herman-Kinney (Lanham, MD: Rowman & Littlefield, 2003), 103. The idea was first formulated in John Dewey, "The Reflex Arc Concept in Psychology," *Psychological Review* 3, no. 4 (1896). See also Strübing, *Pragmatische Wissenschafts- und Technikforschung. Theorie und Methode*, 60–63.

37 Peter M. Hall, "A Symbolic Interactionist Analysis of Politics," *Sociological Inquiry* 42, nos 3–4 (1972): 39. See also Gunther Hellmann, "Creative Intelligence. Pragmatism as a Theory of Thought and Action," in *"Millennium" Special Issue Conference on "Pragmatism in International Relations Theory"* (London 2002).

38 Hopf, "The Logic of Habit in International Relations," 547.

39 Neil Gross, "A Pragmatist Theory of Social Mechanisms," *American Sociological Review* 74, no. 3 (2009): 367.

40 Charles S. Peirce, "The Fixation of Belief," *Popular Science Monthly* 12(1877). See also Bernard M. Meltzer, "Mind," in *Handbook of symbolic interactionism*, ed. Larry T. Reynolds and Nancy J. Herman-Kinney (Lanham, MD: Rowman & Littlefield, 2003), 258–259.

41 Roos, *Deutsche Außenpolitik*, 48–77.

42 Although it should be noted that Jervis indeed concedes that a "simple stimulus-response model rarely will do." He does not elaborate further on this aspect, though. Robert Jervis, "Signaling and Perception," in *Political psychology*, ed. Kristen R. Monroe (Mahwah, NJ: L. Erlbaum, 2002), 293. See also *System effects: complexity in political and social life* (Princeton, NJ: Princeton University Press, 1997), 57–58.

43 Larsen, *Foreign policy and discourse analysis: France, Britain, and Europe*, 5.

44 Robert G. Dunn, "Self, Identity, and Difference," *Sociological Quarterly* 38, no. 4 (1997): 693.

45 Alexander Wendt, *Social theory of international politics* (Cambridge: Cambridge University Press, 1999), 335. See also "On Constitution and Causation in International Relations," *Review of International Studies* 24, no. 5 (1998).

46 Joas, "Praktische Intersubjektivität," in *passim*.

47 This does not imply that identities are easily malleable. See, for example, Jennifer Mitzen, "Ontological Security in World Politics: State Identity and the Security Dilemma," *European Journal of International Relations* 12, no. 3 (2006).

48 Drawing on Emirbayer and Elias, Jackson and Nexon provide a profound social-theoretical elaboration of an anti-substantialist, processual-relational approach to IR. Accordingly, "a focus upon processes and relations rather than substances ... allows a researcher to problematize the existence of the units we observe in world politics at any given time ... and to inquire more systematically into changes in a unit" (Patrick T. Jackson and Daniel H. Nexon, "Relations Before States: Substance, Process and the Study of World Politics," *European Journal of International Relations* 5, no. 3 (1999): 292). See also Bernd Bucher, "Processual-Relational Thinking and Figurational Sociology in Social Constructivism: The Rogueization of Liberal and Illiberal States" (Ph.D. dissertation, St. Gallen: University of St Gallen, 2011).

49 Walsh, "Learning from Past Success: The NPT and the Future of Non-Proliferation," 39.

50 Roos, *Deutsche Außenpolitik*, 64.

51 Regarding the role of pop-cultural representations of politics see, for example: Roland Bleiker, "The Aesthetic Turn in International Political Theory," *Millennium* 30, no. 3

(2001); Matt Davies, "'You Can't Charge Innocent People for Saving Their Lives!' Work in Buffy the Vampire Slayer 1," *International Political Sociology* 4, no. 2 (2010); Nick Randall, "Imagining the Polity: Cinema and Television Fictions as Vernacular Theories of British Politics," *Parliamentary Affairs* 64, no. 2 (2011).

52 Hansen differentiates three different scopes of analysis: (1) a narrow analysis that focuses on governmental documents only; (2) a medium-range analysis that also includes statements issued by non-governmental groups, parties, etc.; and (3) a comprehensive approach that additionally incorporates fictional and literary sources. I do not look at a wider array of different genres or cultural representations and their relation to the political discourse, even though such a more culture studies-inspired approach may yield further interesting insights. The approach therefore resembles Hansen's "Model 2." Obviously, this comprehensiveness is more difficult to achieve in the Libyan case, where the non-democratic political system suppressed or at least severely controlled most forms of participation in political processes. Hansen, *Security as practice*.

53 Interview-based studies moreover have to be taken with a grain of salt, since interviewees tend to provide ex-post-facto rationalizations of historical events (for example, in the light of new insights or reassessments):

> Advocates of interviews typically argue that this approach is beneficial inasmuch as a rich account of the interviewee's experiences, knowledge, ideas, and impressions may be considered and documented…. [However, it] is important not to simplify and idealize the interview situation, assuming that the interviewee – given the correct interview technique – primarily is a competent and moral truth teller, acting in the service of science and producing the data needed to reveal his or her "interior" (i.e., experiences, feelings, values) or the "facts" of the organization.
>
> (Mats Alvesson, "Beyond Neopositivists, Romantics, and Localists: A Reflexive Approach to Interviews in Organizational Research," *Academy of Management Review* 28, no. 1 (2003): 13–14)

54 Paul A. Chilton, *Analysing political discourse: theory and practice* (London; New York: Routledge, 2004), 16–29.

55 Andrew P. Cortell and James W. Davis, "Understanding the Domestic Impact of International Norms: A Research Agenda," *International Studies Review* 2, no. 1 (2000): 76; Thomas Risse-Kappen and Kathryn Sikkink, "The Socialization of International Human Rights Norms into Domestic Practices: Introduction," in *The power of human rights: international norms and domestic change*, ed. Thomas Risse-Kappen, Steve C. Ropp, and Kathryn Sikkink (New York: Cambridge University Press, 1999).

56 John L. Austin, *How to do things with words*, The William James lectures (Cambridge, MA: Harvard University Press, 1962); Jennifer Milliken, "The Study of Discourse in International Relations: A Critique of Research and Methods," *European Journal of International Relations* 5, no. 2 (1999); Holger Stritzel, "Towards a Theory of Securitization: Copenhagen and Beyond," *European Journal of International Relations* 13, no. 3 (2007). Hellmann *et al.*, moreover, write that single instrumental rhetorical interventions can have an impact on the specific speech act situation, but that such intentional, "manipulative" utterances can hardly change a whole discourse: "Vokabulare und die darauf aufbauenden Sprachspiele sind menschliche Erfindungen, Diskurse sind jedoch nur in Grenzen durch einzelne Sprechakte intentional steuerbar" (Hellmann *et al.*, "'Selbstbewusst' und 'stolz'," 657).

57 Neta Crawford, *Argument and change in world politics: ethics, decolonization, and humanitarian intervention*, Cambridge studies in international relations (Cambridge; New York: Cambridge University Press, 2002). Haas and Haas make a similar argument:

Policy-making … is seen as a discursive practice in which different views are offered and modified in conformity with temporarily accepted "true" knowledge. Within consistent democratic practice, policy-making is a learning process about the world and how to alter it. Authoritarian regimes, less reliably and consistently, may also allow the process to occur, but the fate of Soviet genetics reminds us that the absence of dialogue can produce a caricature of knowledge.

(Peter M. Haas and Ernst B. Haas, "Pragmatic Constructivism and International institutions," in *Pragmatism in international relations*, ed. Harry Bauer and Elisabetta Brighi (London; New York: Routledge, 2009))

58 Juha A. Vuori, "Illocutionary Logic and Strands of Securitization: Applying the Theory of Securitization to the Study of Non-Democratic Political Orders," *European Journal of International Relations* 14, no. 1 (2008): 71.

59 Paul A. Chilton, "Introduction," in *Language and the nuclear arms debate: nukespeak today*, ed. Paul A. Chilton (London: F. Pinter, 1985), xv, xvii.

60 Mark Bevir, "How Narratives Explain," in *Interpretation and method: empirical research methods and the interpretive turn*, ed. Dvora Yanow and Peregrine Schwartz-Shea (Armonk, NY: M.E. Sharpe, 2006); Reiner Keller, "Analysing Discourse. An Approach from the Sociology of Knowledge," *Forum Qualitative Social Research* 6, no. 3 (2005). For the original contributions see also Ulrich Oevermann, "Die Struktur sozialer Deutungsmuster," *Sozialer Sinn* 1(2001); Alfred Schütz, *The phenomenology of the social world* (Evanston, IL: Northwestern University Press, 1967).

61 For examples of the different concepts see: Judith Goldstein and Robert O. Keohane, eds, *Ideas and foreign policy: beliefs, institutions, and political change* (Ithaca, NY: Cornell University Press, 1993); J.M. Goldgeier and P.E. Tetlock, "Psychology and International Relations Theory," *Annual Review of Political Science* 4, no. 1 (2001); Rose McDermott, *Political psychology in international relations* (Ann Arbor: University of Michigan Press, 2004); Richard C. Snyder, H.W. Bruck and Burton M. Sapin, *Decision-making as an approach to the study of international politics* (Princeton, NJ: Princeton University Press, 1954); Alexander L. George, "The 'Operational Code': A Neglected Approach to the Study of Political Leaders and Decision-Making," *International Studies Quarterly* 13, no. 2 (1969); K.J. Holsti, "National Role Conceptions in the Study of Foreign Policy," *International Studies Quarterly* 14, no. 3 (1970); Nathan Leites, *A study of Bolshevism* (Glencoe, IL: Free Press, 1953). For a critique of the rationalist conceptualization of ideas and interests see Mark Laffey and Jutta Weldes, "Beyond Belief: Ideas and Symbolic Technologies in the Study of International Relations," *European Journal of International Relations* 3, no. 2 (1997); Jutta Weldes, "Constructing National Interests," *European Journal of International Relations* 2, no. 3 (1996); Doty, "Foreign Policy as Social Construction: A Post-Positivist Analysis of U.S. Counterinsurgency Policy in the Philippines"; Kevin C. Dunn, "Examining Historical Representations," *International Studies Review* 8, no. 2 (2006).

62 Martin Hollis and Steve Smith, *Explaining and understanding international relations* (Oxford and New York: Oxford University Press, 1990), 74.

63 Valerie M. Hudson and Christopher S. Vore, "Foreign Policy Analysis Yesterday, Today, and Tomorrow," *Mershon International Studies Review* 39 (1995): 210.

64 Ole Wæver, "Discursive Approaches," in *European integration theory*, ed. Antje Wiener and Thomas Diez (Oxford; New York: Oxford University Press, 2004), 199.

65 Oevermann, "Die Struktur sozialer Deutungsmuster."

66 Sagan, "Why Do States Build Nuclear Weapons? Three Models in Search of a Bomb," 63.

67 For an elaboration upon the differences between textual analysis and discourse analysis, see, for example, Johannes Angermüller, "Diskursanalyse: Strömungen,

Tendenzen, Perspektiven. Eine Einführung," in *Diskursanalyse: Theorien, Methoden, Anwendungen*, ed. Johannes Angermüller, Katharina Bunzmann, and Martin Nonhoff, *Argument-Sonderband* (Hamburg: Argument Verlag, 2001).

68 Clifford James Geertz, *Dichte Beschreibung. Beiträge zum Verstehen kultureller Systeme*, Theorie (Frankfurt am Main: Suhrkamp, 1983), 7–43.

69 Alexander L. George and Andrew Bennett, *Case studies and theory development in the social sciences*, BCSIA studies in international security (Cambridge, MA: MIT Press, 2005), 205–232.

70 Milliken, "The Study of Discourse in International Relations: A Critique of Research and Methods," 231. For a detailed description of different discourse analytical approaches see, for example: Yoshiko M. Herrera and Bear F. Braumöller, "Symposium: Discourse and Content Analysis," *Qualitative Methods* 2, no. 1 (2004); Stefan Titscher *et al.*, *Methods of text and discourse analysis* (London: Sage, 2000).

71 Juliet M. Corbin and Anselm L. Strauss, *Basics of qualitative research techniques and procedures for developing grounded theory*, 3rd edn (Los Angeles, CA: Sage, 2008); Barney G. Glaser and Anselm L. Strauss, *The discovery of grounded theory: strategies for qualitative research* (Hawthorne, NY: Aldine de Gruyter, 1999); Udo Kelle, "'Emergence' vs. 'Forcing' of Empirical Data? A Crucial Problem of 'Grounded Theory' Revisited," *Forum Qualitative Social Research* 6, no. 2 (2005); Jane Mills, Ann Bonner, and Karen Francis, "The Development of Constructivist Grounded Theory," *International Journal of Qualitative Methods* 5, no. 1 (2006); Anselm Strauss and Juliet Corbin, "Grounded Theory Methodology: An Overview," in *Handbook of qualitative research*, ed. Norman K. Denzin and Yvonna S. Lincoln (Thousand Oaks, CA: Sage, 1994); Anselm L. Strauss and Juliet M. Corbin, *Basics of qualitative research: techniques and procedures for developing grounded theory*, 2nd edn (Thousand Oaks, CA: Sage, 1998); Jörg Strübing, *Grounded Theory. Zur sozialtheoretischen und epistemologischen Fundierung des Verfahrens der empirisch begründeten Theoriebildung* (Wiesbaden: VS, 2004).

72 Milliken, "The Study of Discourse in International Relations: A Critique of Research and Methods," 231.

73 Kathy Charmaz, "Grounded Theory: Objectivist and Constructivist Methods," in *Handbook of qualitative research*, ed. Norman K. Denzin and Yvonna S. Lincoln (Thousand Oaks, CA: Sage, 2000), 515.

74 Glaser and Strauss, *The discovery of grounded theory*, 101–116.

75 Anselm L. Strauss, *Qualitative analysis for social scientists* (Cambridge; New York: Cambridge University Press, 1987), 27–28. For an illustration see also Strübing, *Grounded Theory*, 27.

76 Corbin and Strauss, *Basics of qualitative research techniques*, 104–106.

77 Strauss, *Qualitative analysis for social scientists*, 35.

78 For an abstract and general critique of most of the philosophy of science assumptions underlying my study, see Gary King, Robert O. Keohane, and Sidney Verba, *Designing social inquiry: scientific inference in qualitative research* (Princeton, NJ: Princeton University Press, 1994).

79 Roos, *Deutsche Außenpolitik*, 66; John Gerard Ruggie, "Continuity and Transformation in the World Polity: Toward a Neorealist Synthesis," *World Politics* 35, no. 2 (1983); Ole Wæver, "Identity, Communities and Foreign Policy," in *European integration and national identity: the challenge of the Nordic states*, ed. Lene Hansen and Ole Waever (London: Routledge, 2002).

80 George and Bennett write:

  The method and logic of structured, focused comparison is simple and straightforward. The method is "structured" in that the researcher writes general questions that reflect the research objective and that these questions are asked of each case under study to guide and standardize data collection, thereby making systematic comparison and cumulation of the findings of the cases possible. The method is "focused" in that it deals only with certain aspects of the historical cases examined.

(George and Bennett, *Case studies and theory development in the social sciences*, 67)

81 Harry Eckstein, "Case Study and Theory in Political Science," in *Strategies of inquiry*, ed. Fred I. Greenstein and Nelson W. Polsby (Reading, MA: Addison-Wesley, 1975); see also Howard S. Becker and Charles C. Ragin, eds, *What is a case? Exploring the foundations of social inquiry* (Cambridge: Cambridge University Press, 2000).

82 Levite, "Never Say Never Again: Nuclear Reversal Revisited," 61.

83 Robert J. Einhorn, "Will the Abstainers Reconsider? Focusing on Individual Cases," in *The nuclear tipping point: why states reconsider their nuclear choices*, ed. Kurt M. Campbell, Robert J. Einhorn and Mitchell Reiss (Washington, DC: Brookings Institution Press, 2004), 35.

84 Levite, "Never Say Never Again: Nuclear Reversal Revisited," 69–70.

85 Abraham, "The Ambivalence of Nuclear Histories"; Sheila Jasanoff, "Technology as a Site and Object of Politics," in *The Oxford handbook of contextual political analysis*, ed. Robert E. Goodin and Charles Tilly, Oxford handbooks of political science (Oxford and New York: Oxford University Press, 2006); Gabrielle Hecht, "Nuclear Ontologies," *Constellations* 13, no. 3 (2006).

86 James W. Davis, *Terms of inquiry on the theory and practice of political science* (Baltimore, MD: Johns Hopkins University Press, 2005), 156; John Walton, "Making the Theoretical Case," in *What is a case? Exploring the foundations of social inquiry*, ed. Howard S. Becker and Charles C. Ragin (Cambridge: Cambridge University Press, 2000), 121–122.

87 Table 3.1 draws on Müller and Schmidt, "The Little Known Story of Deproliferation. Why States Give Up Nuclear Weapons Activities; Levite, "Never Say Never Again: Nuclear Reversal Revisited." Additional information was gained from the Nuclear Threat Initiative's country profiles at www.nti.org/e_research/profiles/index.html. For almost all cases it holds true that the realm of nuclear weapons acquisition, nuclear decision-making and nuclear strategy is covered by so much secrecy and non-disclosure that many details remain unknown; this concerns a broad range of issues such as nuclear production and storage sites, extent of research and development programs, magnitude and composition of the arsenal, etc.

88 There is hardly any literature on the Algerian, Chilean and Nigerian cases. Levite claims, for example, that (as of 2003) Algeria was still actively seeking nuclear weapons. It appears difficult to corroborate this assumption. Similarly, for their assessment of Chile and Nigeria, Müller and Schmidt rely on only one study for each case. Therefore, all three cases should be treated with a grain of salt.

89 Belarus, Kazakhstan and Ukraine are customarily grouped under the heading of nuclear reversal, but this categorization appears to be politically motivated – either by politicians in these countries who want to underline their countries' "good behavior" or by arms control proponents who want to emphasize the international community's achievement in peacefully disarming former nuclear states. In fact, all three countries inherited Soviet nuclear weapons following the demise of the Soviet Union. More precisely, Soviet nuclear weapons were deployed on their territory. But neither had one of them ever made any effort to unilaterally establish its own nuclear force; nor were they ever in full command (i.e., in possession of the launch codes) of complete weapons. The three countries should therefore not quite count as "*prime*" examples of nuclear reversal.

90 The range, determination and intensity with which these states strive for nuclear weapons remains unclear; likewise it is difficult to assess how successful they have

been thus far in acquiring the composite technological parts or a crude weapon (in the case of North Korea).

91 As of today, Israel's nuclear status remains officially unconfirmed. In December 2006 the issue received renewed attention when the then Prime Minister Olmert said in an interview: "Iran openly, explicitly and publicly threatens to wipe Israel off the map. Can you say that this is the same level, when they are aspiring to have nuclear weapons, as France, America, Russia and Israel?" ("Olmert's Nuclear Slip-up Sparks Outrage in Israel," *Times Online*, December 12, 2006).

92 Hymans, "When Does State Become a 'Nuclear Weapons State'? An Exercise in Measurement Validation"; Müller and Schmidt, "The Little Known Story of Deproliferation. Why States Give Up Nuclear Weapons Activities."

93 For an explanation of the principle of "maximally contrasting case selection" see: Barney G. Glaser and Anselm L. Strauss, *The discovery of grounded theory strategies for qualitative research* (New York: de Gruyter, 1967).

94 Cf. Freedom House, "Worst of the Worst 2010" (2010), www.freedomhouse.org/sites/default/files/inline_images/Worst%20of%20the%20Worst%202010.pdf.

95 I will consider these societal, political, economic and cultural characteristics in more detail in the following two case chapters.

96 Rudra Sil and Peter J. Katzenstein, "Analytic Eclecticism in the Study of World Politics: Reconfiguring Problems and Mechanisms across Research Traditions," *Perspectives on Politics* 8, no. 2 (2010): 419.

97 Harry Bauer and Elisabetta Brighi, "Introducing Pragmatism to International Relations," in *Pragmatism in international relations*, ed. Harry Bauer and Elisabetta Brighi, *The new international relations* (London New York: Routledge, 2009), 2.

4 Switzerland

The ambivalent neutral

Switzerland's nuclear weapons ambitions have received only scant attention from the international research community. When they are considered at all, these ambitions are mostly refracted through a realist security prism. The rise and fall of Switzerland's nuclear efforts is explained by reference to the country's security environment. I argue, however, that we can gain more comprehensive insights by looking at the case through the pragmatist-interactionist framework previously elaborated. The subsequent analysis consists of two broad parts. The first part encompasses a contextualization and historiographic reconstruction of Switzerland's nuclear weapons research program. The second part provides an actual analysis of frames and narratives that were prominent in the nuclear weapons discourse between 1958 and 1969.

Contextualizing Switzerland's nuclear research program

The case of nuclear decision-making in Switzerland seems well suited to a fuller illustration of the applicability of the pragmatist framework as a lens for understanding the multi-layered and non-linear process of nuclear decision-making in general. The nature of Switzerland's political system, with its direct democracy, means the debate surrounding the acquisition of nuclear weapons has not only been comparatively broad and inclusive, but also relatively transparent.[1] Switzerland is the only country in the world that has held referenda on the issue of nuclear acquisition. Hence, the Swiss debate on the "pros" and "cons" of acquiring its own nuclear force is well documented in publicly accessible sources, making an in-depth study of the underlying processes and discursive shifts possible.

The path to nuclear restraint: dominant readings of the case

Switzerland's nuclear restraint has gained relatively little attention in the theoretical literature on nuclear proliferation, not least because the research focus has long been on those countries that have actually acquired nuclear weapons. Hence, Switzerland has rarely been included in theoretically grounded studies on the causes of (non-)proliferation. Instead, most studies that deal with the Swiss case look at it primarily from a military-historical, single case study angle.[2] The few studies that do deal with the case in a more IR-theoretical, abstract perspective are more or less consistent in their findings. Accordingly, Switzerland's initial move toward its own, genuine nuclear capabilities was triggered by the political and strategic situation in the aftermath of World War II and by the perceived high level of threat. The country thus aimed to secure the autonomy of its defense by acquiring a deterrent.[3]

In line with large parts of the theoretical literature on the subject, Switzerland – like other small neutral states – may be considered a particularly likely candidate for the acquisition of a nuclear weapon capability for at least two reasons. First, the level of its technological and economic development provides the country with the necessary means to acquire or build the infrastructure that is indispensable for a military nuclear complex. Second, the lack of security agreements with other – nuclear-armed – states implies that a neutral state might seem highly vulnerable to exogenous military threats, since it cannot participate in a nuclear umbrella or in nuclear-sharing agreements with other states. Hence, from a theoretical perspective, it appears rather surprising that Switzerland has not acquired a nuclear defense capacity.[4]

In a similar vein, T.V. Paul, who has contributed a major theoretical analysis of the Swiss case, draws on a threat-based explanation to account for it. He traces Switzerland's initial striving for nuclear weapons back to prime security considerations. Accordingly, Switzerland's drive for the development of nuclear weapons was triggered by the perceived necessity of having a reliable deterrence capacity and of improving existing war-fighting capabilities. The underlying rationale was that the existence and possible use of tactical nuclear weapons would dissuade a potential aggressor by keeping the "price of entry" high and thereby compensating for the lack of alliance protection. Hence, when the global political situation became tense in the 1950s (as exemplified by the Berlin crisis, the war in Korea, the uprising in Hungary or the Sputnik crisis), Switzerland "faced an enormous threat"[5] in its strategic environment. This consequently led the government to inquire into the feasibility of a Swiss nuclear weapons program.

Likewise, when the government changed its mind and finally signed the Non-Proliferation Treaty in 1969, this decision, too, was based on military-strategic reasons and a new cost–benefit analysis, Paul maintains:

> Switzerland viewed its immediate region as friendly, with neighboring states having no territorial ambitions against it, and it perceived no need for a nuclear deterrent to withstand threats from them.[6]

Accordingly, the instant necessity of acquiring nuclear weapons was now regarded to be minor. In addition, Paul claims that Switzerland was trapped in the "dilemma" of its neutrality:

> Others, especially potential adversaries, would take nuclear possession as an aggressive step, as it would blur the line between the neutral state's traditional insistence on defensive capabilities and the exigencies of nuclear warfare.[7]

Hence, according to Paul, Switzerland's decision should be regarded as the "result of a conscious cost–benefit analysis" in which security benefits were weighed against neutrality. On the face of it, these readings appear convincing and coherent. They integrate the Swiss case neatly into our familiar IR-theoretical framework and establish a sound connection to concepts such as threat, strategic environment and the like. However, a closer look at the relevant discourses shows that this threat-based explanation glosses over many of the specific particularities that have shaped the development of the Swiss case. These particularities cast doubt on the neat consistency and parsimony of the realist explanation. Instead of merely stating that formerly held threat percep-tions or policy convictions simply disappeared or vanished, a discourse-based analysis can help us to understand *how* the shifts and changes in several crucial beliefs actually occurred in the midst of deep political contestation.

Between nuclear acquisition and restraint: the strategic context

The emerging discussion of the potential acquisition of nuclear forces dates back to – and was deeply embedded in – a larger debate on Switzerland's regional and international security environment in the post-World War II world. At the time, several aspects of the Swiss security situation appeared troubled. As a consequence of Switzerland's strict neutrality and its non-participation in the Allied war against Hitler's Germany, the country was somewhat isolated politi-cally once the war was over. According to Altermatt, the Allies regarded Swit-zerland as a "parasite"[8] that had benefited from the Nazi regime instead of making any significant contribution to its defeat. Switzerland's bilateral diplo-matic relations with the major powers were strained (US) or even non-existent (Soviet Union). As a result, the allied powers did not invite Switzerland to participate in the San Francisco Conference on the establishment of the United Nations.[9]

The emerging Cold War led to further changes in Switzerland's security land-scape, which resulted in a growing fear that the country could inadvertently be drawn into a conflict by the two sides.[10] In addition, despite its neutrality, Swit-zerland was of course affected by the more tangible events of global politics during the Cold War period. The repercussions of global crises such as the Berlin Blockade (1948/1949), the Hungarian Revolution (1956) or the Cuban missile crisis (1962) were similarly felt in Switzerland and repeatedly provoked debates on – and a questioning of – the country's self-positioning within the international system.[11] The perceived Soviet threat increased domestic pressure to seek a closer security relationship with the Western powers. The strong historically anchored tradition of international neutrality, however, proved too persuasive a rationale, and eventually inhibited decision-makers from embarking on this path. Moreover, and somewhat ironically, the further cementation of the Cold War and the seemingly insurmountable – but gloomily stable – superpower stand-off eventually provided Switzerland with some room for maneuver to establish itself more confidently between the two poles.

Another defining strategic aspect of the post-World War II phase concerned the more technology-related issues of the country's security situation. The emergence of new means of warfare (i.e., not only the development and use of nuclear weapons, but also increasingly sophisticated means of fast and long-range military deployment in the post-1945 period) ultimately changed the traditional strategy of warfare and forced the country's military establishment to rethink the goals of the Swiss defense posture and the means of implementing it. During World War II, Switzerland had relied on the strategy of *Réduit*, which called for a retreat and the amassing of large parts of the army into heavily fortified, hard-to-conquer regions in the Swiss mountains in order to establish a center for resistance and counter-attack. Yet this strategy, designed as a means of compensating for the numerical and technical inferiority of the Swiss military to the Axis powers, implied that Switzerland would have to give up large parts of the densely populated and economically important lower mainland. Not only would this come at extreme economic cost; it would also entail giving up large parts of Swiss territory to the invader. This strategy was also becoming increasingly difficult to uphold, given the profound advances in military technology and military equipment at the onset of the Cold War era.[12] The development of more mobile and more accurate artillery, as well as the emergence of tactical nuclear weapons, thus initiated an overhaul of the central pillars of the Swiss defense posture. However, in the early years of this reconceptualizing phase it was far from clear which new strategic orientation should replace the old stance. The defense community was split between proponents of so-called "area defense," who argued for a fairly static and deeply staggered line of protection, and proponents of a "mobile defense" posture, who favored reliance on highly mobile tank and air units and also called for the acquisition of nuclear weapons. It is against this background of technological and strategic change that the nuclearization question came to the fore.

Historiographic reconstruction of the Swiss case

As early as 1945, high-ranking military personnel called for an analysis of the changed security environment and voiced demands for an investigation into the possibilities of a Swiss nuclear force. One of the first high-level sources to voice these new concerns was an official letter from Korpskommandant Frick to the head of the Defense Department.[13] Significantly, the letter did not revolve around the question of whether Swiss security was endangered by the emergence of a new, specific threat. Instead, the author focused primarily on advances in (military) technology and the way in which these advances might change the general, rather abstract terms on which Swiss defense had been built. In addition, while the letter is framed in a very tentative and sometimes even obscure manner – insofar as it does not *explicitly* demand the development of a Swiss nuclear capacity – it certainly suggests that the Swiss military should make use of nuclear technology itself in order to counter possible nuclear attacks.[14] In the months that followed, various governmental departments joined the debate and made several suggestions for the mandate and scope of a study group on the civil and military dimensions of nuclear technology. This led to the official appointment of the Studienkommission für Atomenergie (Study Commission on Atomic Energy, SKA) in June 1946.[15] Kupper reveals that the SKA received considerable funding. From 1947 to 1951 it had 18 million Swiss francs at its disposal – an enormous amount of money compared to other state-funded research projects in Switzerland at that time. He acknowledges, however, that this amount was fairly small compared to the funding available in other countries.[16]

By the time the Commission was officially established, it had (under the auspices of the military department) already initiated its first clandestine investigations into the military and non-military uses of nuclear weapons.[17] This follows from a classified directive issued by Bundesrat Kobelt, then head of the military department. However, what is particularly interesting about this secret directive is again the hesitant and defensive style in which the research mandate is framed. Even though the document was not intended for publication, but solely for intra-agency use, it is circumspect and very cautiously worded. It does not contain the clear and unequivocal task of examining the steps necessary for developing offensive or defensive nuclear forces for the Swiss Army, but focuses instead on how to increase existing knowledge about nuclear weapons research in other countries and on the potentialities of developing protective measures against nuclear warfare. Furthermore, only one member of the Commission was part of the professional military establishment. It is thus debatable if the beginnings of the Swiss nuclear program were indeed as clear-cut and straightforward as assumed, for instance, by Wollenmann.[18] Braun, for example, argues:

> [i]t is worth noting that in the immediate after-war period no proper nuclear strategy was formulated and the question of the military suitability of an atomic armament of the Swiss Armed Forces was not even debated. The determining factor in initiating nuclear technology research was primarily the fear that, sooner or later, this kind of weapon – like any other weapon before – would become a part of the arsenal of all modern armed forces. Switzerland should therefore be prepared too.[19]

Nevertheless, there is little doubt that the research to be undertaken had a primarily military dimension, given that the Studienkommission was institutionally part of the military department. This institutional arrangement contributed to the greater leverage of the military establishment within the nuclear debate. On the other hand, it should be noted that while the extent of military-related research into the uses of atomic energy remained unclear, as did the stage it was at, the fact of its existence had been publicly known since 1946.[20]

Overall, the first years of the Swiss nuclear research program (until the mid-1950s) are characterized by a rather tentative approach to the issue of nuclear weapons acquisition. It was only in subsequent years that the country's efforts took on somewhat greater momentum, not least due to growing private sector interest in nuclear technology. Encouraged by Eisenhower's "Atoms for Peace" speech in December 1953, as well as by an international conference on nuclear technology in Geneva in 1955, Swiss industry increased its effort to use the new technology for civilian purposes. Its first major success was the acquisition of the SAPHIR research reactor, which was bought from the US government and moved to Würenlingen in 1957. In addition, Swiss industry established a private research center, the Reaktor AG, in order to conduct further studies.[21] This basic research eventually led to the development of a distinct Swiss reactor type: the DIORIT reactor[22] – a small, heavy water reactor that used natural uranium instead of enriched uranium. The advantage was clear: Switzerland did not have its own uranium enrichment facilities and was therefore dependent on imports if it wanted to run SAPHIR-type reactors. The DIORIT, on the other hand, operated on the basis of natural uranium, which was much easier to obtain on the global market than enriched uranium. Yet the DIORIT reactor type also offered another advantage: heavy water reactors produce more plutonium as a by-product than light water reactors. This could in turn be used to produce fissile material for manufacturing nuclear weapons.[23] However, it is not clear whether the Swiss government tried to promote the development of reactors suitable for military purposes.[24] When Swiss industry eventually lost interest in developing a distinct Swiss reactor type and instead bought facilities from abroad, the government did little to reverse this trend.

Yet in the meantime – regardless of these industrial developments – the intensified military interest in the acquisition of nuclear weapons unleashed a fierce and heated debate among both the political elite and the wider public. The key document that set the stage for, and marked the prelude to, the nuclearization debate was a government statement which was published in several Swiss newspapers on July 11, 1958. In the document, entitled "Erklärung zur Frage der Beschaffung von Atomwaffen für unsere Armee," the government explicitly and publicly addressed for the first time the question of whether Switzerland should acquire nuclear weapons. The authors argued that Switzerland was faced with a decision regarding its nuclear status because of the increasing number and types of nuclear weapons worldwide, as well as the steady "conventionalization" of nuclear weapons. According to this line of thought, nuclear weapons would soon become a "standard weapon" on the battlefield, barely distinguishable from more conventional weapons. Moreover, it was claimed that nuclear weapons in general, and specific weapons such as atomic mines and nuclear-equipped surface-to-air-missiles in particular, significantly increased an actor's defensive capabilities.

> It is obvious that an army that is equipped with nuclear weapons can defend the country distinctly better than forces that do not possess nuclear weapons.... In accordance with our centuries-old tradition of resistance the Bundesrat therefore holds the view that the army has to obtain the most potent weapons in order to preserve our independence and to protect our neutrality. These include nuclear weapons.[25]

> (my translation)

This statement was perceived as a clear indication of Switzerland's nuclear ambitions both on the domestic and the international level. For contemporary observers there seemed to be little doubt that the country had finally embarked upon a weapons procurement program. The *New York Times*, for example, wrote the next day that the "Swiss will seek nuclear weapons."[26] In a similar vein, US, and above all Soviet, government sources voiced their concern about this potential case of nuclear proliferation, perceiving it as definite evidence of Switzerland's nuclear ambitions.[27] In the light of international disapproval and objection, the Bundesrat reacted by issuing a further public and several private statements clarifying that no final decision on actual procurement had been taken so far. Indeed, there is reason to argue that both domestic and foreign observers alike tended to overrate the government's determination to implement a full-fledged nuclear program, while underrating certain hints that would have shed light on the more hesitant and irresolute nature of the government's deliberations. Most analysts, for example, paid little attention to the fact that the government primarily mandated the Defense Department to further address "questions related to the introduction of nuclear weapons into our army."

The somewhat reluctant technical steps undertaken by the government to start a weapons program further corroborated the hesitancy reflected in the mandate. The government-sponsored research group called "Möglichkeiten einer eigenen Atomwaffenproduktion" (Possibilities of Indigenous Nuclear Weapons Production, MAP), for example, consisted of only three scientists who had the task of enquiring into the possibilities and limits of a genuine Swiss nuclear weapons production program, primarily in their spare time.[28] Moreover, the group was only established in 1963 – more than five years after the government had published its thoughts on acquiring a nuclear force. Similarly, even by 1966 the government had not conducted any meaningful or substantial research on the size of uranium deposits in Switzerland – one of the preconditions of an indigenous program.[29] Given all these factors, this would seem to indicate that the 1958 statement reflects more of an eagerness to investigate the possibilities of acquiring nuclear weapons. It is debatable whether it represented the commencement of an actual procurement project.[30]

What it certainly did instigate, however, was the intensification of a broad public debate, culminating in two referenda on the nuclear issue.[31] The first of these referenda, initiated by the Swiss Movement Against Atomic Weapons (Schweizerische Bewegung gegen atomare Aufrüstung, SBgaA) in April 1958 and put to popular vote in April 1962, demanded that Switzerland forgo and constitutionally prohibit the acquisition of nuclear weapons. The second referendum, put forward by the Social Democratic Party (SPS) in July 1959 and conducted in May 1963, was more moderate in that it only called for an obligatory popular vote in the event of the government ever making the decision to acquire nuclear weapons. The debate took place in a heated and uncompromising atmosphere, with both camps – the proponents as well as the opponents of nuclearization – conducting large-scale campaigns and publicity efforts. The grassroots Movement against Atomic Weapons consisted of more than 15,000 members and included participants from a wide societal spectrum, among them many unionists, intellectuals and figures from different religious groupings. Advocates of nuclearization on the other side were often affiliated with the conservative political spectrum and had strong ties to the military – as illustrated by the Offiziersgesellschaft or the Verein zur Förderung des Wehrwillens.[32] Both referenda were ultimately rejected by a relatively large majority of voters, thereby allowing the government a "free hand" in the further development or acquisition of a Helvetian nuclear force.[33]

However, these results did not induce the Bundesrat to take any major steps toward the actual implementation of the project. This might be considered even more surprising given that the MAP working group had come to the conclusion that indigenous procurement of tactical nuclear weapons was indeed feasible. In their report, the MAP scientists and experts envisioned a three-stage process for acquiring an operational nuclear force. In the first phase, Switzerland would produce 50 bombs with a payload of approximately 60 to 100 kt each for use on Mirage fighter aircraft. In the second phase, this arsenal would be extended to encompass 100 fighter aircraft bombs as well as 50 artillery projectiles (5 kt). The third developmental stage would bring the total up to 100 aircraft bombs (60–100 kt each), 100 artillery projectiles (5 kt) and 100 missile warheads (20 kt). However, the report was kept vague and only covered preliminary estimates; it outlined the need for further clarification and called for additional funding to conduct research on local uranium deposits, the technology of uranium enrichment, as well as plutonium extraction and similar technical challenges.[34]

Despite the MAP board's relatively optimistic assessments, the development of a Swiss nuclear force did not gain significant momentum. Rather than pushing for nuclearization, the government upheld its motto of "having the option" to eventually nuclearize, while at the same time maintaining "freedom of action." This attitude seems to have been the prevalent stance up until the mid- to late 1960s. As late as 1967, the government initiated research projects to examine the possibility and desirability of acquiring nuclear weapons – yet without seriously pushing for their actual acquisition or implementing a full-scale practical research program. The 1967 decision to establish three new research commissions on the Non-Proliferation Treaty reflects this highly ambivalent approach.[35] Moreover, it illustrates that ongoing NPT negotiations increased fear among proponents of a Swiss nuclear option that signing the treaty would even further diminish the "window of opportunity" to finally acquire an indigenous nuclear weapons capability. This underlying fear surfaced in the final report issued by the Study Commission on Strategic Questions:

> Scientifically and technically, Switzerland would by its own means be capable of acquiring a small nuclear force within ten years.... An operational-tactical nuclear force would significantly advance our defense power and thereby also the war-prevention capability of our national defense.... Regardless of the decision on accession or non-accession to the Non-Proliferation Treaty we ought to create and maintain the option to produce nuclear weapons in case of an emergency.[36]

(my translation)

Interestingly, however, the three study commissions also exemplified "en miniature" the various conflicting positions within the Swiss nuclear debate. While the Study Commission on Strategic Questions demanded that the nuclear option be kept open and that Switzerland should not in principle forgo the acquisition of nuclear weapons, the Interdepartmental Working Group on the NPT explicitly recommended joining the NPT to signal support for nuclear disarmament and provide further momentum to the juridification of International Relations in order to increase international stability. This disagreement reflected a more general dissent between the foreign policy community (and the Department of Foreign Affairs) on the one hand, and the defense establishment (represented by the military and the Defense Department) on the other. A third influential player that also shaped the debate was the working group on reactor technology. Mandated to examine the NPT's possible impact on Switzerland's access to nuclear technology, nuclear energy production and other civilian applications of nuclear engineering, the technical experts advocated accession to the NPT notwithstanding some negative economic implications that were to be expected.[37]

It is also worth noting that there was at least one aspect that all groups could agree on, albeit to different degrees: in principle all the actors involved in the Swiss debate acknowledged the weaknesses and problems associated with the NPT, in particular the discriminatory character of the treaty (i.e., the unequal treatment of nuclear weapon states and non-nuclear weapon states) and the insufficient measures of investigation and inspection provided for by the treaty. For the next two years discussions were influenced by the different positions exemplified by the three study groups until, in November 1969, the Bundesrat eventually signed the Non-Proliferation Treaty.[38] However, they did not fundamentally change the course of the decision-making process. On November 27, 1969, the Swiss government finally signed the Non-Proliferation Treaty – one day before the Federal Republic of Germany.[39] It was a further eight years before the treaty was eventually ratified, though. It is also worth noting that even the signing and ratification of the treaty did not lay the matter to rest for good. As a result of domestic, intra-governmental pressures, a covert Working Group on Nuclear Issues – established in April 1969 – continued its research until 1988. Its mandate was the provision of the fundamental technological knowledge necessary to maintain a "surge option" and to break away from the non-proliferation regime should security considerations necessitate such a step. Nevertheless, this working group is perhaps one of the most telling embodiments of Switzerland's nuclear ambitions. On the one hand, it highlights the staunch and almost stubborn interest in nuclear weapons that continued to exist even after the official decision against nuclear weapons. On the other hand, it symbolizes the ultimately decisive languor and ambivalence from which the whole project suffered. During the almost two decades of its existence, the working group met only 27 times "before it was disbanded on its own proposal."[40] The Swiss case thus nicely illustrates one of the key findings of scholars working on the sociology of technology: often, the development of complex technological systems does not progress linearly, but meanders back and forth in an ambivalent, vague manner (both with regard to their beginning and their ending).[41] Moreover, it lends further support to Levite's theory of nuclear hedging. Accordingly, states sign and eventually even ratify the NPT because they know that the inherent obligations are weak enough to allow for a broad range of "nuclear behaviors" – i.e., far-reaching research and development efforts as well as practical applications of nuclear technology – and that exiting the treaty remains legally possible.[42]

Outlining the debate and its key actors

In reconstructing the debate, I will focus primarily on the period between 1958, when a government statement called for the acquisition of nuclear weapons, and November 1969, when Switzerland finally signed the Non-Proliferation Treaty. Yet while the decision to abstain from nuclear weapons only became manifest with the signing of this treaty, public discourse reached its peak in 1963 with the rejection of the referenda and the government's signing of the Partial Test Ban Treaty (PTBT). Hence, the majority of non-government documents analyzed date from 1958 to 1963; they cover the core phase of the debate and reflect the central arguments raised for and against the nuclear program. Moreover, although public attention diminished following the referenda, the issue remained far from settled from the government's perspective and in terms of policy.

The selected documents map out the key players who participated in the debate: government actors exemplified by the Federal Council and the Military Department, pro-nuclear groups such as the Verein zur Förderung des Wehrwillens und der Wehrwissenschaft (VFWW), Schweizer Offiziersgesellschaft (SOG), Aktion freier Staatsbürger, and the influential Aktionskommittee gegen die Atominitiative; while on the other side were the nuclear skeptics or outright opponents from Sozialdemoratische Partei der Schweiz (Social Democratic Party, SPS) and anti-nuclear groups such as Schweizerische Bewegung gegen atomare Aufrüstung and Arbeitsgemeinschaft der Jugend gegen die atomare Aufrüstung.[43]

Understanding the Swiss case: narratives and beliefs

How can we "make sense" of Switzerland's nuclear choice? Given the complexity and multifaceted nature of the decision- and policymaking processes in relation to this particular policy issue and the multitude of actors involved, together with non-linear shifts in the various positions on the issue, a simple (monocausal) threat-based explanation does not seem to provide us with a satisfactory picture. This by no means implies that it would be possible to account for the Swiss case by simply "factoring out" the concept of "threat." It does imply, however, that a complementary, eclectic approach could deepen our understanding of Switzerland's nuclear decision-making process. Such an approach is based on the assumption that neither the level of threat nor security concerns nor any other "condition" are objective determinants of human/state behavior but that these factors are instead mediated by language. Hence, actors give meaning to their environment on the basis of an intersubjective, linguistically mediated exchange of perceptions or views. The emerging "structures of meaning" subsequently enable and guide an actor's self-perception and behavior within this environment. The aim of the following analysis is therefore to "unearth" the dominant structures of meaning inherent in the Swiss nuclear weapons debate. An analysis will be carried out of how these structures have not only shaped the discourse, but also how they have changed over time. These changes find expression in shifting and altering understandings of the environment and also ultimately create changing policy implications and policy outcomes.

In the interest of greater clarity and a more fine-grained description of the discursive shifts and intertextual references, the "discourse universe" is divided into two phases, the first phase being from 1958 to 1963 and the second from 1963 to 1969. This division reflects the course of public debate and is tied to the central aspects of the decision-making process: the government's press release of 1958 marks the beginning of the first phase of the debate. This phase ends in 1963 with the second of the two referenda. In contrast to the second phase, the first phase was characterized by a high level of media and public attention. The analysis therefore draws on a greater number of non-governmental sources. In the second phase, both the media and the public paid less attention to the nuclear question and hence there are fewer documents available on the subject. However, as the above historical reconstruction illustrates, the issue remained on the agenda until at least the late 1960s – formally even until 1988, when the remaining Nuclear Working Group was eventually dissolved.

Phase I: the debate between 1958 and 1963

The first phase of the analysis dates from 1958 to 1963. It thereby incorporates the first official government statement on the nuclear weapons issue, several publications by non-governmental groups for and against the acquisition of nuclear weapons, as well as government publications on broader defense-related issues. The first phase ends with the two referenda in 1963. When asked whether the government should be constrained in its nuclear weapons policy, the public voted "no," thereby allowing the executive to push forward with the acquisition of nuclear weapons, if deemed necessary.

Erklärung zur Frage der Beschaffung

When the government adopted its first public stance on the nuclear question in July 1958,[44] five narratives figured prominently in its statement: wide-ranging references to the Swiss tradition of neutrality and self-defense and, in a similar vein, an emphasis on the defensive character of Swiss nuclear weapons (level 1); a rather vague and fuzzy depiction of Switzerland's security environment and of the threat faced by the country (level 2); a largely deterministic understanding of the spread of nuclear weapons; a technocratic perception of the weapons issue; and the connection between nuclear technology on the one hand and ideas of modernity and progress on the other (level 3). In order to analyze the implications of these structures and how they shape the discourse, I will consider each of these levels of analysis in greater detail below. I will then analyze the way in which these frames differ from those applied by other actors or at other times during the debate.

Level 1: identity and self-perception

The first level of analysis, relating to self-perception and identity, reveals that there are strong references to the notions of neutrality and resistance in the first government statement. The government powerfully frames the issue of nuclearization as a means for the continuation of Switzerland's traditionally neutral approach in the international system. Nuclear weapons, in other words, are depicted as a precondition for the preservation of neutrality and independence.

> In accordance with our centuries-old tradition of resistance … the army should be equipped with the most effective weapons for the preservation of our independence and the protection of our neutrality.[45]
>
> (my translation)

This is a particularly powerful frame given the role of the two concepts of neutrality and resistance in Switzerland's history and also given neutrality's manifestation in the country's constitution.[46] As Riklin points out, Switzerland's self-conception as a neutral state dates back to the seventeenth century when it was first mentioned as one of the country's core foreign policy principles.[47] It served both domestic and foreign policy purposes. By shielding the country from external intrusions, this principle of neutrality helped to integrate the heterogeneous parts of the country's territory, and by ensuring that Switzerland would not interfere or become entangled in foreign quarrels it strengthened the country's own independence, thereby preventing it from being dragged too deeply into the severely unstable and fractured European environment. In a similar vein, Kriesi and Trechsel argue:

> For nearly two centuries, neutrality was – and remains – the ineluctable guiding principle of Switzerland's relations with other states, polities and supra- or international organizations.[48]

Hence, references to these principles serve as a powerful frame that can be easily comprehended and both cognitively and emotionally grasped by readers of the statement.[49] Moreover, the lexical connection between the acquisition of nuclear weapons on the one hand, and the traditional and historically charged concepts of neutrality and independence on the other, integrate the nuclear issue into the long stream of Swiss history. According to this reading, nuclear weapons do not imply a change or even deviation from the key pillars of Swiss foreign and security policy but instead embody a high degree of continuity with its historical policies as well as with its traditional identity and self-conception. In addition,

the reference to neutrality (and the implicit emphasis on the non-offensive attitude of the country) provides further support for the government's assurance that
the weapons it aspires to acquire would – "as everyone knows" – only be used
for defensive purposes and in "acts of self-defense."[50]

Furthermore, we can discern a powerful invocation of the notion of passivity.
Together with the related idea of a deterministic automatism of proliferation,
these references constitute a fairly striking and recurring narrative that appears
to be characteristic of the beginnings of the Swiss debate and of the government
statements in particular. In several instances in the first governmental statement
it is claimed that Switzerland *is faced with* a situation in which the respective
government agencies and institutions are being forced to make a decision
regarding the acquisition of nuclear weapons.[51] The problem is depicted as one
that is not only objectively given, but that also seems to automatically become
aggravated given the likely rise in the number and types of nuclear weapons.

> These weapons increase steadily in number and diversity.... Today the
> number of powers that possess nuclear weapons is limited. Yet there is evid-
> ence that in the not so distant future further states will be added.[52]
>
> (my transation)

Hence, the spread of nuclear weapons appears to be an inevitably occurring phenomenon which causes a global security situation that leaves Switzerland with
hardly any options.[53] What remains obscure, however, is the aspect of agency: it
is not made explicit who is considered responsible for this spread; by the same
token, the authors neglect to specify the mechanism that leads to the growth in
weapon numbers and designs.

Similarly, the government portrays itself as a "passive actor," one that is
incapable of intervening in or changing the perceived automatism of "proliferation." The role of human agency as a force underlying all policies and political
decisions is overlooked. Consequently, the country is depicted not as an actor
choosing a particular policy but rather as a dependant reacting to global trends.
At first glance, this depiction seems surprising: it runs counter to more common
official narratives in which governments usually try to portray themselves as
able and competent. As feminist IR theorists have pointed out, states usually
depict their security policies in masculine terms – as the exercise of power and
self-help.[54] In this document, on the contrary, the government actually subscribes
to a narrative of weakness. Switzerland is thereby pictured as a small and powerless follower in the international system that lacks both the influence and power
to achieve political change.[55]

Level 2: Switzerland's position in the international system

The second level of analysis – regarding Switzerland's role in the world and its
position vis-à-vis other states – contains a narrative that is perhaps the most
important in analytical terms: the notion of threat. Surprisingly, though, this

frame is the least developed and the least concrete throughout the document. Given the established background of IR and proliferation-specific literature, there may be a tendency to assume that the beginning of Switzerland's nuclear weapons program is related to a large degree to a discernible external threat. The assumption might also be made that in order to legitimize the acquisition of nuclear weapons the document would contain more concrete references to a specific foreign actor, or at least more specific references to a definite threat perception. However, any explicit attributions or indications are conspicuously absent from the document at hand. Interestingly, instead of specific references to an external security menace we find several allusions to a rather general but no less illuminating frame of "danger." The government justifies its move towards nuclear weapons by hinting at (a) the global proliferation dynamic. Accordingly, the anticipated increase in the number of weapons, as well as the potential for growth in the number of nuclear armed states, would weaken Switzerland's relative power position should the country refrain from acquiring the same weapons.[56] In addition, the authors delineate a scenario (b), according to which the Swiss territory could (inadvertently) become a theater of hostilities between "foreign powers."[57]

Both examples remain vague and underspecified, though. Just why the further spread of nuclear weapons or a further erosion of the nuclear monopoly would unavoidably represent a threat to Switzerland is not spelled out, for instance. Under what conditions might one expect foreign powers to clash in warfare activities on Swiss territory? Similarly, it remains unclear if any erosion of the nuclear monopoly is considered a threat. Do all potential new nuclear powers represent a threat to Switzerland or are certain powers more threatening than others? Does this also imply that Switzerland does not need to feel threatened by the existing nuclear powers (including the Soviet Union), but only by other potential nuclear-armed states? And which states would they be? Some analysts have argued that Germany's quest for nuclear weapons was the main cause of concern for Switzerland's decision-makers.[58] On the basis of this first document this assumption can neither be explicitly supported nor refuted. It is nonetheless revealing that the authors of this document put such strong emphasis on the feared erosion of the nuclear monopoly. Later on we will see that other supporters of weapons acquisition regard this aspect as being only a secondary issue and focus instead on the perceived danger from communist forces.

Level 3: attributes of civil and military nuclear technology

The third, and most extensive, level of analysis contains specific references to nuclear technology. This analysis reveals that that dominant narrative in the document is the depiction of nuclearization as a primarily technocratic question. This "technocentrism" is compellingly illustrated by numerous references to scientific studies ("Studies have shown that in future wars…"[59]) as well as in the use of a multitude of technical terms and concepts. In addition, this is also underlined by the framing of the nuclear question as "a problem" that has to be addressed, thereby again leaving no room for political choice. By framing the issue in terms of a problem, it is suggested that the government has barely any room for maneuver: it is compelled to act in accordance with the given situation.[60]

What is particularly striking, however, is that the authors of the government report go to great lengths to provide readers with details of future nuclear weapons developments and with examples of different nuclear weapon designs. They refer to the weight and maneuverability of nuclear projectiles, illustrate the defensive character of nuclear mines and describe the protective value of surface-to-air-missiles that are equipped with nuclear warheads.[61] The acquisition of nuclear weapons is thereby framed primarily as a technological step, with political or moral aspects consequently taking a back seat in the discussion. As a result, the decision to acquire nuclear weapons is banished from the realm of political deliberations and instead subordinated to mere technical considerations.

The references to modernity and progress in the document suggest a similar trend. Nuclear weapons are instilled with a normative, symbolic meaning that appears to be only tangentially linked to their strategic or warfare characteristics. Instead, they seem to mirror ideas of what a modern, well-equipped army, and a modern state respectively, should look like. By qualifying the term "nuclear weapon" with adjectives such as "modern" or "standard," the weapons are imbued with a symbolic meaning: they are described as a prestigious, legitimate, state-of-the-art means of warfare.[62] Hence, the acquisition of a nuclear arsenal comes to serve a more symbolic rather than a purely military function. It is a statement about a country's identity as a modern state and an illustration of how progressive, technologically and scientifically advanced it is. Opposing the acquisition of nuclear weapons, in turn, is implicitly framed as backwardness and as an impediment to the nation's development.

In a similar vein, nuclear weapons are described merely as the next developmental stage after conventional weapons. Neither the specifically indiscriminate character of nuclear devices nor their radioactive impact is mentioned.

> In the not-so-distant future on the battlefield, nuclear ammunition will likely be fired off by weapons that hardly differ in weight and mobility from the ones that have been in use until now.[63]

> (my translation)

Instead, it is stressed that future generations of nuclear weapons will increasingly resemble conventional weapons due to ongoing efforts to decrease their size and yield. Hence, the issue is again approached from the very technical angle of "product development" – it is "conventionalized" and thereby "normalized." The technocratization of the nuclear discourse glosses over all other attributes that are inherent in the concept of nuclear technology. It suggests that the acquisition of nuclear weapons is merely a non-political management decision based on mundane, obvious necessities, thereby leaving little room for different political interpretations.

It is important to note that such a representation of nuclear weapons is not merely a scientific, "objective" account of nuclear weapons as such. The portrayal of atomic devices as technologically advanced, modern and pioneering tools also functions as an implicit depiction of the country's aspired identity. A state that is able to command the development of such innovative and progressive technologies must therefore undoubtedly be a modern, progressive state. By the same token, nuclear weapons are described as the *sine qua non* for the "truly modern state." If nuclear weapons are imbued with a connotation of modernity and progress, then any state that develops and possesses these weapons also benefits from this reputation.

It should also be acknowledged that on the one hand such framing was far from unusual during the early post-1945 period. With regard to the discourse in the United States, Tannenwald writes, for example, that "the American public was not particularly bothered by atomic bombs – radiation did not really become an issue until the 1950s – and the atomic bomb was not viewed as a decisive weapon."[64] On the other hand, the invention of nuclear weapons had always been accompanied by voices calling for a stigmatization of this means of warfare. As early as 1946 the UN called for "the elimination from national armaments of atomic weapons and of all other major weapons adaptable to mass destruction."[65] The Russell-Einstein Manifesto, published in 1955, is a further embodiment of the emerging deprecating attitude toward nuclear weapons:

> In view of the fact that in any future world war nuclear weapons will certainly be employed, and that such weapons threaten the continued existence of mankind, we urge the governments of the world to realize, and to acknowledge publicly, that their purpose cannot be furthered by a world war, and we urge them, consequently, to find peaceful means for the settlement of all matters of dispute between them.[66]

Thus, while the rather technocratic, modernity-oriented position put forward by the Swiss government in this first document was not particularly unusual for the early years of the nuclear age, it disregards the more critical stance that was beginning to emerge at the time.

To sum up the analysis of this first document, given the elusiveness of several of the key narratives and of the threat frame in particular, the argumentative power or force of the 1958 document can at least be questioned. Leaving these questions aside, however, there is little doubt that this document, having been widely published by Swiss newspapers on July 11, 1958, set the stage for the ensuing broad public debate. It established an influential interpretation of the nuclear weapons issue that depicted the acquisition of atomic forces primarily as a milestone of modernity and as a fairly conventional, ordinary replacement of military equipment.

Aufruf an das Schweizer Volk

The Schweizerische Bewegung gegen atomare Aufrüstung, which vigorously opposed the government's plan for the acquisition of a nuclear force, reacted soon after and, in April 1959, petitioned for a referendum on the nuclear question. The initiative demanded a constitutional ban on the production or acquisition of nuclear weapons.[67] The petition was part of a large public campaign to counter the arguments put forward by the government and other pro-bomb advocates. In their principal statement, entitled "Aufruf an das Schweizer Volk," the nuclear opponents draw primarily on six narratives: an emphasis on the humanitarian nature of Swiss identity; an activist understanding of Switzerland's role in global political affairs; a view of nuclear weapons as non-conventional and criminal; a depiction of proliferation as dangerous; a perception of nuclear weapons as detrimental to Switzerland's security; and the assertion of antagonism between the ideal of neutrality on the one hand and nuclear armament on the other.

Level 1: identity and self-perception

This statement diverges greatly from the government interpretation of "Swissness," i.e., Swiss identity. What is Swiss? What is at the core of the country's identity? As we have seen in the first document, the government refers to two pillars of identity: the tradition of neutrality and resistance as well as receptiveness to modernity and progress. The anti-nuclear movement, on the other hand, associates Swiss identity above all with the humanitarian heritage of the Red Cross and its founder Henri Dunant.

> Switzerland is the country of respected neutrality; the country that has – through the deeds of Henri Dunant – countered the cruelty of war with the enterprise of worldwide humanity…. The moral credit that Switzerland has gained thanks to its humanitarian mission in the world would be questioned by its own nuclearization. This would indeed do a disservice to national defense.[68]
>
> (my translation)

It thereby creates an implicit but strong emotional and cognitive link between the nuclear question, international humanitarian law and the *ius in bello* conceptions for the protection of civilians during warfare. The acquisition of nuclear weapons would, in other words, contradict Switzerland's humanitarian efforts and hence also run counter to its own identity. What is particularly significant, however, is the implied "deviant" reading of the term neutrality. As we have seen before, the government had created a specific reading of the term neutrality by predicating neutrality on resistance. The opposition, however, challenged this reading and provided an alternative chain of associations that linked the country's status as neutral to the tradition of humanitarianism, the legacy of Henri

Dunant, and the Red Cross. This narrative of charity and philanthropy offers an understanding of Swiss identity that runs counter to the more official martial or "soldierly" reading.

Furthermore, the authors of the "Aufruf" attempt to depict the defensive use of nuclear weapons as "non-Swiss" by making extensive reference to the Winkelried myth, a well-known and prominent folktale with iconic status in Switzerland's national history and the country's fight against domination by the Habsburgs.

> Atomic weapons are suicidal weapons. Suicidal weapons are not defensive weapons. Anyone who uses them brings ruin on himself and his people and does not sacrifice himself as Winkelried did.[69]
>
> (my translation)

According to this fourteenth-century legend, Winkelried, a captain in the Swiss confederate forces, sacrificed himself in order to break the ranks of the enemy, thereby enabling the Swiss forces to attack and defeat the Habsburg forces. Implicitly, Winkelried's deeds are stylized not only as a paragon of virtue but also as the epitome of "Swissness." The idea of using nuclear weapons in an act of self-defense, on the contrary, is criticized as amounting to a perverted version of heroism, given the devastating consequences that such a military effort would have for the country itself. Thus, while the government tried to legitimize the acquisition and use of weapons for defensive purposes, arguing that this was in accordance with the Swiss self-perception of neutrality and resistance, its opponents, too, drew on descriptions of Swiss identity and the country's historical self-perception – albeit with very different results. As is shown below, this oppositional humanitarian trope is then given further strength through a description, several paragraphs long, of the "devastating" consequences of the use of nuclear devices. Referring to a culturally anchored historical myth – a myth that is highly likely to be engrained in the "identity memory" of many readers – is a particularly noteworthy step in the framing process, however. The authors do not cede Switzerland's past to governmental or conservative historiography but instead use these traditional legends and cultural roots for their own purposes. The document thus offers an interesting example of the openness and contestable nature of historical interpretation; it reminds us of the negotiability of cultural and historical memories.

Level 2: Switzerland's position in the international system

The interpretations differ not only with regard to the level of self-perception, though. The international system and Switzerland's relations with "significant others" are also depicted differently by the opponents of the nuclear option. Accordingly, one of the staunchest and most visible discrepancies between opponents and proponents of the acquisition of nuclear weapons focuses on the notion of agency. More concretely, while the government (as shown above) portrays the nuclear question as a problem to which the country can only *react*, the nuclear opponents frame the issue as one that not only allows, but in fact calls for, a high degree of agency and proactive decision-making ("We have to begin the struggle..."). Consequently, the question of whether to obtain nuclear weapons is not forced on to the country or its government but leaves room for maneuver and political deliberation. Hence, the government's emphasis on the external or material and practical constraints on decision-making is not only called into question by the notion of agency and a presumed capacity for action. It is in fact replaced by a normative call for responsible action.

Level 3: attributes of civil and military nuclear technology

Moreover, the opponents of Switzerland's nuclearization provide a contrasting reading of nuclear technology and nuclear weapons (level 3). Drawing on socially shared interpretations of the nuclear bombings of Hiroshima, the authors expound on the impact of radiation on human health and the environment.

> We have not forgotten Hiroshima! One single atomic bomb killed more than 70,000 people with one strike; ten thousands have since then died a miserable death caused by radiation sickness. Apparently healthy parents have gruesome miscarriages. According to estimates by the Japanese medical association another hundred thousand people will be affected.[70]
>
> (my translation)

The logical consequence of this perspective is to oppose the "conventionalization" of nuclear weapons. To recall: the government had framed nuclear devices as simply a further step in the development and modernization of conventional means of warfare. The anti-nuclear camp then argued vigorously and explicitly against this blurring, calling nuclear weapons a "means of eradication." The use of nuclear weapons is thus considered "a crime not only against living humans, but also against our children and grandchildren" – an assertion that is supported by detailed references to the consequences of the bombings of Hiroshima. Hence, in opposition to the government's notion of conventionalism, the anti-nuclear movement underscores the qualitative otherness of nuclear weapons and calls for the criminalization of their use.[71]

A further significant frame in the argument put forward by the nuclear opponents is the depiction of proliferation as dangerous. Again, this runs at least partially counter to the narrative inherent in the government's statement. The government, too, argued that the further spread of nuclear weapons to hitherto non-nuclear countries would represent a threat. However, it drew the conclusion that this trend would force Switzerland to acquire nuclear weapons for its own defense. The opponents of nuclearization, on the other hand, claimed that any spread of nuclear weapons and any form of proliferation posed a danger – not just for Switzerland, but globally – and that proliferation in general therefore had to be prevented. In contrast to the government's focus on Switzerland's particular security needs, this line of argument reflects a more universalist understanding of the weapons issue.

At the same time, however, the "Aufruf" debate is pervaded by another frame that explicitly addresses traditional security considerations. Accordingly, the acquisition of nuclear weapons is considered detrimental to Switzerland's military security and its national defense.

> Even from the standpoint of military national defense, nuclear armament is a menace to our country. Switzerland, as a densely-populated small state, would be even less likely than the spacious great powers to survive a war in which it deployed nuclear weapons.... If Switzerland restricts itself to tactical weapons with a short range, then in the event of a crisis, these weapons would destroy and irradiate our own land, the territory of friendly neighbors, humans, soil, plants and livestock and they would make Switzerland uninhabitable for a long period of time. This has nothing to do with national defense.[72]
>
> (my translation)

Implicitly drawing on the impact of nuclear weapons deployment in terms of explosive power and radiation, the authors argue that a territorially small country like Switzerland would suffer even more from a nuclear war than larger countries. On the basis of this assumption they call for a repudiation of the deployment of tactical nuclear weapons by Swiss forces. In extending this line of argument, the opponents of a Swiss nuclear force furthermore claim that tactical nuclear weapons, in addition to their detrimental radiological impact, have no deterrent effect on major powers. In other words, what we see in this passage is an attempt to undermine the government's strategic rationale for the acquisition of tactical nuclear weapons. While their proponents emphasized the deterrent impact of Swiss nuclear weapons on a potential enemy by highlighting the additional costs the aggressor would have to bear, the opponents frame the military effect of nuclear weapons from a humanitarian perspective. At the core, therefore, lie two differing conceptions of "defense" (and ultimately also of "state survival"): the government's idea of how best to militarily defend the territorial integrity of the country competes with an alternative frame that equates defense with the protection of civilians.[73]

These diverging beliefs about defense, security and endangerment are also apparent in another part of the document. The authors of the "Aufruf" refer to and criticize statements made by "individual industrial and army leaders"[74] who had apparently called for the purchase of "long-range nuclear missiles" that could reach targets in "Paris or Moscow." While the authors are very clear in their rejection of this idea, arguing that this would only provoke preventive strikes against Switzerland, they are less clear in revealing who they are referring to when using the term "individual leaders" and whom exactly they are quoting. Only the reference to "targeting Moscow" is attributable to Oberstdivisionär Primault who had apparently called for long-range bombers to potentially attack targets on Soviet territory. It is not known who called for weapons that could possibly "hit Paris." In any case, however, this passage of the "Aufruf" is enlightening, since it seems to indicate an unclear, distorted and overall rather hazy perception of threat, on both sides of the argumentative line. The government did not succeed in assembling an unambiguous and convincing narrative of threat and danger, ironically thus making it difficult for its opponents to explicitly oppose or counter it.

The last significant structure of interpretation that emerges in the text is an asserted antagonism between the country's "respected neutrality" on the one hand and nuclear armaments on the other. As we have already seen above, the opponents of nuclearization hold a different view of Switzerland's identity and self-perception to the government. As seen in the analysis of the first document, the government had framed the acquisition of nuclear weapons as a necessity in order to maintain and protect Switzerland's neutrality and to ensure its capacity for resistance. The structure of meaning contained in the "Aufruf," however, runs diametrically counter to this frame. Not only is Switzerland's long-established and "respected" neutrality intimately linked with its self-perception as a humanitarian state; humanitarianism is also considered incompatible with the possession of nuclear weapons. Once again, therefore, we find highly divergent notions of the concept of neutrality. On the government's side we see a security- or defense-related conception that interweaves neutrality not only with the principle of non-interference with other states but also with a strong concept of resistance to and defense against external aggression ("bewaffnete Neutralität"). The opposition, on the other hand, promotes a humanitarian conception of neutrality that is intimately linked to universalist ideas of civilian protection, the civilization of warfare and political benefaction. Given the historically grown significance of the concept of neutrality to Switzerland's self-image, it is clear that this frame does not merely concern the legal issue of the rights and obligations of neutral states or the right policy choices of neutrals. It touches upon the very foundations of the country's identity (see level 1). Nuclear weapons are thus predicated as anti-humanitarian and anti-Swiss: they are considered the antithesis of "Swissness."

Anti-nuclear leaflets

While the 1958 "Aufruf an das Schweizer Volk" was perhaps the single most influential, most widely circulated and most comprehensive document published by the peace movement, it was far from the only one. On the contrary, it was supported and supplemented by a large number of leaflets, handouts, pamphlets, newspaper advertisements, as well as mail shots and brochures.[75] Compared to the rather limited number of government publications on the issue, the arguments put forward by the peace movement were naturally much more diffuse, polyphonic and miscellaneous, and less coherently orchestrated. Nevertheless, we can identify at least two other recurring, prevalent narratives that supplement and go hand in hand with the ones already delineated in the "Aufruf":[76] an emphasis on the Swiss tradition of popular sovereignty and direct democracy, as well as an activist notion of foreign policymaking.

Level 1: identity and self-perception

The question of nuclear procurement is integrated into the broader framework of Switzerland's history and identity as an archetypal direct democracy. It is emphasized that the institution of direct democracy and the use of popular initiatives and referenda are integral components of the country's historically grown political identity and that they must not be suspended over the procurement question.[77] Hence, in a move that aims to "re-politicize" the nuclear issue, the opponents of the Swiss nuclear program demand that the debate be maintained and addressed within the institutional structure of direct democracy, instead of entrusting the decision-making prerogative to the executive or the military establishment alone.

> The nuclearization of our military is not merely a military question, but to a much larger extent a political and moral one which touches upon the principal ideas on which our country is built.[78]
>
> (my translation)

The nuclear question, in other words, is portrayed as a pivotal example of and a test case for the vitality and virtues of the political system. It is a reading that runs counter to the one put forward by the government and members of the military establishment who argue that the issue is too crucial to be surrendered to the "passionate atmosphere of a popular referendum."[79] Again, this reveals the two diverging perspectives on the "political dimension" of the nuclear issue: the anti-nuclear movement describes the nuclear armament question as a deeply political issue that is open to deliberation and political agency, while the proponents call into question the political nature of the armaments decision and refer instead to factual constraints and security necessities.

Level 2: Switzerland's position in the international system

The second alternative structure of interpretation advanced by the non-nuclear movement pertains to the second level of our analytical heuristic, i.e., the country's role in the world; its attitudes and relations vis-à-vis significant other states, etc. The interpretive model advanced by the anti-nuclearization movement centers on a call for a particularly activist approach to foreign policy. In contrast to the government's emphasis on passivity and powerlessness due to international obligations and constraints, those on the Left emphasize the government's freedom of action regarding the nuclear issue.[80] They argue that neither the international system nor international law call for or necessitate the acquisition of nuclear weapons by Switzerland.[81] Instead, the authors not only demand the renunciation of all nuclear weapon plans, but call for increased, visionary efforts toward a more activist, peace-promoting foreign and security policy that supersedes the traditional patterns of Machtpolitik. The opponents thus provide a much broader narrative than the government, which focused fairly narrowly on the weapons issue in itself. The government dwelt at great length on the deterministic force of proliferation and framed the issue of nuclearization as an externally given necessity. The anti-nuclear movement, on the other hand, frames its argument more broadly, invoking a generally activist concept of foreign policy-making: it depicts Switzerland as an apparently influential – but militarily self-limited – player that has a duty to influence and shape international relations in accordance with normative considerations.

> Our struggle is an affirmation of the accepted platform of traditional power-political self-limitation that a small state has to take as its starting point in order to contribute in an adequate manner to the constitution of international understanding. Its goal is: to win over the majority of the Swiss people to a new, constructive politics in the service of détente and understanding among nations.[82]

(my translation)

Early on in the debate, therefore, the issue of agency is established as one of the major bones of contention between the opponents and supporters of Swiss nuclearization. From an early stage, the debate went beyond the specific question of nuclear proliferation, and instead touched upon the much broader aspects of Switzerland's foreign policy.

These two narratives complement the anti-nuclear frames – i.e., the call for a proactive foreign policy or the call for a neutrality policy based on humanitarian principles, such as those already outlined in the "Aufruf," for example.

Erklärung der 35

The first phase of the debate was also shaped by at least one other major document: the "Erklärung der 35" – a statement signed by 35 unionists and social democrats which was published in the *Schweizer Metall- und Uhrenarbeiter-Zeitung* newspaper.[83] In general terms, this document is significant for three main reasons: first, for addressing the nuclear issue; second, for its attempt to reunify the fragmented political Left; third, for its pronounced anti-communist standpoint. One of the central arguments of the publication is a call for unity among the working classes and the Social Democratic Party (SP). The 35 signatories were highly critical of the left-wing peace movement; their demand for unity was a reaction to the turmoil and uproar on the Left which had been caused by the formation of the Schweizerische Bewegung gegen atomare Aufrüstung by members of the SP and other peace activists. Hence, the authors of the "Erklärung" made extensive references to the need to re-establish the unity of the Left and repeatedly emphasized their disdain for communist forces – signals which were likely directed not only at SP members, but also at the conservative forces within the political system. Furthermore, the statement served as a "position marker" aimed at voters.[84] What is also interesting is the narrowness of the chain of argument used in this document. All of the main arguments revolve around the idea of anti-communism, which forms the central narrative in this pro-nuclearization statement. As a result, the link between the purported conception of Swiss identity – Switzerland as an anti-communist state – and the call for an anti-nuclear foreign policy is evident here.

Levels 1 and 2: on identity and global role

The authors of the "Erklärung" make considerable efforts to embed the question of nuclearization within a more fundamental depiction of the global confrontation between capitalism and communism. In their statement they use detailed and graphic language to draw a comparison between the two opposing blocs. The East is portrayed as "totalitarian," "predatory," "oppressive," "intimidating" and "hypocritical." The West, on the other hand, is pictured as "free-spirited"; its peoples are characterized as "free." While this style or characterization is in itself not particularly surprising given that the document was drafted during the Cold War, it is important to note that this is the only underlying theme drawn upon by the authors. In other words, in contrast to other documents, the authors of this particular document justify the acquisition of nuclear weapons solely and exclusively by reference to the East–West confrontation.

The narrow but concise argument is further strengthened by two other, secondary structures of meaning. The first, (a), is the interpretation of communism as a direct and actual threat to Switzerland and the West. According to this interpretation, the East is not simply perceived as "the other" or the second force in the global balance of power. It is depicted as a concrete and immediate danger that has the ability to dominate and conquer the "free peoples of Europe and ultimately the whole world." Hence, whereas the other documents thus far analyzed refrained from depicting or failed to depict an imminent danger in order to justify the acquisition of nuclear forces, the "Erklärung" is far more vigorous and outspoken in delineating this perceived threat. And yet it, too, does not provide a detailed threat analysis, remaining instead on an abstract, ideological level.

A second subordinate frame, (b), depicts the Soviet threat not only as imminent and acute, but also as inherent and ultimately "automatic." In other words, the threat need not be aroused or provoked: the totalitarian Eastern bloc is impulse-driven and intrinsically inclined to expand its realm of influence in order to exert dominance over the "free world."

> Experience has taught us that the East, by oppressing its people and eyeing at world dominance, can only be withheld from causing new aggression and from putting the hydrogen bomb in the balance if it is confronted by a nuclear arsenal which is at least equally potent.[85]

(my translation)

In evoking this interpretation, the document shifts the East–West confrontation from the level of political disagreement which can be influenced to the realm of constraints and impulses which cannot be influenced. The potential for meaningful political action is thus eliminated, given the inherent, automatic danger posed by the Eastern enemy. Against the background of this narrative – the international threat environment and the enemy – another major interpretation or frame may be discerned, which exhibits the key attributes of the role of the free Western world within the international environment. In contrast to the expansive policies attributed to the totalitarian bloc, the West is depicted as inherently passive and defensive. Accordingly, the predicates used to describe the West's behavior and its role in the world are purely defensive in nature, the main ones being "defense preparedness," "defense capacity" and "means of defense."

In summary, the document approaches the issue of Switzerland's nuclearization from a very different perspective, one that is mainly ideological and universalist. The call for the acquisition of nuclear weapons is embedded in a more abstract and general depiction of the confrontation between East and West, the incongruity of the two systems and the perceived inherent aggressiveness of the Soviet Union.

The documents analyzed thus far have been central in delineating the argumentative realm of the debate on the acquisition of nuclear weapons by the Swiss government. However, as will be shown by the interpretation of further documents, the debate was by no means static or even fixed following this first exchange of arguments. Instead, as will become apparent in the further course of this analysis, the central frames and interpretations, as well as underlying notions and meanings, changed throughout the debate.

Three further important documents were issued by the Swiss government during this first phase (up until 1963): a military strategy report on the organization of the army, the "Truppenordnung"[86] (1960); a Bundesrat statement on the first anti-nuclear weapons initiative (1961),[87] as well as a statement (including an addendum) on the second initiative (1962).[88] Given that the government issued only relatively few public statements on the issue of nuclear weapons acquisition (and even fewer in the years after 1963), all three publications are highly relevant, although they deal with the nuclear question to varying degrees.

Truppenordnung

The "Truppenordnung" only touches upon the nuclearization question within the larger context of the Swiss military doctrine at the beginning of the 1960s. The document integrates the nuclear question into a more comprehensive analysis of the changing strategic environment and calls for a fundamental reform and reorganization of the Swiss military. Moreover, as illustrated above, the issue of nuclear weapons acquisition was closely interwoven with general questions regarding the future structure and strategic posture of the Swiss military. It is thus insightful to closely analyze the contextual threads and the larger defense framework in which the possible acquisition of nuclear weapons was embedded.

The document is dominated by four key narratives or argument threads that give a further spin to the ongoing debate. They refer to or contain the following aspects: recurring references to the country's neutrality and independence;

a discourse of modernity and military-technological progress; depictions of the changing military and strategic environment; and several allusions to Switzerland's threat environment and its threat perception.

Level 2: Switzerland's position in the international system

The text does not contain many explicit statements relating to the level of identity and self-perception (level 1). Rather, the narratives of neutrality and independence are part of a broader depiction of the country's role in the international world and its structures. The document delineates how these structural constraints shape the global arena in general and the government's range of choice in particular (level 2). Referring to the Swiss constitution, the authors argue that the government has to subordinate its policies to the major foreign policy goal of maintaining the country's independence. Moreover, it is claimed that the country has to conform to the obligations (Neutralitätspflichten) that arise from its status as a permanent neutral state.

> Swiss foreign policy uses permanent neutrality as the primary vehicle for reaching its goal. Hence, certain particular demands concerning the organization of the army arise. It has to be capable of meeting the obligations of neutrality.[89]

(my translation)

This reference works well to emphasize the government's limited freedom of action. The framing suggests that Switzerland is not in a position to autonomously determine its military policies, but instead has to follow certain duties and responsibilities imposed upon it by the international system and codified in international law. More explicitly, it is claimed that Articles 1, 5 and 10 of the 1907 Hague Convention embody an obligation to maintain the integrity of the territory and that they unambiguously call for the acquisition of the "necessary military instruments of power" to do so.[90] It should be noted, however, that the authors concede that this does not imply an obligation to pursue nuclear weapons per se, but that it may also be understood as a call for a strong, upgraded and conventionally equipped army that is able to deter and dissuade any potential adversaries.[91] These references to the "obligations of neutrality," together with a range of other publications published during that period, form a specific intertextual web. In them, several authors discuss the future characteristics of Switzerland's neutrality in the broader context of international law and international security. The most important contributor to the debate was Rudolf Bindschedler, who acted as legal counsel for the Swiss Foreign Ministry during the 1950s. In what came to be known as the Bindschedler-Doctrine, he maintained that a neutral state had the obligation to use all means to defend its territory and to avoid being drawn into a military conflict.[92]

In a comparatively lengthy description of the fundamental facets of the international system, the authors then set out to justify their claims for a strong,

modernized army, claiming that true ("tatsächlich," i.e., military) power is necessary if the country wants to defend its existence and freedom under the conditions of "self-help." What is also significant about this line of argument is the
equation of national strength with military strength. Military might, it is argued,
is necessary to protect a country's economic, social and cultural values, and is
essential if the country is to remain an active international subject:

> Even if a state only wants to defend its existence and freedom, it must have
> the necessary power. This includes an army so that it can repel a violent
> attack in the most extreme of cases. The unarmed and weak will not be able
> to survive in the long run; such a country will go from being a subject to
> being the object of politics. And although the power of a state – understood
> in the broadest sense – is co-determined by intellectual, economic, social
> and cultural factors, it is manifest that power, in the narrower sense of the
> word, is necessary in order to protect these values and enforce them.[93]

(my translation)

Accordingly, the issue of military reform and modernization is justified by
embedding it into a larger narrative of international anarchy, self-help and
survival.

Despite these broad sketches of the international system and of the inherent
perils to Switzerland's national security there are no specific allusions to concrete threat perceptions. Similarly, there is no mention of specific enemies or
threats, or of vital national interests that had to be protected. It thus remains
unclear which threat perceptions influenced the draft of the "Truppenordnung"
document and which scenarios were to be covered by the envisioned military
reform. This vagueness and the incoherence of the underlying threat perception
become even more apparent given that certain scenarios are almost explicitly
ruled out by the authors. While they generally concede that the use of nuclear
weapons in future acts of warfare is probable,[94] they describe a nuclear war
against Switzerland as unlikely. "We cannot envision a military-political situation" which would make a full-scale nuclear war against Switzerland reasonable for any enemy, they argue.

> Should we be attacked by nuclear weapons ... one could theoretically assume
> the possibility that our people and our army would be exterminated.... Yet
> we cannot envision a military-political situation, which would make such
> action appear reasonable – neither in the light of the current constellation,
> nor in the light of a future, possibly different grouping of powers.[95]

(my translation)

Yet, in a section entitled "The menace to Switzerland," the authors write that the
"use of all means, including nuclear weapons" has to be expected.[96] While such
a framing is not necessarily contradictory, it suggests that the underlying security
rationale was far from precise and unequivocal.

Level 3: attributes of civil and military nuclear technology

In addition, this document is particularly significant due to its rather comprehensive and lengthy depiction of the ongoing developments at the time in the area of military security and strategy. The impact of technological developments on Switzerland's defense and security concept is described in great detail. While most of this description refers to technological developments in general, we also find several statements that relate to the specific issue of nuclear weapons technology (level 3). Under the heading of "The general development of warfare and war technology," the authors describe how two global developments – the introduction and deployment of nuclear weapons, and developments in fire power and mobility – have fundamentally altered the country's security landscape.[97] Against the backdrop of these developments, they call for significant changes to the military's equipment, organizational structure and its operational strategy in order to catch up with this evolution. As a consequence the authors demand a reduction in the size of the Swiss military, greater mobility and increased fire power through the deployment of faster, higher caliber weaponry.

Moreover, this reference to ongoing developments in the realm of military technology is closely interwoven with and constitutive of the related narrative of modernity. As noted earlier in this chapter, this narrative was also prevalent in the 1958 "Erklärung zur Beschaffung." In this narrative the acquisition of new means of warfare is endowed with a symbolic meaning of modernity and public progress. The underlying mechanism is the lexical association between "modernity" and "new technologies of warfare." Building upon a general narrative of military modernization, nuclear weapons are regarded as the "climax of progress" in terms of fire power and as an icon of modern means of warfare.[98] Nonetheless, as will be elaborated in more detail below, the authors concede that it may also be possible to defend the country without having the most modern weapons (i.e., nuclear weapons) at the military's disposal.[99]

Three aspects of this set of argumentative frames seem particularly striking. First, the process is rhetorically described as one of "catch-up modernization." In other words, Switzerland is portrayed as currently being on the boundary of modernity and backwardness in its military technology. If it does not make serious efforts to upgrade the military and acquire new weapons, the country cannot be an equal player on the international scene.[100] Second, the process is again pictured as one that is *forced upon* Switzerland: the country apparently has little room for maneuver and is instead only reacting to external pressures and constraints[101] – a rhetorical device that we have also seen in other government publications on similar issues. Third, the depiction of the new security environment and of the utility of nuclear weapons as a supplement to existing means of warfare lacks any reference to the detrimental environmental and health effects of these weapons. Issues such as radiation, nuclear contamination or other hazards that go hand in hand with nuclear warfare are not mentioned at all throughout the text. Instead the authors limit their description to the positive strategic effects these weapons would have in war. This omission is astonishing, given that the "Truppenordnung" was published amid heated public debate on the harmful effects of nuclear weapons, among other issues. The disregard is also irritating because it indicates that the authors of the study disregard the necessity of protecting their own military against the possible fallout of a nuclear attack during acts of warfare: they neither demanded additional sources of funding in order to acquire special protective gear for the troops, nor did they outline particular strategic or tactical responses to acts of nuclear warfare. This raises the question of whether the possible use of nuclear weapons by enemy forces was given any serious consideration at all at this point or if it merely functioned as a frame for national modernity and progress rather than as a starting point for a serious reassessment of a new warfare scenario.

Overall, the document thus shows a certain imprecision and vagueness regarding the exact nature of the threat faced by Switzerland and the role of nuclear weapons within this new security environment. This ambiguity or even incoherence could be interpreted as an indication of the authors' struggle to bind together and integrate several diverging threat perceptions and strategic cultures prevalent within the military establishment. It appears that fault lines between the different branches of the armed services – for example, between the army and the air force – come to the fore in this rather heterogeneous document. It all amounts to a rather half-hearted call for nuclearization.

> We are therefore convinced that building up its arms increases the security of a country to an extent that proves much greater than the amount and quality of the war-fighting equipment would lead one to expect – even though the arsenal thus created might not allow the small state to achieve success on its own in the long run, and even though the arsenal might not encompass the most modern weaponry. The upgrading of armaments boosts security disproportionally.[102]

> (my translation)

While the air force might have an interest in emphasizing the significance of nuclear weapons (given its envisaged role as the bearer of Switzerland's strategic nuclear forces), the army has an interest in highlighting the continued relevance of conventional, non-nuclear means of defense and in affirming the general usefulness of increased conventional defense efforts.

Bericht des Bundesrates über das Volksbegehren (1961)

Interestingly, many of the schemes of interpretation that may be identified in the "Truppenordnung" are also prevalent in the next document published by the government on the nuclear issue: the "Bericht des Bundesrates über das Volksbegehren für ein Verbot von Atomwaffen."[103] In addition to the 1958 "Erklärung," this report is perhaps the one document that most vigorously and comprehensively exemplifies the government's arguments in favor of acquiring a nuclear force. In other words, the 1961 report, more vehemently than any other document, calls for the introduction of nuclear weapons into the Swiss defense posture. It does this not least by systematically rejecting the counter-arguments brought to the fore by opponents of the nuclear option.[104] Moreover, a closer analysis shows that the report indeed combines and builds upon the different micro-components of the debate: it emphasizes some of the key arguments put forward by the nuclear proponents and discounts objections by the non-proliferation movement in order to carve out a coherent argumentative narrative in support of nuclearization.

What is particularly striking about this document and its argumentative force is that it comes down much more vehemently in favor of a Swiss nuclear force although its analysis of the country's strategic and security environment is similar to that in the "Truppenordnung" document. In both documents the authors outline a comparable threat perception: a large-scale nuclear attack on Switzerland leading to the country's nuclear annihilation is considered an unlikely scenario. Similarly, the authors regard it as "plausible" that given the existing balance of power and for political and psychological reasons, local wars or limited wars on the European continent will remain conventional wars.[105] Should the nuclear equilibrium be distorted, however, it is claimed that the actual deployment of nuclear weapons would become more likely.[106]

Against this background, how does the government justify its own call for the acquisition of nuclear weapons? The position is based on three[107] decisive argument narratives: first, the creation of a link between Switzerland's quest for nuclear weapons and its self-proclaimed tradition as a neutral and resistant country; second, the predicted end of the nuclear equilibrium and of the great powers' nuclear monopoly; and third, a legal and ethical case outlining the acceptability and desirability of (Swiss) nuclear weapons.

Level 1: identity and self-perception

It is argued that the procurement of nuclear weapons does not undermine, but actually conforms to the country's "centuries-old tradition of resistance."[108] While opponents of Switzerland's nuclear proliferation claim that nuclear weapons are qualitatively different from conventional devices of warfare, supporters of nuclearization oppose this view. From their perspective, nuclear weapons should not be considered a qualitatively different step in terms of strategic thinking and military procurement. Rather, nuclear weapons symbolize continuity and military coherence. By making a lexical connection between nuclear weapons and predicates such as "tradition," "resistance" and "defense," the authors depict nuclearization as a means for the continuation of Switzerland's traditionally neutral, non-offensive attitude toward its opponents in the international system. Nuclear weapons, in other words, are characterized as a precondition for maintaining neutrality and independence. Again, and in accordance with the 1958 "Erklärung," the authors make use of a powerful and culturally well-established historical narrative in order to justify their policies.

Level 2: Switzerland's position in the international system

The 1961 "Bericht" dealing with Switzerland's situation in the international system and its relationship toward other countries expands on the previous document. Agreeing with the threat assessment provided in the "Truppenordnung," the authors argue that while an all-out nuclear attack against Switzerland is barely conceivable, they perceive the greatest threat as stemming from the uncertain future of the global distribution of nuclear weapons. Although it remains possible that future wars, too, may be fought by conventional means only, this prospect is considered uncertain. Even more blatantly, the authors write that "a renunciation of nuclear weapons is hardly to be expected, unfortunately, not least because an international ban on the use and production of nuclear weapons has not been reached so far."[109]

This argument amounts to a veritable paradox, however: the Swiss government justifies its own procurement of nuclear weapons, or its pursuit of a "nuclear option" to phrase it more tentatively, by pointing the finger at those actors in the international system who upset the nuclear equilibrium by attempting to procure nuclear weapons for themselves (although, once again, it is not explicitly spelled out who they would be). The authors seem to acknowledge this inconsistency. In order to address it they explicitly emphasize that *Switzerland's pursuit of nuclear weapons would not add to insecurity and tensions in the international system*, "as it is universally known that we do not pursue a policy of expansionism" – a statement that reveals crucial insights into the prevalent self-perception of Switzerland's role in the international system:

> Equipping our army with nuclear weapons seems only thinkable today under the precondition that the current nuclear monopoly held by the great powers is breached. It is rightly feared that an extension of the circle of nuclear powers would lead to greater insecurity and danger. The fear is of nuclear chaos.... Nuclear weapons in the hands of unstable, predatory expansionist governments would be political dynamite. This raises the question of whether a nuclear-armed Switzerland would add to this insecurity and whether it would increase international tensions. It has to be said that the acquisition of nuclear weapons would take a fairly long time. Eventually, there would be clarity if the world powers were successful in sustaining the nuclear monopoly.... The chances are low. We have to expect the disappearance of the monopoly and we have to be prepared. It is hardly conceivable that the ambitions of our country would lead to additional tensions, given that it is universally known that we do not pursue a policy of expansionism.[110]

> (my translation)

It shows a strong, idiosyncratic – and arguably incoherent – narrative underlying Switzerland's quest for nuclear weapons and also, in more general terms, its foreign policy and security thinking. More precisely, it pictures the country as both seriously affected by developments in the international system and the strategic environment, as well as oddly disconnected from the "usual" dynamics. Switzerland's security moves are considered inconsequential to other states' perceptions, while the country itself justifies its own move toward nuclearization by reference to other states' behavior. It is this self-proclaimed "other-worldliness"[111] that serves as a prominent justification for the country's policies and that is reinforced by the narrative of neutrality and resistance (level 1).

Level 3: attributes of civil and military nuclear technology

The first two narratives furthermore provide the basis for the culmination of the argument. This is contained in the third frame, which deals with the judicial and ethical acceptability and desirability of Swiss nuclear weapons. This is a particularly powerful frame, as it not only interweaves key arguments in support of nuclearization, but also explicitly tries to undermine the claims that were brought to the fore by the anti-nuclear movement. The argument starts by providing a fairly detailed scientific and technical description of the impact and ramifications of nuclear weapons deployment. The authors cover the issues of "light flash," "heat," "blast" and "radiation," with radiation being addressed in most detail. They concede that radiation released in an explosion "damages the living cells" of organisms. In one of the report's subsequent paragraphs, the authors address the concerns of the anti-nuclear movement and admit that the deployment of nuclear weapons would lead to the radioactive contamination of a "considerable" area of terrain. It is, moreover, acknowledged that long-term effects on human health such as leukemia and cataracts can occur even years later.[112]

Yet, notwithstanding these indications of the detrimental effects of nuclear warfare, the text retains a clear pro-nuclear tenor. It continues to suggest strongly that the negative repercussions elicited by nuclear weapons may be controlled and "confined." Three main characteristics of the report reinforce this suggestion. First, the authors devote a great deal of attention to the possible protective measures to be taken in order to decrease the impact of radiation. In an astonishingly vague but optimistic fashion they argue, for example, that "the impact can be reduced strongly, if people stay inside houses, basements or shelters during the first hours to days and leave the shelters only for a short time afterwards."[113] Likewise, the authors describe gas masks and dust filters as an "appropriate means of protection"[114] against the inhalation of radioactive dust. The provision of technical details and specific figures documenting radiation levels renders the text particularly "authoritative" and putatively convincing – although a closer reading casts doubt on some of the proclaimed logical conclusions and certainties.

Second, the authors relativize the impact of military-triggered nuclear radiation by comparing it to naturally occurring radiation. Accordingly, radiation caused by the deployment of nuclear weapons should be viewed within "the general framework of naturally occurring radiation."[115] To further support this claim, the report contains several examples of natural, artificial and medical sources of radiation, as well as references to respective scientific studies. While the report claims that further nuclear test explosions would not significantly increase global levels of radiation, no such calculations are provided to back up this assertion or demonstrate the impact of actual nuclear weapons use – yet it is asserted that a nuclear war would always lead to the release of radioactivity, regardless of whether Switzerland actually contributed by deploying its own weapons. This framing strikes a similar chord to the one described earlier: the country not only seems to portray itself as being somewhat disconnected from the main stage of international affairs; it also paints its own deeds as inconsequential and negligible.

Allusions to the devastating radioactive impact of deployed nuclear weapons are thus countered by juxtaposing the risk posed by nuclear weapons with natural risks and with risks that would arise if the country were to forgo nuclearization. Radiation is portrayed as the lesser evil compared to sacrificing "appropriate armament." This de-emphasizing of the negative ramifications of nuclear weapons in favor of their strategic military benefits culminates in the idea that such weapons could even be used for strikes *within* the boundaries of Switzerland, should the enemy manage to break through the lines of defense:

> At first glance, the consideration for our civilian population – unconditionally justified on moral, psychological and political grounds – suggests that the deployment of our own nuclear weapons within our territory cannot be recommended. After the breakthrough of enemy forces into our territory, however, there would be a multitude of targets in the heartland. In most cases, such targets would be in areas that had already suffered from nuclear attack or that had been abandoned by the civilian population due to belligerent actions.... Additionally, there would be multifarious valuable targets to support counter-attacks by the mobile forces of our army.[116]
>
> (my translation)

Defending the territorial and political integrity of the country is rated higher than the protection of the civilian population and its natural habitat. According to this cost–benefit analysis, the prime goal of all defense efforts is the protection and preservation of the country's territorial integrity as well as its political status, regardless of the cost to the population.

Third, the authors paint an "optimistic" picture of the future trend in weapons development. They suggest that nuclear warheads are likely to become both "cleaner" (in terms of radiation) as well as smaller (in terms of yield). This appraisal mirrors the characteristic belief in the opportunities and feasibility of technological development, progress and modernization which appears in similar frames in other pro-nuclearization documents. Moreover, it questions the established perception of "weapons of mass destruction," since it suggests that science will soon develop a type of nuclear weapon that shares all the main characteristics of conventional means of warfare: low yield, little radiation, usability in tactical combat situations and, above all, narrowness and predictability of impact. According to the authors, the fundamental qualitative distinction between nuclear and conventional weapons would thereby be eliminated, turning nuclear devices into merely a particular category of conventional means of warfare. Against this background of "conventionalizing" tactical nuclear weapons, it is then a fairly coherent – albeit highly disputable – move to actually consider their deployment legal.

> There is no doubt concerning the legality of their tactical use, i.e., against military objects, or any doubt concerning weapons whose range can be calculated and limited to the target. It cannot be disputed that nuclear weapons represent a further development in the field of armaments.[117]
>
> (my translation)

Nonetheless, this third frame on the legal and ethical "acceptability" of Swiss nuclear weapons encompasses more than a "conventionalization" of nuclear weapons and a downplaying of the detrimental environmental and health effects of radiation. It also tackles the strong narrative of humanity invoked by the opponents of Switzerland's nuclear weapons acquisition. The authors explicitly mention and address the opponents' claim that Switzerland should renounce its interest in acquiring nuclear weapons for ethical and humanitarian reasons; indeed, they turn it around by arguing that it is for these very humanitarian reasons that the country *should* acquire nuclear weapons. According to their thread of argumentation, Switzerland is forced to acquire its own nuclear weapons capability in order to protect both its independence and its humanitarian stance. Thus, while sharing the narrative of Switzerland's humanitarian identity, the authors draw the opposite conclusion. The humanitarian actor must not relinquish nuclear weapons, but, on the contrary, must acquire a "realistic" (i.e., nuclear) defense capacity in order to retain his capacity to further pursue ethically correct, humanitarian policies. Hence the possession of nuclear weapons is not only reconciled with ethical imperatives, but it is also turned into a precondition for meeting these ethical requirements. Becoming a nuclear power in order to "fight evil" is framed as a moral obligation imposed upon Switzerland. Noticeably, Switzerland's nuclear ambitions are again (as in other government documents) portrayed as an imposed duty, rather than as an active, voluntary move. This amounts to an inherent paradox: on the one hand the government calls for the acquisition of nuclear weapons in order to ensure it is capable of actively, independently and responsibly fighting evil; on the other hand it justifies the move on the grounds of dictated obligations and global trends of proliferation.[118]

In sum, this document gains its specific argumentative strength not only by addressing (and rebutting) several of the arguments put forward by the anti-nuclear movement, but even more so by constructing a powerful, all-encompassing alternative (and almost counter-intuitive) structure of interpretation. This draws upon a particular moral obligation for nuclear armaments and justifies the very acquisition of nuclear weapons by interweaving the notion of humanity with multiple references to Switzerland's long-standing self-image as a neutral, benevolent state.

Bericht des Bundesrates über das Volksbegehren (1962)

Neither of the two further government documents[119] that were published in this first phase of the debate was comparable in their assertiveness and, above all, in their comprehensiveness; neither of them shaped the debate in the same way; neither of them contributed such a broad and cogent narrative. Instead, both dealt primarily with constitutional, legislative and juridical issues in the context of nuclear procurement and clarified why the federal institutions, rather than the electorate, should be responsible for deciding whether to pursue a nuclear weapons program.[120] What is nonetheless remarkable, however, is the way in which the executive characterizes the issue of nuclear acquisition: it is depicted as above all a technological matter, presumably very similar to any other – conventional – procurement decision.[121] The notion of a fundamental qualitative difference between nuclear and conventional weapons, which has long been (and continues to be) a key argument of the anti-nuclear movement, is then refuted or at least called into question.[122] Moreover, the issue of whether Switzerland should have the option to initiate its own weapons program is removed from the political realm and ultimately reduced to a merely practical question regarding the modernization of the Swiss military.

Pro-nuclear publications

The government, however, was not the only player calling for a nuclear weapons research program. The military-industrial complex, above all the Verein zur Förderung des Wehrwillens und der Wehrwissenschaft (Association for the Advancement of Military Will and Science) and the Schweizerisches Aktionskomitee gegen die Atominitiative (Swiss Action Committee against the Nuclear Initiative), lobbied powerfully for the acquisition of nuclear weapons.[123] As the following analysis of some of the major structures of interpretation will indicate, these lobbying groups were in fact far more blunt and assertive in their demands and positions than the government. What is more, they criticized the anti-nuclear movement in a very assertive and outspoken manner. A synopsis of the relevant publications reveals three central, persistent frames: recurring references to Switzerland's identity as a neutral and resistant country; a fierce depiction of the communist threat; an ethical argument centering on both the obligation for self-defense as well as on the acceptability of nuclear weapons.

Level 1: identity and self-perception

In many of the pro-nuclear leaflets and publications analyzed, the authors make a case for the acquisition of nuclear weapons by appealing to Switzerland's long-standing identity as a neutral, resistant and independent international actor. Drawing on many references to Switzerland's claimed defiant attitude and unyielding stance in the past, the country is portrayed as a model of fortitude and virtue. This characterization culminates in a depiction of Switzerland as virtually the "antithesis"[124] of the "normal" actors of the international system.[125] "Armed neutrality" is not merely regarded as a well-tried foreign policy practice but as the integral and distinguishable – almost mythical – backbone of the country's self-proclaimed identity.

However, the acquisition of nuclear weapons is not merely justified by reference to Switzerland's identity and history as a neutral state but also on the grounds of its legal rights and obligations as a neutral actor. Accordingly, the country's neutral stance is defined as necessarily and irrefutably an "armed" one. A renunciation of the "best weapons available" would therefore substantially threaten, undermine and ultimately "obliterate" this stance, the authors claim. Under the slogan "wanting to be neutral means having to be strong," the authors claim that a renunciation of nuclear weapons would "devalue, even undermine, our perpetual, comprehensive and armed neutrality in its substance as well as in its rights and obligations under international law."[126] Even though the Hague Convention's provisions on neutrality are not explicitly mentioned, they provide the legal justification for this claim.

As already shown, similar references may be found in the government documents, but the framing used in the non-governmental nuclear advocates' writings is somewhat different: because of its history as a "neutral" *and* "benign," "peace-loving," "defensive" state, the country is said to have every right to acquire the weapons it needs in order to guarantee its continued existence. "From a religious, ethical, and moral perspective, the equipping of our military with controllable nuclear weapons of limited power is permissible, once this is necessary for defending our freedom," the proponents of nuclearization hold.[127]

Furthermore, rather than merely referring to the concept of neutrality, which has evolved historically, the notion invoked is much broader and more comprehensive. It also relates to several other qualities that are considered essential to define Switzerland as a nation.

> The reason that our people may need to envisage the acquisition of these weapons in a nuclear-armed world is not born of fear but the brave and biblically imperative belief of a small, resistant nation in its obligation to defend itself against any possible threat.[128]

> (my translation)

In the same passage it is further contended that the procurement of nuclear weapons is in line with the country's practice of credible neutrality and its "historical peace mission." The use of a large number of adjectives with a positive connotation to describe Switzerland is thus an effort to portray the country as a benevolent actor ("a peace-loving people that detests war") which is merely determined to withstand the pressure from its hostile communist antagonists. Subsequently, its actions are not simply justified on legal or historical grounds, or on the basis of international law (neutrality), but even more so by virtue of the intrinsic features of its identity. This practice of predication in the writings of the pro-nuclear movement becomes particularly suggestive and cogent, as it connects well with the ethical argument regarding the obligation for self-defense and the acceptability of nuclear weapons (level 3, below).

Level 2: Switzerland's position in the international system

The second narrative describes Switzerland's involvement in the international political situation in the late 1950s and early 1960s. According to the arguments of the pro-nuclearization movement, the international system is shaped by a powerful struggle between good and evil, and between the free and open societies of the West and the suppressed totalitarian communist countries in the East. In contrast to those of the government, the documents issued by non-government nuclear proponents reveal a far more unambiguous and explicit stance regarding the perceived threat environment and the global strategic situation. Not only do they describe communism as an inherently expansive, totalitarian, violent force, they also call for the procurement of nuclear weapons in order to fight the spread of communism.[129] In a similar vein, the vast majority of documents that were published by the advocates of a Swiss nuclear program included references to the juxtaposition of "communism" and the "free world" as well as references to the global bloc confrontation.[130] Hence, anti-communism – and the perceived threat posed by communism – may certainly be considered to be the most frequently and vigorously articulated narrative in that it arguably provides the thread that weaves together the other, more specific, structures of meaning. Moreover, it functions not only as one of the defining characteristics in the portrayal of Switzerland's role in the world and for devising the county's foreign and security policy, but it is also used as a vehement rhetorical tool and a means of political differentiation and even defamation on the Swiss domestic political scene: members of the anti-nuclear movement are described as "pacifist, leftist socialist and crypto-communist"[131] and "useful idiots,"[132] and it is frequently suggested that these "defeatists" are collaborating with or at least have fallen prey to the demagogy of communist forces abroad:

> It has to be pointed out to the defeatists that the guarantee for our survival in freedom depends on the strength of our army.[133]

(my translation)

Level 3: attributes of civil and military nuclear technology

The moral and ethical case in favor of the acquisition of nuclear weapons is based on two main arguments, revolving around the pre-eminent characteristics of nuclear weapons: the assumed conventionalization of nuclear weapons and the moral obligation to protect and defend the country. More specifically, it is argued that further scientific progress in the realm of nuclear physics and weapons design will make it possible to devise small (tactical) nuclear weapons that release hardly any radiation. Future nuclear weapons would moreover be designed to accurately target enemy forces without causing unintended devastation among the civilian population.

> It is generally recognised today that the deployment of small-caliber tactical weapons can for the most part be handled in a manner which will ensure that the population in the battlezone will not be recklessly wiped out. The damage from contamination can be heavily localized. Moreover, in the not so distant future one will possess projectiles that are completely or almost completely 'clean', which will avert the existing dangers of contamination. This means the possible procurement of small nuclear munitions for our army is not immoral.[134]
>
> (my translation)

The notion of "ethically acceptable nuclear weapons" is thus related to a strong idea of scientific progress, modernity and feasibility.

In a similar vein, the ethical argument is also linked to the right of self-defense.[135] This leads the debate away from a singular focus on the environmentally and medically detrimental effects of nuclear radiation and toward the question of deterrence and retaliation. In this way, the possession and potential deployment of nuclear means of warfare is framed as ethically justified if it is needed in order to protect the greater good – namely the survival of the state.

> It is precisely because of our peace mission that we, the Swiss people, take our commitment to perpetual, unconditional and resistant neutrality seriously and make immense sacrifices for our territorial defense. No moral justification is required to do this for it is the vital imperative and ethical obligation of a free country to protect our right to live and to shield our people: resistance to the world of evil, violence and injustice.[136]
>
> (my translation)

Nuclear weapons are therefore evaluated not necessarily on the basis of their intrinsic characteristics, but as a means to an end in which the defense of the country is defined as a superior good. Accordingly, there are two complementary readings of the "ethical frame": the use of nuclear weapons is morally justified if the weapons are small, controllable and clean, or if the deployment is warranted in order to protect and defend the existence of the country.[137]

Phase II: the debate after 1963

Against this background it is hardly surprising that the debate became so fierce and heated in the early 1960s. Given the comprehensive and suggestive metanarratives deployed by both the government (defense of neutrality and independence) and the non-governmental nuclear advocates (anti-communism), it is arguably fairly understandable that the two referenda on the nuclear question were turned down by a majority of voters in 1962 and 1963 respectively, subsequently allowing the government a "free hand" in the nuclear issue.

These supporting circumstances notwithstanding, Switzerland never actually developed nuclear weapons but remained latently under the nuclear threshold. It did not even drastically intensify or expand its military research efforts regarding the development of nuclear weapons. The analysis of the "phase II" documents, which cover the period from 1963 (the post-referenda era) to 1969 (when the government signed the NPT), reveals why the quest for nuclear weapons did not gain further momentum following the rejection of the anti-nuclear referenda. I will focus on three sets of documents in order to describe and elaborate upon the shift in the relevant narratives.

Botschaft des Bundesrates betreffend PTBT

The first document to be analyzed is the Federal Executive's report to the General Assembly regarding the Partial Test Ban Treaty (PTBT).[138] The report contains a six-page opinion piece which accompanies the text of the treaty. In this statement the Bundesrat describes both the treaty's genesis and the main provisions of the treaty, before commenting on the agreement's "significance" as well as its weaknesses. What makes the present document so significant for this case study is the authors' balanced and systematic discussion of the issues raised in the treaty and of its strengths and deficits. The authors concede that the agreement reveals major flaws in terms of its legal composition, since it contains neither verification measures, nor provisions for the establishment of a court of arbitration; the treaty obligations are described as incomplete.[139] Moreover, the authors criticize – albeit rather subtly – the discriminatory nature of the treaty, insinuating that the three depository countries (the Soviet Union, the United States of America and the United Kingdom) had unfair motives that went beyond the goals of the treaty.[140] Why did the Bundesrat then decide to join the treaty against this background of flaws and shortcomings? We can discern two frames that seem particularly crucial in order to understand the decision: a narrative concerning the detrimental effects of radioactivity and a reference to the country's self-proclaimed humanitarian nature.

Level 3: attributes of civil and military nuclear technology

In contrast to the government documents analyzed thus far, the key argumentative thread in this report is an unambiguous and undeniable admission of the detrimental environmental and health repercussions of nuclear weapons. More precisely, the agreement is characterized as "significant because it seeks to end the further radioactive contamination of the elements, air and water, which are vital for humankind."[141] In two consecutive paragraphs the authors then describe in more detail the ramifications of nuclear (test) explosions. Evaluating these detrimental environmental and health effects, the authors conclude that these aspects alone justify signing the treaty.[142] Compared to the previous documents we thus see the government explicitly admitting for the first time the harmful effects of nuclear radiation and plainly welcoming measures to reduce this negative impact. The frame of radiological contamination and nuclear hazards has clearly gained a new impetus as one of the major narratives within the discourse on nuclear weapons. This becomes even more striking given that other possible rationales for signing the treaty (such as the juridification of international affairs or the potential curbing of further global nuclear proliferation) receive only negligible argumentative attention throughout the accompanying text. Instead, the argument centers on the radiation issue, thereby promoting a new line of argument that diverges from previous documents.

Level 1: identity and self-perception

Likewise, the second major concept that may be identified in the statement – the reference to the country's humanitarian nature and identity – does not represent a clear and unambiguous continuation of former interpretations.

> Let us now consider the reasons that justify a positive Swiss opinion. Given the strong aspirations of all peoples to détente and peaceful co-existence – aspirations that have so far always been disappointed – it befits Switzerland, with its humanitarian tradition, to welcome every concrete step towards a reduction of the menace of total war and to support such steps with the modest means it commands.[143]

(my translation)

While at first this may look as though this is simply continuing an idea that had already been raised in the publications issued during the first phase, a closer look reveals a certain dissimilarity of degree. In previous government documents Switzerland's humanitarian nature was always linked to its equally important stance as a resistant, neutral state. In other words, the three attributes formed a specific web of significations that not only delineated significant characteristics of Switzerland's identity, but also supported and constituted each other. The narrative provided in the 1961 government report, for example, construes a strong connection between the country's humanitarian stance and the need (or even obligation) to acquire nuclear weapons. According to this argument, the humanitarian actor must not relinquish nuclear weapons, but instead must acquire a sufficient, possibly nuclear defense capacity in order to further pursue ethically correct, humanitarian policies.[144] Hence, the possession of nuclear weapons is not only reconciled with ethical imperatives but also turned into a precondition for meeting these requirements. Becoming a nuclear power in order to "fight evil" is thereby described as a moral responsibility imposed upon Switzerland. In this accompanying letter to the PTBT, however, such a rationale is not mentioned. The very nexus between humanitarianism and military might is not explored; nor is there any mention of the military usefulness or desirability of nuclear weapons.

However, this must not lead the reader to assume that the 1963 document already constituted a complete break from the nuclear ambitions previously voiced by the government. Instead, the strong emphasis given to the treaty's exit option and the possible terminability of the PTBT again clarifies that at the time of the signing of the treaty the government was still very keen to maintain the option of nuclearization. It is emphasized several times that membership of the treaty may be recalled by each country at any time should the highest national interests be endangered.[145] The government's "freedom of action"[146] would hence not be impaired by joining the agreement.

This thread of continuity notwithstanding, the two prevalent narratives in the PTBT's accompanying statement should be regarded as a fairly significant first shift in the debate on Switzerland's possible acquisition of nuclear weapons. Both the emphasis on the detrimental effects of radiation and the underscoring of the country's humanitarian obligations (without linking it to a strong military posture) undermine the hitherto cogent and paramount argumentation in favor of nuclear weapons, by conceding "argumentative space" for objections and doubts. In other words, while the government had previously tried to systematically counter the peace movement's objections to the nuclear weapons option – for example, by playing down the hazards of radioactivity – it now incorporates these very anti-nuclear arguments into its statement in order to justify the signing of the PTBT. This suggests that the emerging international regime against nuclear weapons and the government's support for the test ban treaty changed the tone of the debate by forcefully highlighting the detrimental environmental and health impact of nuclear weapons. Moreover, it should not be underestimated that the international agreement on the PTBT symbolized a rapprochement – albeit delicate and frail – between the two global superpowers. Both countries recognized not only the need to decrease global nuclear fallout, but also discovered a common interest in using the test ban to impede the emergence of additional nuclear weapon states. The treaty was thus the first indication of potential common interests between hostile antagonists, thereby allowing for a relaxation of the East–West confrontation and providing room for a tentative reconsideration of the global security environment which had been previously taken for granted. A closer analysis of three further documents issued by the government on that topic will reveal that this discursive shift was not a single occurrence but actually mirrors a larger transformation in the argumentative pattern which appears to have eventually formed the basis for the renunciation of the weapons option in 1969.

Konzeption der militärischen Landesverteidigung (1966)

The second major official publication in the second phase of the Swiss nuclear debate is a report on issues of national defense published by the executive in 1966.[147] Together with the 1960 "Truppenordnung," it is the central document on the concept of Switzerland's defense posture in the 1960s and early 1970s. Moreover, this defense report is the first major publication on defense issues since the Mirage scandal in 1964. As already described in the historiographic reconstruction, in 1961 the Swiss government had agreed to acquire 100 Dassault

Mirage III fighter airplanes from France in order to facilitate the implementation of a new defense doctrine based on the concept of mobile defense.[148] These airplanes were intended to play a major role by providing combat support for defensive ground operations and also by delivering nuclear strikes against enemy troops. However, the originally allocated budget of 800 million Swiss francs was soon exceeded due to massive technical modifications and customization needs. As a consequence, the Bundesrat had to solicit an additional 400 million francs from Parliament to cover the unexpected costs. Parliament, however, refused this loan, and instead instituted a parliamentary investigation committee in order to clarify causes of the massive financial overrun and where responsibility for it lay. Detecting grave instances of mismanagement and violations of mandatory supervision, the commission called for the resignation of several high-ranking members of the military and ultimately also brought about the resignation of Chaudet from the Bundesrat in 1968.[149] Moreover, Parliament scaled down the procurement plan so that only 57 of the originally planned 100 airplanes were actually acquired. This in turn severely undermined the adjustment of the defense strategy and the implementation of the new mobile defense blueprint.

An analysis of the 1966 national defense report shows that the Mirage affair left a deep imprint on the military establishment and significantly influenced the country's defense conception. Two frames exemplify the major subsequent conceptual changes: a less militaristic and more humanistic understanding of Switzerland's national defense and a diminished belief in the adequacy of large-scale military modernization projects.[150]

Level 1: identity and self-perception

The fundamental change that took place with respect to the country's defense conception becomes clearly visible when we recall the doctrinal terms of reference that were provided in earlier documents. In the "Bericht des Bundesrates über das Volksbegehren für ein Verbot von Atomwaffen" published in 1961, the government had strongly argued in favor of a nuclear defense component in order to raise the "entry-level price" any potential enemy would have to "pay." It had been claimed that the army *had to be equipped* with nuclear weapons, as these "not only serve the attacker but also significantly strengthen the resistive power of the defender."[151] This framing not only embodies a clear and unambiguous call for nuclear weapons, but also reveals an exclusively militaristic understanding of defense – culminating in the idea that the Swiss military could even use its nuclear defense forces to attack "valuable" targets on Swiss territory in order to harm the enemy.[152]

The 1966 report diverges considerably from these conceptual assumptions and firmly emphasizes the civilian requirements of all national defense efforts. In a long paragraph on the concept of "total national defense" the authors argue that the needs and requirements of the civilian population have to be taken more seriously. This reframing, however, undermines the fundamental belief in the appropriateness of a nuclear-based defense.

It is inevitable that military planning must be adjusted more strongly to the needs of the civilian population.... Both the coordination of military territorial defense, with its civilian aspects, and the feasibility of better support of the civilian population by the military are the subjects of a comprehensive study conducted by an appointee of the Swiss Military Department.[153]

(my translation)

Hence, what we see is a re-evaluation of the goals and objectives of the country's defensive measures and an enhanced focus on alternative means that ought to be more in line with the goal of protecting the civilian population.

In a similar vein, the second prevalent frame casts doubt on the potency and efficacy of large-scale military defense and mirrors a diminished belief in the adequacy of monumental military modernization projects. In a passage several paragraphs long, the authors explicitly concede that the Mirage scandal triggered a reassessment of both the general defense concept and the appropriate procurement measures. As a consequence, procurement measures that are "judged necessary have to be put into the framework of what is feasible."[154] Thus, besides the mere organizational and personnel changes outlined above, the Mirage affair also impelled some more fundamental transformations in the civil–military relationship and seriously eroded voters' trust in the military. The belief that the military was capable of fully and comprehensively protecting the country if it was sufficiently equipped with a modern, up-to-date means of warfare was disputed to an ever greater degree. Accordingly, the almost mythical faith in the Swiss military (nurtured, as has been shown, by recurrent references to its history) and the unchallenged pervasiveness of the military in Swiss politics and Swiss everyday life was contested and perhaps even replaced by a more critical reading that emphasized the dangers inherent in a culture of exalted militarization and expanding armament.[155]

Both of the dominant frames in this document thus add up to an increased skepticism regarding the usefulness and feasibility of Swiss nuclear weapons, culminating in "the question of to what extent and under which preconditions nuclear weapons could increase our combat power."[156] Strikingly, the authors do not even attempt to sketch concrete global security scenarios that might provide an answer to this question or that might deliver a rationale for the acquisition of nuclear weapons. Instead, they merely call for further investigations into "when the further proliferation of nuclear weapons could force us to acquire them."[157] Against the background of these changing frames, it appears that the "window of opportunity" for acquiring nuclear weapons is slowly but steadily closing; even maintaining the option to go nuclear in the future becomes less and less justifiable given the discursive shift toward a renunciation of nuclear weapons.

Interpellation Binder

A parliamentary exchange of views between the President of the Federal Council Willy Spühler and CVP politician Julius Binder in 1967 lends further support to this view.[158] Answering an official interpellation by Binder, President Spühler provided an assessment of the possible legal, political, economic and military consequences of the Non-Proliferation Treaty. This specific debate in Parliament is particularly important, as the government had hardly published any proliferation-related documents in the post-1963 period. Hence, there are not many official documents for the years between 1963 and 1969 in which the executive shares its views on the future political course with regard to nuclear weapons.

Binder's interpellation is also significant, as it neatly reflects many of the key arguments that had been voiced previously by both sides of the debate. Generally identifying himself as a proponent of the NPT, Binder argues that the treaty should be supported "if and insofar as it takes into account the vital interests of the non-possessing states."[159] Overall, his tentative statement of approval provides a careful – and yet perhaps slightly contradictory – analysis that is based on three central aspects: the claim that Switzerland has an obligation to actively support international peace; a word of caution against the potential loss of sovereignty; and an emphasis on the requirements of neutrality. Thus, on the one hand Binder claims that "Switzerland, as a small and neutral state, has a particular commitment to a policy of peace."[160] Criticizing the government's apparently passive attitude, he goes on to claim that the country should have pursued the idea of a non-proliferation treaty proactively and much earlier.

Yet, in the same statement he emphasizes the legal obligations that a neutral state has to meet according to international law:

> We must assume that we have to observe the principle of neutrality in our foreign policy. However, the neutral state is obliged to defend its territory in a credible and reasonable manner. Question: Is an effective national defense possible without nuclear weapons? Today, this question has to be answered in the affirmative. No one thinks that our army has to be equipped with nuclear weapons now. Yet the situation can change.... For this reason, our country has to retain its freedom of action, even with respect to nuclear weapons.[161]

(my translation)

In several places Binder refers to the question of sovereignty. He asks the government how and whether the envisioned treaty is reconcilable with the requirements of national sovereignty and equality among nations. In referring to the discriminatory provisions of the NPT – regarding the right to possess nuclear weapons and the designated inspection regime – Binder describes the treaty as a grave intrusion into Swiss sovereignty.[162] His verdict is clear: If Switzerland joins the treaty, "it will be surrendering part of its sovereignty."[163]

In his reply, Spühler, then president of the Federal Council, goes to great lengths in order to justify why the country should join the agreement, despite the NPT's discriminatory character and despite its intrusiveness.[164] What seems even more significant for the course of this analysis, however, is the further transformation of the discourse on nuclear weapons that becomes apparent in his statement. Starting with the question of whether the possession of nuclear weapons could improve the security of a small country, Spühler delivers arguments based on two broad interpretive frames: the issue of equal rights among nations (level 2); and the – military, political, economic and environmental – damage done by nuclear weapons (level 3).

Level 2: Switzerland's position in the international system

At the very beginning of his reply, Spühler acknowledges that the NPT may indeed be regarded as a discriminatory, unjust treaty.

> The treaty will be discriminatory. And given that Switzerland does not possess nuclear weapons, these discriminations will work against us if we join the treaty. Therefore it has to be examined whether the advantages of the treaty are such that they compensate for the legal approval of this discrimination.[165]

> (my translation)

What is striking, however, is that he instantaneously subverts this judgment by rhetorically asking: "Is non-proliferation preferred to non-discrimination?" This question illustrates the crucial divergence of views between proponents and opponents of the treaty: while they might all share the judgment that the nuclear regime is indeed based on unequal rights and a fundamental discrimination between nations, they differ profoundly in their conclusion. Spühler and the executive have come to the conclusion that equality and unconditional sovereignty need to be sacrificed in order to counter the menace of unhindered nuclear proliferation. However, by making this concession they not only forfeit Switzerland's legal status as an indisputable equal; they also – and this may even outweigh the legal aspect for many observers and participants in the debate – sacrifice the country's reputational and ideational standing. They concede that Switzerland, together with many other countries, has had to accept its inferior position in order to contribute to world peace. The sacrosanct roles of sovereignty and equality among nations are hence questioned. What is arguably coming to the fore here is an altered self-perception and a new notion of statehood and participation in the international system.

Level 3: attributes of civil and military nuclear technology

The second frame that Spühler draws on is the description of the harmful – or at best negative – effects of nuclear weapons. Referring to the major nuclear advantage of the superpowers as well as to the hazardous ramifications of both tactical and strategic nuclear weapons, Spühler argues that nuclear weapons in the hands of the Swiss state would not provide the country with any deterrent effect. First, given the numerical advantages acquired by America and the Soviet

Union, both superpowers would hardly be discouraged by the small nuclear arsenals of small states. What is more, the development of a means of intercepting incoming missiles would soon make it impossible even for the medium nuclear powers to "strike vital targets in America or Russia," thus rendering nuclear weapons "useless" for deterrent purposes.[166] Second, the harmful and potentially devastating effects of the deployment of nuclear weapons render them "unusable," even in locally limited theaters of war. Quoting from a UN report Spühler says:

> "One can state with certainty that the use of tactical nuclear weapons would lead to the devastation of the complete battlefield.... It is utterly clear that the devastation and disorganization caused by the so-called tactical nuclear war yields effects that would hardly differ from a strategic nuclear war in that respective zone." Therefore it seems that in Europe nuclear weapons would only have a weak effect against a superpower and would be useless in a locally limited clash.[167]
>
> (my translation)

According to this analysis, the threat and possible use of nuclear retaliation in Europe is considered unlikely. Nuclear weapons are described as non-deployable – an assessment that questions the whole notion of deterrence.

Spühler does not limit his depiction to the lack of deterrence, however. He goes on to outline the detrimental effects on the economy and global security resulting from nuclear proliferation. In contrast to previous governmental documents[168] in which Switzerland's possible nuclearization was described as non-deleterious to international security due to the country's benign character and its peaceful, defensive intentions, "any further increase in the number of nuclear-equipped states or any further amplification of existing nuclear arsenals"[169] is now regarded as damaging to international peace and security. Even in economic terms, Spühler now refers to nuclear weapons as outright "dangerous." Thus, for the first time, the government mentions the negative economic consequences of nuclear proliferation:

> Nuclear proliferation is dangerous not only from a military and political point of view; it also is economically so.[170]

These examples mirror a profound and almost radical change in the framing of the nuclear issue. There is little mention of the wide range of positive notions of neutrality, resistance, independence and even humanity that had previously been associated with nuclear weapons. Instead, the emphasis is now on the environmentally, politically, militarily and even economically negative implications of nuclear proliferation.

In summary, it may be said that the second phase of the Swiss nuclear debate brings profound changes in the predominant narratives and frames. The initial enthusiasm for the military and strategic benefits of nuclear weapons gives way to a narrative that centers on the environmentally detrimental repercussions of Switzerland's nuclear weapons acquisition and of further proliferation in general. However, this is not the only considerable discursive shift that may be observed; two other developments appear to be crucial. First, the narrative of Switzerland's identity changed from one that emphasizes the country's "resistant neutrality" to one that primarily revolves around notions of "humanitarian neutrality." A brief reminder: in the first phase the prevalent frame construed a strong connection between the neutral state's humanitarian stance and the need to acquire nuclear weapons. According to this argument, the humanitarian neutral must not forgo nuclear weapons but should acquire a "realistic," possibly nuclear defense capacity in order to be able to retain and defend its political stance. In the second phase, however, we see a different web of significations: the focus is now put on a proactive foreign policy that aims to reduce global conflicts and that promotes "concrete steps toward a reduction of the menace of total war." Thus, the dominant narrative now stresses Switzerland's obligation to promote peace and stability. Likewise, it emphasizes the country's role as a more active subject on the international scene.

Second, we can observe a diminishing belief both in the feasibility and effectiveness of military defense as well as in the appropriateness of large-scale military procurement projects. Against the background of a menacing (global) nuclear war, the utility of a Swiss nuclear defense capacity is called into question. A primarily military notion of defense that focuses on the protection of statehood and territorial integrity thus recedes and gives way to a more civilian ideal that calls for the safeguarding of the population.

Notably, this did not lead the government to formally and irrevocably reverse its nuclear course and to abolish its (rudimentary) nuclear bureaucracy: the working group on nuclear issues remained in place until the end of the 1980s. However, the change in key socially shared political and normative beliefs that took place in the 1960s severely constrained the government and eventually thwarted the acquisition of a nuclear deterrent.

Switzerland's nuclear reversal: conclusion

This analysis illustrates that an explanation that draws solely upon realist security reasoning does not adequately account for Switzerland's nuclear reversal, as it oversimplifies the multiple dimensions of the political disagreement that took place during the 1950s and 1960s. It was not the emergence and subsequent disappearance of an objectively given, concrete external threat or a threat perception – as realism would like us to think – which primarily shaped the Swiss interest in and later dismissal of a military nuclear capability. On the contrary: while the perceived threat remained present throughout the debate, it was rather vague und ill-defined. Thus the Swiss debate was always interwoven with perceptions of threat and danger. Yet these perceptions were far from unambiguous or clearly articulated. While the executive mainly focused on the dangers posed by an expected spread of nuclear weapons and a disruption of the nuclear monopoly, conservative forces and large parts of the Swiss populace predominantly emphasized the threat embodied by the "perilous" and "inherently expansive" nature of the Soviet Union.

Likewise, the argument that once the threat disappeared, the government decided to forgo its nuclear ambitions remains unconvincing. More precisely: if the perceived menace from the Soviet Union was the crucial variable in Switzerland's defense calculations, why then did the government eventually abandon its nuclear plans in 1969 – only a few months after the Soviet Union had brutally crushed the Czechoslovak reform movement? Against the background of these political events it seems rather unconvincing to account for Switzerland's decision by referring solely to the diminished Soviet threat. Rather, it would appear from the documents that the articulated threat perception always remained graspable. Even in the 1960s, when the decision was made not to undertake concrete steps toward nuclearization, official documents embodied a sense of insecurity and endangerment. Hence, pointing to the country's security environment alone seems insufficient for a full comprehension of the course of events.

Similarly, the present analysis of central beliefs and narratives has found little evidence for the centrality of economic or bureaucratic interests. Neither economic considerations nor bureaucratic pressures alone are sufficient to explain either the commencement or abandonment of Switzerland's nuclear weapons research. This is not to say, however, that these aspects were absent from the debate. Rather, the documents from the second phase suggest that economic interests contributed to and further solidified the repudiating attitude that had already begun to emerge. Thus economic considerations fed into an ongoing contestation of several interwoven and intricate beliefs and assumptions regarding the country's role and identity, regarding its position within the international security environment, as well as regarding the value and acceptability of nuclear weapons.

In the light of these findings, understanding the Swiss debate on nuclear weapons seems only possible if we manage to grasp the changing meaning of nuclear weapons in relation to the country's self-proclaimed concept of its own identity. This allows us to discover a shift in meaning: the weapons' attributed characteristics shifted away from being a symbol of progress and modernity, an "almost conventional" device of warfare and an ethically justified means of protection, and toward an interpretation of nuclear weapons as "useless" and "harmful." Within less than ten years the dominant interpretation of nuclear weapons and the attributed predicates changed from a modern, prestigious, legitimate, clean and ethically justified means of warfare to their depiction as inappropriate, ineffective and even militarily, politically, economically and environmentally dangerous. In other words, the discourse on nuclear weapons and nuclearization had shifted from an emphasis on the benefits of nuclear weapons to one that primarily highlighted their adverse effects.

However, it is not only the interpretation of nuclear weapons that changed, but also the notions of neutrality, role and, as a consequence, of national defense. The idea of neutrality changed from an alleged obligation to acquire neutral weapons due to the country's status as a neutral state to a more humanitarian understanding of neutrality.[171] The long-held mystified, ideological representation of Swiss neutrality was increasingly questioned and ultimately replaced by a less idealized, critical reading of Switzerland's history and its role in the international environment. The focus shifted from a fairly legalistic interpretation of neutrality toward a material interpretation that was more concerned with the actual politics of neutrality. While many contributions at the beginning of the debate referred to the provisions of international law in order to emphasize the country's obligation to acquire the most effective weapons available, this belief lost much of its appeal in the 1960s. Against this background, the procurement of nuclear weapons – given their non-discriminatory, detrimental effects – slowly appeared to be at odds with a modern, more humanitarian concept of neutrality and thus with one of the fundamental aspects of the country's self-perception.[172]

With this change in the notion of neutrality also came a shift in Switzerland's self-perceived role in the world. The country's self-perception shifted from being a strong isolationist pillar of resistance and virtually the antithesis of the European powers to being a more proactive agent of neutrality – for example, through humanitarian contributions, good offices and mediation in negotiations.[173] What is particularly interesting about this new belief is that it vividly exemplifies the discursive shift that took place over the course of the debate: early on in the controversy about Switzerland's nuclear policy the opponents of nuclear weapons acquisition had lobbied the Swiss government to adopt an active, peacemaking foreign policy. The proponents of the nuclear option, on the other hand, had argued that if the country remained a mere bystander, it would be forced into a purely passive, reactive role. They reasoned that Switzerland, too, had to acquire nuclear weapons, as it would otherwise ultimately be incapable of influencing the international political scene. The government documents issued during the second phase, however, seem to suggest that the anti-nuclear movement's call for a more proactive foreign policy and a Swiss contribution to peacemaking did eventually resonate, since in its later documents the government itself envisioned a more actively humanitarian foreign policy for Switzerland.

In a similar vein, the blueprint for national defense underwent a significant change: from a focus on the protection of the country as a military-political entity to a more civilian-oriented notion of defense, emphasizing the need to protect the population. As a reminder: the military had actually originally envisioned the deployment of tactical nuclear weapons on Swiss territory should the enemy manage to break the lines of defense: "After the breakthrough of enemy forces into our territory there would be a multitude of targets in the heartland," it was argued in 1961. Later documents reveal a considerable re-articulation of the principles of defense. In the 1966 defense concept, the protection of civilians took center stage. Accordingly, it was argued that the needs and requirements of the civilian population had to be taken more seriously.

It appears that this latter shift is closely linked to Swiss domestic developments. As detailed in the historiographic reconstruction, the Mirage crisis seems to have triggered a fundamental loss of confidence in state institutions in general and in the military's grandiose projects in particular. As a result, the military lost its previously uncontested role as the sole provider of protection, defense and security, as the population not only became increasingly skeptical of the ongoing militarization and of large-scale defense technology procurements, but also increasingly questioned the effectiveness of military defense in the face of a nuclear threat.

This development and discursive shift, however, can only be fully understood if we also take into account the change in opinion regarding the nature and impact of nuclear weapons. Originally, the debate was strongly influenced by pro-nuclear voices of all political affiliations, with a strong belief in the military benefits of nuclear weapons and in the controllability of their possibly harmful side effects. Opponents, however, explicitly refuted this optimistic view of the military benefits, emphasizing instead the weapons' devastating and non-discriminatory environmental effects and the utter vulnerability of the population in the case of nuclear war. The analysis indicates that the loss of confidence in the military and in its ability to protect was reinforced by a re-evaluation of the perceived uncontrollable effects of nuclear weapons.

On a more abstract level and against the background of these findings, the analysis of the Swiss case also seems to validate the usefulness of the pragmatist lens of inquiry. It reveals that the decision-making process for the (non-)acquisition of nuclear weapons occurred in a multi-layered and non-linear manner. Instead of merely reacting to objectively given exogenous impulses or inputs, the decision was based on an intersubjective, linguistically mediated exchange of perceptions and views. The result was an ongoing renegotiation of the meaning of key issues and concepts such as the country's security environment and threat perception, its identity and role perception and the attributes of nuclear weapons.

It is beyond the scope of this study to illustrate in detail how the shifting discourses in Switzerland were linked to the discursive shifts which were taking place on the international or European scene. The broader pattern seems to be clear, though. It is a convincing assumption that the multilateral negotiations leading up to the PTBT or the negotiations which led to the agreement on the NPT not only spurred a shift in the global perception of nuclear weapons but also left an imprint on Swiss domestic debates. These negotiations highlighted the detrimental effects of nuclear weapons and challenged the conventionalization argument. In a similar vein, it seems reasonable to argue that the dramatic events of the Cuban missile crisis not only heightened an awareness of the dangers inherent in a nuclear standoff, but also downgraded the hitherto dominant positive security connotations attached to nuclear weapons. The adverse attitude toward nuclear weapons in Switzerland and the emerging global norm against nuclear weapons influenced and strengthened each other in a mutually productive manner.[174]

This finding is very much in line with our theoretical knowledge of the domestic significance and the effects of international norms.[175] The widespread – although not dominant – negative attitude toward nuclear weapons resonated well with an increasingly critical global outlook. Rublee, for example, writes with regard to her analysis of Japan, Sweden and Germany that in each of these cases,

> significant elements of the political elite wanted an independent nuclear deterrent. However, in each case, portions of the domestic population lobbied heavily against an indigenous nuclear weapons program, activating the emerging international norm against nuclear weapons to strengthen and add credibility to their arguments.[176]

The "cultural match"[177] between domestic and global perceptions reinforced the non-nuclear weapons norm in Switzerland once the global regime evolved and became institutionalized. Political forces in Switzerland were thus able to draw on the idea of global non-proliferation in order to make their case in the domestic debate. They thereby contributed to the growing salience of the non-proliferation norm and to a gradual shift in the discourse on nuclear weapons. The narratives that emerged against the background of these presumably global – as well as domestic – discursive shifts subsequently shaped the shared perception of Switzerland as a non-nuclear weapon state. They increasingly constrained a pro-nuclear policy and eventually enabled the materialization of a policy of nuclear forbearance. While this multifaceted causal narrative may not lend itself to establishing a general model, it certainly helps us to elucidate less obvious, but equally important, aspects of Switzerland's nuclear reversal.

Notes

1 Laurent Goetschel, Magdalena Bernath, and Daniel Schwarz, eds, *Schweizerische Aussenpolitik Grundlagen und Möglichkeiten* (Zürich: Verlag Neue Zürcher Zeitung, 2002), 10; Andreas Ladner, "Das Parteiensystem der Schweiz," in *Die Parteiensysteme Westeuropas*, ed. Oskar Niedermayer, Richard Stöss, and Melanie Haas (Wiesbaden: VS Verlag für Sozialwissenschaften, 2006); Lionel Marquis and Pascal Sciarini, "Opinion Formation in Foreign Policy: The Swiss Experience," *Electoral Studies* 18, no. 4 (1999); Adrian Vatter, "Vom Extremtyp zum Normalfall? Die schweizerische Konsensusdemokratie im Wandel: Eine Re-Analyse von Lijpharts Studie für die Schweiz von 1997 bis 2007," *Swiss Political Science Review* 14, no. 1 (2008).
2 Dominique Benjamin Metzler, "Die Option einer Nuklearbewaffnung für die Schweizer Armee 1945–1969," *Studien und Quellen* 23(1997); Jürg Stüssi-Lauterburg, *Historischer Abriss zur Frage einer Schweizer Nuklearbewaffnung* (Bern: Jürg Stüssi-Lauterburg, 1995); Theodor Winkler, *Kernenergie und Aussenpolitik die internationalen Bemühungen um eine Nichtweiterverbreitung von Kernwaffen und die friedliche Nutzung der Kernenergie in der Schweiz* (Berlin: Berlin Verlag, 1981).
3 Reto Wollenmann, *Zwischen Atomwaffe und Atomsperrvertrag. Die Schweiz auf dem Weg von der nuklearen Option zum Nonproliferationsvertrag (1958–1969)*, Zürcher Beiträge zur Sicherheitspolitik und Konfliktforschung (Zürich: ETH, 2004).
4 Paul, *Power versus prudence*, 84.
5 Wollenmann, *Zwischen Atomwaffe und Atomsperrvertrag. Die Schweiz auf dem Weg von der nuklearen Option zum Nonproliferationsvertrag (1958–1969)*, 33.

6 Paul, *Power versus prudence*, 96.

7 Ibid.

8 Urs Altermatt, "Vom Ende des Zweiten Weltkrieges bis zur Gegenwart (1945–1991)," in *Neues Handbuch der schweizerischen Aussenpolitik*, ed. Hans Haug, Alois Riklin, and Raymond Probst (Bern: Haupt, 1992), 62.

9 In addition, the Swiss Federal Council decided in 1946 that UN membership was not compatible with Switzerland's neutral status. Cf. Regula Ludi, "Demystification or Restoration of Neutrality? Confronting the History of the Nazi Era in Switzerland," *Holocaust Studies: A Journal of Culture and History* 11, no. 3 (2005): 30. See also Daniel Möckli, *Neutralität, Solidarität, Sonderfall. Die Konzeptionierung der schweizerischen Aussenpolitik der Nachkriegszeit, 1943–1947*, ed. Kurt R. Spillmann and Andreas Wenger, vol. 55, Zürcher Beiträge zur Sicherheitspolitik und Konfliktforschung (Zürich: Forschungsstelle für Sicherheitspolitik und Konfliktanalyse der ETH Zürich, 2000); Max Petitpierre, "321. Exposé relatif à la Conférence des Ambassadeurs de 1947," *Diplomatische Dokumente der Schweiz* Bd. 17, Nr. 26 (dodis.ch/321).

10 For a different take, see Andreas Wenger, "Swiss Security Policy: From Autonomy to Co-operation," in *Swiss foreign policy, 1945–2002*, ed. Jürg Martin Gabriel and Thomas Fischer (Basingstoke; New York: Palgrave Macmillan, 2003).

11 Christoph Breitenmoser, "Strategie ohne Aussenpolitik zur Entwicklung der schweizerischen Sicherheitspolitik im Kalten Krieg" (Diss phil Zürich, 2002), 42–43.

12 Marko Milivojevic and Pierre Maurer, *Swiss neutrality and security: armed forces, national defence, and foreign policy* (New York: St. Martin's Press, 1990), 15–17.

13 Oberstkorpskommandant Hans Frick: Brief an den Chef des Eidgenössischen Militärdepartments, Herrn Bundesrat Dr. Kobelt, 15.8.1945, in *Diplomatische Dokumente der Schweiz*, vol. 16, no. 24 (1997). Within military circles the question was raised even earlier – see, for example, Ernst Uhlmann, "Die Zielsetzung unserer Landesverteidigung," *Allgemeine schweizerische Militärzeitschrift* 121, no. 4 (1955).

14 Peter Braun, "Dreaming of the Bomb. The Development of Switzerland's Nuclear Option from the End of World War II to the Non-Proliferation Treaty," Conference Paper: *Uncovering the Sources of Nuclear Behavior. Historical Dimensions of Nuclear Proliferation* (Zurich 2010), 4.

15 Bundesrat, "1513. Schweizerische Studienkommission für Atomenergie, 8. Juni 1946 [Swiss Study Commission for Nuclear Energy, 8. June 1946]," *Diplomatische Dokumente der Schweiz* (1946); Nationalrat, "5074. Förderung der Atomforschung, 18. Dezember 1946 [Support for nuclear research, December 18, 1946]," *Amtliches Bulletin der Bundesversammlung* 5 (1946); Ständerat, "5974. Förderung der Atomforschung, 16. Oktober 1946 [Support for nuclear research, October 16, 1946]," *Amtliches Bulletin der Bundesversammlung* 4 (1946); "5074. Förderung der Atomforschung, 8. Oktober 1946 [Support for nuclear research, October 8, 1946]," *Amtliches Bulletin der Bundesversammlung* 4 (1946). Unofficially, the commission had already been in place since November 1945.

16 Patrick Kupper, "Sonderfall Atomenergie. Die bundesstaatliche Atompolitik 1945–1970," *Schweizerische Zeitschrift für Geschichte* 53, no. 1 (2003).

17 Eidgenössisches Militärdepartement, "Richtlinien für die Arbeiten der S.K.A. auf militärischem Gebiet, 5. Februar 1946," in *Diplomatische Dokumente der Schweiz* (Bern 1997).

18 Wollenmann, *Zwischen Atomwaffe und Atomsperrvertrag. Die Schweiz auf dem Weg von der nuklearen Option zum Nonproliferationsvertrag (1958–1969)*.

19 Braun, "Dreaming of the Bomb. The Development of Switzerland's Nuclear Option from the End of World War II to the Non-Proliferation Treaty," 3.

20 Bundesrat, 5074. Botschaft des Bundesrates an die Bundesversammlung zum

Entwurf eines Bundesbeschlusses über die Förderung der Forschung auf dem Gebiete der Atomenergie, 17. Juli 1946 [Report of the Federal Council to the Federal Assembly on the draft of a Federal Decision regarding the funding of research in the field of atomic energy, July 17, 1946]. *Bundesblatt*, vol. II (1946): 928–935.

21 Tobias Wildi, Der Traum vom eigenen Reaktor die schweizerische Atomtechnologieentwicklung 1945–1969 (Zürich: Chronos, 2003), 59–63.

22 The reactor that was later established in Lucens (completed in 1968) resembled the DIORIT heavy water design.

23 Wildi, *Der Traum vom eigenen Reaktor die schweizerische Atomtechnologieentwicklung 1945–1969*, 72.

24 Winkler, *Kernenergie und Aussenpolitik die internationalen Bemühungen um eine Nichtweiterverbreitung von Kernwaffen und die friedliche Nutzung der Kernenergie in der Schweiz*, 87; Wildi, *Der Traum vom eigenen Reaktor die schweizerische Atomtechnologieentwicklung 1945–1969*, 74; 128.

25 Eidgenössisches Militärdepartement, "1208. Erklärung zur Frage der Beschaffung von Atomwaffen für unsere Armee, 11. Juli 1958 [Statement on the question of nuclear weapon procurement for our military, July 11, 1958]," *Diplomatische Dokumente der Schweiz* (dodis.ch/16065).

26 "Libyan WMD: Tripoli's Statement in Full," BBC News, December 20, 2003.

27 Winkler, *Kernenergie und Aussenpolitik die internationalen Bemühungen um eine Nichtweiterverbreitung von Kernwaffen und die friedliche Nutzung der Kernenergie in der Schweiz*, 153–154; Braun, "Dreaming of the Bomb. The Development of Switzerland's Nuclear Option from the End of World War II to the Non-Proliferation Treaty," 11.

28 Eidgenössisches Militärdepartement, "753.4/63. Möglichkeiten einer eigenen Atomwaffen-Produktion (MAP-Bericht), 15. November 1963 [Possibilities of an indigenous nuclear weapon production (MAP-Report), November 15, 1963]," *Diplomatische Dokumente der Schweiz* (dodis.ch/30592): 46.

29 Stüssi-Lauterburg, *Historischer Abriss zur Frage einer Schweizer Nuklearbewaffnung*, 25–26.

30 Braun, for example, argues that the military did not actively seek the acquisition of nuclear weapons, but merely tried to maintain a "surge opportunity": "The point was rather to keep the option of an independent nuclear armament open in case the three existing nuclear powers would lose their monopoly" (Braun, "Dreaming of the Bomb. The Development of Switzerland's Nuclear Option from the End of World War II to the Non-Proliferation Treaty," 10).

31 Interpellation Gitermann, "7649. Ausrüstung der Armee mit Atomwaffen," *Amtliches Bulletin der Bundesversammlung* 4 (1958).

32 The pro-nuclear efforts benefited enormously from initiatives and lobbying by the Farner public relations agency. Established in the 1950s by Rudolf Farner (who also founded the "Verein zur Förderung der Wehrwissenschaft und des Wehrwillens"), the company had strong ties with both high-ranking military personnel and private businesses. For an illustration, see Constantin Seibt, "Die Macht der PR-Agentur Farner," *Tagesanzeiger*, November 25, 2009.

33 Cf. Bundesrat, "8468. Botschaft des Bundesrates an die Bundesversammlung über das Ergebnis der Volksabstimmung betreffend das Volksbegehren für ein Verbot von Atomwaffen, 4. Mai 1962 [Report of the Federal Council to the Federal Assembly on the outcome of the referendum concerning the petition for a ban on nuclear weapons, May 4, 1962]," *Bundesblatt*, vol. I (1962); "8816. Bericht des Bundesrates an die Bundesversammlung über das Ergebnis der Volksabstimmung vom 26. Mai 1963 betreffend das Volksbegehren für das Entscheidungsrecht des Volkes über die Ausrüstung der schweizerischen Armee mit Atomwaffen, 19. Juni 1963 [Report of the Federal Council to the Federal Assembly on the outcome of the referendum of

May 26, 1963 concerning the petition for the decision-making power of the people regarding equipping the Swiss military with nuclear weapons, June 19, 1963]," *Bundesblatt*, vol. II (1963). Accordingly, the first referendum was rejected by 537,138 to 286,895 votes. On the second occasion 274,061 electors supported the initiative, while 451,238 opposed it. While the margin in both cases was clear and indisputable, it may nevertheless come as a surprise how many voters actually favored nuclear abstention or at least constraint. Cf. Rolf Eberhard, "Die Abstimmung über die Atominitiative I," *Jahrbuch der Schweizerischen Vereinigung für politische Wissenschaft* 3(1963); Hugo Kramer, "Die Schweiz und die Atomwaffen," *Neue Wege* 57, no. 6 (1963).

34 Winkler, *Kernenergie und Aussenpolitik die internationalen Bemühungen um eine Nichtweiterverbreitung von Kernwaffen und die friedliche Nutzung der Kernenergie in der Schweiz*, 157–158.

35 These included: (1) Studienkommission Strategische Fragen (Study Commission on Strategic Questions); (2) Interdepartementale Arbeitsgruppe Sperrvertrag (Interdepartmental Working Group on the NPT); (3) Ad-Hoc Arbeitsgruppe Reaktortechnik (Ad-hoc working group on reactor technology).

36 Studienkommission für strategische Fragen, *Grundlagen einer strategischen Konzeption der Schweiz* (Bern 1969), 107–108.

37 Wollenmann, *Zwischen Atomwaffe und Atomsperrvertrag. Die Schweiz auf dem Weg von der nuklearen Option zum Nonproliferationsvertrag (1958–1969)*, 77–81.

38 According to the findings of the present study, the reactor accident at Lucens in January 1969 did not fundamentally change or impact upon the nuclear weapon decision-making process: by the time the accident happened, the decision had already been made.

39 Braun provides an additional explanation for why the treaty was only signed in 1969:

> The international tension following the Soviet intervention in Czechoslovakia in spring 1968 gave the federal government the pretext to dodge for a while the US pressure to accede to the treaty as soon as possible, and to delay its signature until mid-November 1969.
> (Braun, "Dreaming of the Bomb. The Development of Switzerland's Nuclear Option from the End of World War II to the Non-Proliferation Treaty," 20)

40 Braun, "Dreaming of the Bomb. The Development of Switzerland's Nuclear Option from the End of World War II to the Non-Proliferation Treaty," 21.

41 Abraham, "The Ambivalence of Nuclear Histories"; Flank, "Exploding the Black Box: The Historical Sociology of Nuclear Proliferation"; MacKenzie, "Missile Accuracy: A Case Study in the Social Processes of Technological Change."

42 Levite, "Never Say Never Again: Nuclear Reversal Revisited."

43 It should be noted, however, that this categorization in terms of group runs the risk of oversimplification, as will become clearer in the course of this analysis. At least the SP defies an easy labeling in the nuclear debate.

44 Eidgenössisches Militärdepartement, "1208. Erklärung zur Frage der Beschaffung von Atomwaffen für unsere Armee, 11. Juli 1958 [Statement on the question of nuclear weapon procurement for our military, July 11, 1958]."

45 "1208. Erklärung zur Frage der Beschaffung von Atomwaffen für unsere Armee, 11. Juli 1958 [Statement on the question of nuclear weapon procurement for our military, July 11, 1958]," 2.

46 Neutrality is contained in two different articles (Art. 173 and Art. 185); nevertheless, the concept has never been defined in the constitution, suggesting a certain amount of fluidity and vagueness and, above all perhaps, a certain degree of flexibility in its practical and political application.

47 Alois Riklin, "Die Neutralität der Schweiz," in *Schriftenreihe der Schweizerischen*

Gesellschaft für Aussenpolitik, ed. Hans Haug, Alois Riklin, and Raymond Probst (Bern: Haupt, 1992), 192.

48 Hanspeter Kriesi and Alexander H. Trechsel, *The politics of Switzerland. Continuity and change in a consensus democracy* (Cambridge: Cambridge University Press, 2008), 18.

49 The emotional and cultural significance of neutrality and resistance as the two key historical myths of Switzerland are also well illustrated by an anecdote mentioned by Breitenmoser. One of the central architectural features at the international "Expo 64" exhibition in Lausanne (1964) was a stylized figure/building in the shape of a hedgehog depicting the well-fortified, impregnable Switzerland. Breitenmoser, "Strategie ohne Aussenpolitik zur Entwicklung der schweizerischen Sicherheitspolitik im Kalten Krieg," 61–62.

50 Eidgenössisches Militärdepartement, "1208. Erklärung zur Frage der Beschaffung von Atomwaffen für unsere Armee, 11. Juli 1958 [Statement on the question of nuclear weapon procurement for our military, July 11, 1958]," 2. What is particularly striking about this frame (at least from today's perspective) is the ostensible "naivety" that shines through these phrases: the government does not seem to be deeply concerned or even aware of possible unintended consequences of its striving for nuclear weapons. This may also reflect the state of strategic thinking (at least outside the US) at that time: strategic misperceptions, nuclear arms dynamics or the consequences of shifts in the offense–defense balance had not yet been fully taken into account. Or, if one favors a more charitable reading, the Swiss government was so deeply convinced of Switzerland's peaceful identity that it did not spare a thought for other countries' "misperceptions."

51 "1208. Erklärung zur Frage der Beschaffung von Atomwaffen für unsere Armee, 11. Juli 1958 [Statement on the question of nuclear weapon procurement for our military, July 11, 1958]," 1.

52 "1208. Erklärung zur Frage der Beschaffung von Atomwaffen für unsere Armee, 11. Juli 1958 [Statement on the question of nuclear weapon procurement for our military, July 11, 1958]," 1; Winkler, *Kernenergie und Aussenpolitik die internationalen Bemühungen um eine Nichtweiterverbreitung von Kernwaffen und die friedliche Nutzung der Kernenergie in der Schweiz*, 153.

53 Eidgenössisches Militärdepartement, "1208. Erklärung zur Frage der Beschaffung von Atomwaffen für unsere Armee, 11. Juli 1958 [Statement on the question of nuclear weapon procurement for our military, July 11, 1958]," 1.

54 J. Ann Tickner, "Feminist Perspectives on International Relations," in *Handbook of international relations*, ed. Walter Carlsnaes, Thomas Risse-Kappen, and Beth A. Simmons (London; Thousand Oaks, CA: Sage, 2002), 283.

55 Taylor and Kinsella note that this is not an unusual move in framing processes on nuclear weapons and nuclear technology.

> Due to the high stakes controversies surrounding nuclear weapons development, most – if not all – of its associated scenes are characterized by competition between multiple frames and narratives. Of particular interest to communication scholars are the ways in which military, scientific, and government elites use nuclear rhetoric (e.g., technical rationality) to accomplish politically regressive outcomes. These outcomes include: mystifying audiences; obscuring the contingency, historicity, and human agency underlying policies and operations; promoting hierarchical and authoritarian institutions (such as nuclear "priesthoods"); and neutralizing dissent.
>
> (Bryan C. Taylor and William J. Kinsella, "Introduction: Linking Nuclear Legacies and Communication Studies," in *Nuclear legacies: communication, controversy, and the U.S. nuclear weapons complex*, ed. Bryan C. Taylor *et al.* (Lanham, MD: Lexington Books, 2008), 4–5)

56 Eidgenössisches Militärdepartement, "1208. Erklärung zur Frage der Beschaffung von Atomwaffen für unsere Armee, 11. Juli 1958 [Statement on the question of nuclear weapon procurement for our military, July 11, 1958]," 1.
57 "1208. Erklärung zur Frage der Beschaffung von Atomwaffen für unsere Armee, 11. Juli 1958 [Statement on the question of nuclear weapon procurement for our military, July 11, 1958]," 2.
58 Stüssi-Lauterburg, *Historischer Abriss zur Frage einer Schweizer Nuklearbewaffnung*, 91.
59 Eidgenössisches Militärdepartement, "1208. Erklärung zur Frage der Beschaffung von Atomwaffen für unsere Armee, 11. Juli 1958 [Statement on the question of nuclear weapon procurement for our military, July 11, 1958]," 1.
60 Ibid.
61 Ibid.
62 Ibid.
63 Ibid.
64 Tannenwald, *The nuclear taboo*, 90.
65 Ibid., 101.
66 Bertrand Russell and Albert Einstein, "The Russell-Einstein Manifesto," (London, 1955).
67 Bundesrat, "7854. Bericht des Bundesrates an die Bundesversammlung über das Volksbegehren für ein Verbot der Atomwaffen, 19. Mai 1959 [Report of the Federal Council to the Federal Assembly regarding the referendum on the prohibition of nuclear weapons, May 19, 1959]," *Bundesblatt*, vol. I (1959).
68 Schweizerische Bewegung gegen die atomare Aufrüstung [Swiss Movement against Atomic Armament], "Aufruf an das Schweizervolk [Appeal to the Swiss people]" (1958).
69 "Aufruf an das Schweizervolk [Appeal to the Swiss people]."
70 Ibid.
71 Ibid.
72 Ibid.
73 Notably, this dissent was already discernible in one of the early public documents regarding the nuclear question. In the course of the parliamentary "Interpellation Gitermann" divergent understandings of defence strategies (and of the appropriate means to reach these objectives) came to the fore. Gitermann, "7649. Ausrüstung der Armee mit Atomwaffen."
74 According to Wollenmann, this refers to a statement given by Oberstdivisionär Etienne Primault who had apparently called for the acquisition of long-range means of delivery in order to be able to hit targets within the enemy's country instead of only hitting enemy forces deployed at the Swiss border or indeed already on Swiss territory. Wollenmann, *Zwischen Atomwaffe und Atomsperrvertrag. Die Schweiz auf dem Weg von der nuklearen Option zum Nonproliferationsvertrag (1958–1969)*, 36.
75 In the analysis I considered approximately 30 such anti-nuclear documents (leaflets, newspaper advertisements, etc.)
76 To recap, these were: (1) an activist understanding of global political affairs; (2) an emphasis on the humanitarian character of the Swiss identity; (3) a non-conventionalization and criminalization of nuclear weapons; (4) a depiction of proliferation as dangerous; (5) a perception of nuclear weapons as detrimental to Switzerland's security; and (6) an asserted antagonism between neutrality and nuclear armaments.
77 Schweizerische Bewegung gegen die atomare Aufrüstung [Swiss Movement against Atomic Armament], "Noch ist es Zeit!" (1963); "Vertrauen zur Demokratie!" (1963).
78 "Atombulletin Nr. 16" (March 1962).

79 See, for example: Bundesrat, 8509. Ergänzungsbericht des Bundesrates an die Kommission des Nationalrates betreffend das Volksbegehren für das Entscheidungsrecht des Volkes über die Ausrüstung der schweizerischen Armee mit Atomwaffen, 15. November 1962 [Additional report of the Federal Council to the commission of the National Council concerning the petition for the decision-making power of the people regarding equipping the Swiss military with nuclear weapons, November 15, 1962]. *Bundesblatt*, vol. II (1962).

80 Schweizerische Bewegung gegen die atomare Aufrüstung [Swiss Movement against Atomic Armament], "Millionen Menschen in allen Ländern der Welt," (1962); "Noch ist es Zeit!"

81 "Das Schweizervolk ist gewarnt!" (1962).

82 "Atombulletin Nr. 23" (April 1963).

83 "Erklärung der 35," *Schweizerische Metall- und Uhrenarbeiter Zeitung*, June 11, 1958.

84 The "Erklärung" provoked fierce objections from large parts of the Left. See, for example, Gertrud Woker, "Atomaufrüstung auch in der Schweiz? Zur Erklärung von 35 prominenten Sozialdemokraten und Gewerkschaftern," *Neue Wege* 52, nos 7–8 (1958).

85 "Erklärung der 35."

86 Bundesrat, "7987. Botschaft des Bundesrates an die Bundesversammlung betreffend die Organisation des Heeres (Truppenordnung), 30. Juni 1960 [Report of the Federal Council regarding the Reorganization of the Armed Forces, June 30, 1960]," *Bundesblatt*, vol. II (1960).

87 8273. Bericht des Bundesrates an die Bundesversammlung über das Volksbegehren für ein Verbot der Atomwaffen, 7. Juli 1961 [Report of the Federal Council to the Federal Assembly regarding the referendum on the prohibition of nuclear weapons, July 7, 1961]. *Bundesblatt*, vol. II (1961).

88 8509. Bericht des Bundesrates an die Bundesversammlung über das Volksbegehren für das Entscheidungsrecht des Volkes über die Ausrüstung der schweizerischen Armee mit Atomwaffen, 18. Juni 1962 [Report of the Federal Council to the Federal Assembly regarding the referendum on the decision-making power of the people regarding equipping the Swiss military with nuclear weapons, June 18, 1962]. *Bundesblatt*, vol. II (1962).
"8509. Additional report of the Federal Council to the commission of the National Council concerning the petition for the decision-making power of the people, 1962." For an account of the debate, see moreover Nationalrat, "8509. Ausrüstung der schweizerischen Armee mit Atomwaffen, 17. Dezember 1962 [Equipping the Swiss army with nuclear weapons, December 17, 1962]," *Amtliches Bulletin der Bundesversammlung*, vol. IV (1962); "8509. Ausrüstung der schweizerischen Armee mit Atomwaffen, 18. Dezember 1962 [Equipping the Swiss army with nuclear weapons, December 18, 1962]," *Amtliches Bulletin der Bundesversammlung*, vol. IV (1962).

89 Bundesrat, "7987. Report of the Federal Council regarding the Reorganization of the Armed Forces, 1960." See also Winkler, *Kernenergie und Aussenpolitik die internationalen Bemühungen um eine Nichtweiterverbreitung von Kernwaffen und die friedliche Nutzung der Kernenergie in der Schweiz*, 165.

90 Bundesrat, "7987. Report of the Federal Council regarding the Reorganization of the Armed Forces, 1960," 325.

91 Ibid., 326. As will be elaborated later on, this inconclusiveness could be a subtle indication of diverging interests within the military establishment (between the proponents of a mobile defense posture on the one hand and an area defense on the other).

92 See, for example, Rudolf L. Bindschedler, *Die Neutralität im modernen Völkerrecht* (Stuttgart: Kohlhammer, 1956).

93 Bundesrat, "7987. Report of the Federal Council regarding the Reorganization of the Armed Forces, 1960," 322.
94 Ibid., 324, 31.
95 Ibid., 324.
96 Ibid., 333.
97 Ibid., 331.
98 Ibid., 338.
99 Ibid., 323, 25.
100 Ibid., 321, 22, 31.
101 Ibid., 323.
102 Ibid., 325.
103 "8273. Report of the Federal Council to the Federal Assembly regarding the referendum on the prohibition of nuclear weapons, 1961."
104 For example, the problem of radiation or the possible global impact of Switzerland's quest for a nuclear capability.
105 Bundesrat, "8273. Report of the Federal Council to the Federal Assembly regarding the referendum on the prohibition of nuclear weapons, 1961," 216.
106 Ibid.
107 Arguably, one can even discern a fourth frame which touches upon the issue of national modernity and technological progress. However, this frame seems to play a slightly subordinate role in the 1961 report compared to other documents.
108 Bundesrat, "8273. Report of the Federal Council to the Federal Assembly regarding the referendum on the prohibition of nuclear weapons, 1961," 203.
109 Ibid., 215.
110 Ibid., 221.
111 On page 215, the authors refer to it as "exceptionalism" ("Sonderstellung").
112 Bundesrat, "8273. Report of the Federal Council to the Federal Assembly regarding the referendum on the prohibition of nuclear weapons, 1961," 204–209.
113 Ibid., 207.
114 Ibid.
115 Ibid., 208.
116 Ibid., 218–219.
117 Ibid., 213.
118 Ibid., 220.
119 "8509. Additional report of the Federal Council to the commission of the National Council concerning the petition for the decision-making power of the people, 1962"; "8509. Report of the Federal Council to the Federal Assembly regarding the referendum on the decision-making power, 1962."
120 "8509. Report of the Federal Council to the Federal Assembly regarding the referendum on the decision-making power, 1962," 21.
121 Ibid.
122 "8509. Additional report of the Federal Council to the commission of the National Council concerning the petition for the decision-making power of the people, 1962", 1159.
123 Their major, frequently distributed publication outlet was the "Pressedienst": a regular collection of statements, commentaries and analyses by different authors and nuclear proponents. It may be assumed that the Pressedienst was influential in shaping public debate, since it was specifically targeted at and sent to publicists, journalists, opinion leaders and the like. Overall, I analyzed approximately 45 documents of the pro-nuclear movement.
124 Breitenmoser has coined this fitting and sound depiction: Breitenmoser, "Strategie ohne Aussenpolitik zur Entwicklung der schweizerischen Sicherheitspolitik im Kalten Krieg," 39.

125 Cf. Schweizerisches Aktionskomitee gegen die Atominitiative [Swiss Action Committee against the Nuclear Initiative], "Pressedienst Nr. 4" (1962).

126 "Neutral sein wollen, heisst stark sein müssen!" "Pressedienst Nr. 3" (1962); "Pressedienst Nr. 10" (1962).

127 Verein zur Förderung des Wehrwillens und der Wehrwissenschaft, "Stellungnahme: Aktuelle Militärpolitik" (1962).

128 Schweizerisches Aktionskomitee gegen die Atominitiative [Swiss Action Committee against the Nuclear Initiative], "Pressedienst Nr. 12" (1962); "Pressedienst Nr. 7" (1962).

129 Pamphlet published by Aktion freier Staatsbürger, March 1962; "Pressedienst Nr. 4."

130 "Pressedienst Nr. 1" (1963).

131 "Pressedienst Nr. 3; "Pressedienst Nr. 5" (1962).

132 "utili idioti": "Pressedienst Nr. 9" (1962).

133 "Pressedienst Nr. 9" (1963).

134 "Pressedienst Nr. 5" (1962).

135 "Pressedienst Nr. 6" (1962).

136 "Pressedienst Nr. 11" (1962).

137 For a substantial theoretical analysis of the complex Christian perspective on nuclear weapons – and an implicit refutation of this pro-nuclear argument – see Nigel Biggar, "Christianity and Weapons of Mass Destruction," in *Ethics and weapons of mass destruction: religious and secular perspectives*, ed. Sohail H. Hashmi and Steven P. Lee, The ethikon series in comparative ethics (Cambridge: Cambridge University Press, 2004).

138 Bundesrat, 8831. Botschaft des Bundesrates an die Bundesversammlung betreffend die Genehmigung des in Moskau geschlossenen Abkommens über das Verbot von Kernwaffenversuchen in der Luft, im Weltraum und unter Wasser, 13. September 1963 [Message of the Federal Council to the Federal Assembly regarding the approval of the agreement signed in Moscow on the prohibition of nuclear weapons tests in the air, in space, and underwater, September 13, 1963]. *Bundesblatt*, vol. II (1963).

139 "8831. Report of the Federal Council to the Federal Assembly regarding the Moscow test ban treaty, 1963," 618.

140 The authors remain rather vague on this point. While they explicitly state that the three signatories attempted to prevent the spread of nuclear weapons to other countries, they only conspicuously claim that the three also had other motives outside the realm of the treaty. "8831. Report of the Federal Council to the Federal Assembly regarding the Moscow test ban treaty, 1963."

141 "8831. Report of the Federal Council to the Federal Assembly regarding the Moscow test ban treaty, 1963," 617.

142 Ibid.

143 Ibid., 620.

144 "8273. Report of the Federal Council to the Federal Assembly regarding the referendum on the prohibition of nuclear weapons, 1961," 214–215.

145 "8831. Report of the Federal Council to the Federal Assembly regarding the Moscow test ban treaty, 1963," 619.

146 Ibid., 621.

147 "9478. Bericht des Bundesrates an die Bundesversammlung über die Konzeption der militärischen Landesverteidigung, 16. Juni 1966 [Report of the Federal Council to the Federal Assembly on the concept of military national defense, June 16, 1966]," *Bundesblatt*, vol. I (1966).

148 The acquisition of another 100 jets was envisaged to take place two or three years later. "8153. Botschaft des Bundesrates an die Bundesversammlung über die Beschaffung von Kampfflugzeugen (Mirage III S), 25. April 1961 [Report of the

Federal Council to the Federal Assembly regarding the acquisition of combat aircraft (Mirage III S), April 25, 1961]," *Bundesblatt*, vol. I (1961).

149 Given that these proponents of the mobile defense concept were also the ones who had been lobbying for the nuclear option, their resignations significantly weakened the nuclear advocate camp within the government and the military establishment.

150 Despite these changes in strategic and military thinking among large parts of the public, parts of the military remained attached to the idea of a Swiss nuclear deterrent. See, for example, Gustav Däniker, "Kleinstaatliche Abschreckung," *Allgemeine Schweizerische Militärzeitschrift* 132, no. 9 (1966).

151 Bundesrat, "8273. Report of the Federal Council to the Federal Assembly regarding the referendum on the prohibition of nuclear weapons, 1961," 203.

152 Ibid., 218–219.

153 "9478. Report of the Federal Council to the Federal Assembly on the concept of military national defense, 1966," 870.

154 Ibid., 866.

155 Ludi provides a convincing account of the origins of this military myth:

> By the end of the 1940s, a particular national memory emerged which associated resistance with neutrality and identified the latter with the army.... Being seen as the main guarantee of neutrality, the military served as the most important symbol of Swiss coherence and identity, not least because of its presumed ability to bridge social distinctions and cultural gaps.... In foreign relations this discourse took pride in splendid isolation. In the face of rapid modernisation in the 1950s, however, this myth gradually turned into a nostalgic longing for a lost world.
>
> (Ludi, "Demystification or Restoration of Neutrality? Confronting the History of the Nazi Era in Switzerland," 32)

For a critical reflection see Breitenmoser, "Strategie ohne Aussenpolitik zur Entwicklung der schweizerischen Sicherheitspolitik im Kalten Krieg," 78–84. Insights into the original discussion regarding the "readjustment of the defence conception" may be derived from Interpellation Hubacher, "Atombewaffnung der Armee," *Amtliches Bulletin der Bundesversammlung*, vol. III (1966).

156 Bundesrat, "9478. Report of the Federal Council to the Federal Assembly on the concept of military national defense, 1966," 871.

157 Ibid., 872.

158 Interpellation Binder, "Stellungnahme zum geplanten Atomsperrvertrag," *Amtliches Bulletin der Bundesversammlung*, vol. IV (1967).

159 Ibid., 594.

160 Ibid.

161 Ibid., 595.

162 As is shown in the following chapter, the similarities to the Libyan case could hardly be more striking: the Libyan discourse, too, is interwoven with a narrative of global inequality and discrimination. However, it is not only the rather unexpected parallel between Switzerland and Libya that makes this finding so striking. It is also that even today – four decades later – this theme regularly comes up in ongoing debates on the NPT and the inherent, unequal obligations for nuclear and non-nuclear states.

163 Binder, "Stellungnahme zum geplanten Atomsperrvertrag," 595.

164 Many observers feared that the treaty could hamper Switzerland's progress in the realm of peaceful nuclear technologies and thwart the economic exploitation of civilian nuclear applications, especially if the treaty was not universally adhered to.

165 Spühler in Interpellation Binder, "Stellungnahme zum geplanten Atomsperrvertrag," 596.

166 "Stellungnahme zum geplanten Atomsperrvertrag," 596.

167 Ibid.

168 As a reminder, see, for example, Bundesrat, "8273. Report of the Federal Council to the Federal Assembly regarding the referendum on the prohibition of nuclear weapons, 1961."

169 Spühler in Interpellation Binder, "Stellungnahme zum geplanten Atomsperrvertrag," 596.

170 Ibid.

171 Ludi, "Demystification or Restoration of Neutrality? Confronting the History of the Nazi Era in Switzerland."

172 This finding gains additional support from a different perspective: Strasser's study on the link between Switzerland's scientific policies and its role as a neutral state underlines the fact that the country's science and technology policies and the idea of neutrality were mutually reinforcing and co-constitutive:

> The neutrality of science and the state have never been givens; rather, they represent a process of negotiation which is taking place in historically-specific contexts, aimed at deflecting particular political forces.... States such as Switzerland defined being neutral as being permanently engaged in the process of finding a path along the delicate line balancing the necessity of active involvement in international affairs and the refusal to commit to political alliances aimed at shifting balances of power. Given the paramount importance of political alliances of all kinds in political affairs, the Swiss were hard pressed to find domains that could be made to fit this agenda. Scientific cooperation was one of these domains, along with cultural, humanitarian and social cooperation. By actively attempting to depoliticize and demilitarize these international affairs, Switzerland could affirm publicly how much it cared about its neutrality policy. These actions were not cynical manipulations of the neutrality idea.... Indeed, Switzerland's neutrality was not only a useful fiction employed by the government to defend its foreign and economic policies but also a central tenet of the nation's identity.
>
> (Strasser, "The Coproduction of Neutral Science and Neutral State," 186–187)

173 Raymond Probst, "Die 'guten Dienste' der Schweiz," Annuaire de l'Association Suisse de Science Politique = Jahrbuch der Schweizerischen Vereinigung für politische Wissenschaft 3(1963).

174 The global impact of the Swiss debate must certainly not be overestimated. Yet it seems a convincing assumption that the changing attitude to nuclear weapons in Switzerland did at least leave an imprint on the global debate. For illustrative purposes one might compare it to the more recent case regarding the future of nuclear energy. Here, too, we see that Germany's 2002 decision to phase out its nuclear power plants attracted global attention and led to increased debate at least in like-minded countries, although it did not instigate a global de-nuclearization movement.

175 See, for example, Andrew P. Cortell and James W. Davis, "How Do International Institutions Matter? The Domestic Impact of International Rules and Norms," *International Studies Quarterly* 40, no. 4 (1996).

176 Rublee, *Nonproliferation norms. Why states choose nuclear restraint*, 202.

177 Jeffrey T. Checkel, "Norms, Institutions, and National Identity in Contemporary Europe," *International Studies Quarterly* 43, no. 1 (1999): 86. Referring to the concept of "cultural match," Checkel writes:

> I thus define it as a situation where the prescriptions embodied in an international norm are convergent with domestic norms, as reflected in discourse, the legal system (constitutions, judicial codes, laws), and bureaucratic agencies (organizational ethos and administrative procedures). So defined, cultural matches vary across issue areas. Cultural match is not simply a dichotomous variable (yes, one has it or not); rather, it scales along a spectrum.

5 Libya

The stateless state

On December 19, 2003, after almost four decades of WMD procurement efforts, the Socialist People's Libyan Arab Jamahiriya announced its unilateral relinquishment of all types of weapons of mass destruction and of ballistic missiles with a range of over 300 km and a payload of more than 500 kg. The declaration had been preceded by several months of intense secret negotiations limited to a small circle of Libyan, British and US government officials, and took most non-proliferation analysts, practitioners and politicians by surprise. Given Muammar Gaddafi's typically confrontational and rather deviant behavior toward the international community, very few observers had thought it likely that the Libyan leader was about to forgo the country's weapons of mass destruction.[1] Thus, Libya's rollback of its nuclear weapons program is one of the prime examples of nuclear reversal and deserves major attention both from a theoretical and policy perspective. This is even more true given the recentness of the development: no other country has since performed a similar about-face in its general foreign and security policy and in its nuclear policy in particular. However, the analysis that follows will also reveal that Libya is not only an interesting case in terms of its initial interest in and later dismissal of the nuclear option. An aspect of the Libyan case that is at least equally striking – and one that deserves further attention – is the inconsistent political commitment to the nuclear weapons program and the rather volatile government support it received.[2]

The analysis begins with a depiction of Libya's political, strategic and ideological context. This is followed by a historiographic reconstruction of the country's nuclear program. The principal readings of the case are explicated; potential weaknesses in the currently prevailing explanations, as well as gaps in research, are identified and described. In the second part of the chapter, the Libyan case is then examined through a "pragmatist lens." It is argued that the country's proliferation policy was not simply based on purported, objective threats or on the state's pre-defined situation within its security environment, but on intersubjectively shared beliefs regarding Libya's identity, its position in the international system and its role conception. Thus, the goal is to uncover how threat perceptions, interests or preferences – which ultimately led to the non-acquisition of nuclear weapons – emerged.

Clearly, the particular analytical challenge of this case study arises from the nature of the Gaddafi regime as an oppressive, inhuman and brutal dictatorship. This endeavor to understand the ideational underpinnings of such a political actor may easily be misconceived by readers as a cynical attempt to academically justify or legitimize the regime's deeds. This, however, is far removed from what the chapter actually seeks to achieve. Rather than analyzing the regime's (presumably manipulative) justifications, this analysis tries to establish the intersubjectively (i.e., socially) shared beliefs underlying the actual proliferation decision. In other words: the study by no means aims to exonerate the regime, but to understand how intersubjectively shared beliefs or narratives (regarding the state's identity, its security perceptions, etc.) make particular policies possible in the first place. Hence, while positivist-realist studies usually trace a proliferation/nuclearization decision back to apparently fixed security constraints and necessities, I argue, on the other hand, that there is no automatism: states' decisions and policies are rooted in socially shared understandings of "what the state is," what "role" it occupies in the international system and the way in which it perceives its security environment. Arguably, these narratives and beliefs are "tenacious" and "sticky"; they do not change easily. And yet they are not fixed either. Hence, it is by analyzing these narratives that we are able to understand how certain policies become possible. Moreover, we can illustrate potential arenas for the articulation of reflections, disagreements and counterviews which may ultimately – under favorable political conditions – instigate policy change.

Libya's political and strategic context

Compared to the previous analysis of Switzerland's nuclear reversal, the Libyan case could hardly be more different. While Switzerland is commonly considered to be the role model for direct democracy and a prime example of functioning state institutions successfully underpinning a heterogeneous confederation, Libya is seen as the epitome of a "stateless state": for most of its modern history, Libya was formally a sovereign country with "virtually no stable state apparatus," as Anderson and several other authors have put it.[3]

Moreover, the level of interregional cooperation and interaction has been low, especially between the tribal hinterland and the urbanized coastal areas. In addition, the emergence of closer economic, cultural, communicational or political ties has been hindered – not least by Libya's Italian colonizers.[4] The cultural, and above all tribal, genealogical differences that have existed among Libya's three constituent regions – Tripolitania, Cyrenaica and Fezzan – since ancient times have significantly shaped the country and continue to shape even the modern state, thereby preventing the emergence and fostering of a local *classe politique*.[5] For the majority of Libyans, the main political arena consisted of traditional decision-making procedures based on local and regional groupings, while social cohesion was primarily based on tribal structures and kinship linkages – or, in a wider sense, based on the common Islamic faith. These also remained the primary sources of identity even after the country's independence in 1951.[6] The establishment of the monarchy – a political concept that did not root in Libya's political culture – did little to change this situation: the entrenchment of the national state and its political and administrative institutions within the local population remained weak.[7] In addition, the dismal economic situation – before the discovery of vast oil and gas resources in the late 1950s – further contributed to the structural weakness of the state.[8]

The revolution and its ideological tenets

In terms of domestic institutions, the situation was further aggravated by Muammar Gaddafi's September 1969 revolution. Fundamentally rejecting the principles of Western representational multi-party democracy, the revolutionaries established direct democratic forms of self-governance. Although officially justified by noble grassroot-democratic motifs, it could barely conceal the regime's suppressive, violent nature, as reflected in both the government's domestic and foreign policies. In addition, a dense network of partly overlapping security forces and secret police units ensured that opponents of the regime were identified and "sidelined," either through the threat of force or through the actual use of violence.[9] Informal, paralegal structures of power furthermore guaranteed that major political issues were beyond the realm of the democratic institutions, being instead dealt with exclusively by a small unofficial circle of Gaddafi's trusted aides, the majority of whom originated from or were affiliated with the Qadhadhfa tribe. This invalidated ideals of equality or grassroots governance and clearly limited any sort of people power.[10]

The lack of functioning political and state structures further undermined the political entity and the Libyan state. The bifurcation between institutionalized and defined mechanisms of people power on the one hand, and informal – indeed still tribal – structures of government on the other is indicative of the emergence of a more broadly idiosyncratic and highly ambiguous form of statehood that was to become so typical of Libya.[11] This reflects Libya's struggle between two types of ambition: on the one hand it wanted to establish a mature and modern state that was capable of redistributing the vast amounts of revenue generated by oil exports and of securing the regime, while on the other hand there was a desire to maintain an essentially traditional, pre-bureaucratic, non-state entity. Ultimately, what did emerge was a vast bureaucratic apparatus typical of a rentier state. Rather than a political structure, there was a relatively formal, administrative structure, whose primary goal was to redistribute large oil revenues in order to foster regime security.[12] Country-wide political institutions remained weak, while tribes retained their influence and maintained a crucial function, acting not only as (local) political and government institutions, but also as a source of identity and a defining influence on Libya's political culture.[13]

> [F]rom the creation of the monarchy onward, there existed in Libya a tension between the pursuit and maintenance of an earlier form of political community – based on family and tribe – and the exigencies of a modern

state.... Particularly after 1969, the rhetoric and flamboyance of the regime obscured a more profound and unique process by which it attempted to avoid the burdens of extending the mechanisms of a modern state. Instead, it enunciated a vision of statelessness that was carefully wrapped in a cloak of nostalgia for earlier times, when family and tribe provided solidarity, equity, and egalitarianism.[14]

In broader political terms, the 1961 revolution was not primarily a response to the monarchy's specific policies, but rather a rebellion against developments and attitudes in the country in general: against the monarchy itself, which was regarded as an imposition by foreign powers and considered un-Arabic; against cronyism, corruption and decadence; against the influence of foreign oil companies; but also against King Idris' pro-Western stance in terms of foreign policy (manifested in the continued military cooperation with British and US forces and in the provision of military basing rights to both countries) and his apparent disregard for volatile issues such as the Palestinian question or other matters of Arab cooperation against perceived Western political and cultural domination.[15]

Gaddafi's policies – and his foreign policy in particular – have often been judged erratic and capricious.[16] Nonetheless, the ideological "superstructure" implemented by the revolutionaries was fairly consistent and reflected certain key beliefs with regard to the future depiction of Libyan society. This portrayal was based on the three central notions of *freedom from colonialism and oppression*, *Arab unity* and *Arab socialism*. Unmistakably, these tenets exemplify the close proximity of the revolutionaries' goals to the Egyptian model, as the Libyan ideological triad resembled the ideals proclaimed by Gamal Abdel Nasser in 1952.[17]

Thus, both in rhetorical and policy terms, the fight against colonialism and Western political, cultural and economic dominance, and for Arab unity and global equality became the keystones of Gaddafi's reign – and central to both his domestic and foreign policy initiatives. Burgat explains that in ideational terms these ideas are deeply anchored in Beduin history and culture:

> [T]he quest for Arab unity is also the pursuit of a dream – the dream of an adolescent growing up under the reign of a complacent Idris, who took the full measure of the political decadence and economic dependence of his native Libya. Unity provides a magic answer to colonial domination and postcolonial dependence. For the deracinated Bedouin, the myth of unity is also a means by which to exorcise the disillusions of modernity. It cushions the impact of cultural alienation, for only by recovering their lost unity can the Arabs achieve reconciliation with themselves, with their values, including those of their mythical past.[18]

Notably, Islamic principles were not at the center of the revolutionary movement, yet the movement had to ensure that it was not in open breach of religious traditions and prescriptions. At the same time, Islamic thought provided legitimacy to the regime's social and economic policies and granted a spiritual underpinning to the notion of *Arab socialism*, thereby "transforming Libya into a large-scale replica of the consensual, egalitarian, and collective values that typify traditional life."[19]

As the following paragraphs illustrate, these principles not only shaped much of Libya's domestic politics but also provided legitimacy for the country's deviant and largely violent and aggressive foreign policy.

Ideational foundation of Libya's foreign and security policy

For much of the Cold War, Libya's international position and behavior was shaped significantly by the confrontation between the two great powers. On the one hand, the Gaddafi government was eager to expel British and American forces from bases in Libya and to free the country, and with it the whole Arab region, from what was perceived to be "modern colonial domination" by the West; quite naturally, therefore, the Soviet Union seemed to be the logical ally. Yet, on the other hand, Libya was afraid to lose its long-fought-for independence to another dominator. Moreover, the revolutionaries emphasized the ideological differences between Soviet communist ideology and their idea of "Arab social-ism." These differences notwithstanding, the Soviet Union was indeed Libya's closest ally for most of the Cold War, providing Libya with large stockpiles of weapons as well as with nuclear technology (see below). The fortitude and fixity of Libya's position between the two superpowers should not be overestimated, however. As late in the Cold War as 1979/1980, Gaddafi undertook several attempts to reach a rapprochement with the Carter administration, even if they were only timid or half-hearted. This policy revision seems to have been trig-gered by two main factors. First, the Soviet Union's costly and destructive involvement in Afghanistan caused Libya to fear that it was steadily losing Soviet support – both in political as well as military terms. Second, Gaddafi faced mounting domestic opposition, primarily from the military but also from militant Islamist groups.[20]

Yet, not only did his reconciliatory steps toward the US government fail, but relations between the two countries deteriorated even further in the 1980s, not least due to the change of president from Carter to Reagan. While the tensions at first seemed to be limited to several small-scale military standoffs in the Medi-terranean, the year 1986 saw an escalation of events. On April 4 a bomb exploded in Berlin at La Belle, a discotheque frequented by US military person-nel, killing three people. Twelve days later, US President Reagan ordered air strikes against Benghazi and Tripoli in retaliation for the La Belle incident. Two years later, Libya's international terrorist activities escalated, with the bombing of two civilian airliners, Pan Am flight 103 over Lockerbie (Scotland) and the UTA flight 772 over Ténéré (Niger), leaving more than 400 people dead. In 1992 the international community reacted to these incidents by politically isolating Libya and imposing a relatively strict sanctions regime on the country with the aim of forcing Libya to extradite the two key suspects in the bombings and to end its support for all forms of international terrorism.[21] The sanctions regime, which was based on several UN Security Council Resolutions, banned all air travel with Libya, prohibited arms exports to Libya and proscribed the sale of certain technologies and oil industry-related equipment. However, the sanctions did not include a complete ban on Libya's oil exports, not least due to pressure from Europe.[22] In spite of these loopholes, the sanctions did have a severe impact upon Libya's economy and ultimately played at least a part in the Gaddafi regime's changing behavior and hence also its renunciation of the WMD option in 2003.[23]

Libya's foreign relations with the Arab region as well as with its African neighbors are closely intertwined and are difficult to disentangle from the Cold War constellation of power. Besides simple power calculations, however, there is also a strong ideological and religious component – particularly with regard to Libya's attitude toward the Arab world: as indicated above, the notion of Arab unity must not be underestimated as one of the driving forces behind Libya's foreign policy. The September 1 revolution was indeed based on the drive to unite the Arab region against the perceived dominance of and interference by the Western powers. While Joffé reminds us to analyze Libya's foreign policy not only through an "Islamist lens," he nevertheless emphasizes its significance:

> Particularly since 1974, certain common strands can be identified which stem directly from the domestic role played by Islam in Libya. Libyan foreign policy is anti-Zionist, anti-imperialist, supportive of radicalism in the African world, and integrative in its efforts to obliterate colonial boundaries. Practically all these objectives combine a Nasirist legacy with Islamic legitimization and are even buttressed by specific Islamic objectives involving the extension of Islamic values. They derive from the three basic principles of the September revolution – freedom, unity, and socialism.[24]

Following the death of Egypt's President Nasser in 1970, Gaddafi had proclaimed himself Nasser's heir and the new leader of the Arab world; several attempts to create bilateral or multilateral federations and to strengthen regional cooperation underline these efforts.[25] However, Egypt's revised stance on the Israel–Palestine conflict in the mid-1970s and its concomitant rapprochement with the United States drove a deep wedge between Libyan–Egyptian relations and undermined the vision of Arab–Islamic unity.[26] That the Arab world, moreover, did little to condemn the imposition of international sanctions further estranged Gaddafi from his former partners.

Consequently, he turned toward the Maghreb and sub-Saharan Africa in his search for new allies – a step that was certainly more pragmatic than ideologically compelling, since it clearly diverged from Gaddafi's revolutionary and belligerent Africa policy as well as from the country's pan-Arab stance in earlier decades.[27] On the other hand, it must be taken into account that Gaddafi's fight against colonialism and Western dominance and for global equality did strike a chord with many African citizens and politicians. Gaddafi was therefore able to extend his egalitarian international vision and to arouse the support of many African leaders. As a result, and not least due to the promise of large Libyan investments in African states' infrastructure projects, several African governments politically supported Gaddafi and his quest for a lifting of the sanctions. In June 1998 the Organization of African Unity issued a declaration calling for the suspension of all anti-Libyan sanctions. Furthermore, in the following weeks more and more African states started to violate the air travel ban against Libya, thereby undermining the strict policy enforced by the United States and the United Kingdom.[28] At the climax of Gaddafi's call for pan-African unity, he declared that "we Libyans are Africans. Africa is our continent."[29] However, it should also be noted that following the lifting of international sanctions at the same time as renewed efforts to establish a Libyan–European partnership, Gaddafi lost some of his interest in the African continent.[30]

Historiographic reconstruction of Libya's nuclear program

Libya's announcement in 2003 that it was to abandon its biological, chemical and nuclear warfare program, as well as its ballistic missile program, marked the end of a decades-long endeavor to acquire WMD capabilities. Gaddafi sought to acquire nuclear weapons as early as 1969, soon after the revolutionary takeover of the government. His first attempt to purchase "off-the-shelf" weapons from China was rejected by the Chinese government.[31] Yet, as Bowen points out, the Libyan administration was not particularly discouraged by these setbacks. In contrast, the 1970s saw increased efforts by Libyan government officials to "tap" alternative sources of nuclear technology: Libya signed a cooperation agreement with Argentina on the first steps of the nuclear fuel cycle such as uranium prospection and the further mining and processing of the raw material; it maintained a scientific exchange program with Egypt; it attempted to buy a ready-to-use nuclear research reactor as well as a turnkey power reactor both from France and the United States; it concluded an agreement with India covering the exchange of oil for civil nuclear technology; and it entered into a nuclear deal with Pakistan, in which Libya would provide uranium (apparently from Niger) and funding in return for technology and scientific expertise.[32] During the 1980s, the country sought further to buy technological components from Bulgaria, Yugoslavia and Belgium.[33]

While the Libyan government justified all these efforts by emphasizing that it was solely interested in the civilian use of nuclear technology, most of the possible supplier states were concerned about the regime's actual intentions. Indeed, the United States – being highly skeptical of Libya's peaceful motives – increased its pressure on supplier states to make them refrain from exporting technology to or entering into nuclear deals with Libya. Hence most countries either immediately refused to cooperate with Libya or ultimately backed down and withdrew from already signed agreements due to mounting US pressure in the 1970s.[34] As a result, the Soviet Union became Libya's most important source of nuclear technological assistance at least during the first decade of Libya's activities. In 1975 it provided the ten-megawatt nuclear research reactor, as well as the necessary fuel, for the Tajura Nuclear Research Center, located in the coastal region east of Tripoli and in operation since 1980. A further joint project for a nuclear power plant at Sirte never materialized.[35] It is important to note that the Soviet Union, too, was not wholeheartedly convinced by the Libyan government's benign intentions and therefore made its cooperation in the nuclear field conditional upon Libya's ratification of the NPT and its acceptance of the additional IAEA Safeguard Agreement.[36]

In addition to possible hesitancy on the part of the suppliers to deliver the required nuclear technology, the acquisition of fissile material posed a similar, if not greater challenge for the Libyan nuclear plant. In the 1970s and 1980s, large-scale explorations for natural sources of uranium on the Libyan territory proved unsuccessful, which meant that the country's leadership realized it had to rely on foreign resources if it was ever to obtain sufficient means for civilian or military applications of nuclear technology. It is widely assumed in the literature on the subject that this lack of access to domestic uranium deposits was one of the reasons for the Libyan government's occupation of the Aouzou Strip in northern Chad in 1973.[37] Moreover, it spurred the emergence of an intricate, multidirectional trade network between Libya, Niger and Pakistan: Libya purchased uranium from Niger, which it then transferred to Pakistan where the material was fed into Pakistan's covert enrichment program. In addition, Libya provided financial means to support Pakistan's clandestine research on civil and military nuclear technology. In return, the government in Tripoli expected to obtain access to this research, as well as actual components for its nuclear weapons program.[38] Yet, as Bowen indicates, this hope did not seem to have materialized in this early period of Libya's nuclear endeavor:

> Despite the lack of clarity on the exact nature of the nuclear relationship during this period, it appears that Pakistan did provide Libya with at least some technical assistance in the form of training and personnel exchanges.... However, it does not appear that Libya received significant amounts of sensitive technology during this early period.[39]

Thus, at least during this first phase of its exploration of the prospects of civil and military nuclear technology applications, Libya was primarily reliant upon support from the Soviet Union, which, however, was hesitant to share nuclear technology with the Gaddafi regime. As a result, Libya's nuclear complex made somewhat limited progress in areas such as uranium enrichment, uranium conversion or plutonium separation – not least because the country had a severe shortage of qualified scientific personnel and, more generally, lacked the necessary research infrastructure for further indigenous research efforts.[40] This also explains why many steps undertaken by the Libyan government seem rather incoherent and disorganized – an assessment that is also illustrated by the following anecdote. Libya had managed to order specific components for uranium conversion from a company based in Japan. However, when the delivery finally arrived in Libya in 1986 without instructions on how to assemble and operate them, the parts were simply left unpacked and stored for more than a decade.[41] This seems to validate one of the "classical" arguments of the sociology of technology – namely that technological development often occurs in a somewhat non-linear, obscure and non-deterministic manner. The country's nuclear aspirations suffered from a lack of guidance and oversight, which in turn was mainly due to a lack of the scientific infrastructure needed to integrate the different research components into a more coherent whole.

Furthermore, this explains why Libyan officials became increasingly convinced during the 1990s that the acquisition of nuclear weapons would only materialize if the country managed to procure the technology from abroad. However, given the reluctance of potential supplier states to provide dual-use technology to Libya, it also became clear that the Gaddafi regime would need to tap clandestine supply routes. The opportunity for doing so was provided through the Pakistani-based but internationally operating A.Q. Khan network. According to the detailed account provided by Albright, the first contact between Khan and the Libyan authorities had already been established in 1984 when the Pakistani scientist offered to sell centrifuge technology to Libya. Five years later, negotiations between the two partners were renewed, and an agreement was reached in 1991 for the purchase of P1 centrifuges for uranium enrichment by Libya. The deal seems to have been beneficial for both sides as Khan's vast nuclear complex in Pakistan was modernizing its facilities and therefore had an abundance of old P1 centrifuges it wanted to phase out. In total, Libya apparently procured 20 P1 centrifuges together with most of the components needed to manufacture a further 200. It also ordered 10,000 more sophisticated P2 centrifuges from Khan, the first of which were delivered in 2002.[42]

What is particularly remarkable, however, is the once again ambivalent nature of Libya's steps: we know that as far back as the early 1990s Libya had already tentatively signaled its willingness to abandon its nuclear weapons program. And yet at the same time it continued negotiations with black market vendors to procure further nuclear building blocks, despite its increasingly poor economic situation. There seem to be at least two possible explanations for such behavior. Either the program was so dispersed and badly managed that senior-level managers were able to covertly continue their efforts without government authorization. This is not necessarily implausible, based on the many insights we have from technology studies. Alternatively, and perhaps more likely, the government deliberately pursued a "two-track nuclear insurance policy ... in which the pursuit of nuclear weapons was continued as a back-option in case rapprochement with the US could not be achieved."[43]

However, later IAEA inspections revealed that the centrifuges which Libya received from the Khan network were never completely assembled, installed or used in Libya.[44] Nevertheless, it should be taken into account that – if it functioned – "the plant would produce approximately one hundred kilograms of weapon-grade uranium a year, enough nuclear material for several nuclear warheads a year."[45] Given that the Khan network also provided Libya with a blueprint for manufacturing and assembling a nuclear weapon (based on the weapon design developed by China in the 1960s that was later also used by Pakistan), it is possible to assume that the country did in fact acquire many of the essential pieces of the complete nuclear puzzle.[46] And while the lack of an indigenous scientific and technological base certainly hampered the country's progress on the path toward building a nuclear bomb, Bowen points to another factor that might help us better understand why Libya ultimately failed in its nuclear endeavor:

> By the time the Gaddafi regime opted to abandon its nuclear aspirations in December 2003, Libya had procured most of the technical pieces of the nuclear weapon jigsaw. However, despite spending millions of dollars purchasing "off-the-shelf" centrifuge equipment, UF_6 [uranium hexafluoride, U.J.] and detailed information on weapon fabrication, Libya had not stockpiled or even produced any weapons-grade uranium, let alone manufactured nuclear warheads.... At one level, the nuclear programme was evidently not well managed.... *Poor management may, to an extent, have been the result of a lack of political continuity accorded to the programme over the years* [emphasis added].[47]

Thus, more than three decades after Libya's first attempt to acquire a nuclear weapon capability, Gaddafi officially ended a program that on the one hand was characterized by vast financial resources from Libya's oil exports, and on the other by little scientific progress. And while the exact status of the country's program in 2003 remains a matter of debate,[48] it seems safe to assert that Libya has ultimately achieved relatively little considering the time and resources invested in the program: not only did it not manage to produce any workable nuclear warheads or bombs, it also failed to even produce the fissile material necessary for the production of nuclear weapons. Likewise, the country had only very limited technological capabilities for delivering non-conventional warheads in that it did not maintain a research and development program for missile delivery systems suitable for nuclear warheads.[49]

Nevertheless, the reason for Libya's announcement in 2003 that it would relinquish its WMD and ballistic missile program remains a puzzle both from a more general IR perspective as well as from the narrower proliferation perspective. As Müller points out, the volte-face was not brought about by internal revolutionary change; nor was it triggered by coercive force or by extensive external pressure.[50]

Mapping key actors

Unsurprisingly, the Libyan case is in stark contrast to the previous case of nuclear decision-making in Switzerland. While the Swiss case, as illustrated previously, was characterized by a lively and, to a large extent, transparent debate that included not only the political elite and members of state institutions, but also a wide range of non-governmental actors, the situation in Libya was characterized by a definite lack of any such debate in the common understanding of the term. If we understand the term "debate" to mean something along the lines of a free, open contest of arguments in which at least two opposing parties deliberate on, attack or defend a certain position, then we have to conclude that this was not the case in Libya – neither at the beginning of the country's nuclear aspirations nor at the end. And yet, while we cannot find traces of an open, societal discussion of the nuclear issue, this does not mean that the issue was simply "off the table" or solely dealt with behind the scenes. For the years between 1969 and 2003 we do find a number of public documents that provide us with hints and evident statements on the nuclear weapons issue. The principal difference between the Libyan and the Swiss case, however, is, that only very few actors participated in this "debate."

Given the dictatorial, suppressive nature of the revolutionary regime, it might be tempting to argue that the statements issued by the regime merely reflect attempts to rhetorically justify or even conceal "true" – and supposedly malign – intentions. This is a problematic assumption, since not only does it purport a very particular truth claim (namely that *we* as scientists have privileged access to truth and can hence easily discern true and untrue statements), it also disregards the ever-productive, meaning-making power of language – a concern that provides the basis for any discourse analysis.

> If one stretches discourse analysis to telling us what people think, and why they do what they do, at first one gains a lot in explanatory reach, but then numerous problems and unjustified interferences emerge. What is often presented as a weakness of discourse analysis with psychological or cognitive approaches, or a commonsensical assumption that the "real" motives must be what we are all interested in, and texts can only be a (limited) means to get to this. Not so! Structures within discourse condition possible policies. Overall policy in particular must hold a definite relationship to discursive structures, because it is always necessary for policy makers to be able to argue where "this takes us" (who they have to argue this to depends on the political system, but they are never free of this obligation) and how it resonates with the state's "vision of itself."[51]

It is both the productive power of language, as well as the political dictates of justifying policies and political decisions, that find expression in official documents and make the analysis of discourses so valuable and insightful – ultimately regardless even of the political system.[52]

It is, however, obvious that the Libyan "discursive landscape" does not resemble the one we are familiar with from the Swiss case. Instead of what is, for the most part, an open, transparent, diverse and comprehensive public debate (which culminated in two referenda), we are faced here with a rather "monologic discourse" that is predominantly shaped by statements made by Muammar Gaddafi and a few other public officials. The lack of publicly visible opposition means we can find very few dissenting views and can rely less on the idea of a feedback loop in order to visualize the way in which shifting discourses lead to different policies. However, this does not necessarily mean that there is no opposition or that policymaking indeed occurs in a completely autarchic, individualistic or self-contained manner through Gaddafi alone. Rather, and according to a pragmatic understanding of social phenomena, it seems important to emphasize that Gaddafi (or any other autocratic leader for that matter), regardless of our perception of his actual character traits, should not be conceptualized as a "loner" who derives his policies and decisions simply from introspection or reverie. Such a methodological individualist perspective underestimates or even ignores the social embeddedness of social actors. Moreover, a detailed analysis of the documents reveals that even a dictatorial, brutal ruler like Gaddafi makes references and allusions to dissenting or non-conformist views and deviating ideas – if only to condemn these voices or justify the regime's chosen political path.[53] Therefore, one of the essential goals of a discourse analysis is to discern the way in which the statements relate to and are embedded within a broader discursive realm and how they are intertextually interwoven. This will help us arrive at a more informed view of socially or interpersonally shared narratives and ideas which in turn provide the grounds for political action – be it in autocratic or democratic political systems.

The likely objection to this chosen methodological approach is that an authoritarian ruler should not be taken "at face value" and that his statements are mere "rhetoric." This objection is unwarranted. All types of public declarations – even lying and deception – have "an impact." They all produce intelligibility, construe "reality" and justify policies – no matter how inhuman or oppressive these policies are. They make certain thoughts and social practices thinkable and discredit others. This holds true regardless of the political system or regime type of the government in question and it also holds true regardless of the statement's truth content. Consequently, the study does not aim to convict a speaker of lying or to "measure" the verisimilitude of an utterance. It seeks to uncover how intersubjectively shared narratives "pseudo-legitimize" and enable specific policies – without justifying or exonerating the culprits.

Explaining Libya's nuclear weapons program: dominant readings

As stated before, realists provide the most compelling and prevalent account not only of proliferation in general, but also of the Libyan case. They argue that Libya's drive for nuclear weapons is far from surprising, given the country's threat environment: according to this reading, the Gaddafi regime maintained strained if not bellicose relations not only with the US, but also with several of its immediate neighbors such as Israel, Egypt, Algeria, Sudan and Chad, which in turn compelled Libya to pursue a nuclear capability. And yet this explanation seems far-fetched at best. When, in 1969, the revolutionary regime first attempted to acquire nuclear weapons, Israel did not pose an existential threat; it was not particularly hostile toward Libya. Rather, it was Gaddafi's subsequent behavior – in particular his support for anti-Zionist movements and anti-Israeli policies in Africa and the Middle East – that increased tensions.[54] This is certainly not to downplay the importance that the "Palestinian issue" has always held for Libya's revolutionaries:

> Nothing is more emblematic than the Palestinian question.... First of all, from the perspective of Arabism, the Palestinian people have been depicted as the victims of one of the most cynical colonial operations in history, and since the Palestinians are considered to belong to the Arab nation, therefore it follows that all the Arab world has undergone such violence. Moreover, Arab perceptions, inserting in the Arab "homeland" an alien presence, useful to the West, in order to maintain the West's grasp on the whole area, is seen simply as the persistence of a colonial presence and as a continuous challenge against the Arab world with the purpose of denying its identity, its cultural and historical specificity.[55]

In other words, the significance of Israel for Libya's foreign and security policy can hardly be overstated. However, it is implausible to maintain that as early as 1969 relations between the two countries had deteriorated into outright enmity, thus forcing Libya to strive for nuclear weapons.

Likewise, tracing the emergence of Libya's nuclear program back to its relations with Egypt would seem to be a serious dismissal of the chronological context: when the Gaddafi regime first examined the possibilities of acquiring nuclear weapons, relations between the two neighbors were amicable. In fact, as described above, Gaddafi regarded himself as a staunch proponent of Arab unity and as the ideological heir of Gamal Abdel Nasser. The "Tripoli Charter" that was signed in 1969 to create a federation between Libya, Egypt and Sudan illustrates their common goals.[56] Again, as in the case of Israel, this account is not to deny that relations later began to deteriorate, not least due to Egypt's rapprochement with the United States. And yet until 1973 at least, Libya had good and peaceful working relations with both Egypt and Sudan.[57] Hence, Libya's early interest in nuclear weapons cannot be adequately traced back to its relations with these neighbors. Moreover, and given Gaddafi's deep belief in pan-Arabism and Arab unity, it seems to be at least debatable whether Libya's interest in nuclear weapons was ever directed against its Arab neighbors.

In sum, therefore, the security threat explanation seems inadequate to account for the inception of Libya's nuclear endeavor in 1969.[58] Again, this is not to claim that security considerations never played a role during the course of the three-decades-long attempt to acquire a nuclear capability. A careful analysis of the Libyan nuclear weapons case indicates that the deteriorating relations with the United States (from the mid-1980s onward) and Israel did contribute to Libya's perceived need for a deterrent. However, the analysis suggests that this explanation is too narrow to comprehensively account for Libya's policy.

This also seems to be the case when it comes to explaining Libya's nuclear reversal in 2002/2003. Initially, many commentators and policy analysts argued that the Gaddafi regime's new course was the direct result of heightened

US pressure. Accordingly, it was claimed that Gaddafi renounced his nuclear ambitions once he realized that he might suffer the same fate as Saddam Hussein. Consequently, the Libyan case is often taken as proof of the effectiveness and success of the George W. Bush administration in its policy of threatening the pre-emptive use of force, as well as in creating effective counter-proliferation measures.[59] However, Jentleson and Whytock demonstrate in great detail that this account is rather biased and that it only partially reflects the historical developments of the case. They conclude that the possible use of force was only one of many factors that led to the ultimately peaceful resolution of the Libyan stalemate.[60]

And Takeyh, writing in 2001, had already pointed out that Libya was undergoing significant political change at least since the mid-1990s, when extensive UN sanctions as well as plummeting oil prices had triggered a drastic economic downturn and deteriorating living conditions for large parts of the population. Moreover,

> in the 1990s, certain events pressed Qaddafi toward a pragmatic redefinition of his nation's interests. The collapse of the Soviet Union deprived Libya of its main counterweight to the United States and exposed it to the kind of unified international pressure that was once impossible. As Qaddafi became isolated, his ideology and methods came to be seen hopelessly anachronistic. The colonel's anti-imperialism was eclipsed as the nonaligned bloc turned its attention to securing its position in the global economy.[61]

Rost Rublee comes to a similar conclusion, arguing that neither the American threat position nor the sanctions regime provide a plausible explanation for Libya's moves. According to her analysis, Libya experienced a significant change in its domestic political landscape during the 1990s which gave rise to the emergence of new political views. Two main beliefs came to the fore of the political debate – "a desire to see the Libyan economy improve, and a desire to see Libya leave behind its pariah status and become a constructive member of the international community."[62] Libya's abandonment of nuclear weapons is thus portrayed as the result of Gaddafi's search for "a new paradigm,"[63] i.e., a new idea of "what Libya is" and what it aims to achieve.

Both Harald Müller and Etel Solingen offer a range of additional alternative explanations.[64] Solingen argues that Libya's desire for nuclear weapons was the result of Gaddafi's political and personal zeal[65] and that they served as a useful – material and symbolic – tool to increase the regime's reputation and status at home and abroad, specifically in the Arab world. On a more abstract level, she argues that Libya's attempted nuclearization has to be understood through the prism of regime security and survival: accordingly, nuclear weapons strengthened the revolutionaries' grip on power and their domestic legitimacy.

> Qadhafi's shifting models of political survival explain both Libya's nuclearization and denuclearization. Soon after assuming power he pursued nuclear

weapons as a central pillar of his populist, nationalist inward-looking model.... Qadhafi's model made the attainment of nuclear weapons a centerpiece of his drive for domestic control through Jamahiriyya and related international, grandiose and ultimately personal ambitions.[66]

While many of the arguments put forward by Solingen to explain Libya's nuclear trajectory are convincing, her more general conclusion is debatable. She argues that Libya under Gaddafi was interested in nuclear weapons because it was an "inward-looking country."[67] However, this view seems to underestimate not only the country's strong focus on the export of oil, but also the role of pan-Arabism in Gaddafi's ideological stance: Müller stresses that pan-Arabism and the fight for liberation from Western domination were crucial characteristics of Libya's outward-looking stance and also spurred Gaddafi's nuclear ambitions. Nonetheless, the two studies are valuable in that they direct our attention away from (neorealist) security explanations and instead point us toward domestic dynamics that appear significant for an explanation of proliferation. This certainly allows for a more complete picture of Libya's attempted nuclearization as well as its eventual decision to abandon its WMD program.

Drawing on a multi-causal analysis, Braut-Hegghammer provides perhaps the most detailed account of Libya's changing nuclear ambitions and the actual process involved, and she, too, partly rejects traditional realist security-based assumptions. Instead, she argues that "Libya's initial desire to become a nuclear weapons state was rooted in the Gaddafi regime's regional and revolutionary zeal."[68] She also states, however, that the government's decision to later renounce its weapons program was based on a reassessment of Libya's prime interests, ambitions and needs, and on a realization of the "negative consequences of the pursuit of nuclear weapons on regime security."[69] While this does not explain – and nor does it try to – the underlying social-theoretical practices and the shifting beliefs regarding Libya's role in the world, Braut-Hegghammer's analysis provides crucial insights into the decision-making processes of the Libyan administration and investigates the role of key actors – "nuclear entrepreneurs" – within the Libyan nuclear establishment. She argues that

> successful states [i.e., states that manage to acquire nuclear weapons] are driven by a strong entrepreneurial alliance comprised of "nuclear entrepreneurs" (technocrats from nuclear bureaucracies) and government sponsors who enhance the political sustainability of the nuclear weapons program. Their prospects for success in securing the necessary political, organizational and financial resources are defined, but not determined, by the security environments facing their states.[70]

In disciplinary terms, the present, pragmatist-inspired approach complements existing studies: it seeks to shed light on the underlying ideational dimensions of the decision-making processes. Hence, at the center of the study is not (as, for example, in Braut-Hegghammer's or Walsh's models) the multitude of particular decision-making steps that over the course of the years lead to a particular outcome. Rather, my aim is to elucidate the integral, basal narratives that shape Libya's security perception vis-à-vis other states, its role in the world as well as prevalent views on the usefulness and appropriateness of nuclear weapons technology. Consequently, the study complements rather than questions existing accounts.

Understanding the Libyan case: narratives and beliefs

The underlying question that guides the research process for the Libyan case naturally resembles the one posed at the beginning of the previous chapter: How can we "make sense" of Libya's nuclear choice? I argue that – given the complexity and multi-layered nature of the decision-making and policymaking processes and given the multitude of actors and non-linear shifts in position – a monocausal threat-based explanation does not seem to provide us with a satisfying picture. Yet again, this is not meant to imply that we can make sense of Libya's policies and moves by simply ignoring the idea of "threat" or the country's security environment as a viable explanatory category. However, I argue that neither threat nor security nor any other "condition" are objectively given determinants of state behavior. They are mediated by language, and are thus open to interpretation and different responses.[71] The aim of the analysis is therefore to once again reveal how the central actors give meaning to their environment on the basis of an intersubjective, linguistically mediated exchange of perceptions or views and how these meanings shift over time, thereby enabling and restraining changing policies and altering types of political behavior.[72]

In accordance with previous studies on the Libyan case[73] and also in order to facilitate a better access to the documents, this analysis divides the events and developments of the case chronologically into three distinct phases:

1   Phase I (1969–1986): Development of an initial interest in acquiring nuclear technology; acquisition of "nuclear building blocks" (technological precursors).
2   Phase II (1986 to mid-1990s): Lack of access to relevant technology; clandestine procurement efforts.
3   Phase III (1995–2003): Nuclear indecisiveness; incoherent, ambivalent behavior oscillating between rapprochement with the international community and "nuclear insurance."

Phase I: Libya's initial interest in nuclear weapons (1969–1986)

The narratives that were predominant and authoritative in the first phase[74] of Libya's nuclear ambitions may be grouped into three broad categories: (1) frames and narratives that revolve – in the broadest sense – around attributes of self-perception such as the idea of Libya as a small, tribalistic, Islamic, anti-capitalist pioneer; (2) narratives that refer to Libya's position in the international system (e.g., its security outlook, but also its role as a power pushing for world revolution and anti-colonialism), its relations to "the international world," its threat perception; (3) references to and statements on the (national/Libyan or global) role of nuclear weapons and nuclear technology in general.

Level 1: identity and self-perception

Various documents from the first phase contain references to particular characteristics and attributes of the country that, when interwoven and seen in relation to each other, present a fairly specific and coherent depiction of "what Libya is" and how the participants in the discourse – in this case above all the Gaddafi government – see it (1). One of the pre-eminent sets of attributes in this category is the recurring reference to Libya as a non-capitalist, socialist, humanitarian country whose identity is staunchly based on Islamic principles.

> [T]he people of the Libyan Arab Republic were able to lay down the foundations of the socialist society, the humanitarian society and the Moslem society.[75]

This set of references is significant, since it establishes early on two key ideological characteristics of the Libyan state under Gaddafi: its deep entrenchment in and reference to Islam on the one hand and its "socialist" position on the other. However, both attributes call for a more nuanced understanding than might be afforded them at first sight. Unlike, for example, the Iranian revolution, the Libyan revolution was never a religious, Islamic undertaking; the enforcement or implementation of Islamic traditions, laws or rituals was not a priority for Gaddafi and his followers, even though "an austere morality was introduced with new laws to ban alcoholic consumption, prostitution, and nightclubs, laws on halal slaughtering of imported meat, the conversion of churches into mosques, and the introduction of an official Islamic calendar."[76] These concessions notwithstanding, the regime change can hardly be called an Islamic revolution. In addition, as many studies have shown, the Islamic community of scholars was at times even considered a potential threat to the revolutionaries' grip on power – which explains why Gaddafi incrementally undermined their authority by promoting an idiosyncratic, non-hierarchical understanding of Islam.[77] However, this is not to say that Gaddafi's statements on the role of Islam and on the rootedness of the "new state" in the Islamic tradition were merely rhetorical devices designed to mislead the masses. Quite on the contrary, the new leadership was immersed in Islamic thought and religious traditions, which provided "the cultural mosaic"[78] or the ideational framework in which the revolution took place. At the same time, however, the appeal to religious principles did, quite naturally, help to increase the new regime's legitimacy, not least by setting it apart from the previous regime, whose practices had been perceived by many Libyans, especially in rural areas, as fairly impious and corrupt.[79] The focus on Islam as one of the ideational pillars of Libyan society is also one of the key aspects that distinguished Libyan or Arab socialism from more mainstream European connotations of the word as well as from communism.[80]

What the idea of a "third way" and a new "universal theory" – as an alternative to capitalism and communism – suggest moreover is Libya's self-designed role as a global pioneer in the vanguard of change. Instead of following the examples of other states or ideological traditions, the revolutionary government depicts Libya as the motor of fundamental changes – changes that are not limited to Libya or the neighboring region, but have a universal dimension. Given the frequency of statements that explicitly or implicitly refer to Libya as a "pioneer" and "model for other countries" or to the country's role in "representing" and "serving mankind," it seems important not to underestimate the strength and influence of this self-representation: basically all the relevant documents from the first phase contain multiple references to this particular set of representations, which strike a link between – on the one hand – Libya's "unconventional," idiosyncratic political and economic system, and – on the other hand – its regional and even global role as a motor of change. While the implications of this self-perception are rarely made explicit, it may certainly be argued that attributes such as "vanguard," "model" or "motor" not only serve to describe domestic uniqueness or to mobilize the masses for the cause of the revolutionary regime. They also provide the grounds for – even call for – a more active role in Libya's external relations with other states – "serving mankind" can hardly be confined to Libya alone. As we will see below, the country's self-perception as a unique state and as a champion of Islamic socialism bridges the two analytical spheres of self-perception and international role insofar as it is used time and again as a justification for a proactive foreign policy:

> In its capacity as a revolutionary force, the LAR [Libyan Arab Republic] believes that our duty is not confined to our country, but goes beyond the LAR borders and includes the Arab homeland, the Islamic world and the Third World.[81]

However, the "avant-garde" attribute is, perhaps surprisingly, only partially interwoven with metaphors of progress and modernity. While many of the speeches analyzed do contain descriptions of the economic and material improvements that have been achieved since the revolution, there are as many other references that emphasize Libya's tribal roots, its natural inhospitality and its limited wealth:

> We are only a small country, a small and poor people with economic problems and problems in the field of development and the unification of its scattered nation.[82]

[W]e are not rulers: We came from the desert barefoot and naked. We attacked this base [Umm 'Atiqah Airbase] when I was a lieutenant with our soldiers sitting around here barefooted. We attacked it because we came from among the people. We are not rulers and did not come to power by inheritance.... We are only barefooted and naked people.[83]

While these and many similar statements reveal ideas of economic and material progress and improvements for the people, we do not see a well-defined, suggestive narrative that interweaves these advancements with the notion of a strong nation state. Rather, the ideas of progress and betterment revolve around the improvement in the people's living conditions. Neither the Libyan state as such nor its institutions play a prominent role in most of the speeches; the discourse does not seem to suggest a vision of an increasingly strong and powerful nation state. Libya, in other words, is described as the "vanguard" or the "motor," but it ultimately seems to remain a disembodied idea.

This rather unexpected finding, which runs counter to our traditional assumptions regarding the emergence and accretion of states and nation states, gains further support if we take a closer look at the concept of nationalism which figures prominently in many of the speeches. The following quote embodies the importance of the notion of nationalism for the revolutionary regime:

We must return to religion and nationalism.... None of us can get rid of these two factors, religion and nationalism ... it is clear that history is motivated by religions and nationalism.[84]

At first glance these quotes might contradict the previous findings, which implied a weak concept of the nation state. When we put the nationalism quote into perspective, however, it becomes clear that "the nation" has a particular, non-Libyan connotation. Rather than the Libyan state or the Libyan people, the government seems to mean the "Arab nation" when it talks about "the nation." In fact, literally every one of the documents of the first phase refers in one way or another to the "Arab homeland," "pan-Arabism," "Arab unity" or the "Arab nation." Nationalism, in other words, is never understood as "Libyan nationalism." Several references not only capture all these different interpellations; they also document an explicit distinction between Libya as the "domestic level" and the Arab region as the "national level."[85]

This leads to the assumption that a "Libya-centered" nationalism was not part of the public discourse and that the idea of Libyan statehood remained somewhat vague and undefined. Instead, the frame of reference and allegiance was predominantly the Arab nation. On the basis of the documents analyzed, it is thus evident that the discourse on Libya's self-perception lacks a strong narrative of Libyan nationhood and provides little indication of a vision of the Libyan state. Against the background of this "discursive emptiness," it is hardly surprising that Libya always remained what Anderson called the "stateless state": a state that lacks both comprehensive authority and strong, capable, effective institutions. The fact that even the formal constitutional position of Gaddafi as the leader of the Revolutionary Command Council and as official head of state was abolished in 1977 – thereby de jure (but of course not de facto) disempowering him – is thus more than a quirky little anecdote: it once more underscores the fundamental statelessness and the institutional void of the Libyan state.[86]

In sum, what this analysis shows is that the self-perception of the Libyan state was predominantly shaped by frames and narratives emphasizing Libya's role as a tribal, non-capitalist, non-communist state which sets itself apart from any other political or economic system. And although the country is portrayed as a motor of regional and even global change, we find hardly any depictions of institutional strength; similarly, the notion of the Libyan state remains somewhat hollow and undefined. Instead, the central frame of reference is the country's identity as an Islamic Arab state and as a member of the larger Arab nation. The following analysis of narratives referring to Libya's position in the international system shows in more detail how closely interwoven both the country's self-depiction and its assumed international role are.

Level 2: Libya's position in the international system

The discourse on Libya's role in the international world (2) is characterized by two central, prevalent features: the country's deeply rooted and permanently re-articulated eagerness to achieve Arab unity and its striving for freedom, de-colonization, non-suppression and international equality.

The almost mythical longing for Arab unity can hardly be considered surprising given Libya's widely expressed self-perception as an Arab state and as a member of the Arab nation. It figures prominently in every document of the first phase and is widely covered and elaborated upon. The following quotes exemplify the manner in which the idea of Arab unity is framed:

> The Libyan people believed that socialism must be achieved throughout the vast Arab land.... If we want to build this society we cannot live within narrow regional borders which are fabricated and fake, fabricated by imperialism and perpetuated by the reactionaries. We must look outside these borders and look at the entire Arab area in which prosperity must prevail and in which Arab socialism must be built.[87]

> We believe in Arab unity. Arab unity is not an emotional demand. Arab unity is the destiny of the Arab nation. It is necessary for the life and freedom of the Arab.... The Arab map must change. The Arab state of affairs must change for the better. Arab civilization must be revived. The banner of Islam must be raised anew.[88]

A closer look at these quotes reveals the multitude of rationales behind the idea of Arab unity. In the first statement, Arab unity is primarily justified as a means of achieving economic strength and of integrating as many states as possible into the Arab socialist economic system. In more abstract terms it is argued that the dissolution of artificial borders between the Arab states and the implementation of the socialist "experiment" would increase prosperity and protect the Arab nation from becoming a "pawn in the hands" of the major powers. Yet, as the other statements clarify, the economic rationale is but one of several justifications which are prevalent within the discourse and which call for increased efforts toward Arab integration and unity. The second prominent rationale is the reference to a shared cultural and religious history and the implication of a common Arab civilization. In this reading, Arab unity is justified not only on the grounds of past historical achievements and experiences, but also as a vow to revive the "grandiose heroic past." Lastly, Arab unity is called for as a strategic means of opposing Western imperialism and Western interference in the Arab region and of fighting "the Zionist state in Palestine." This frame is primarily based on the assertion that the region should staunchly fight any kind of intrusion by "external" powers and protect, or rather restore, its asserted territorial integrity. Interestingly, Israel is not continually and consistently described as a threat, but often as more of a "sting" or "bridgehead" of global imperialism: it acts as "the other" that is needed to spur the emergence of the unified Arab self. At the same time, Gaddafi unwaveringly denies Israel any kind of right of existence. The confrontation with Israel is thus not framed as a struggle between differing or opposing interests, but rather as an unsolvable, existential clash. Thus, on an abstract, analytical level, Israel plays an almost ironic role for Libya. On the one hand Libya denies Israel's right of existence; on the other hand it urgently needs the country as the central source of identity creation through altercasting; namely by "forcing" Israel into the role of a hostile adversary, Libya seeks to legitimize its own identity as a revisionist power.

While these references provide a strong ideological backbone for the Libyan discourse, their stringency and discursive effectiveness is at times undermined by a parallel set of statements that refer to and condemn US–Arab cooperation. Frustrated by practical failures on the road to achieving Arab unity and by a lack of support for further steps in intra-Arab cooperation, Gaddafi claimed in 1984:

> The Arab states are entering the war against the Iranian revolution on America's behalf.... Recently, we found these regimes conspiring against us – the Arab regimes. On American orders they are training saboteurs and terrorists and supporting them, in order to liquidate us. Who is the loser in this? The losers are the Arab regimes to whom we extended a hand; the losers are the Arab rulers who bet on the cards in their hands. Now these cards have been burned. The unity by stages, the unity of economic integration, the peaceful unity, Arab solidarity, the purification of Arab atmosphere – all these cards are now invalid.[89]

This reference is particularly important for two reasons. The tone adopted in this speech is much fiercer and more fervent than in the speeches of the early years of his reign; we can in fact observe a significant deterioration in intra-Arab relations and a growing frustration due to the mounting isolation that he faced within the Arab world. Furthermore, the above statement provides a much longer and more detailed account of the Libyan perspective on impediments to Arab unity than do other, earlier documents. This again underlines the Libyan regime's dissatisfaction with Arab affairs in the early 1980s. Yet it also reveals the importance of the "Arab unity" issue for Libyan politics: the varying levels of success of Arab integration were for many years the central frame of reference for Libya's foreign policies.

The second key narrative regarding Libya's role in the world centers on the country's fierce and sweeping political (and at times military) battle for freedom, decolonization, non-suppression and international equality. All the analyzed documents – particularly from the first, but also, as will be seen later, from the second phase – contain references to Western oppression, colonialism, dependence, lack of freedom, global inequality and other, similar notions. In one of its very first statements, the new regime justifies the 1969 revolution by arguing that it helped to liberate the country from the United States.[90] Accordingly, the fight against American influence and interference in Libyan politics became one of the founding myths of the new Republic.

However, early on in the post-revolutionary era the frame of reference was already being extended to encompass not merely the fight against American bases and the US-British military presence on Libyan territory, but also to cover a broader, more comprehensive striving for decolonization, anti-imperialism, and equal rights:

> Those who promote democracy and the democratic world are like those who promoted the free world. They are imperialists if they want, on this basis, to push the land of small peoples into spheres of political, economic or military influence.[91]

> I support the fight for freedom and just cause in the world. And America, of course, is against freedom, against the freedom of all the people in the world because America is an imperialist power who wants to dominate the world. And I oppose this imperialist policy in the world and support the struggle of all the fighters of freedom in the world.[92]

This historical representation can – in one form or another – be uncovered in all the documents of the first phase. With its allusions to dignity and non-humiliation, it provides a potent narrative, for two reasons. First, it contributes to a shared historical ground and a common identity for the Libyan people and establishes the ideational *raison d'être* for the new Libyan Republic. According to this reading, the revolution restored the people's dignity, stature and self-respect by liberating it from foreign aggressors. Second, the narrative provides a broader – regional and even global – context and justification for the revolutionaries' fight against American influence by claiming that it is not merely and genuinely a Libyan struggle against foreign intervention. Rather, the struggle is integrated and arranged into the universal post-World War II fight for decolonization and anti-imperialism, thereby granting it further legitimacy.[93]

Given the character of the speeches and the occasion of their delivery, it is perhaps unsurprising that the narrative of liberation, freedom and anti-imperialism remains rather vague and ill-defined. Historical and geographical specificities are brushed aside, and cases are interwoven even though they exhibit striking differences. In this narrative of imperialism, Israel's "occupation of Palestine" figures as a prominent example, as does the "British occupation of Ireland" and America's military basing policy in Libya.[94] Yet these historiographical inadequacies aside, the narrative is a persuasive one, since it provides a large set of emotional and ideational points of reference. These seem to suggest that the Libyan people's struggle against external interference is not a solitary campaign, but instead emblematic of a much broader cause. As with the narrative of Arab unity the frame of freedom and liberation from imperialism figure prominently in all the speeches of the first phase. Their significance for the construction and envisioning of Libyan politics can thus hardly be overstated.

In terms of concrete foreign policies, the two narratives seem to enable two specific "strategic attitudes": a reliance on neutrality, as well as support for asymmetric forms of conflict as a means of resistance.[95] The discourse of the first phase exhibits a number of references to the idea of neutrality and non-alignment. In a broad sense this positioning between the major global blocs of power has ideological roots insofar as it mirrors Libya's "third way" – its commitment to a non-communist and non-capitalist social and economic system (see above). Hence, while the revolutionary regime outspokenly rejected capitalism, it likewise opposed many facets of the European or Soviet notions of socialism and communism such as the lack of religious principles or the denial of private property. On the other hand, Libya's orientation toward (Arab) socialism is indicative of a closer ideational affiliation between the North African state and the Soviet Union. Thus it is striking to see that the early documents of the first phase exhibit a strong and explicit wariness toward clear alignment with either of the two superpowers:

> We are committed to our stand with the Black Moslem Movement in America and with the Moslems in the Philippines, as well as with the rebels in Ireland. We are in solidarity with the peoples of Latin America, Africa and Asia which are struggling for their freedom. We consider the Third World front the only front hostile to imperialism. The major powers must be outside this front. The Third World camp is the camp hostile to imperialism *because imperialism could come from the East or the West or from any other direction* [emphasis added].[96]

These statements reveal that – despite the presumed ideational affinity between Libya and the Soviet Union – the Gaddafi regime was primarily concerned with guaranteeing Libya's independence and its freedom from external interference. In other words, the struggle for liberation and freedom seems to have overruled the search for ideological partners and allies, at least during the early years of the revolutionary era.

In later speeches we can see an altered understanding of neutrality and non-alignment – and eventually even a renunciation of the concept. In 1975, for example, Gaddafi introduced the notion of "positive neutrality" – but without clearly establishing or defining its meaning:

> Our interest lies in positive neutrality. If we could neutralize the United States this would be an important accomplishment. Our main enemy is Israel, not the friends of Israel. I also told him [Egypt's President as-Sadat]: If we throw ourselves in the laps of the Soviet Union, this would make the United States go to extremes in supporting Israel.[97]

This new framing of Libya's strategic situation illustrates the visibly complicated security environment that the country faced during the early 1970s: while Israel was increasingly clearly depicted as an enemy, a clear alliance with the Soviet Union did not seem to provide a promising solution since it was perceived to be provoking a harmful US reaction. An analysis of further documents supports the assessment that Libya's foreign policy in the first five to ten years after the revolution was far from defined and fixed. There was neither a clear and unambiguous depiction of an existential threat, nor a conclusive designation of friends and foes.[98] Most revealing is a statement that Gaddafi made in an interview in 1976. While he prides himself on the steadily improving Libyan–Soviet relations, an underlying eagerness to positively develop Libya's relations with the United Kingdom may also be discerned:

> We are always trying on our side to develop a relationship with the British; it was the British side which hindered this. But at the end of Mr. Wilson's era constructive and positive talks took place between the two sides and we hope that we shall resume such talks under the new prime minister.[99]

It may even be argued that the narrative which delineates the country's position toward the US seems to contain some discursive inconsistencies: on the one hand we find a strong condemnation of "American imperialism" and a characterization of America as the "arch-enemy." On the other hand, this apparently closed narrative exhibits its non-fixity and potential flexibility in statements such as that made by the government: "We did not want any confrontation with America. We are only a small country."[100] This suggests that even core categories and frames, such as the notions of enemy, imperialism and ally, leave some room for reinterpretation and a shift in meaning. This holds true at least if there is a possibility that the dominant readings are challenged by influential participants in the discourse. We will come back to this aspect later.

What we should register, however, is that Libya's foreign policy attitude in the first years following the revolution was shaped by a preference for neutrality or non-determination. While there may have been an ideological affinity toward the Soviet Union, this was overruled by a strong fear of external interference and imperialism – whether from the West or the East. A quest for independence, freedom and sovereignty was thus the all-defining foreign policy trait of the first years of post-revolutionary Libya – and it was apparently stronger than any clear threat perception.

The second specific foreign policy (besides "neutrality") that is legitimized in the narratives on Libya's international role is its explicit support for asymmetric forms of violence as a means of resistance against "oppression" and "colonialism." An analysis of the dominant structures of meaning reveals that this frame is time and again used as a justification for Libya's recourse to or support for international terrorism and liberation movements.[101] This is a clear commitment to asymmetric means of warfare and to international aggression as a "legitimate" tool in international affairs. This interpretation of Libya's role in the international arena is in fact quite consistent with its self-perception as a small and rather resource-weak state – a state that lacks the means to face the major powers on a level playing field. It is similarly consistent with Libya's view of the international system: as seen above, the prevalent narrative regarding the international system characterizes both superpowers – and the US in particular – as potentially threatening to Libya's independence. Moreover, it depicts the struggle against what is perceived as imperialism, neo-colonialism and suppression as the key driving force in both domestic and international politics, thereby contextualizing Libya's own struggle into a global historical effort. The country's recourse to asymmetrical or even illegal means of warfare is thus justified by the argument that it is the only response available for countering imperialism and suppression. What is surprising, however, is that this frame of being a renegade in the international system is far from consistent. Instead, several instances reveal that the seemingly clear "roguish" foreign policy attitude of the Libyan regime was time and again questioned and toned down by calls for dispute arbitration by international courts or international organizations. Hence, while the narrative of being a "revolutionary freedom fighter" and "anti-colonialist power" seems to have been dominant, it was at times undercut by a far more passive and appeasing stance that cherished the benefits of international organizations as well as international law and juridification.

Level 3: attributes of civil and military nuclear technology

In the final part of the analysis of the first phase we now turn to those discursive frames that refer explicitly to the role of nuclear weapons and nuclear technology (3). We will analyze the frames that dominate the Libyan discourse on military and civilian uses of nuclear technology, both by Libya itself and by the international community. This analytical and interpretive step seems to be the most challenging: the "nuclear" narratives and frames are less clear-cut, less definite and less precise than, for example, the frames on neutrality or anti-imperialism. Instead, we find partially inconsistent references, linguistic ambiguities and even contradictions. Moreover, for several years after the revolution there seems to be no reference to Libya's nuclear weapons ambitions, even though we have strong reason to assume that the new regime developed an interest in nuclear technology very early on. The first mention of nuclear weapons dates back to 1972. However, the reference that the government made at that time only alluded to and condemned the storage of American nuclear weapons on Libyan territory. A comparable frame is visible in another speech, when Gaddafi claims that "there are nuclear bomb stockpiles in the Mediterranean, which should be a sea of trade and economy between the continents in order to serve mankind."[102] In another instance the regime refers to nuclear weapons only in the context of capitalism, arguing that there is a causal relation between a capitalist economy and nuclear proliferation, whereas Islamist principles prohibit the production of nuclear weapons.[103] It is striking, however, that this negative and adverse framing of nuclear weapons contradicts the above-mentioned reports, which seem to prove a Libyan interest in nuclear weapons as early as 1969/1970.

In the years that followed we can observe a significant change in the framing of nuclear issues. The outright dismissal of nuclear weapons as the "work of the devil" recedes, thus allowing for the emergence of an alternative narrative: from 1975 onward the spread of nuclear technology is depicted as a basically naturally occurring and necessary process of development and progress:

> [O]ne day nuclear power will become as necessary as electric power. This will become something natural just as has happened with other things. Just as now it is being said this country has 50 planes while that country has 500 planes, the day will come when it will be said this country has three atomic bombs and that country has 10 atomic bombs.... In the future nuclear power will no longer be a monopoly or a secret. The Arab nation has a vast potential and many scientists who are capable of achieving anything if given the right atmosphere. In Libya we decided to build a township for Arab scientists so that the Arab nation will benefit from them and so that they will not remain scattered around the world.[104]

> Soon the atom will have no secrets for anybody. Some years ago we could hardly procure a fighter squadron. Tomorrow we will be able to buy an atom bomb and all its parts. The nuclear monopoly is about to be broken.[105]

While still not explicitly revealing Libya's acute interest in the acquisition of nuclear weapons, this utterance is nevertheless enlightening: it sets the stage for the emergence of a comprehensive frame on nuclear technology and nuclear weapons. This comprehensive "nuclear frame" touches upon and revolves around three central aspects: the notion of "spread" and automatism; a call for development and equal rights; and a link between Arab unity and "Arab nuclear weapons." While the regime rejects accusations that it has already obtained a nuclear device, it depicts the further spread of both civilian and military nuclear technology as inevitable and natural. Likewise, the spread of technological resources – and the inherent thaw of the nuclear oligopoly – are described as a welcome and desired step toward global equality and toward the empowerment of developing nations, both in technological and military terms.[106]

> We want to use nuclear power for peaceful purposes.... You know that efforts all over the world are to use nuclear power for peaceful purposes. As developing countries we want to use it for peaceful purposes. All our efforts are in this direction. We want to exploit oil and the wealth that oil produces to build up other resources to sustain our economy.[107]

Later speeches – for example, by the country's special representative at the UN General Assembly – indicate, however, that the Libyan perception of its security environment has changed, prompting the regime to argue that the country is indeed threatened and that the development and deployment of nuclear weapons may be "justified":

> The decision to launch aggression which will be carried out jointly by the United States war machine and Israel against the Jamahiriya is as obvious as anything can be, and the ceaseless statements made by Israel and the United States confirm, more than ever, that a decision to that effect has been taken.[108]

> It is difficult for Libya to obtain nuclear weapons, and it is not our policy to do so. We are against nuclear weapons in the world and we call to destroy all nuclear bombs in the world. But to use them against Israel may be a different story.[109]

Thus, as a result of public speculation over Israel's nuclear arsenal, the prevalent Libyan threat perception changed in the early 1980s, with justifications starting to emerge regarding the possible acquisition and deployment of nuclear weapons against a nuclear-armed Israel. The common thread, however, is again provided by the interpellation of "the Arab nation" – as in almost all the nuclear-related statements of the first phase: the "nuclear subject" (i.e., the actor most often referred to) is rarely the Libyan state as such. Rather, Libyan speakers refer to the "Arab nation" as the envisioned acquirer of nuclear technology and nuclear weapons. If mentioned at all, Libya merely figures as an "agent" of empowerment for the Arab world or as a "motor." Hence, the acquisition of nuclear weapons is seldom justified on national, Libyan grounds – as a means of Libyan defense, for example – but rather in terms of an Arab obligation or necessity and as an indispensable step toward further regional development.

There is little to indicate that there were altruistic reasons for this reference to the "Arab nuclear frame" – certainly Libya did not intend to strengthen any of its regional competitors by providing them with nuclear weapons. Rather, the documents suggest that the acquisition of nuclear weapons *by* Libya *together with* or *on behalf of* the Arab nation was seen as providing a potential boost to Libya's role in the region. However, the range and frequency of references to the "Arab nation" signify the weight carried by the notion of pan-Arabism. It appears that in order to fully comprehend Libya's nuclear moves the analysis must not be limited solely to domestic motivations. Instead, it seems important not to underestimate pan-Arabism as a driving force behind Libya's nuclearization attempts in the first 15 years after the revolution. As seen above, for many years, pan-Arabism provided one of the Libyan state's main identity-constituting notions; the country perceived itself as being inextricably integrated into the region and into its cultural sphere. Strengthening the region as such and deepening its societal and intra-state connectedness, coherence and external influence was thus a prime political concern.[110] It is thus not surprising that this concern is also mirrored in the narratives relating to nuclear weapons and civil nuclear technology, providing a strong ideological underpinning and justification for Libya's nuclear ambitions.

In sum, we see that the Libyan discourse in the first 15 years following the revolution was shaped by a set of prevalent narratives which depict both the country's identity and self-perception as an actor within the international system as well as its attitude toward nuclear proliferation. On the level of Libya's self-perception the discourse is strongly shaped by attributes that portray the nation as small, tribalistic and deeply Islamic. At the same time it is depicted as the global pioneer of anti-capitalism. This set of references is significant, since it establishes early on two key ideological characteristics of the Libyan state under Gaddafi: its entrenchment in Islam on the one hand and its "socialist" position on the other. What is striking, however, is the lack of a more fully fledged notion of Libyan statehood and more explicit references to the nation state. Both seem to be rather absent from the discourse of the first post-revolutionary phase. The idea of the Libyan nation remains somewhat vague and disembodied.

The second set of narratives refers to the country's position within the international system and its relations with other actors. The country's deeply rooted and permanently re-articulated eagerness to achieve Arab unity and its striving for freedom, decolonization, non-suppression and international equality are omnipresent. The two narratives are supported by Gaddafi's recurring self-stylizations as a world revolutionary and as a motor and pioneer of both the struggle for unity and liberation from oppression.

Another set of frames refers more or less explicitly to the role of nuclear weapons and civil nuclear technology. As mentioned above, this aspect seems to be more difficult to decipher given that the analysis uncovered a range of inconsistencies and contradictions. Despite these challenges we can discern two key aspects. First, the framing of the nuclear discourse changed during the first decade and a half from one condemning nuclear weapons as the "work of the devil" to one that depicts the spread of nuclear technology as a naturally occurring and necessary process of development and progress.

Second, the interpellation of "the Arab nation" provides the common thread for almost all the relevant statements on nuclear proliferation of the first phase: the "nuclear subject" (i.e., the actor that Gaddafi refers to) is rarely the Libyan state as such. Rather, Gaddafi refers to the "Arab nation" as the envisioned acquirer of nuclear technology and nuclear weapons. If mentioned at all, Libya merely figures as an "agent" of empowerment for the Arab world or as a "motor." In other words, the acquisition of nuclear weapons is hardly ever justified on national (i.e., Libyan) grounds, but rather in terms of an Arab obligation – as a means of collective Arab self-defense against Israel. The acquisition of (peaceful and/or military) nuclear technology is characterized as a necessary and indispensable step toward further regional development – both in political/military and economic terms. The next section will provide an analysis of how these narratives shift or consolidate in the second phase of Libya's nuclear program (1986–1995).

Phase II: arrested development (1986 to mid-1990s)

In order to render our findings accessible and comparable with the findings of the first phase, we will continue to proceed in accordance with the three-level framework of analysis. We will thus examine (1) frames and narratives that describe the country's self-perception; (2) narratives that refer to Libya's position in the international system and to its threat perception; and (3) references and statements that touch upon the issue of nuclear weapons and nuclear technology in general. Again, the aim is to analyze how major Libyan actors give meaning to the country's environment and how these meanings solidify or shift over time, thereby enabling and restraining shifts in policies and altering types of political behavior.[111]

Level 1: identity and self-perception

As we have seen in the analysis of the first phase, many documents contained references to particular characteristics and attributes which, when interwoven and related to each other, present a fairly specific and coherent depiction of "what Libya is" (1). One of the pre-eminent sets of attributes was the recurring description of Libya as a non-capitalist, socialist, humanitarian country whose identity is staunchly based on Islamic principles.[112] These depictions are still discernible in the second phase, yet they have become less prominent – more than 15 years after the revolution there seems to be less need for the ideological justification and political legitimization of the upheaval. The ideological underpinnings and the "socio-political meaning" of the Jamahiriya appear to have been successfully established and need not be permanently renegotiated.

The far-reaching oppressive mechanisms of the revolutionary institutions, moreover, provide additional leverage with which to influence, control and mobilize the masses while at the same time preventing the rise of oppositional forces that could otherwise challenge the dominant domestic discourse on Libya's identity as a socialist, Islamic country. Hence, the lack of vocal and influential domestic challengers of the dominant discourse allows the regime to spend less energy on defining and elaborating what the new Libyan state stands for in domestic terms, since both the political and economic characteristics of the post-revolutionary state are sufficiently established. As we will see later on, this allows the discursive focus to shift on to the second level, i.e., Libya's role in the international system.

There is, however, one narrative that had a rudimentary presence in the first phase and which becomes more significant and explicit in this second phase: it is a narrative that combines the idea of (grassroots) political empowerment, self-determination and statelessness. As we have seen in previous analytical steps, the discourse on Libya's self-perception lacked a comprehensive narrative of nationhood; the documents provided little indication of a vision of the Libyan state. Instead, the understanding of the state was predominantly shaped by frames and narratives which emphasized Libya's role as a tribal and decentralized entity. This notion of "statelessness" becomes even more visible in the years between 1986 and 1995, since it is interconnected with a strong and recurring call for empowerment and grassroots political autonomy. In a rather unorthodox and unconventional speech given in 1987, Gaddafi went to great lengths to deconstruct and demolish any kind of political, religious or educational authority and hierarchy (as well as Western representative democracy) within the country while at the same time calling for the mobilization, self-government and sovereignty of the masses.[113]

We do not find precise traces of a narrative that defines or enriches the idea of the Libyan nation state in any of the documents. Instead, "Libya" and the nation state remain abstract terms that are not sufficient to mobilize the masses – either by generating a strong sense of belonging or by upholding a powerful and inclusive national myth. In lieu of a compelling call for allegiance to the state, Gaddafi instead adds to the notion of institutional weakness and "anti-étatism" by calling for the emancipation and empowerment of the masses – as is particularly apparent in the following quote:

> *There is no such thing as a state.* This is a Jamahiriya, the state of the masses. These are the masses [emphasis added].[114]

If we also take into account the above-mentioned regional and topographic fragmentation of the country and the diverse historical roots of the main regions, it becomes apparent that the lack of a national narrative is likely to further impede the proper functioning of the central state. Again, however, the proposed anti-étatism appears to be a coherent idea if we assume that the prevailing interpretations and narratives are ultimately anchored in the country's history and in the Islamic Bedouin culture: kin-based groups and tribes strive for autonomy and independence; they refuse to be subordinate to hierarchical political authorities, since this would question and undermine the key tenets of autonomy and equality and would endanger the tribe's dignity and honor.[115] Hence it may be argued that the vision of statelessness and the seeming dismissal of a hierarchical political order can be traced back to deeply anchored egalitarian Bedouin traditions. And while it is important not to romanticize and idealize Bedouin life and tribalism or to ignore cultural differentiations in Libyan society (for example, between urban dwellers and the rural population), it seems indispensable to pay attention to these cultural traits in order to gain a better understanding of the political dimensions of modern Libya. Likewise, examining underlying cultural and historical currents certainly helps us to avoid an oversimplification of Libyan politics under Gaddafi as merely "irrational, bloodthirsty, megalomaniac."[116] The lack of functioning, far-reaching state institutions and of a convincing state narrative may therefore be explained not by allusions to Gaddafi's seemingly impulsive, irrational and arbitrary behavior, but rather by a socially shared and culturally inspired skepticism toward state authorities and the central/nation state.

What does this mean for the analysis of Libya's nuclear program? Although I do not want to draw premature conclusions, it seems plausible to argue that the lack of "statehood" severely hampered the implementation of a comprehensive nuclear research and development program. Moreover, Libyan society did not share a convincing, inclusive and inspiring idea of the Libyan state. The idea of Libya as a powerful, centralized entity that could amass and allocate resources and stimulate an effective research enterprise – a precondition for a successful weapons program – did not really exist. Thus, although Itty Abraham is right to assume that "new cities, enormous dams, soaring skyscrapers, ballistic missiles, space programs, and nuclear power are universal techno-political means by which modern states seek to visualize their power and express their authority,"[117] the Libyan case seems to be a fascinating exception to this rule. There was seemingly "not enough of a state" in Libya to express authority and visualize power.[118] Libya, in other words, failed to institutionalize a coherent, well-organized and fully fledged nuclear weapons program and to maintain sufficient momentum, not least because the notion of the state and thus the state itself was too weak. Again, this does not imply that nuclear technology and modern technology in general were absent from the Libyan discourse. On the contrary, as we have seen in the analysis of phase I and as we will see later from further analyses of phases II and III, nuclear weapons were icons – but more icons of general scientific technological progress of modern developing states than icons of national – Libyan – scientific achievements.[119]

Moreover, the discourse of modernity and progress lacks a certain degree of coherence and comprehensiveness; it was time and again undermined and destabilized by rather unconventional, unexpected references to an almost mythical ideal of life in Libya's pre-modern, agrarian countryside. For example, referring to the danger posed by a potential nuclear strike from the United States, Gaddafi explains:

> We have deserts and wide areas that would absorb many an atom bomb. We are not densely populated. As for the cities, we would leave the combatants in them and move out to the countryside and the suburbs which we would use for building farms and breeding livestock. We would then live as sultans; we would confront the United States while singing and dancing.[120]

Level 2: Libya's position in the international system

However, the idea of grassroots empowerment and emancipation from authority that figures so prominently on the level of self-perception and identity is also interesting and significant for another reason: it resembles and alludes to a similar frame that describes Libya's position in the international system, (2). As we have already seen in the analysis of the first phase, Libya's role in the world was described as that of a liberator and emancipator of the disadvantaged and oppressed. Repeated allusions to the idea of empowerment and self-determination suggested this narrative during the first phase, but also in later years.

The narrative of empowerment, emancipation and liberation from authority thus provides an ideational common thread that connects the level of self-perception with the level of the international environment. It not only describes a particular vision of Libyan society; it is also used to endow the Libyan regime with a justification for conducting a revisionist, "rogue" foreign policy that seeks to revise and alter the existing international order. Accordingly, the claim of empowering the "disempowered," of liberating the "oppressed" and of creating equality is applied not just as a domestic idea, but is also turned into a leitmotif of Libya's foreign policy. This becomes particularly evident in the aftermath of the US attacks on Tripoli and Benghazi in April 1986:

> The Americans must understand that they are facing a stubborn challenger and they will never find respite in their war against us. They must also understand that they have only one course – to recognize our rights and to negotiate with us *on equal footing* [emphasis added].[121]

While the specific foreign policy measures stemming from this frame remain vague and perhaps even disjointed, the importance of the "empowerment" narrative as such must not be underestimated: it seems to provide one of the few overarching ideas that guide Libyan politics under the Gaddafi regime. Moreover, the idea of a global fight for equality serves to legitimize the application of asymmetric means of confrontation. In other words: as long as major powers refuse to deal with the less powerful states on an "equal footing," the notion of resorting to asymmetric measures is characterized as just.

Hence, what we see from this analysis is the growing significance and exposition of a frame of empowerment and equality – both in domestic and foreign policy terms. This has two main implications for Libya's foreign policy. First, the narrative enables a resolutely revisionist attitude toward the international order and further contributes to Libya's self-perception as the motor of a global liberation movement. Second, the notion of empowerment is applied as a justification for the deployment of asymmetric means of warfare, such as terrorist attacks against both civilians and military personnel. The Libyan authorities do not even try to deny their involvement in some of the most brutal incidents of international terrorism – such as the Lockerbie bombing or the La Belle attack.[122] Rather, they explicitly justify these actions by referring to the unjust international system and the lack of alternative means.

Arguably, then, the Libyan case calls for an extension and refinement of the current literature on renegade or rogue regimes.[123] While Libya shares many of the attributes that are commonly used to characterize "renegades" – norm-breaking, attempted acquisition of WMD, resort to terrorism, aggressive foreign policy and the undemocratic, authoritarian nature of the regime – the motives for its revisionist attitude seem to differ from several assumptions in the literature on the subject. The analysis of the Libyan documents suggests that the Gaddafi regime's renegade behavior was not primarily motivated by economic, religious, ethno-nationalist or ideological considerations. It was instead driven by an almost excessive, deeply rooted myth of equality and egalitarianism in the international system – a vision that was all the more powerful and compelling as it drew so intimately on notions of dignity, self-esteem and respect.[124] At the same time it becomes all the more obvious that neither Libya's continuous disregard of Israel's right of existence nor Libya's interference with its neighbors ever mirrored these concerns for respect and equality.

Yet, as mentioned earlier, the discursive emphasis shifted in the second phase: Libya's foreign policy and its role in the international system receive more attention. Besides the narrative of empowerment and global equality, what are the other major frames or structures of meaning that describe the country's attitude toward the international system?

A second significant structure of meaning for the years between 1986 and 1995 is – again – the notion of Arab unity. This is hardly surprising given the narrative's centrality in previous years. However, a closer analysis reveals that the picture during these years was more complicated. On the one hand, the desire to achieve Arab unity remains one of the central goals of Libyan foreign policy:

> Arab Unity is the sole solution to safeguarding the existence of the Arab nation and its future.[125]

Gaddafi then goes on to describe at great length the specific goals and advantages of Arab unification in political, military, economic and cultural terms, and he finally outlines what he envisions to be the institutional and structural shape of the "Arab Union." This vision of unification is hence clearly in line with many other statements from previous years which had explicitly called for the integration of the Arab world. It even goes beyond earlier statements in terms of clarity and specificity.[126]

On the other hand, this strong vision of a unified Arab nation must not disguise the regime's growing dissatisfaction both with Libya's regional neighbors and with the lack of progress that had been achieved on the way to unification. The documents of the post-1986 period clearly suggest that the Libyan regime found itself increasingly at the margins of the Arab world; with the exception of various short-lived and limited attempts at regional unification it did not manage to steer a significant number of states toward integration. On the contrary, from the mid-1980s onward the somewhat regressive mood is even mirrored in public statements by the Libyan leadership condemning the lack of official high-level support from the majority of the Arab regimes:

> I would like to say that the Arab official position is unable to oppose the aggressors.... Brothers, we should reconsider our international policy. On the Arab level, if the Arab governments are unable, we should ally ourselves with the masses, with the revolutionary forces, and with the Palestinian revolutionary movements inside the Arab nation. We should ally ourselves with the Islamic revolutionary forces, and with the Jihad movements.[127]

An analysis of the dominant structures of interpretation thus shows a gradual but clearly visible change compared to earlier years: while the Gaddafi regime still maintained that unification of the Arab states was a necessity and that Libya should be the motor and vanguard of the unification movement, its frustration at the lack of support in the aftermath of the 1986 raids against Tripoli and Benghazi had a heavy impact on its foreign policy attitude in the second half of the 1980s. This frustration and dissatisfaction seemed to reach a climax in the early 1990s, when for several years the discourse lacked any concrete reference to the project of Arab unity.[128]

Nevertheless, in the late 1980s and early 1990s the Libyan regime continued to place Libya's fate within a broader international political context: the prevalent narrative revolved around the notions of "liberation from oppression" and "liberation from colonialism" as well as the call for Third World empowerment. It only gave way on very few occasions to an interpretation that focused on a global crusade and religious confrontation. In these few instances, Libya's conflict with the West is no longer framed as a fight for liberty and universal equality, but rather as a global war between Islam and Christianity:

> The issue is a crusade. Hatred for the Arab nation; hatred for the Islamic East. Therefore we call on one billion Muslims to confront the tenth crusade which is led by the United States. The issue is not one of terrorism; it is an issue of jihad and a crusade aimed against Islam and aimed at destroying Islam and stopping it from developing.[129]

However, despite these allusions to Islam and Islamic traditions, we do not find a coherent and influential narrative of global jihad. At first sight this may seem surprising, given Gaddafi's constant attempt to embed Libya's cause within the broader international frameworks of anti-colonialism, liberation or Arab unity. However, two broad currents seem to have undermined and disabled any potential strength that a "crusade narrative" had within Libyan politics. The first was the regime's at times instrumental use of Islam for domestic purposes (for example, the disempowerment of the ulema, i.e., the community of Islamic scholars), as well as its idiosyncratic interpretation of central religious texts and traditions, whereby Libya's reputation as a religious model was undermined.[130] Second, the lack of global Islamic unity (so clearly exemplified by the Iran–Iraq war in the 1980s) meant that there was not enough breeding ground for Libya's "jihad narrative." Hence, while we see some allusions and references to Islam and to Libya's Muslim roots, there are no strong traces of an inclusive and coherent narrative of crusade, jihad and a confrontation between Christianity and Islam (either in phase I or phase II).[131]

There are two further – interwoven – narratives related to Libya's position vis-à-vis the international system: the first relates to the country's threat perception; the second refers to its alignment policy. It may be argued that the threat perception during the first 15 years following the revolution was primarily shaped by a general and rather vague feeling of vulnerability in the face of the "imperialist aggressors." In the second phase (i.e., after 1986), the identified threats remain the same, but the feeling of vulnerability appears to be more defined and acute – a development that is hardly surprising given the military events of 1986. In the light of the US raids against Tripoli and Benghazi, the danger of further US military strikes is described more explicitly. Likewise, we find several references to the alleged danger posed by Israel, as well as more explicit depictions of the danger posed by the use of nuclear weapons – either by Israel or by the US – against Libya.[132]

What is surprising, however, is the (again) incoherent self-positioning and the disjointed alignment policy that stems from this threat perception. In the immediate aftermath of the 1986 attacks on Libya, the alignment policy seemed obvious: the Gaddafi regime pledged allegiance to the socialist world, appealed to the Soviet Union for further support and called for Libyan–Soviet alliance arrangements in order to defend world peace.[133]

The discourse of the first phase exhibited a number of references to the idea of neutrality and non-alignment which mirrored the country's initial attempt to position itself between the major global blocs of power and even questioned the non-imperialist nature of the Soviet Union. On the contrary, then, the second phase seems to be shaped by a clear change in attitudes and by an explicit turn toward the Eastern bloc. However, Libya's position on its alignment, even in the aftermath of the 1986 events, is much less coherent than one might assume. Only several weeks after the US bombings, Gaddafi implies that a shift in Libya's position is conceivable:

> We are uniting the Arab nation. If the United States helps us in uniting the Arab nation, then this unity will be a friend to the United States. If the USSR is the one who helps us to unite the Arab nation, then this unity will be a friend to the USSR. Our enemy is whoever stops the establishment of our unity.[134]

In a similar vein, a close analysis of the key documents indicates that the country's vigorously confrontational attitude toward the international system is time and again undermined by seemingly incongruous invocations of conflict-resolution mechanisms, international law and international organizations – a characteristic that we have already seen in earlier years.

We are fully convinced of the integrity and fairness of the International Court of Justice, because it is the highest international judiciary body.... We will comply with the International Court of Justice's ruling, whether it is in our favor or against us, because we are confident of its integrity.[135]

These quotes suggest that neither the attitude of a vigorous rogue and revisionist state nor the alignment with the Soviet bloc were always maintained in a consistent and stringent manner. Instead, a number of breaks and withdrawals from the "renegade script" may be discerned. Accordingly, these statements exhibit the non-fixity and fluidity of seemingly closed narratives. This might again suggest that even core categories and frames, such as notions of ally or enemy, ultimately leave some room for reinterpretation and for a shift in meaning.

Level 3: attributes of civil and military nuclear technology

In the next step, we turn to those discursive frames of the second phase that refer explicitly to the role of nuclear weapons and non-military nuclear applications (3). We will analyze which frames are prevalent in the Libyan discourse on military and civilian uses of nuclear technology in the years between 1986 and 1995.

As we saw in the analysis of earlier documents, Libya's attitude toward nuclear weapons underwent some kind of change. The initial characterization of nuclear weapons as the "work of the devil" receded; instead, a frame emerged that touched upon and revolved around three central aspects: the notion of "spread" and automatism, a call for development and equal rights, and a link between Arab unity and "Arab nuclear weapons." The further spread of both civilian and military nuclear technology was depicted as inevitable and natural. Likewise, the spread of the technological wherewithal – and with it the inevitable thaw of the nuclear monopoly – were described as a welcome and desirable step toward global equality and toward the empowerment of developing nations, both in technological and military terms. The acquisition of nuclear weapons through the "Arab nation" was now considered justified.

Against this background, it is not surprising that the second phase was also strongly shaped by a call for Arab nuclearization:

I would say on this occasion that the Arabs should possess the atom bomb. For the first time, we declare that we must not ever be embarrassed by working day and night to possess the atom bomb. While we do not want to play with the atom bomb, if others want to play with the atom, they must not play against the Arab people or the future of the Arab people and the safety of the Arab homeland.... Now that the Israelis possess the atomic bomb, the Arabs have no alternative but to work day and night to possess an atomic weapon in order to defend their existence.... There is accordingly nothing left for the Arabs except to declare that they must possess the atomic weapon in order to defend themselves – and this is a legitimate action.[136]

Two aspects are particularly important in this context: the reference to Israel and its assumed acquisition of nuclear weapons, and the call for an Arab nuclear weapon. Both aspects also figured prominently in the early documents, as we have seen. Once again, it is the "Arab nation" that is the envisioned acquirer of nuclear technology and nuclear weapons, and not necessarily Libya. Moreover, nuclearization is justified on the grounds that Israel, too, possesses a nuclear capability. In other words, nuclear weapons are considered a legitimate means of self-defense against an external threat.

While these statements seem to suggest that Libya and/or other Arab states were already working on the development of nuclear weapons – an assumption that is (as illustrated above in the historiographical reconstruction) confirmed by other sources – the assessment becomes more difficult when we take later documents into account. Only three years later, in an interview with the German magazine *Der Spiegel*, Gaddafi makes an utterance that fundamentally calls into question the hitherto prevalent view. Asked by a reporter how far the development of the "Islamic nuclear bomb" has progressed, he replies:

> The idea of the Islamic bomb already died with Pakistani Premier Bhutto. Do not unearth Bhutto and the bomb. The idea is finished.[137]

From an analytical perspective this statement is quite challenging. Taking it at face value, one might be led to assume that in the space of just three years the regime's position toward the acquisition of nuclear weapons underwent a complete change. A different interpretation may be that Libya simply backed away from an "Islamic bomb"[138] – for example, one produced together with Pakistan – while still supporting an "Arab bomb." Interpreting and assessing this issue becomes even more complicated if we include additional documents in the analysis.

> Why are the Americans permitted to produce nuclear bombs or chemical weapons and I am not? It is impossible that one state may do everything, while the others are not permitted to do anything.... As long as Israel is given a free hand to produce all sorts of weapons of destruction, chemical and nuclear weapons, I also have to strive for them, in order to be able to defend myself.[139]

While this statement could be understood as an indication of an already existing nuclear weapons program, other quotes by the administration call such a reading into question.

> [W]e are not concerned with the nuclear issue and we do not have any nuclear programs. We do not have the capability or resources for this. We are benefiting from the atom for peaceful purposes only. We have called for establishing a zone free of weapons [not further specified, FBIS] in the Mediterranean and the Middle East.[140]

Anyone may construct a nuclear bomb. Everybody has the right to construct one if he wishes. If Libya wished to have one, it would have been very easy to obtain considerable funds. Should we spend billions? We have billions. We prefer to use them for the protection of the environment, to construct a big artificial river, for education, and health care.[141]

Thus, if we look at the broader nuclear narrative which prevails in the years between 1986 and 1995, we can discern two central aspects that shape the discourse, albeit to varying degrees: the question of "agency" and the idea of equality.

The question of agency is particularly important if we compare the narrative of the second phase with the previous analysis of the first phase. To recall: we established that for the period between 1969 and 1986 the main "nuclear actor" (i.e., the acquirer of nuclear weapons) was meant to be the "Arab world." The Libyan authorities regarded Libya as merely a proxy or at best a "motor" of Arab nuclearization. The interpellation of "the Arab nation" that figured in almost all nuclear-related statements of the first phase suggested that the "nuclear subject," i.e., the actor to which Gaddafi refers, was rarely meant to be the Libyan state. Hence, the acquisition of nuclear weapons was almost never justified by reference to genuinely national, Libyan needs, but as an Arab obligation or necessity and as an indispensable step toward further regional development. It is noticeable but – given the above-mentioned political developments – hardly surprising that this aspect of the nuclear narrative is much weaker in the years between 1986 and 1995. We find far fewer allusions to the idea of Arab nuclearization and to the "Arab nation" as a future nuclear power. The Libyan regime's frustration over lack of Arab support in the aftermath of the 1986 raids thus seems to have left its imprint on the nuclear discourse: the lack of political unity clearly called into question and undermined the idea of Arab nuclear cooperation. To put it differently: the appeal and mobilizing force of "Arab unity" and Arab progress – in political, economic and military terms – had decreased significantly, thereby weakening both the original rationale of nuclearization as well as its practicability. This suggests that during the 1990s it became increasingly uncertain who could and would be the main driver and beneficiary of nuclearization. The lack of a clear vision of agency started to undermine the viability of the program.

The second crucial aspect that shines through in the narrative on nuclear weapons and nuclear technology is the recurring invocation of global equality and equal rights. Given the frequency with which the idea of equality appeared in the discourse on both Libya's foreign and domestic policy and its great importance in that discourse, its appearance in the discourse on nuclear weapons is consistent and to be expected. Tellingly, of course, the discourse once again includes the condition that Israel is excluded from any such call for equality. Consequently, in several statements, the Libyan regime voices its refusal to accept the global nuclear order (as exemplified in the NPT) which distinguishes between legitimate nuclear weapon states on the one hand and compulsory non-nuclear weapon states on the other.

[T]he Arab countries do not have atomic bombs, they do not have the capability to manufacture atomic bombs, and yet they go to sign the Nuclear Nonproliferation Treaty [NPT] as though they have atomic weapons when they do not have them, and they do not have the capability to manufacture them. Why is this extravagance? Why is this exaggeration in insulting and humiliating themselves before the Zionist and imperialist forces? This is humiliation.... Either atomic weapons are forbidden for everyone or everyone has the right, according to his capabilities, to possess the weapons with which to defend his children.[142]

Hence, once again we see the pre-eminent role that allusions to global equality and equal rights play within the relevant Libyan discourse. It is this motif that the Libyan regime uses to justify both its abstention from the NPT and its condemnation of the global nuclear order of legitimate nuclear weapon states and non-nuclear weapon states. Even the reference to Israel and its possession of nuclear weapons has to be interpreted through this lens: a nuclear-armed Israel is certainly perceived as a potentially existential threat to Libya; but even more, it is considered a grave injustice and humiliation that Israel is the only country in the region with the tacit right to possess nuclear weapons while Libya and the Arab states have to give up this option. In more abstract terms it may be argued that the concept of equality and non-hierarchy, so deeply rooted in Libyan traditions and cultural practices, again plays a major role in shaping the country's foreign and security policy: it calls for a nuclear weapons policy that consequently opposes what is perceived as an unjust, hierarchical international order and persistently emphasizes "equal nuclear rights" for all state actors in the international system.[143]

There is, however, one further aspect that is noteworthy for the Libyan discourse on nuclear weapons between 1986 and 1995. The conventional assumptions of political scientists regarding the symbolism of nuclear weapons as an emblem of modernity lead us to believe that states acquire nuclear weapons as a vigorous demonstration of their technological progress and a display of their society's participation in the achievements of the modern age. The Libyan discourse partly seems to run counter to this idea. The ideational role of nuclear weapons and nuclear technology as a symbol of Libyan modernity, technological advancement and scientific progress barely features in the discourse on nuclear weapons between 1986 and 1995. Instead, we even find traces of a counter-narrative – one that seeks to identify progress with a different set of achievements:

If Libya wished to have one [a nuclear weapon] it would have been very easy to obtain considerable funds. Should we spend billions? We have billions. We prefer to use them for the protection of the environment, to construct a big artificial river, for education, and health care.[144]

The Libyan case thus forces us to draw our conclusions with care when it comes to the prevalent assumptions about the symbolic nature of nuclear proliferation.

While the idea of state modernity and scientific, technological progress does not figure prominently in the Libyan discourse, other ideational and symbolic aspects of nuclear proliferation play a significant role: the idea of global equality and the equal rights of sovereign states are a central aspect of the discourse on nuclear weapons in Libya. The – refused – right to possess nuclear weapons, in other words, symbolizes the hierarchical global order. Nuclear weapons, then, do have a symbolic meaning – but it is one that alludes more to people's rights, equality and egalitarianism than to progress and modernity.

Overall, we may conclude that the second phase of Libya's nuclear ambitions (1986–1995) exhibits discursive continuities as well as changes and modifications compared to earlier years; moreover, several frames and narratives exhibit a certain degree of inconsistency and self-contradiction. The country's self-perception continues to be shaped by attributes that depict the nation as small, tribalistic and Islamic. Likewise, the dominant frame depicts Libya as the global pioneer of anti-capitalism and Islamic socialism. However, there does seem to be at least a partial decrease in the use of these characteristics. Instead, a new narrative of empowerment, autonomy and anti-étatism gains more prominence – both on the domestic and the international level of analysis. This is particularly noticeable for two reasons. On the one hand, this narrative provides further legitimacy for a foreign policy that continues to challenge the status quo and that calls for an "empowerment of the powerless" on the international level; it lends additional ideological support to a confrontational, change-seeking foreign policy. On the other hand, the empowerment frame, and the related questioning of authorities and hierarchies, also has a domestic aspect: it further undermines the idea of strong and powerful national authorities and inhibits the emergence of a strong Libyan central state. Against this background it is hardly surprising that the discourse on nuclear weapons does not contain references that equate the development of nuclear weapons with the notion of a strong Libyan state. In the Libyan discourse, nuclear weapons never achieve a symbolically laden status as emblems of *national* technological and scientific progress or as emblems of *national* achievement. This may be partly because there is no coherent idea of the desirability of modernity: while Libya is time and again characterized as a motor or in the vanguard of social and political change, we also find several instances that emphasize the country's tribal, pre-modern traits. As a result, there is no strong and convincing narrative linking the possession of nuclear weapons with state power and state aptitude.

Rather, the acquisition of nuclear (military or civilian) technology is depicted as a symbol of global (in-)equality: it is suggested that the *Arab world* ought to possess nuclear weapons in order to overcome the existing inequality of the global nuclear order and to draw level with the nuclear weapons states, above all with the US and Israel. However, growing frustration over the lack of progress toward Arab unity reveals how weak an actor the "Arab nation" is considered to be. A multitude of fault lines and conflicts among the Arab states results in the joint venture of an "Arab bomb" seeming more and more out of reach during the 1980s and 1990s.

Arguably, the very lack of a state narrative was a significant factor in the ultimate failure of Libya's nuclear endeavors. There was no compelling national frame to spur broad-based national efforts and to provide sufficient momentum in order to maintain a fully fledged research program over several decades. Alternative frames that could have justified a weapons program – such as the notion of equality or the narrative of an Arab bomb – were either too weak to justify the vast financial and political cost of a comprehensive program, or eventually crumbled in the face of detrimental political developments.

If we furthermore take into account that the second-phase discourse also reveals certain inconsistencies and fluctuations with regard to such fundamental matters as Libya's threat assessment and its perceived position within the international world, it seems almost inevitable that the country's nuclear weapons policy was rather incoherent and disorderly.

In the following section we will examine how the discourse developed further during the third phase of Libya's nuclear experiments, i.e., between 1996 and 2003. How did the definition of the situation of key decision-makers change, resulting in the unexpected and remarkable renunciation of nuclear weapons in 2003? Can we discern new and different patterns of interpretation within the discourse on nuclear armament? Do we find traces of a changed identity or self-perception?

Phase III: nuclear indecisiveness (mid-1990s–2003)

In December 2003, Muammar Gaddafi announced publicly – and to the surprise of many observers – the end of Libya's WMD and ballistic missile research and development programs. Can the analysis of additional documents from these final years yield further insights that help us to understand this step better? Which dominant structures of meaning were prevalent in the years before the Libyan administration decided to abandon its WMD activities? How did particular frames and narratives evolve or stabilize? These questions will be addressed in the following pages. We will again proceed in three steps in order to analyze (1) patterns of self-perception; (2) attitudes toward the international system, and (3) frames relating to issues of nuclear technology.[145]

Level 1: identity and self-perception

Analysis of the first two phases has revealed the prevalence of a fairly specific and coherent depiction of "what Libya is" (1). A central facet of the discourse is the recurring description of Libya as a non-capitalist, socialist, humanitarian country, rooted in widely shared Islamic principles.[146] These depictions were most obvious in the first two decades of post-revolutionary Libya (between 1969 and 1986), but had already become less discernible by the second phase (1986–1995). In later years (1996–2003) these attributes seem to have faded even further. Three decades after the revolution the ideational underpinnings and the "socio-political meaning" of the Jamahiriya rarely appear in the discourse on

Libya's self-perception. Arguably, the dissolution of the Warsaw Pact and the demise of the Soviet Union deprived the northern African state of its ideological "cousin"; socialism had lost much of its appeal. Only the description of Libya as a global motor, in the vanguard of change, remains in place. Even this idea, however, takes on a rather altered meaning: during the first three decades after the revolution the discourse had above all characterized Libya as a pioneer of revolutionary global change, of social justice and equality. The country was depicted as the leader of a new social order, as the spearhead of the Third Way and as the legitimate agent of a revolutionary, revisionist, proactive foreign policy. The documents of the third period, however, reveal a rather subtle but nevertheless crucial change in Libya's self-perception. The country is still depicted as a motor of change, but the frame now relates to Libya's self-perceived role as a pioneer and pacifier of international relations:

> Let us build international relations on the principles of respect, understanding and joint cooperation in the service of humanity.... *Libya was the first country* which officially called for the convening of an international conference to combat and eliminate terrorism. It also called for the holding of a special session of the UN General Assembly for this purpose. It still insists on the need to intensify all efforts in order to lay down firm and strong foundations for peace and security in the world and eliminate violence, terrorism, tyranny, injustice and human aggression against brother humans.[147]

> [Libya] believes that the arms race will neither serve its security nor the region's security and contradicts its (Libya's) great concern for a world that enjoys peace and security. *By taking this initiative, it wants all countries to follow its steps*, starting with the Middle East, without any exception or double standards[emphasis added].[148]

Libya is still portrayed as a motor and pioneer, yet the "policy script" has changed. The self-perception of being a radical, revolutionary actor – a maverick of the international system – fighting vigorously against colonialism, inequality and suppression has given way to an identity conception which depicts Libya as integrative, benign and peaceful.

This novel depiction is complemented by a second frame: the characterization of Libya as a member of the international community. Contrary to the prevalent narratives in former years, the key actors in the debate now portray Libya as a constitutive part of the international arena. In other words, Libya is no longer the revolutionary, revisionist rogue it used to be in former years, but instead seeks to alter the international arena from within. In most documents of the third phase, this change in frames is fairly subtle and implicit. Speakers refer, for example, to referents such as "humanity," "children of humankind" or "humankind" – notions which naturally include Libya as well as any other social actor. A 2003 article by Saif Gaddafi (Muammar Gaddafi's son) in *Middle East Policy*, however, makes this altered self-conception very explicit by comparing Libya's historical role as a revolutionary force with its new cooperative attitude.

> [T]rouble began soon after the Libyan revolution of 1969, when the new government under the direction of Colonel Qadhafi, seeking to assert national independence, expelled American military bases from our territory. We were a more radical country then. Colonialism had forced us to adopt radical policies even after we were nominally free.[149]

Given the author's (informal) political weight, the significance of this detailed explication and bluntly fundamental revision of Libya's identity and its policies can hardly be overestimated. It amounts to an official renunciation of policy principles that formerly took center stage and reflects a comprehensive reconsideration of Libya's role in the world. The article comes to a climax with the following words:

> At this crossroads of history, Libya recognizes America's special role as a superpower.... Libya is now ready to transform decades of mutual antagonism into an era of genuine friendship. This is not to say that Libya regrets the policies it long followed to preserve its independence.[150]

What we see is an essential reframing of Libya's identity and its role in the world: the former pariah "holds out its hand" to its previous enemy and seeks to overcome the rifts that once barred it from the international community. Libya's view of the world and the perception of its own role have changed dramatically; the hitherto dominant narrative of Libya as a fierce revolutionary fighter has been replaced by a notion of cooperation, consideration and benignity.[151]

This new motif is in harmony with another – long-established – frame of self-perception which depicts Libya as a "small," "defensive" and "peaceful" country, and a "small" and "peaceful" people respectively. Notably, the attributes "small" and "resource-poor" were apparent in earlier years (as seen above) and they now reappear in many of the documents of the third phase.[152]

Level 2: Libya's position in the international system

What is so striking about this narrative of smallness, resource scarcity and weakness is the evolving link to Libya's foreign policy and its position within the world (2). Libya's foreign policy and its attitude toward the world is described and justified as a mere defense of its genuine and legitimate interests. The following quote from a rambling interview with Gaddafi illustrates both the self-perception as a small and weak actor as well as the resulting foreign policy stance:

> America always beset our country, always run after this small people who don't know why. It is very shameful for America as a superpower.... We

are not afraid. We have to defend our country, and we have the right to live free and peacefully under the sun and on the earth. And America has no right to act as international bullies.[153]

Other sources complement and expand on this narrative, thereby leading to the emergence of an "interpretation of the world" in which Libya is described as a rather powerless, defensive actor that is merely and justifiably trying to protect its own interests. Any offensive foreign policy intentions on the part of the Gaddafi regime are thus denied. Somewhat surprisingly, however, it is admitted that this foreign policy posture gives rise at times to misinterpretations by Libya's adversaries:

We have not erred against the West. We are defending our interests. This defense is usually interpreted as harming their interests.

Moreover, these statements illustrate the prevalent threat perception that dominates the Libyan discourse in this period between the mid-1990s and 2003. This is that "the West" (i.e., the United States, together with its main ally, Israel, and the United Kingdom) present a grave threat to Libyan security and to the country's crucial interests, not least because they (allegedly) possess weapons of mass destruction:

[Libyans] are the victim of organized international terrorism and of an unjust aggression used skillfully by the United States against the Libyan people.... The fact that the United States is supplying Israel with nuclear, biological, and chemical weapons and advanced missiles and planes proves the extent of the US–Israeli alliance against the states of the region.[154]

If we compare this frame with the results of our previous analyses, however, we find some significant differences. To recall: the documents of the earlier years contained several explicit justifications for Libya's resort to terrorist activities. The central reasoning was that due to the unequal structure of the international system and Libya's lack of sufficient military and economic means, it had the "right" to take advantage of alternative – asymmetric – policies in order to compensate for its weakness and to defend itself. In a multitude of Libyan sources we found explicit support for asymmetric forms of violence as a means of resistance and a recurring justification for Libya's recourse to or support for international terrorism and liberation movements.

In this new phase, however, we seem to be witnessing a change in Libya's attitude toward the international system. While the definition of the situation remains more or less the same – the international system is still characterized as unjust and unfair, America is portrayed as an imperialist power, and Libya feels threatened by the West and Israel – Libya's reaction becomes less "roguish." We find fewer and fewer statements justifying Libya's "maverick" behavior or the recourse to terrorism; instead, several of the documents of the third phase depict

Libya as a member of the international community and call for joint efforts to tackle regional and international problems under the auspices of international institutions such as the UN. The most obvious and explicit statement in this regard is again Saif Gaddafi's 2003 article in *Middle East Policy* – it outright embodies the fundamental change. Yet it is far from being the only statement:

> We always urge dialogue with all world states whenever there is confusion or misunderstanding over any issue, be it a political, economic, or security issue.[155]

> Let us build international relations on the principles of respect, understanding and joint cooperation in the service of humanity.[156]

> We are facing real terrorism on this occasion [the spread of Anthrax in the US in fall 2001].... The issue needs an international meeting in which the world's consciousness and wisdom are represented away from the moral and emotional considerations which are ineffective at this hour.[157]

Hence, alongside the change in Libya's self-perception – from being a maverick or pariah state toward being a member of the international community – comes a change in the country's foreign policy behavior. This change is not least exemplified by the interpellation of "we" and "us," which symbolize Libya's attempt to become part of the international community. The previous self-portrayal as a revolutionary, revisionist outsider thus gives way to an inclusive, integrative notion of being a member and partner. This new interpretation led the country to tacitly and rather self-righteously signal its openness to cooperation and negotiations with its former arch-enemies and to allude to common interests.

It would take a more specific, detailed analysis of the discursive structures to determine the exact time frame within which this change happened; on the basis of the present analysis, however, it may be assumed that the crucial transformation materialized in or around 1996. In any case, the alteration took place way prior to 2003 when Gaddafi officially announced the end of Libya's WMD efforts. This undermines the claim that the Gaddafi administration only backed down in the face of US military pressure following the fall of Saddam Hussein. At the same time, however, it should be taken into consideration that Libya's "new approach" was originally far from coherent and unified: even in the late 1990s, when the Gaddafi regime had already signaled its revised stance, we find statements that repeat old threat perceptions and that reveal a hostile attitude toward the West. Hence, the discursive shift from a hostile mindset toward a more benevolent stance did not materialize immediately and in a linear fashion, but "zigzagged" over a longer period of time. What we see is in fact a "competition" between interpretive frames and resulting policy options: in the background we can see a fairly constant and stable narrative which depicts the international world as inherently unjust and unequal. At the same time, there are two contradictory policy frames in the foreground: one justifies and even calls for terrorist means to assert Libya's interests in the world; the other outlines possibilities of cooperation and negotiations with Libya's opponents. Only in the late 1990s did the "cooperation frame" become predominant, thus allowing the Libyan regime to reach out to its former enemies.

There is one further aspect of Libya's "attitude toward the world" to which we should pay closer attention; that is the concept of partnership and alliance. As has been described extensively above, Libya's key point of reference in terms of allies and partners used to be its Arab neighborhood. The feeling of being embedded within this region was so prevalent that the almost mythical notions of "Arab nation" and of "Arab unity" even replaced any strong sense of the Libyan nation state. The longing for Arab unity was explained on the grounds of past historical and cultural achievements, but it also contained a vision to revive the "grandiose heroic past." Thus, Arab unity was not only one of the central ideological tenets of the Libyan state following the revolution in 1969 and one of the most prominent narratives in all the relevant documents, but also embodied a strategic idea of opposing perceived Western "imperialism" and interference in the Arab region.

While Gaddafi had always been dissatisfied by the slow progress toward Arab unity, his criticism became fiercer and more serious in the second half of the 1980s (triggered by the perceived lack of support in the aftermath of the 1986 attacks). In the years between 1996 and 2003 we observe a further erosion of the idea of Arab unity within the Libyan discourse, and consequently a reorientation toward new, alternative partners, namely Africa – a step that is intimately linked with a reconsideration of Libya's regional identity.

> Libya is in the Middle of North Africa, not in the periphery. Its location is like South Africa and more so. If Libya wants to avoid the evil of enemies from outside, it will seek protection in Africa.[158]

Again, however, the changed interpretation is not fixed and conclusive, but unstable and open to renegotiation. Other utterances still contain references to Libya's Arab identity or its allegiance to the Arab world. In comparison to former years, however, the importance of "Arabism" as a defining trait of Libya's identity and as a justification for specific policies has decreased dramatically. Even in those documents that still make allusions to Arab unity and pan-Arabism, these ideas are rarely used to justify or explain Libya's foreign policy or to mobilize support. They do not seem to be aiming to develop significant momentum to instigate policies or to steer Libya's policymaking in one direction or another. At the end of the twentieth century, it seems, Libya lacked a precise idea of its communal identity and its regional belonging.

Level 3: attributes of civil and military nuclear technology

In the final step we will analyze the significant patterns of interpretation that may be discerned with regard to level 3 of our analytical framework, i.e., the question of nuclear weapons and nuclear technology.

A first, cursory look at the documents reveals that the "nuclear frame" is significantly less obvious and less complex than in previous phases. In fact, nuclear weapons figure less prominently in the discourse than in the first two phases. More specifically, there are hardly any allusions to notions of modernity or progress: while we saw that even in earlier years the discourse of modernity and progress lacked a certain degree of coherence and that it was time and again undermined and destabilized by somewhat unconventional, unexpected references to an almost mythical ideal of life in Libya's pre-modern, agrarian countryside, even these fractured allusions to "nuclear modernity" are now absent. Similarly, we do not find any references to metaphors of "nuclear spread" and "nuclear growth" which could provide a rhetorical justification for a "quasi-natural" proliferation of nuclear weapons to hitherto non-nuclear states. Moreover, and in notable contrast to earlier phases of the discourse, references to the "Arab nuclear weapon" frame are tacit and less compelling:

> [T]he Arab states are entitled to possess all weapons which are available in the world and which are in Israel's possession. If these weapons are available to the United States and other states, why should the Arabs not acquire them? And to prevent Israel from threatening us with such a dangerous weapon, we should possess the same weapon.[159]

These frames differ remarkably from the imperative wordings we have seen previously. In the light of our previous analyses it appears reasonable to assume that the ongoing decrease in momentum for the idea of Arab unity further undermined both the political as well as the ideological driving force behind Libya's attempted acquisition of nuclear weapons. In other words, if there was no such thing as Arab unity and if there was never going to be some kind of joint Arab agency then why and how should Libya pursue the idea of an Arab-Islamic nuclear bomb? The decreased significance of the idea of Arab unity thus has grave implications for the nuclear dynamic, since it calls into question both the program's feasibility as well as its designation.

At the same time, the analysis reveals that another frame within the nuclear discourse is gaining importance: the call for a WMD-free zone in the Greater Middle East. While this idea had already been voiced in the early 1990s, it is more frequently articulated from 1996 onwards, although it later ebbs and flows – thus contradicting the at times still-existent idea of an Arab nuclear weapon. The following quote perfectly illustrates this incongruous stance:

> Libya announced its position some years ago on the importance of removing all types of mass-destruction weapons from the Middle East and Africa.... [However] the Arab states are entitled to possess all weapons which are available in the world and which are in Israel's possession. If these weapons are available to the United States and other states, why should the Arabs not acquire them? And to prevent Israel from threatening us with such a dangerous weapon, we should possess the same weapon.[160]

In a similar vein, Libya is characterized as an active proponent of arms control and disarmament ambitions:

> [T]he Jamahiriyah has always been first in calling for the eradication of anything that may jeopardize international peace and security, particularly weapons of mass destruction, whatever they are, and whatever they are called. Libya has signed the international agreements regarding the prevention of nuclear arms proliferation and all forms of mass destruction weapons.[161]

> Libya is not making any efforts, does not have plans, and is not thinking of possessing what is known as weapons of mass destruction because Libya is a signatory to the agreements on the non-proliferation of nuclear weapons. It also signed the agreements prohibiting chemical and biological weapons and is committed to them.[162]

These frames provide several interesting clues regarding the role of nuclear weapons in Libya's thinking on foreign and security policy. The disappearance of a clear and strong conception of Arab unity undermined the key designation of nuclear weapons. To recall: many of the previous documents revealed that Libya was not primarily interested in a "Libyan nuclear weapon," but was hoping more to develop nuclear weapons for and together with its Arab neighbors. Once the idea of Arab agency and cooperation began to totter, the central driving force behind the weapons idea lost much of its appeal. At the same time, an alternative frame – that of a WMD-free zone – became more prevalent. Again, this is hardly a surprising development given Libya's fundamental belief in egalitarianism and equality: we are led to believe that the Gaddafi regime would have voluntarily agreed to reverse its nuclear ambitions, if other countries in the region – above all of course Israel – had agreed to follow suit. Hence, Libya's insistence on a WMD-free zone in the Middle East may only partly be explained by security considerations. Rather, the idea of establishing a zone free of weapons of mass destruction served two purposes: as a demand for Israeli disarmament and the disabling of the perceived nuclear threat it posed to Libya; and to satisfy the regime's demand for global recognition and "equal nuclear rights" among states. Arguably, when the Gaddafi regime realized that the acquisition of nuclear weapons was hardly feasible and that "nuclear equality" was not achievable by deploying an Arab nuclear force, the commitment to a WMD-free zone grew more significant. The documents suggest that it was not merely the result of eagerness to break the Israeli nuclear threat, but that Libya's policy was equally spurred by a desire to achieve some form of equality.

Yet, the discourse of this last period is not only significant in terms of the interpretations it contains, but also because of the narratives and frames that are missing from it. For example, the frame of modernity and progress, which had always been rather obscure and vague in the Libyan case, plays an even smaller role in the last period under examination. In fact, the documents analyzed for the years between 1996 and 2003 do not include any reference to the idea of "nuclear modernity." In the period under scrutiny, nuclear weapons do not figure as an epitome of technological and scientific progress or as a symbol of a modern, advanced state. Likewise, we do not find allusions to a "proliferation automatism" or to national or joint research and development projects. All these frames, which at times figured prominently in the Libyan discourse, seem by now to have disappeared.

Instead, it is apparent that the Libyan discourse on nuclear weapons narrows considerably in the years after 1996. It basically revolves around only one aspect: the question of equality. The key reasoning here is that if the US, Israel and the UK – or for that matter any other state – have the right to possess nuclear weapons (and, more generally, weapons of mass destruction) and to use these weapons to exert a threat, then Libya and the Arab states should have the right to do the same – both for military and ideational reasons. Thus the possession of nuclear weapons by these states is considered a threat to Libya's security and its survival. But even more so, it is considered an embodiment of a hierarchical, unjust and non-egalitarian global order that promotes certain states at the expense of others. This interpretation, which has already figured prominently in the previous phases of Libya's nuclear history, is still emphatically present in this last period.

The narrative does not appear to be powerful enough, however, to enable a straightforward, far-reaching nuclear enterprise. On the contrary: the documents from the third period reveal a set of somewhat incoherent, and partly even conflicting frames and interpretations that seem to make a coherent and systematic foreign policy unlikely or at least more difficult. On the one hand, Libya's foreign policy and its nuclear ambitions are still shaped by a deep-seated call for global equality and egalitarianism – the international world is still considered unjust and discriminatory. Likewise, the possession of nuclear weapons by some states acts as the basis of Libya's threat perception, thus nurturing the country's nuclear ambitions. On the other hand, however, its self-perception as a revolutionary pioneer has decreased; its attitude toward the world has become less hostile and its overall stance vis-à-vis the international community has become more benevolent. Similarly, the dominant interpretation of Libya is no longer that it is a global maverick, but rather an actor that has agreed to reach out to the international community. If we furthermore take into account the fact that other interpretations have disappeared from the Libyan nuclear discourse – for example, the narrative of nuclear weapons as symbols of development and as symbols of equality and "democratization of technology" – and that the idea of Arab unity has lost its appeal, it is hardly surprising that Libya's nuclear efforts lost much of their momentum in the 1990s. The country's impetus to achieve nuclear parity – either through Libya's acquisition of nuclear weapons or through the establishment of a WMD-free zone – is not sufficiently strong to fuel and sustain a broad, all-encompassing nuclear program. In fact, Libya's nuclear ambitions compete with – and eventually lose out against – its aspiration to become an accepted member of the international community. Thus it is this reinterpretation of the country's security environment and of its self-perception that ultimately spur a policy of tacit rapprochement with the West.

Libya's nuclear reversal: conclusion

How can we make sense of Libya's nuclear weapons ambitions? Why did the regime attempt to acquire a nuclear capability – and why did the same administration decide to abandon its efforts three decades later? In line with the theoretical framework developed in the first chapters, it is argued that we need to understand the underlying structures of meaning that guide any state action. In line with the results provided by Solingen, Müller and others I argue that we should not merely look for security threats that were allegedly given, and that might have caused the decision to go nuclear, or for presumably clear-cut cost–benefit calculations. Instead we should attempt to gain a broader understanding of the prevailing identity conception, the dominant role perception and world-view as well as the specific ideas regarding nuclear weapons and nuclear technology on which the government's decision-making – its pondering of different policy options – is based. Again, the danger is that such an approach is seen as a justification for the policies of a brutal dictatorship. However, the study at hand is not about exonerating the regime, but about understanding how intersubjectively shared beliefs or narratives regarding Libya's identity, its security perceptions and its interests enabled particular policies in the first place. Thus, unlike positivist-realist studies that merely trace proliferation/nuclearization decisions back to apparently given security constraints and strategic necessities, I argue that there is no proliferation automatism: states' decisions and policies are based on and stem from shared understandings and beliefs of "what the state is," which "role" it occupies in the international system, and as how threatening it perceives its security environment to be. If we want to understand how a particular course of action evolves and to gain a more comprehensive understanding of political action, we need to analyze this underlying ideational "layer."

Thus, against the background of these theoretical assumptions, what conclusions may we draw? The analysis reveals that Libya's self-perception in the years following the revolution was shaped by a set of narratives which characterize the nation as small, tribalistic and deeply rooted in Islamic traditions. At the same time it is depicted as the global pioneer of anti-capitalism and as a motor of global change toward equality. Despite its smallness and its limited power, Libya thus sees itself as an active player on the global scene – as an actor that has the right and the duty to fight against global inequality and post-colonial suppression. Thus, it is this self-perception and identity conception that fuels much of Libya's aggressive foreign policy behavior, its interference in regional and global politics, and its nuclear ambitions. However, what is particularly significant for the Libyan case, and what distinguishes Libya's identity discourse from other examples, is the clear lack of explicit references to the nation state and the absence of a narrative of Libyan statehood. The idea of the Libyan nation remains rather vague and disembodied.

Instead, we find overwhelming traces of a narrative of empowerment, autonomy and anti-étatism which has an effect both on the domestic and the international level of analysis. First, this narrative provides further legitimacy for a foreign policy that continues to challenge the status quo and that calls for an "empowerment of the powerless" on the international level; it lends additional ideological support to a confrontational, revisionist and equality-seeking foreign policy – or what Müller calls the "truculent revolt against Western superiority."[163] While the aggressive vehemence of many Libyan statements on this issue is certainly unusual and striking, the mere existence of these allusions is rather unsurprising. We know from other studies that, for example, the Indian discourse on nuclear proliferation also contains a large number of references to the ideals of global equality and parity.[164] In this narrative nuclear weapons come to symbolize equality, status and international prestige. Undoubtedly this is one of the most frequent and elaborate narratives within the Libyan discourse, and it relates strongly to the ideals of equality and parity that are entrenched in local cultural habits. Accordingly, nuclear weapons are imbued with a notion of sovereignty and equal rights.

Second, however, the empowerment frame, and the related questioning of authorities and hierarchies, also has a domestic facet – one that appears to be fairly detrimental to the nuclear endeavor: The idea of local empowerment and decentralization seems to have further undermined the idea of strong and powerful national authorities and inhibited the emergence of a strong Libyan central state. This is not only striking from an identity point of view or from a comparative politics perspective; it is also a crucial aspect if we are to understand Libya's nuclear proliferation history. Given that there is no compelling narrative of the Libyan nation, it is hardly surprising that the discourse on nuclear weapons does not contain references that equate the development of nuclear weapons with the notion of a strong Libyan state. Nuclear weapons are not symbolically elevated to function as epitomes of statehood.

In a similar vein, in the Libyan discourse nuclear weapons never achieve the symbolically laden status of emblems of national technological and scientific progress or emblems of national scientific achievement. This may also be because there is no coherent view of Libya's relation to modernity: while the country is time and again characterized as a motor of social and political change and in the vanguard of such change, we also find several instances that emphasize the country's tribal, pre-modern traits. This double-edged nature of the country's characterization – Müller even calls it "regression into premodernity"[165] – inhibited the emergence of an elaborate and convincing narrative linking the possession of nuclear weapons with state modernity, state power and state aptitude.

"Despite pursuing nuclear weapons for over three decades the Libyan regime never seemed to fully commit to this endeavor,"[166] Braut-Hegghammer writes. I agree: it is this lack of commitment that presents the real puzzle – and it is indeed a puzzle that has hardly been explained by most studies of the Libyan case. I believe, however, that an analysis of the basal narratives on Libya's identity and its self-perception does provide many telling insights. Arguably, the very lack of a state narrative contributed significantly to the eventual failure of Libya's nuclear endeavors: there was no persuasive national frame that could have spurred broad-based national efforts and that could have provided sufficient momentum for the maintenance of a fully fledged research program over several decades.[167] In other words, without a convincing and coherent narrative of "what Libya is," all the efforts to establish a Libyan nuclear weapons program eventually suffered from insufficient political momentum.

For several years, at least, the lack of a state narrative was successfully compensated for through the alternative frame of Arab unity and Arab nationalism. The interpellation of "the Arab nation" provides a powerful ideological pillar – in addition to socialism and equal rights – for much of Libya's foreign policy behavior. It is one of the fundamental and most frequently invoked frames in all the documents of the first two decades. Moreover, the idea of Arab unity and of the Arab nation is the common thread for almost all the relevant statements on nuclear proliferation during the first two decades: the "nuclear subject" (i.e., the actor that is most often referred to) is rarely the Libyan state as such. Rather, the "Arab nation" is the envisioned acquirer of nuclear technology and nuclear weapons. If mentioned at all, Libya merely figures as an "agent" of empowerment for the Arab world or as a "motor."[168] In other words, the acquisition of nuclear weapons is rarely justified on national (i.e., Libyan) grounds, but rather in terms of an Arab obligation. The acquisition of (peaceful and/ or military) nuclear technology is characterized as a necessity and as an indispensable step toward further regional development – both in political-military and economic terms. It is also framed as a step toward equality with the existing nuclear weapon states: the Arab world has to possess nuclear weapons in order to overcome the inequality of the global nuclear order and to draw level with the nuclear weapons states, above all with the US and Israel. Hence, the possession of nuclear weapons by these states is considered to be not only a threat to the security and survival of Libya and the Arab world. It is, even more, considered to be the embodiment of a hierarchical, unjust and non-egalitarian global order that promotes certain states at the expense of others. Only if the Arab world possesses a nuclear force can it achieve parity and equality with the dominant West. Nuclear weapons thus carry a strong symbolic meaning – they epitomize status and prestige. However, the disappearance of a clear and convincing conception of Arab unity in the 1980s – due to a multitude of fault lines and conflicts among the Arab states – not only severely weakened Libya's natural strategic alignment, but also undermined the key designation of nuclear weapons. Once the idea of joint Arab agency and cooperation began to evaporate, the central driving force behind the weapons idea lost much of its appeal and the "Arab bomb" became increasingly out of reach during the 1980s and 1990s.

It was also at this time that Libya's foreign and security policy in general, and its nuclear policy in particular, began to alter – most likely due to a "strategic hopelessness" after the vanishing of Arab unity and the dissolution of the Soviet

Union. Several instances within the discourse reveal that in the early 1990s the Libyan regime tentatively accepted a more cooperative attitude toward the international system. More specifically, an alternative nuclear frame – a WMD-free zone – emerged. Again, this change may be traced back to a culturally anchored belief in egalitarianism and equality: seemingly, the Gaddafi regime would have agreed to reverse its nuclear ambitions if other countries in the region – above all, of course, Israel – had agreed to follow suit. Moreover, calling for a WMD-free zone in the Middle East seemed to offer Libya a chance to save face at a point when it seemed more and more unlikely that the country would be able to acquire its own nuclear capability. This suggests again that Libya's insistence on a WMD-free zone in the Middle East may only partly be explained by security considerations. Rather, the idea to establish a zone free of weapons of mass destruction served two purposes: it embodied a demand for Israeli disarmament and for the disabling of the perceived nuclear threat posed to Libya; and it represented a desire to augment Libya's status by establishing equality and "equal nuclear rights" among states. Arguably, when the Gaddafi regime realized that its own acquisition of nuclear weapons was hardly feasible and that "nuclear equality" was not achievable by deploying an Arab nuclear force, the commitment to a WMD-free zone grew more significant. The documents suggest that it was not merely an eagerness to break the alleged Israeli nuclear threat, but that Libya's policy was likewise spurred by a desire to establish some form of equality.

From an IR perspective it is, moreover, important to pay sufficient attention to two other aspects: first, the role of the nuclear regime; second the security and threat paradigm. The non-proliferation regime does not play a very prominent role in the Libyan discourse. It only shines through in regard to the narratives of global inequality and injustice. Describing the regime as discriminatory, biased and unjust, Gaddafi maintains that Libya and the Arab states should refrain from signing or ratifying the Non-Proliferation Treaty. According to this framing, the treaty is merely an instrument for the suppression of non-nuclear states and an embodiment of the inequitable global order. However, even though the non-proliferation regime and the treaty do not figure prominently in the discursive protocols analyzed, the historiographical reconstruction of the case reveals the regime's importance with regard to Libya's weapons ambitions. The nature of the existing regime and the prohibition on sales of nuclear weapons technology meant that Libya's access to relevant materials was at the very least complicated. In fact, Libya had to rely on obscure, dubious dealings to procure the necessary building blocks. This was even more necessary given the largely erratic and impulsive attitude of the Libyan government, which hindered the establishment of a sufficiently complex and well-developed industrial base in the nuclear sector. Thus, in the absence of a coherent, long-range strategy for an indigenous nuclear program, the "off-the-shelf" procurement of a ready-made bomb became the only viable option – yet it was an option that was severely hindered by the global non-proliferation regime. The NPT regime, in other words, did at least work partially: while it did not prevent Libya from acquiring nuclear building blocks from the Khan network, it certainly aggravated Libyan access and slowed down the program.

The analysis confirms furthermore that the threat perception – most notably the perceived threat posed by the US and its regional ally, Israel – figures prominently within the Libyan discourse on foreign and security policy. More specifically, the Libyan perception seems to shift from a rather broad but vague apprehension of vulnerability during the first phase (1972–1986) toward a more concrete and specific fear of attack by the US during the second phase (1986–1995). However, three aspects need to be taken into account. First, it appears that the security question was not the crucial factor behind the initiation of Libya's nuclear program. While the documents reveal that Libya did feel insecure – due to the unstable situation in the region, its hostilities with Israel and above all the US, shifting relations with its neighbors and its historical experience of colonial suppression – we do not find evidence of an existential threat in the early years of Libya's nuclear ambitions. The country did not face a threat grave enough to immediately necessitate nuclearization.[169] The security paradigm alone therefore seems to be too weak an explanation for Libya's initial interest in nuclear weapons; it only reaches its climax in the post-1986 phase, but even then it seems at times to be slightly ambivalent and ill-defined. Second, the analysis does not reveal an increased threat perception during the late 1990s or even in 2002/2003. While further studies may be necessary to confirm this argument, it does seem apposite to claim that Libya's renunciation of its WMD program was not induced by a heightened sense of danger from abroad. In other words, we do not find sufficient evidence to argue that the Gaddafi administration revoked its efforts because it feared that it would suffer the same fate as Iraq. This does not imply that such fear was absent; rather, the perception was fairly constant and it did not increase noticeably. Hence, this does not lend support to the Bush administration's claim that the example of Iraq led to a policy change in Libya. On the contrary, it seems that the decision to abandon the nuclear program was merely another step in a development that had already begun very tentatively in the mid-1990s.[170] Third, the analysis reveals that even fundamental political categories such as threat, enemy, ally and security are rarely fixed and settled. Instead, we see several instances that suggest a potential for the reopening and renegotiation of these core variables. Hence, both the threat narrative as well as the alignment motif is less coherent and consistent than one might conventionally assume.

The consequences for the Libyan case appear to be twofold. The security narrative was not sufficiently powerful and, hence, not convincing enough to spur far-reaching, wholesale and sustained efforts to acquire nuclear weapons. At the same time, it was open and fluid enough to allow a reconsideration and reframing of Libya's specific foreign and security policies in the 1990s, and thereby eased the country's rapprochement with the international community.

Notes

1 Yehudit Ronen, *Qaddafi's Libya in world politics* (Boulder, CO: Lynne Rienner, 2008), 65.
2 For a similar claim see Målfrid Braut-Hegghammer, "Nuclear Entrepreneurs: Drivers of Nuclear Proliferation" (dissertation manuscript) (London School of Economics, 2009).
3 Lisa Anderson, "The State in the Middle-East and North-Africa," *Comparative Politics* 20, no. 1 (1987): 3; "Tribe and State: Libyan Anomalies," in *Tribes and state formation in the Middle East*, ed. Philip S. Khoury and Joseph Kostiner (Berkeley: University of California Press, 1990); Jacques Roumani, "From Republic to Jamahiriya – Libya Search for Political Community," *Middle East Journal* 37, no. 2 (1983); Dirk J. Vandewalle, *A history of modern Libya* (Cambridge and New York: Cambridge University Press, 2006).
4 Anderson, "Tribe and State: Libyan Anomalies," 293.
5 Vandewalle, *A history of modern Libya*; Roumani, "From Republic to Jamahiriya – Libya Search for Political Community."
6 Vandewalle, *A history of modern Libya*; Fred Halliday, "The Politics of the Umma: States and Community in Islamic Movements," *Mediterranean Politics* 7, no. 3 (2002); Ali Abdullatif Ahmida, *The making of modern Libya: state formation, colonization, and resistance, 1830–1932* (Albany: State University of New York Press, 1994), ch. 5.
7 Frank R. Golino, "Patterns of Libyan National Identity," *Middle East Journal* 24, no. 3 (1970): 348; John Wright, *Libya, a modern history* (Baltimore, MD: Johns Hopkins University Press, 1982), 80; Anna Baldinetti, *The origins of the Libyan nation: colonial legacy, exile and the emergence of a new nation-state*, Routledge studies in Middle Eastern history (London and New York: Routledge, 2010), 143.
8 Waniss A. Otman and Erling Karlberg, *The Libyan economy economic diversification and international repositioning* (Berlin: Springer, 2007); World Bank, *The economic development of Libya* (Washington, DC,1960).
9 Nathan Alexander, "Libya – the Continuous Revolution," *Middle Eastern Studies* 17, no. 2 (1981): 218. On the foreign policy scene, a similar trend of ruthless and brutal behavior found its manifestation in the decade-long support for terrorist attacks, often primarily targeted against civilians as in the Lockerbie bombing or in the explosion of UTA flight 772, as well as in the covert support of insurgencies in many African and Middle Eastern states.
10 Anderson writes: "Qadhafi was obviously and very profoundly ambivalent about tribes. Early on he made clear that he was simultaneously opposed to tribalism as a principle of political organization and proud of his own origins in a saintly, though not noble or wealthy tribe, the Qadadfa" (Anderson, "Tribe and State: Libyan Anomalies," 297–298). See also Vandewalle, *A history of modern Libya*, 105.
11 The most elaborate analysis of this aspect may be found in Lisa Anderson, *The state and social transformation in Tunisia and Libya, 1830–1980* (Princeton, NJ: Princeton University Press, 1986).
12 The weakness in the way the military functioned illustrates this particularly well: while – according to several accounts – the government had acquired an extraordinary, large arsenal with a variety of weapons, the military's performance in most of Libya's foreign policy "adventures" is often described as "poor" or "unimpressive." One reason for these failings seems to be the particularly weak organizational structure of the military: "Most of the problems can be traced to a single political choice: the army is organized to assure one thing before all else, its inability to overthrow the regime" (William J. Foltz, "Libya's Military Power," in *The Green and the black: Qadhafi's policies in Africa*, ed. René Lemarchand (Bloomington: Indiana University Press, 1988), 67.

13 Anderson, "Tribe and State: Libyan Anomalies," 300.

14 Vandewalle, *A history of modern Libya*, 3.

15 Anderson, *The state and social transformation in Tunisia and Libya, 1830–1980*, 257; Vandewalle, *A history of modern Libya*, 75. For a harsher and more radical critique of Libya's socio-political situation on the eve of the revolution see Geoffrey L. Simons, *Libya and the West: from independence to Lockerbie* (Oxford: Oxford University Press, 2003).

16 For an analysis of these depictions, see René Lemarchand, "Beyond the Mad Dog Syndrome," in *The Green and the black: Qadhafi's policies in Africa*, ed. René Lemarchand (Bloomington: Indiana University Press, 1988), 1–3.

17 Ronald B. St. John, "The Libyan debacle in sub-Saharan Africa 1969–1987," in *The Green and the black: Qadhafi's policies in Africa*, ed. René Lemarchand (Bloomington: Indiana University Press, 1988), 92.

18 François Burgat, "Qadhafi's 'Unitary' Doctrine. Theory and Practice," in *The Green and the black: Qadhafi's policies in Africa*, ed. René Lemarchand (Bloomington: Indiana University Press, 1988), 20.

19 E.G.H. Joffé, "The Role of Islam," in *The Green and the black: Qadhafi's policies in Africa*, ed. René Lemarchand (Bloomington: Indiana University Press, 1988), 44–45. Roumani writes in a similar vein:

> Socially, Libyan hinterland culture was inspired by egalitarian Islamic orthodoxy and necessitated by economic scarcity…. Though nearer to Marxist ideals, the Jamahiriya's social ideology is based on Islamic principles derived from the Quran and reinterpreted by Qadhdhafi without reference to established Muslim traditions.
>
> (Roumani, "From Republic to Jamahiriya – Libya Search for Political Community," 166)

See also Muammar Qaddafi, The green book: the solution to the problem of democracy, the solution to the economic problem, the social basis of the third universal theory (Reading, MA: Ithaca Press, 2005); Alexander, "Libya – the Continuous Revolution"; 'Umar Ibrāhīm Faṭḥalī and Monte Palmer, Political development and social change in Libya (Lexington, MA: Lexington Books, 1980).

20 Ronen, *Qaddafi's Libya in world politics*, 19.

21 The Libyan regime denied any involvement in the cases; moreover, it claimed that the call for surrendering the suspects was undermining its sovereignty and hence supporting the post-colonial attitude of the United States and the United Kingdom, since none of the countries had an extradition treaty with Libya (*Qaddafi's Libya in world politics*, 45). In 2010 the issue gained renewed attention due to the early release of one of the culprits.

22 In order to unilaterally increase pressure on Libya, the United States imposed its own, extended sanctions regime in 1996, the Iran and Libya Sanctions Act (ILSA). It thereby further curtailed business relations with Libya and punished any foreign company dealing with the Gaddafi regime or making investments exceeding $40 million. Vandewalle, *A history of modern Libya*, 171.

23 On April 5, 1999, Libyan authorities finally yielded to the mounting pressure and extradited the suspects for trial in the Netherlands. The "neutral" location of the court allowed the Gaddafi regime to save face; moreover, it was agreed that the trial would also inquire into the suspects' personal involvement in the bombings, while the government's role remained more or less unquestioned. As a reward for surrendering the suspects, UN sanctions were immediately lifted; the unilateral US sanctions, however, remained in place until April 2004. See Ronen, *Qaddafi's Libya in world politics*, 54, 68.

24 Joffé, "The Role of Islam," 47.

25 Lemarchand, "Beyond the Mad Dog Syndrome," 7.

26 Ronen, *Qaddafi's Libya in world politics*, 16.
27 Luis Martínez, *The Libyan paradox* (New York and Paris: Columbia University Press, 2007), 107–111. See also Ronen, *Qaddafi's Libya in world politics*, ch. 9, *passim*.
28 *Qaddafi's Libya in world politics*, 53, 186.
29 Quoted in ibid., 188.
30 Ibid., 196.
31 Even today it is not quite clear *when* Gaddafi undertook *which steps* in order to obtain access to nuclear weapons. Müller, for example, writes that the Libyan head of state had actually approached Egypt *even before* making enquiries of the Chinese government. Harald Müller, "Libyens Selbstentwaffnung. Ein Modellfall?," *HSFK-Report* 6 (2006): 7. Given the close political relations at that time between Gaddafi and Nasser this assumption does not seem far-fetched. Indeed, it is undisputed that the two states cooperated. However, according to Bowen, the cooperation occurred in the early 1970s and mainly encompassed an exchange of ideas and scientific personnel. Moreover, their mutual efforts were deemed to have come to an end when bilateral relations deteriorated in the aftermath of Nasser's death in September 1970.
32 Wyn Q. Bowen, *Libya and nuclear proliferation: stepping back from the brink*, Adelphi paper (Abingdon and New York: Routledge, 2006), 26–31. Bowen's publication is one of the best and most detailed analyses of Libya's nuclear efforts currently available.
33 *Libya and nuclear proliferation*, 33.
34 Ibid., 27–28.
35 International Atomic Energy Agency (IAEA), "GOV/2004/12. Implementation of the NPT Safeguards Agreement of the Socialist People's Libyan Arab Jamahiriya. Report by the Director General" (2004).
36 Libya had already signed the Non-Proliferation Treaty in 1968 during the Idris regime; the new revolutionary government, however, postponed its ratification. Similarly, the Safeguard Agreement pursuant to the NPT only entered into force in July 1980 (see "GOV/2004/12. Implementation of the NPT Safeguards Agreement of the Socialist People's Libyan Arab Jamahiriya. Report by the Director General"). For a comprehensive analysis of the origins of the Soviet Union's nuclear export policy and the conditions applied see Gloria Duffy, "Soviet Nuclear Export," *International Security* 3, no. 1 (1978). Herein Duffy argues:

> Based upon its high level of concern about proliferation to certain countries, the Soviet Union maintained tight controls over its own exports of nuclear technology. The Soviet Union has limited its nuclear exports to a variety of reactor which is least susceptible to accumulating fissile material, has forced client countries to accede to international nonproliferation protocols, has maintained control over the spent rods from its fuel exports, and until quite recently has limited the number of countries eligible to Soviet nuclear aid.

It should, however, be borne in mind that this rather tentative approach to nuclear collaboration was attributable to the deteriorating Sino–Russian relations that had formerly encompassed intense cooperation in the nuclear realm (p. 84).
37 Gavin Cawthra and Bjoern Moeller, "Nuclear Africa: Weapons, Power and Proliferation," *African Security Review* 17, no. 4 (2008).
38 Bowen, *Libya and nuclear proliferation*, 30–31.
39 Ibid., 31.
40 Bahgat, for example, concludes that:

> Libya's technological capabilities and infrastructure are very limited and underdeveloped compared with other regional powers such as Iran or Iraq before the 1991 Gulf War. Accordingly, the country's efforts to build WMD capabilities largely rested on foreign suppliers. In other words, in terms of material,

equipment, and expertise, Libya relied heavily on foreign countries to acquire non-conventional capabilities.

(Gawdat Bahgat, "Proliferation of Weapons of Mass Destruction: The Case of Libya," *International Relations* 22, no. 1 (2008): 110)

41 International Atomic Energy Agency (IAEA), "GOV/2004/12. Implementation of the NPT Safeguards Agreement of the Socialist People's Libyan Arab Jamahiriya. Report by the Director General," 4; Bowen, *Libya and nuclear proliferation*, 35.

42 David Albright, *Peddling peril: how the secret nuclear trade arms America's enemies* (New York: Free Press, 2010), 116–117.

43 Braut-Hegghammer, "Nuclear Entrepreneurs." At the same time Braut-Hegghammer contradicts assumptions that Libya only maintained its crude nuclear programme in order to have a bargaining chip for when it came to direct negotiations with the US:

The idea that Libya was not seriously committed to its pursuit of nuclear weapons in the 1990s, but did so only as a bargaining strategy, does not appear to be backed by evidence. The hypothesis that the nuclear project was considered a bargaining tool runs the risk of reading history backwards.

(p. 259)

For a "first-hand" account of US–Libyan relations in the 1990s see also Gary Hart, "My Secret Talks with Libya, and Why They Went Nowhere," *The Washington Post*, January 18, 2004.

44 The IAEA assessment states:

Libya started importing L-1 centrifuges in 1997 through foreign intermediaries. Libya has declared that a total of 20 complete L-1 centrifuges, and most of the components for an additional 200 L-1 centrifuges, except for aluminium rotors and magnets, were acquired by Libya from a supplier State.... Libya has declared that two L-2 test centrifuges, together with small UF6 cylinders, were imported in September 2000 from the supplier State. Agency discussions with the supplier State have confirmed this information. These imports were also arranged through the offices of foreign intermediaries. Libya has stated that it had placed an order for 10,000 additional L-2 centrifuges, the first components of which started to arrive in December 2002 from elsewhere through the clandestine procurement network.

(International Atomic Energy Agency (IAEA), "GOV/2004/33. Implementation of the NPT Safeguards Agreement of the Socialist People's Libyan Arab Jamahiriya. Report by the Director General," (2004), 5–6)

What is striking about this sequence of events and the planned establishment of the enrichment facility is the fact that the plant was only designed to accommodate 5,832 P2-centrifuges. The remaining more than 4,000 centrifuges were calculated as spare parts, since it was assumed that many of them might get damaged when Libyan technicians tried to operate the machine. Albright, *Peddling peril*, 123.

45 *Peddling peril*, 123.

46 Bowen, *Libya and nuclear proliferation*, 43.

47 Ibid., 44. This is similar to Hymans' general assessment of proliferation failures:

The great proliferation slowdown can be attributed in part to U.S. and international nonproliferation efforts. But it is mostly the result of the dysfunctional management tendencies of the states that have sought the bomb in recent decades. Weak institutions in those states have permitted political leaders to unintentionally undermine the performance of their nuclear scientists, engineers, and technicians.

(Jacques E.C. Hymans, "Botching the Bomb: Why Nuclear Weapons Programs Often Fail on Their Own – and Why Iran's Might, Too," *Foreign Affairs* 91, no. 3 (2012), 45)

48 After conducting inspections in Libya in late 2003, the IAEA concluded that the country's nuclear weapons program was only "in its initial stages." This assessment, however, clearly contradicted the Bush administration's view, which held that Libya had made much greater progress on its way toward developing a military nuclear capacity. See Bowen, *Libya and nuclear proliferation*, 73.

49 John Hart and Shannon N. Kile, "Libya's Renunciation of Nuclear, Biological and Chemical Weapons and Ballistic Missiles," in *SIPRI Yearbook 2005*, ed. SIPRI (Oxford: Oxford University Press, 2005), 646–647.

50 Harald Müller, "The Exceptional End to an Extraordinary Libyan Nuclear Quest," in *Nuclear Proliferation and International Security*, ed. Morten Bremer Mærli and Sverre Lodgaard (Abingdon: Routledge, 2007), 73.

51 Wæver, "Identity, Communities and Foreign Policy," 27.

52 In order not to give rise to doubts, it should be stated again that different political systems do of course have differing impacts upon the structure of the discourse – on the number and range of participants, on freedom of expression, the transparency of the debate and so forth. However, even in the case of closed authoritarian political systems such as North Korea, it would be valuable to examine the official discourse on a specific policy issue. While we would find hardly any dissenting voices, it still seems worthwhile to analyse how the regime justifies its behavior, how it depicts the country's role in the world or how it envisions the country's future – and how it makes sense of the world, so to speak.

53 For an example see: "Al-Qadhdhafi Ridicules 'Coup Attempt' Reports," *Foreign Broadcast Information Service*, November 2, 1993; "Al-Qadhdhafi warns no leniency for 'traitors'," *Foreign Broadcast Information Service*, August 4, 1994. Mål-fried Braut-Hegghammer writes furthermore:

> Hardly any information has emerged to shed light on individuals inside the Libyan nuclear establishment or how decisions about the nuclear project were made. Apart from official statements, virtually no Libyan sources shedding light on the nuclear weapons project have been made publicly available. In my field-work and archival searches I have uncovered information about regime debates, actors and perspectives that shed some light on the domestic drivers of the Libyan nuclear weapons project.
>
> (Braut-Hegghammer, "Nuclear Entrepreneurs," 89)

54 Ronald Bruce St. John, "Redefining the Libyan Revolution: The Changing Ideology of Muammar al-Qaddafi," *The Journal of North African Studies* 13, no. 1 (2008).

55 B. Scarcia Amoretti, "Libyan Loneliness in Facing the World: The Challenge of Islam?," in *Islam in foreign policy*, ed. Adeed I. Dawisha (Cambridge and New York: Cambridge University Press, 1983), 62–63.

56 Between 1969 and 1972, there were in fact three unification or cooperation agreements between Egypt and Libya.

57 Mary-Jane Deeb, "The Primacy of Libya's National Interest," in *The Green and the black: Qadhafi's policies in Africa*, ed. René Lemarchand (Bloomington: Indiana University Press, 1988), 33.

58 For a similar assessment, see Solingen, *Nuclear logics*, 214–215. Solingen explicitly writes: "In sum, of all Middle East nuclear aspirants, Libya arguably provides the least support for neorealism" (p. 215).

59 Andrew Gumbel, "Libya Weapons Deal: US Neo-Conservatives Jubilant over WMD Agreement," *Independent*, December 22, 2003.

60 B.W. Jentleson and C.A. Whytock, "Who 'Won' Libya? The Force–Diplomacy Debate and its Implications for Theory and Policy," *International Security* 30, no. 3 (2005).

61 Ray Takeyh, "The Rogue Who Came In from the Cold," *Foreign Affairs* 80, no. 3 (2001): 63–64.

62 Rublee, *Nonproliferation norms. Why states choose nuclear restraint*, 159.
63 *Nonproliferation norms. Why states choose nuclear restraint*, 161.
64 Müller, "Libyens Selbstentwaffnung. Ein Modellfall?"; Solingen, *Nuclear logics*, 213–228.
65 *Nuclear logics*, 226.
66 Ibid.
67 Ibid.
68 Mâlfrid Braut-Hegghammer, "Libya's Nuclear Turnaround: Perspectives from Tripoli," *Middle East Journal* 62, no. 1 (2008): 72.
69 "Libya's Nuclear Turnaround," 72.
70 "Nuclear Entrepreneurs," 11.
71 It should be emphasized again that the interpretation is mostly based on documents that were translated from Arabic to English and not on primary sources in Arabic. Obviously, some of the original conscious or unconscious meaning of language is lost in this process. It would be interesting to see which further (or even differing?) results an Arab-speaking analyst would generate by interpreting the original sources (instead of translations).
72 Again, it is important to underscore that this study does not seek to legitimize or trivialize Gaddafi's actions or make them look harmless. On the contrary, it aims to delineate and interpret the basal narratives that make his policies possible in the first place.
73 I am drawing on the chronological frameworks applied by Bowen, *Libya and nuclear proliferation*; Braut-Hegghammer, "Nuclear Entrepreneurs."
74 "Al-Qadhafi: Evacuation Anniversary Fete," *Foreign Broadcast Information Service*, June 11, 1972; "Al-Qadhafi: Youth Conference Address," *Foreign Broadcast Information Service*, May 14, 1973; "Al-Qadhafi: Interview with Lebanese Newspaper," *Foreign Broadcast Information Service*, January 13, 1975; "Al-Qadhafi: Interview with Reuters," *Foreign Broadcast Information Service*, January 19, 1975; "Al-Qadhafi: Interview with Sunday Telegraph (London)," *Foreign Broadcast Information Service*, May 2, 1976; "Al-Qadhafi: Interview with Indian Magazine," *Foreign Broadcast Information Service*, May 2, 1976; "Al-Qadhafi: Interview with Jana (Tripoli)," *Foreign Broadcast Information Service*, June 7, 1980; "People's Bureau for Foreign Liason: Statement on US Decision to Close People's Bureau," *BBC Summary of World Broadcasts*, May 7, 1981; "Al-Qadhafi: Rally at Umm 'Atiqah Airbase," *Foreign Broadcast Information Service*, June 11, 1984; "Ali Abd as-Salam, Speech to the Non-Aligned Meeting in Malta," *BBC Summary of World Broadcasts*, September 11, 1984; "Libyan General People's Congress Resolutions," *Foreign Broadcast Information Service*, March 2, 1985; "Al-Qadhafi: Interview with NHK Television (Tokyo)," *Foreign Broadcast Information Service*, June 3, 1985; "Communique from the People's Committee of the People's Bureau for Foreign Liaison to UN General Assembly ", *UN General Assembly*, December 31, 1985.
75 "Al-Qadhafi: Evacuation Anniversary Fete." See also "Al-Qadhafi: Youth Conference Address"; "Al-Qadhafi: Interview with Sunday Telegraph (London)."
76 Joffé, "The Role of Islam," 42.
77 "The Role of Islam." Therein Joffé argues that the revolutionaries were well aware that their regime would only survive if it could also destroy the prestige of the existing religious elites.
78 "The Role of Islam," 41.
79 Ibid.
80 "Al-Qadhafi: Youth Conference Address."
81 "Al-Qadhafi: Interview with Indian Magazine."
82 "Al-Qadhafi: Rally at Umm 'Atiqah Airbase."
83 Ibid.

84 "Al-Qadhafi: Youth Conference Address."
85 "Al-Qadhafi: Evacuation Anniversary Fete."
86 Vandewalle, *A history of modern Libya*, 119–120. Spinning this idea of statelessness even further, Gaddafi argues, moreover – in an utterly straightforward but from an analytical perspective absurd and even tautological fashion – that the lack of state institutions also rules out the need for any political opposition within Libya. Asked if his regime was facing any domestic opposition, Gaddafi replied:

> [W]e did not face any political opposition, as there can be no political opposition since there is no government or ruling party or president. What we are facing are remnants of an old society, a society of exploitation, enslavement, dictatorship and classes.
>
> ("Al-Qadhafi: Interview with Jana (Tripoli).")

In a similar vein:

> There is no single Libyan who has a justification for opposing his country now that authority is in the hands of its people, its wealth has reverted to its people, and its weapons are being given to its people to train with.... Affairs in Libya are all very convincing and do not provide any justification or any right for anyone with a minimum of logic to oppose his country. Libya is not a reactionary state. This is not a dictatorship. There is no injustice in Libya. There is no one single section in Libya ruling the remainder of the people.
>
> ("Al-Qadhafi: Rally at Umm 'Atiqah Airbase")

87 "Al-Qadhafi: Evacuation Anniversary Fete."
88 "Al-Qadhafi: Evacuation Anniversary Fete." See also "Al-Qadhafi: Interview with *Sunday Telegraph* (London)"; "Al-Qadhafi: Rally at Umm 'Atiqah Airbase."
89 "Al-Qadhafi: Rally at Umm 'Atiqah Airbase."
90 "Al-Qadhafi: Evacuation Anniversary Fete."
91 "Al-Qadhafi: Evacuation Anniversary Fete." See also "Al-Qadhafi: Rally at Umm 'Atiqah Airbase."
92 "Al-Qadhafi: Interview with NHK Television (Tokyo)"; "Ali Abd as-Salam, Speech to the Non-Aligned Meeting in Malta."
93 As will be seen in the analysis of phase II documents, this narrative (of decolonization and liberation) gains a slightly different connotation in later years when the Gaddafi government aligned itself more closely with its African partners.
94 See, for example: "People's Bureau for Foreign Liason: Statement on US Decision to Close People's Bureau"; "Ali Abd as-Salam, Speech to the Non-Aligned Meeting in Malta."
95 The basic principles of Libya's foreign policy goals of this first phase are summarized in "Libyan General People's Congress Resolutions."
96 "Al-Qadhafi: Evacuation Anniversary Fete." See also "Al-Qadhafi: Youth Conference Address."
97 "Al-Qadhafi: Interview with Lebanese Newspaper."
98 Braut-Hegghammer comes to a similar conclusion:

> In short, there seems to be good reason to assume that national security concerns did play a role in inspiring the al-Qadhafi regime's nuclear weapons ambition. This has been taken to suggest that the national security motive was the main, and perhaps the only, cause of Libya's initial interest in nuclear weapons and the trigger of its efforts to acquire them. However, if we look closer at the Libyan regime's security concerns and challenges it becomes clear that these were neither imminent nor necessary threats necessitating a nuclear weapons option. I will argue that Libya's initial pursuit of nuclear weapons was

not triggered by specific security needs or military requirements. Despite the regime's stated security concerns it is not clear how and why these threats made nuclear weapons seem so desirable.

(Braut-Hegghammer, "Nuclear Entrepreneurs," 95–96)

99 "Al-Qadhafi: Interview with *Sunday Telegraph* (London)"; "Libyan General People's Congress Resolutions."
100 "Al-Qadhafi: Rally at Umm 'Atiqah Airbase."
101 "People's Bureau for Foreign Liason: Statement on US Decision to Close People's Bureau"; "Libyan General People's Congress Resolutions."
102 "Al-Qadhafi: Youth Conference Address."
103 "Al-Qadhafi: Youth Conference Address." In the same speech Gaddafi also claims: "The manufacturing of atom bombs, intercontinental missiles and germ weapons, the aggression against peoples and the looting of their wealth and the threat to occupy the sources of their income are the work of the devil."
104 "Al-Qadhafi: Interview with Lebanese Newspaper."
105 "Al-Qadhafi: Interview with Reuters."
106 It should be emphasized again, however, that the Libyan regime's statements on whether it wants to acquire nuclear weapons or merely civilian applications of nuclear technology remain incoherent and contradictory.
107 "Al-Qadhafi: Interview with *Sunday Telegraph* (London)."
108 "Communique from the People's Committee of the People's Bureau for Foreign Liaison to UN General Assembly." See also "Al-Qadhafi: Rally at Umm 'Atiqah Airbase." Unsurprisingly, this threat perception becomes more defined and concrete two years later: UN General Assembly, "Verbatim Record of the 32nd Meeting" (1986).
109 "Al-Qadhafi: Interview with NHK Television (Tokyo)." It should be noted, however, that FBIS included a note questioning the correctness of the translation of the last sentence.
110 See, for example, "Libyan General People's Congress Resolutions."
111 The documents analyzed for this second period are: "Al-Qadhafi: Rally in Benghazi," *Foreign Broadcast Information Service*, May 8, 1986; "Al-Qadhafi: Speech at 'expulsion of US' anniversary," *Foreign Broadcast Information Service*, June 11, 1986; "Verbatim Record of the 32nd Meeting"; "Al-Qadhafi: Students Revolution Anniversary," *Foreign Broadcast Information Service*, April 7, 1987; "Al-Qadhafi: 1 September Revolution Anniversary," *Foreign Broadcast Information Service*, September 1, 1987; "General People's Congress: Political Communique," *Foreign Broadcast Information Service*, March 10, 1990; "Interview with Jadallah Azzuz al-Talhi, Secretary of the People's Bureau of the Libyan People's Committee for Foreign Liaison, AL-HAWADITH," *Foreign Broadcast Information Service*, March 16, 1990; "Al-Qadhafi: Interview with *Der Spiegel*," *Foreign Broadcast Information Service*, November 12, 1990; "JANA Editorial on Al-Qadhdafi Weapons Remarks," *Foreign Broadcast Information Service*, June 19 1990; "Al-Bishari Interview with AL-HAWADITH," *Foreign Broadcast Information Service*, August 9, 1991; "Al-Bishari: Interview with AL-AHRAM," *Foreign Broadcast Information Service*, March 22, 1992; "Al-Qadhafi: Interview with *Le Figaro*," *Foreign Broadcast Information Service*, March 28, 1992; "Al-Bishari Addresses UN General Assembly (JANA)," *Foreign Broadcast Information Service*, October 6, 1992; "Interview with Umar Mustafa al-Muntasir, Secretary of the Libyan People's Bureau for Foreign Liaison and International Cooperation, AL-DIYAR," *Foreign Broadcast Information Service*, May 6, 1993; "Permanent Mission of the Libyan Arab Jamahiriya to the United Nations Addressed to the Secretary-General," *UN Security Council*, June 23, 1993; "Al-Qadhafi: Speech in Ghadamis," *Foreign Broadcast Information Service*, April 21, 1995.

112 Likewise, the characterization of the country as a small and ultimately fairly power-less actor is retained: "We are a small country, a small and peaceful people. Our resources cannot be compared to those of the major nuclear countries" ("Al-Bishari: Interview with AL-AHRAM").

113 "Al-Qadhafi: Students Revolution Anniversary." What is furthermore striking from a Libyan domestic political perspective is that Gaddafi also uses his idea of empowerment and self-determination to undermine the religious authority of the *ulama*:

> One can just go the mosque and learn the Koran. All mosques should be open for learning the Koran. Anyone who wants to learn the Koran can go to any mosque; he can go and see any religious scholar who would teach him the Koran. One can take the Koran and study it individually.

Without questioning the fact that Libyan society is deeply rooted in Islam, Gaddafi subtly challenges the role of the religious elite in interpreting and teaching the Koran.

114 "Al-Qadhafi: 1 September Revolution Anniversary."

115 See, for example, P. Baehr and P.C. Salzman, "Tribes and Terror in the Middle East: A Conversation with Philip Carl Salzman," *Society* 46, no. 5 (2009): 396. See also Halim Isber Barakat, *The Arab world: society, culture, and state* (Berkeley: University of California Press, 1993), 50–53.

116 Deeb, "The Primacy of Libya's National Interest," 29.

117 Abraham, "The Ambivalence of Nuclear Histories," 64.

118 Of course (and as mentioned in the historiographical reconstruction of the case), Libya maintained a brutal and vigorous network of secret service and secret police institutions to control and suppress its citizens. These institutions, however, aimed to guarantee regime survival and not to guarantee the emergence of a strong Libyan state in a politically comprehensive, inclusive understanding of the term (quite to the contrary, in fact).

119 Carol E. Harrison and Ann Johnson, "Introduction: Science and National Identity," *Osiris* 24(2009).

120 "Al-Qadhafi: Speech at 'Expulsion of US' Anniversary." In a similar vein, the government acknowledges several times that it has failed to achieve its modernization and development ambitions; for example: "our aspiration to achieve development has been facing some difficulties" ("Al-Bishari Addresses UN General Assembly (JANA)").

121 "Al-Qadhafi: Speech at 'Expulsion of US' Anniversary." See also "Al-Qadhafi: Rally in Benghazi" and "Permanent Mission of the Libyan Arab Jamahiriya to the United Nations Addressed to the Secretary-General."

122 "Al-Qadhafi: Rally in Benghazi."

123 Cf. Miroslav Nincic, *Renegade regimes: confronting deviant behavior in world politics* (New York: Columbia University Press, 2005).

124 See, for example, Ibrahim Al-Bashiri, Chairman of the Libyan General People's Committee for Foreign Liaison and International Cooperation: "We are ready to die for our freedom and dignity" ("Al-Bishari: Interview with AL-AHRAM").

125 "General People's Congress: Political Communique."

126 "Al-Qadhafi: 1 September Revolution Anniversary."

> [I] wish to put forward a plan for an Arab union.... This is because the Arab nation is in danger except through Arab unity. I ask for nothing from this Arab unity other than two things: First, that there should be a defensive capability for defending the Arab homeland, Arab sovereignty, and Arab life from the outside threat; second, that all Arab economic capabilities be pooled for building an Arab economic force for realizing a better life for the Arab people.

127 "Al-Qadhafi: Rally in Benghazi"; "Al-Qadhafi: Speech at 'Expulsion of US' Anniversary."

128 "Interview with Jadallah Azzuz al-Talhi, Secretary of the People's Bureau of the Libyan People's Committee for Foreign Liaison, AL-HAWADITH."

129 "Al-Qadhafi: Rally in Benghazi." See also "Al-Qadhafi: Speech in Ghadamis"; John Lancaster, "Libyan Pilgrimage Flights Challenge Sanctions," *The Washington Post*, April 20, 1995.

130 Joffé, "The Role of Islam," 44.

131 This finding is also interesting from the point of view of language theory and IR theory, since it calls for a refined understanding of the role of language and rhetoric in IR. The allusions to jihad in Gaddafi's Ghadamis speech seem to suggest that "jihad" is indeed merely used as a rhetorical tool that is supposed to arouse and mobilize the masses, in the particular case of this speech. It does not, in other words, unfold into a dominant framing of reality within the Libyan discourse. To use the terminology of language psychology and psychological studies on rhetoric, one could say: the notion of jihad seems to be only infrequently applied, and mainly in order to influence the "peripheral route" of persuasion – it arouses the sentiment of the audience without developing into and providing an argumentatively sound and logically stringent frame ("central route"). Cf. Michael Billig, "Political Rhetoric," in *Oxford handbook of political psychology*, ed. David O. Sears, Leonie Huddy, and Robert Jervis (Oxford and New York: Oxford University Press, 2003). Hence, the jihad notion may be successfully applied in one specific instance, without evolving into a well-developed, entrenched interpretation of a historically and socially complex situation. Such a metaphor, however, has the potential to develop into more far-reaching cognitive devices to structure and interpret "reality," as Chilton illustrates. Paul A. Chilton, *Security metaphors: cold war discourse from containment to common house*, Conflict and consciousness (New York: Peter Lang, 1996).

132 "Al-Qadhafi: Rally in Benghazi"; "Al-Qadhafi: Speech at 'Expulsion of US' Anniversary."

133 "Al-Qadhafi: Rally in Benghazi"; "Al-Qadhafi: Speech at 'Expulsion of US' Anniversary."

134 "Al-Qadhafi: Speech at 'Expulsion of US' Anniversary."

135 "Al-Bishari: Interview with AL-AHRAM." In a speech to the UN General Assembly, al-Bishari moreover stated: "Mr. President, you can rely on my country's cooperation with you" ("Al-Bishari Addresses UN General Assembly (JANA)"). See also "Al-Qadhafi: Speech at 'Expulsion of US' Anniversary."

136 September 1, 1987, Gaddafi: September 1 Revolution Anniversary.

137 November 12, 1990, Gaddafi: Interview with *Der Spiegel*.

138 The idea of an "Islamic bomb" in itself offers an interesting avenue for further research: so far not much has been written about the link between Islamic traditions and the religious and ethical (un-)acceptability of nuclear arms. One of the few theoretical analyses is the contribution by Sohail Hashmi. He writes that "Muslim scholars have yet to explore in a detailed and systematic fashion how nuclear, chemical, and biological weapons relate to the Islamic ethics of war." However, Hashmi also argues that much of the WMD-related concern voiced by Muslims is not primarily spurred by a desire to acquire an "Islamic" nuclear capacity, but rather stems from "the broader third world critique of the double standards applied by the West" (Sohail H. Hashmi, "Islamic ethics and Weapons of Mass Destruction. An Argument for Nonproliferation," in *Ethics and weapons of mass destruction: religious and secular perspectives*, ed. Sohail H. Hashmi and Steven P. Lee (Cambridge: Cambridge University Press, 2004)).

139 "Al-Qadhafi: Interview with *Der Spiegel*." See also "JANA Editorial on Al-Qadhdafi Weapons Remarks."

140 "Al-Bishari: Interview with AL-AHRAM." See also "Interview with Umar Mustafa al-Muntasir, Secretary of the Libyan People's Bureau for Foreign Liaison and International Cooperation, AL-DIYAR."

141 "Al-Qadhafi: Interview with *Le Figaro*."

142 "Al-Qadhafi: Speech in Ghadamis."

143 Elsewhere, the Libyan regime denounces the international sanctions as "a living example of the policy of double standards" and as proof of a "discriminatory attitude against a Member State to deprive it of its right to take advantage of the technical cooperation programmes" ("Permanent Mission of the Libyan Arab Jamahiriya to the United Nations Addressed to the Secretary-General").

144 "Al-Qadhafi: Interview with *Le Figaro*." Strikingly, however, other statements paint a different picture: "Neither Libya's material and manpower nor its technological progress allows us to build nuclear weapons" ("Interview with Umar Mustafa al-Muntasir, Secretary of the Libyan People's Bureau for Foreign Liaison and International Cooperation, AL-DIYAR").

145 The following documents are interpreted in this section: "Foreign Minister Denies Chemical Weapons Plant (MENA)," *Foreign Broadcast Information Service*, April 11, 1996; "Al-Muntasir: Interview with Al-Sharq Al-Awsat," *Foreign Broadcast Information Service*, April 13, 1996; "Al-Qadhafi: Interview with CNN," *Lexis Nexis*, April 15, 1996; "Al-Qadhafi: Speech in Sirte (Qadhafi comments on trial of Lockerbie suspects, African troops for Congo)," *BBC Monitoring Middle East*, October 1, 1998; "Statement by Abuzed Omar Dorda to the 2000 NPT Review Conference," *2000 Review Conference of the Parties to the NPT, Final Document*, April 25, 2000; "Al-Qadhafi Comments on Spread of Anthrax in USA (JANA)," *BBC Monitoring Middle East*, October 18, 2001; "Al-Shawish Statement to JANA," *BBC Monitoring Middle East*, December 25, 2002; "Libyan Foreign Ministry: Statement to JANA," *BBC Monitoring Middle East*, March 22, 2002; "Libyan WMD: Tripoli's Statement in Full; Saif Aleslam Al-Qadhafi, "Libyan–American Relations," *Middle East Policy* 10, no. 1 (2003); "Al-Fazzani: Interview with Al-Sharq Al Awsat," *Foreign Broadcast Information Service*, April 7, 1997; "GPC Foreign Liaison: Statement to JANA," *BBC Summary of World Broadcasts*, May 9, 2000.

146 Likewise, the characterization of the country as a small and ultimately somewhat powerless actor is retained: "We are a small country, a small and peaceful people. Our resources cannot be compared to those of the major nuclear countries" ("Al-Bishari: Interview with AL-AHRAM").

147 "GPC Foreign Liaison: Statement to JANA." See also "Al-Muntasir: Interview with Al-Sharq Al-Awsat"; "Libyan Foreign Ministry: Statement to JANA."

148 "Libyan WMD: Tripoli's Statement in Full."

149 "Libyan–American Relations," 36.

150 Ibid., 44.

151 It is important to keep in mind that the article was written in late 2002 or early 2003 at the latest. This casts doubt on the view that Libya only changed once the Gaddafi regime had "learnt its lesson" from the Iraq war in 2003.

152 "Al-Qadhafi: Interview with CNN." See also "Al-Fazzani: Interview with Al-Sharq Al Awsat."

153 "Al-Qadhafi: Interview with CNN."

154 "Al-Fazzani: Interview with Al-Sharq Al Awsat." See also "Al-Qadhafi: Interview with CNN."

155 "Al-Muntasir: Interview with Al-Sharq Al-Awsat."

156 "GPC Foreign Liaison: Statement to JANA."

157 "Al-Qadhafi Comments on Spread of Anthrax in USA (JANA)."

158 "Al-Qadhafi: Speech in Sirte."

159 "Al-Muntasir: Interview with Al-Sharq Al-Awsat." See also "Al-Qadhafi: Interview with CNN."

160 "Al-Muntasir: Interview with Al-Sharq Al-Awsat."

161 "Libyan Foreign Ministry: Statement to JANA."

162 "Al-Shawish Statement to JANA."

163 Müller, "Libyens Selbstentwaffnung. Ein Modellfall?," I.
164 Latham, "Constructing National Security: Culture and Identity in Indian Arms Control and Disarmament Practice."
165 Müller, "Libyens Selbstentwaffnung. Ein Modellfall?," 23.
166 Braut-Hegghammer, "Nuclear Entrepreneurs," 89.
167 Jasanoff's phrase aptly captures this challenge: "A successful nation has to be able to produce the idea of nationhood as an emergent, intersubjective property; without this connection of belief, it remains a hallow construct, ruling without assent, and hence unstably" (Sheila Jasanoff, "Ordering Knowledge, Ordering Society," in *States of knowledge. The co-production of science and social order*, ed. Sheila E. Jasanoff (London: Routledge, 2006).
168 Müller describes this as the "high ambition to play a leading role in the Arab world and for the Arab cause and to neutralize Israel's nuclear weapons potential" (Müller, "Libyens Selbstentwaffnung. Ein Modellfall?," I (my translation)). See also Rublee, *Nonproliferation norms. Why states choose nuclear restraint*, 161.
169 This verdict is supported by a statement made by Gaddafi in 2004 (after the sample period of this study): "In 1969 and early 1970s we did not reflect on where or against whom we could use the nuclear bomb. Such issues were not considered. All that was important was to build the bomb" (quoted in Braut-Hegghammer, "Libya's Nuclear Turnaround," 60–61).
170 Lisa Anderson, for example, argues that Libya's nuclear reversal is "consistent with a whole set of things the Libyans have been doing for the last couple of years, all of them intended to bring Libya back into the family of what we call 'civilized nations.' It's another significant step along that road" (Lisa Anderson, "Libyan Expert: Qaddafi, Desperate to End Libya's Isolation, Sends a 'Gift' to President Bush"). See also Ronald Bruce St. John, "Libya Is Not Iraq: Preemptive Strikes, WMD and Diplomacy," *The Middle East Journal* 58, no. 3 (2004).

Conclusion

Why do some states acquire nuclear weapons whereas others abandon their nuclear aspirations? This question was the starting point for the present study. I have argued that current theoretical approaches to nuclear (non-)proliferation leave us ill-equipped to understand the complexities and intricacies of nuclear reversal. A pragmatist-interactionist account was devised in order to give us a different perspective on the nuclear trajectories of states. What are the potential benefits of a pragmatist approach to the study of nuclear (non-)proliferation? And what are the broader implications both for theory-building in IR and for our practical dealings with potential proliferators? I use this final chapter to summarize and weave together key theoretical and empirical findings. I start by recapping the characteristics and premises of a pragmatist view of (state) action. The next section then presents the core findings of the case studies on nuclear reversal in Switzerland and Libya. Finally, I outline how these findings could be applied in order to supplement and enrich existing non-proliferation efforts.

Theoretical premises

Pragmatism starts from the assumption that all human activity is based on a set of beliefs or interpretations that we develop in order to understand a situation and to understand the particular environment in which our action takes place. Before we can act, we need to define and interpret the situation and outline possible courses of action. This implies that human beings do not act solely upon an objectively given stimulus, but come to it with a set of beliefs – about the situation, about their counterparts, about their own role, about their means. These beliefs then provide the background against which human actors construct their behavior – they are "rules for action." But how do these beliefs emerge in the first place – what are the central characteristics of this phase of defining and interpreting the situation?

To recall, I have argued that five empirical concerns are key to the pragmatist approach to IR. First, a strong emphasis on process means that the phenomena of the social world are conceptualized as being non-static, permanently in flux and open to change. Consequently, social life is depicted as an ongoing interactive – and mutually constitutive – process between the environment (whether social or natural) and human agents. Second, pragmatism's focus on meaning-making, interpretation and language urges us to conceptualize human action as a process of permanent interpretation (semiosis), in which the actor gives meaning to the components of his or her environment. Meaning, however, is regarded neither as an inherent property of an object, nor is it established solely by the individual's cognitive psychological or mental processes. Likewise, meaning is never completely fixed once and for all, but contains the possibility of change and alteration. Third, pragmatism stresses the intersubjective and social character of meaning-making and ensuing action. Accordingly, meaning-making is not the result of purely individual cognitive-psychological processes. Nor is human action merely the outcome of solipsistic choices. Instead, the individual, and with this any social action, is densely and co-constitutively tied into the sociality that surrounds the actor. The notion of intersubjectivity, then, comprises two aspects: the form of communicative action between social actors in which objects and their meanings and possible courses of action are continuously renegotiated; and the likewise ongoing co-constitution of the actors involved. Fourth, these aspects allow for a recovery of human agency, since it is assumed that the individual does not merely react to a given stimulus, but selects, negotiates and interprets it first before acting upon it. In a similar vein, human action does not happen on the basis of pre-established needs. Nonetheless, most action occurs in the form of ritualized habits: action takes place on the basis of internalized rules or behavioral patterns. Only if this habit or routine is disrupted by doubt (i.e., by an unknown, challenging crisis situation) do actors have to ("creatively") re-evaluate and redefine the situation in order to develop a new belief concerning the future course of their actions. Fifth, these assumptions lead to and are supplemented by more sophisticated, multi-layered notions of actorness, self and identity. The identity of the self (or of any other actor) is assumed not to be fixed, but is instead constructed as part of an ongoing process. This means that identity is never static, predetermined or fundamentally given, but is always open to change. It is therefore a process rather than a stable structure, since it has to be reworked and regenerated; it has to be "achieved" in interplay with and taking into consideration other actors. Such a conceptualization prohibits us from reducing identity to little more than a stable, given variable. Instead, it enables the integration of non-essentialist intersubjectivity into the analysis, thereby allowing a relational understanding of the interplay between actors and their social and material environment.

In sum, a pragmatist-interactionist framework of analysis overcomes the positivist notion of a given, fixed reality and instead presupposes that threats, national interests and political "re-actions" are understood as socially constructed and created. In doing so, this approach emphasizes the contingency and language dependency of meaning and brings political agency – that is, the creative, mindful behavior of social/political actors – back into our analysis.

Metatheoretically, these empirical principles are accompanied by a deeply embedded call for an anti-foundationalist approach to social science which stresses that knowledge is always preliminary and contingent, and which discards the search for universal grand theories. According to these claims, social science research cannot achieve secured, universal truth claims, since scientists lack access to a detached, objective and neutral "Archimedean" point of judgment. "Science is social practice."[1] Hence, scientific knowledge is not merely discovered "out there" in a mind-external world, but "enacted from a particular viewpoint"[2] and with the help of our linguistically mediated analytical toolkit. The absence of metatheoretical certainties implies, moreover, that we need to reconsider "what to expect" from social science undertakings. Rather than conceptualizing scientific progress in a linear fashion, seeing it as a ladder that ultimately leads ever closer to "the truth," we should picture the increase in scientific knowledge as a net that becomes ever more densely knotted and that allows us to construe more comprehensive, convincing readings of the phenomenon under scrutiny.

As a follow-up to the debates between positivists and non-positivists outlined at the beginning of this book we can thus argue that a pragmatist approach would help us to overcome the quarrels that have long shaped the development of IR. Metatheoretical feuds are put on hold, since we cannot ultimately establish an answer to the question "what is"; nor can we define conclusively how to best think about the world. And yet, to suspend these debates is not to imply that theorizing about the world is impossible from a pragmatist point of view. On the contrary: the fact that we do not know what "really exists" merely means that we should settle for what we perceive to be real. "If men define situations as real, they are real in their consequences"[3] – this is perhaps the most succinct way to phrase the pragmatist core. In other words: we act upon what we believe to be real – no matter if it is "the really real."[4] Ultimately, this notion of social science enables us to bridge the gap that has emerged between metatheorizing on the one hand and problem-solving on the other.[5] Being a theory of action, pragmatism explicitly calls for a suspension of infinite metatheoretical quarrels and for more attention to the complexities of "real world" problems and concrete political challenges – yet in a theoretically reflexive way. Furthermore, instead of elaborating transhistoric, universal grand theories, pragmatist research affirms the historic contingency of truth and knowledge. "[M]eaningful understanding, social critique and emancipation"[6] thus replace theory-building, forecasting and prediction as the primary goals of social science.

Theoretical implications

What follows from these theoretical premises? I argue that pragmatism gives rise to two implications. First, it calls for "theoretical modesty" and for the abandonment of large-scale, universal causal theories. Second, it delivers the potential for cross-paradigmatic dialogue and perhaps even synthesis in IR. I will address each of these dimensions in turn.

Contingent generalizations and scenarios

Theory-building in social science is characterized by two opposing views. On the one hand, researchers aim to establish generalizations that allow the making of meaningful statements which cover a larger number of like-events and like-issues. To achieve this goal they are prepared to reduce the complexity and density of their explanatory accounts and to focus on a specific cut-out of the issue at stake in order to achieve comparability. Non-positivists, on the other hand, maintain that universal, transhistoric theories in social science are either impossible or "close to trivial."[7] This view often attracts support from historians, who point to the singularity and contingency of events and issues, and urge us to pay sufficient attention to the actual details of social processes. These two contradictory expectations of social science theorizing represent the existing extreme poles of the debate.

Pragmatism advocates a middle-ground position between the two poles of the debate. Its emphasis on the complexity of agency and identity as well as its highlighting of intersubjective processes of meaning-making call into question (positivist) attempts to establish large-scale, transhistoric, universal causal laws. According to pragmatist reasoning, it is not possible to immediately test our research results against a given external reality. In a similar vein, we do not detect knowledge about the social world, but rather enact it through our (academic) interventions. Rejecting, moreover, the artificial distinction between clear-cut causes and effects or dependent and independent variables, pragmatism calls for increased attention to be paid to the complexities and intricacies of social phenomena. These qualifications notwithstanding, pragmatism does not relinquish theoretically sound and stringent knowledge production to other social science approaches. While certainly opposing the positivist ideal of large-scale theorizing, pragmatism does not subscribe to the "nihilist" counter-position either. However, from a pragmatist perspective we are urged to pay tribute to human agency, reflexivity and historical contingency. This cannot be accomplished in large-scale, grand theoretical accounts that aspire to parsimony, causality and universality, and that "define away" those parameters that do not fit into their projection. Instead of achieving "systematic simplification,"[8] our research should mirror "the messiness of a given 'real world' problem in all its complexity."[9] Only when we have managed to increase our "orientation in the field" can we proceed to map classes of phenomena or recurring typologies.[10]

Against the background of these premises it appears necessary to limit our explanation and theory-building efforts to the development of – always preliminary, revisable – contingent generalizations and middle-range theories. This may well imply that we should draw extensively on a single case in order to excavate the vast and interconnected intricacies and "the wealth of historical experiences that are represented in each individual case."[11] It also implies that we should refrain from using history merely as a pool of "stylized facts"[12] that we conveniently draw upon in order to substantiate our universalist claims. The pragmatist accentuation of "creativity" demands instead that we acknowledge that human action is situated in contingency and potential openness.[13]

Such an understanding of human action also has deep implications for social scientists' attempts to predict and forecast future courses of action. It also affects the way in which we can make our academically generated knowledge amenable to political practitioners. If we indeed take the pragmatist ethos of relevance seriously, then it is expedient to suspend our efforts to give policy advice based on concrete, rigorous prediction.[14] It is better to rely on *scenarios* or *explanatory narratives* instead, since these make for more comprehensive and richer forward reasoning in that they acknowledge contingency.[15] Rather than trying to pinpoint the outcome of one or a few variables, both scenarios and narratives outline possible plots or stories regarding the way in which a specific issue is likely to develop in the future. The resulting "sketch of the future" will contain a complex and multi-layered web of probable "cause and effect" mechanisms rather than a clear-cut causal relationship. More fundamentally, they differ from classical predictions in that they emphasize contingency and uncertainty and question the achievability of point prognosis. Bernstein *et al.* describe the benefits of a scenario-based approach in the following way:

> Scenarios are not predictions; rather they start with the assumption that the future is unpredictable and tell alternative stories of how the future may unfold.... Scenarios are impressionistic pictures that build on different combinations of causal variables that may also take on different values in different scenarios. Thus it is possible to construct scenarios without pre-existing firm proof of theoretical claims that meet strict positivist standards. The foundation for scenarios is made up of provisional assumptions and causal claims. These become the subject of revision and updating more than testing. A set of scenarios often contains competing or at least contrasting assumptions.[16]

If we follow this approach to forward reasoning, we will be able to formulate more complex descriptions of how a certain issue is likely to develop – under specified circumstances – in the future. Undoubtedly, such scenarios will *not* contribute to precision and simplification; they will *not* provide strict guidance and certainty on which to base policy decisions. However, they generate a more "accurate" picture of the complexities and the muddiness of the "real world" and remind us of the inherent openness of social action.

IR synthesis?

In IR disciplinary terms, pragmatism has, moreover, the potential to initiate cross-paradigmatic dialogue that may lead to the accommodation of existing paradigms and perhaps even careful, partial synthesis among them. Drawing on Katzenstein and Sil's pioneering work on "Analytic Eclecticism,"[17] I briefly outline how pragmatism contributes to this undertaking and what the benefits of such an approach to IR could be.

Katzenstein and Sil's point of departure is the often-voiced lament that the discipline of IR has lost sight of its key objects of study, and that it has contributed little to the understanding of crucial global political developments of the last decades.[18] One of the primary causes that they (in line with many other authors, as we have already seen in Chapter 1) identify is the attention-consuming intra-disciplinary wrangle over metatheoretical questions. They claim furthermore that adhering to a predefined research tradition merely privileges inquiry into those aspects that are easily amenable to this particular school of thought. Aspects of the social world that run counter to the mainstays of each approach are, on the other hand, often sacrificed and disregarded, since they do not fit within the given scope of research. Ultimately, this leads to the reification of existing accounts rather than to the discovery of new insights and previously unknown explanations. In addition, while a narrow approach is advantageous for the establishment of parsimonious, lean and "crisp" generalizations, it is necessarily accompanied by a high level of simplification that makes a more thorough understanding of multifaceted issues impossible – and which appears to be somewhat incongruous, given the complexities of "real life." Katzenstein and Sil's concept of analytic eclecticism is consequently based on the assumption that the stringent singular approaches currently dominant in IR are limited in their capacity to uncover the complex web of interactions that surround social phenomena. Instead, they assert, in order to overcome these restrictions a "multi-perspective" research strategy is needed. The analysis of Switzerland's and Libya's nuclear policies certainly lends support to this demand for a multi-perspective research approach: both cases illustrate that we cannot sufficiently account for the decisions by merely focusing on one theoretical school. This does not imply that we need to "reinvent the wheel." On the contrary, our analysis will benefit more if we manage to integrate and draw upon existing rationales.

While the call for dialogue and synthesis in IR is not new,[19] most previous attempts at synthesizing have in fact attempted more to subsume "deviant" approaches under the dominant metatheoretical – positivist – paradigm. The goal was to homogenize the field rather than to draw upon its plurality. A pragmatist-inspired dialogical approach, on the other hand, could help us to accommodate existing approaches without merely subsuming them under an already-existing dominant heading. Precisely because pragmatism suspends unsolvable metatheoretical disputes and calls for more attention to be paid to the practical problems that we encounter along the way, it allows for the combination of seemingly opposing or even incommensurable concepts and theories. It does not, in other words, abolish existing theories and accounts, but rather draws upon them and engages them in order to develop a wider account of overlapping and interrelating explanatory components. A pragmatist analytic eclecticism thus "offers complex causal stories that incorporate different types of mechanisms, as defined and used in diverse research traditions."[20] It does so by starting its research inquiry with a given problem rather than with a predetermined set of theoretical tools: instead of forcing the subject matter of our study into a predefined analytical framework, we should pay tribute to the potential complexities of social life and allow a greater scope for our analysis. As a consequence, an inquiry based on analytic eclecticism probably delivers an explanation that involves:

> a more complex configuration of mechanisms than is typical in most social scientific research. But greater complexity is precisely what policy-makers and ordinary actors contend with as they address substantive problems in the course of everyday politics. Scholars who wish to have their research speak to such problems must also be willing to contend with complexity.[21]

Empirical findings

The empirical findings of both analyses suggest that we can gain valuable supplementary knowledge regarding the foundations of states' nuclear decision-making by looking at the cases through a pragmatist-interactionist lens. The close examination of underlying narratives and frames reveals insights that remain hidden if we merely proceed from a rational actor model of utility maximization. It is important to note that a pragmatist-inspired analysis does not necessarily refute existing theoretical accounts, but rather complements and extends them. This is perhaps most visible with respect to the broad theoretical literature on identity as a key driver of nuclearization. Both case studies reveal that a comprehensive explanation of the countries' nuclear ambitions does indeed need to encompass the "identity dimension" if it is to deliver a convincing account. However, the pragmatist analysis of shifting frames and meanings also indicates that "identity" is a concept too vague to allow for any meaningful conclusions. In a similar vein, a pragmatist analysis questions the realist notion of objectively given threats and interests; it instead directs our attention to the processes of linguistic construction and interpretation. The analyses of the two cases thus support the claim that simply alluding to traditional security rationales seems insufficient to account for the nuclear behavior of either Switzerland or Libya. This does not imply that the security environment in which each of the countries was embedded did not matter at all. On the contrary, in both discourses we find multiple allusions to threats and perceived insecurities. However, these references were often fairly incoherent and vague; they did not provide a comprehensive narrative of existential threats. Moreover, in both countries the security frame was just one of many others that figured even more importantly.

The present analysis also speaks to and connects with those studies that draw on economic rationales or on the role of norms. We do not find much evidence in support of a liberal, economy-oriented explanation of either the Swiss or the Libyan case. Neither Switzerland nor Libya has abandoned its nuclear weapons research program for purely economic reasons. Both cases suggest, nevertheless, that the economic advantages of nuclear reversal were at least taken into account. The influence of a non-proliferation or non-nuclear norm is similarly complex and ambivalent. It seems reasonable to conclude that in neither of the two cases were decision-makers immediately reacting to a neatly distillable norm; in other words, in neither case did a norm clearly trigger a specific course of action. Yet it appears that, at least in the Swiss case, the global normative discourse on the detrimental effects of nuclear weapons influenced the debate over time.

These findings, too, underline the benefits of an analytical approach that sheds light on the processes of meaning-making and interpretation. Merely referring to rational actor assumptions that explain purposive human behavior as little more than utility maximization does not provide a sufficiently comprehensive picture. Rather, the cases reveal that notions such as identity or prestige, which both figure prominently in the literature on nuclear proliferation, are crucial building blocks for an explanation of the two cases – but that we need to dissect them more carefully. Thus the analysis shows that in both cases, for a comprehensive understanding of the developments we need to use more refined and detailed analytical tools to trace the emergence of and shift in these concepts and their meanings over time and to disentangle the way in which the discourses are shaped through a contestation between dominant and challenging political forces. The recourse to an alternative, pragmatist mode of reasoning is compelling if we wish to generate new insights that are able to complement existing accounts. The following summary of the key results of each case supports this claim.

Nuclear reversal in Switzerland

Looking at the Swiss case through a pragmatist-shaped lens reveals a number of aspects that appear crucial if we want to more fully understand why Switzerland initially showed a significant interest in nuclear weapons, but eventually decided not to carry these plans into effect. A realist analysis cannot convincingly account for these developments during the 1950s and 1960s. Such an explanation would lead us to assume that the evolution of Switzerland's nuclear ambitions was triggered by a clearly discernible, existential threat. Likewise, the later abandonment of these plans accordingly resulted from the disappearance of such a threat perception. Indeed, the Swiss debate was interwoven with perceptions of threat and danger. Yet these perceptions were far from unambiguous and well defined, or even clearly articulated. Rather, the analysis suggests that while the perceived threat remained substantial over the course of the debate, it was vague and ill defined. The executive's focus on the dangers posed by the expected disruption of the nuclear monopoly and the subsequent spread of nuclear weapons was matched by a deep fear of communist expansion among a large part of the population. Given this ambiguity, it is also unconvincing to argue that once the threat disappeared, the government decided to forgo its nuclear ambitions. Neither the historiographic reconstruction nor the discursive analysis supports such a distinct conclusion. And, indeed, if we recall the great volatility of the East–West security situation in the late 1950s and 1960s, it seems at least questionable to assume that a feeling of protection and safety found its way into Switzerland's security calculation and ultimately caused the country to abandon its interest in nuclear weapons. To put it differently, it seems at least disputable that a country that had long felt existentially threatened would suddenly forgo nuclearization just because it had experienced a couple of years of tentative global relaxation.

Instead of merely limiting our explanation to abstract and presumably pre-defined security considerations, we should thus pay more attention to the domestic interpretation of the nuclear weapons question. The realist pursuit of theoretical parsimony necessarily leads to a disregard of the broad political contestation that took place in Switzerland during the early 1960s. However, an analysis of the central beliefs and narratives helps us to make sense of this contestation and brings to light two broad ideational strands which explain how the changing course of action became possible. First, the idea of neutrality changed from a notion that focused on isolationist neutrality toward one that emphasized more humanitarian duties. In the early years the debate regarding Switzerland's self-perception was predominantly influenced by two central frames: proponents of the nuclear weapons option alluded to Switzerland's "heroic" history as staunchly neutral ("armed neutrality"); they referred to the provisions of international law in order to substantiate the country's legal obligation to acquire "the most effective weapons available." The country was thus pictured as a defensive, but resistant and "hardy" neutral that was required to deploy the best military means available.

During the 1960s, however, the focus of the debate shifted and a different frame gained predominance: the fairly legalistic interpretation of (the obligations of) neutrality gave way to a politics-oriented interpretation, which saw a more proactive and above all humanitarian foreign policy role for Switzerland. This newly emerging interpretation of neutrality led to a questioning of the rightfulness and appropriateness of nuclear weapons as a means of defense. Ultimately, the belief gained hold that a humanitarian notion of neutrality was incongruous with the possession and deployment of nuclear weapons.

Along with this revised concept of neutrality came a reconsideration of Switzerland's foreign policy role. The debate in its early phase was mainly forged around notions of passivity, caution and (political) powerlessness; only the anti-nuclear movement recurrently outlined a proactive foreign policy stance and emphasized the country's potential and duty to become involved in global matters and to strive for global peace. Later documents show, however, that this more active, "peace-mongering" vision became integrated into the discursive mainstream. The prevalent self-perception was one that envisioned a more involved and active role for Switzerland; it gave more weight to "proactivity" in foreign affairs.

A third narrative related to the altered ideas of neutrality and foreign policy centered on the country's defense posture. Again, we see that this narrative underwent significant change: the focus shifted from the protection of the country as a military-political entity toward a more civilian notion of defense. The new defense concept that emerged in the mid-1960s reflects this change, since for the first time it called for the protection of the civilian population. This is a major modification compared to earlier manifestations. To recap: originally, the military had envisioned the deployment of tactical nuclear weapons even on Swiss territory, should the enemy manage to breach the lines of defense. In later documents we find a clear revision and reconsideration of these principles. In the 1966 defense blueprint the protection of civilians took center stage; accordingly it was argued that the needs and requirements of the civilian population had to be taken more seriously. The Mirage affair of 1964 caused a fundamental loss of confidence in state institutions in general and in the military's grand power projects in particular, and thus certainly contributed to these changed defense principles. The military appears to have lost its previously uncontested role as the sole provider of protection, defense and security, as the population not only grew more and more skeptical of the ongoing militarization and of large-scale defense technology procurements, but also increasingly questioned the effectiveness of military defense means in the face of nuclear war.

These developments and discursive shifts, however, may only fully be understood if we also take into account another major aspect that was uncovered in the analysis: the altered view of what nuclear weapons *are* and the effects they cause. In the early years of the debate, pro-nuclear voices of all affiliations claimed that the military benefits of nuclear weapons outweighed any harmful side-effects and that the negative impact was controllable. Opponents, on the other hand, rebutted this optimistic view and focused instead on the weapons' non-discriminatory environmental and health effects. Furthermore, they emphasized the fact that the population could not be protected against them. In the course of the debate the prevalent interpretation then changed: the weapons ceased to be viewed as a symbol of progress and modernity, as an "almost conventional" device of warfare, and as an ethically justified means of protection, and came to be predominantly viewed as "useless" and "harmful." Within less than a decade, therefore the attributes of nuclear weapons changed from modern, prestigious, legitimate, clean and ethically justified, toward inappropriate, ineffective and militarily, politically, economically and environmentally dangerous.

In sum, these altered interpretations of Switzerland's self-perception, of its defense conception and the role of nuclear weapons provide a web of frames that need to be taken into account if we want to reach a better – more comprehensive – understanding of the country's nuclear reversal.

Nuclear reversal in Libya

The Libyan case obviously differs from the Swiss example in terms of the organization and composition of the discursive realm. The number of participants is clearly limited; for much of the time frame under consideration Muammar al-Gaddafi (and a small circle of government officials) occupied the position of central speaker. As a consequence, the publicly accessible and traceable textual protocols are far less diverse than in Switzerland. A detailed analysis of the Libyan case nevertheless indicates that a pragmatist-inspired approach can uncover insights that remain outside the scope of more traditional inquiries. The following aspects stand out.

In the immediate post-revolutionary years, Libya's self-perception was shaped by a set of narratives which characterize the nation as small, tribalistic and Islamic. On the other hand, and despite its smallness and limited power, Libya saw itself as an active player on the global scene. It was depicted as a pioneer of socialism and anti-capitalism and as a global power in the fight against inequality and oppression – hence as an actor with the right and the duty to fight against perceived global injustices such as post-colonial suppression. It is this self-perception and identity conception that fueled much of Libya's foreign policy behavior and its self-righteous interference in regional and global politics. Together with a narrative of empowerment, this self-perception provides the justification for a "revolutionary" foreign policy – a policy which challenges the global status quo and which calls for an "empowerment of the powerless." From this perspective it makes sense that we find a large number of references calling for Libyan involvement in world politics or that vehemently criticize the distribution of power within the international system.

However, what is particularly important about the Libyan case, and what distinguishes Libya's identity discourse from other examples, is the clear lack of explicit references to the nation state and the absence of a narrative of Libyan statehood. The idea of the Libyan nation remains vague and disembodied. The Libyan state did not manage to instill and spread among its citizens the idea of Libyan statehood as socially shared property that is to be cherished. This could also explain why the Libyan discourse on nuclear weapons never incorporated references to nuclear weapons as emblems of *national* technological and scientific progress or as emblems of *national* achievement. To put it differently, in the Libyan discourse nuclear weapons never achieved a symbolically laden status as embodiments of the state's expertise and technological competence. Rather, the possession of nuclear weapons was regarded merely as a symbolic expression of global equality. This may also be due to the fact that there is no evidence of a coherent view of Libya's relation to modernity: while the country is time and again characterized as a motor and vanguard of social and political change, we also find several instances where the country's tribal, pre-modern traits are emphasized. This double-edged characterization undermines the rise of an elaborate and convincing narrative that could link the possession of nuclear weapons with state modernity, state power or state competence. Arguably, this very lack of a state narrative contributed significantly to Libya's eventually unsuccessful nuclear endeavors, since there was no compelling national frame to provide sufficient momentum for a fully fledged, decades-long research program.

At least for several years, the lack of a state narrative was successfully compensated for by the alternative frame of Arab unity and Arab nationalism. The interpellation of "the Arab nation" provided a powerful ideological pillar – in addition to those of socialism and equal rights – for much of Libya's foreign policy behavior. It is one of the fundamental and most frequently invoked frames in all the documents of the first two decades. Moreover, the idea of Arab unity and of the Arab nation is the common thread between almost all the relevant statements on nuclear proliferation during the first two decades. It is the "Arab nation" that is the envisioned acquirer of nuclear technology and nuclear weapons. If mentioned at all, Libya merely figures as an "agent" of empowerment for the Arab world or as a "motor." The acquisition of nuclear weapons is hardly ever justified on Libyan national grounds, but rather in terms of an Arab requirement. Unsurprisingly, then, the disappearance of the "Arab nation narrative" in the 1980s thus symbolizes the moment when Libya's foreign and security policy in general and its nuclear policy in particular began to alter. Several instances within this later phase of the discourse reveal a tentatively more cooperative attitude toward the international system.

Two additional aspects are important from an IR theoretical perspective. First, the non-proliferation regime does not play a very prominent role in the Libyan discourse insofar as it does not trigger Libyan nuclear reversal. However, the regime is repeatedly invoked in the context of the already depicted narratives of global inequality and injustice. Accordingly, Libya and the Arab states should refrain from signing or ratifying the Non-Proliferation Treaty, since it is characterized as discriminatory, biased and unjust. The treaty is merely considered as an instrument for the suppression of non-nuclear states and a further manifestation of the inequitable global order. This facet is particularly striking, as it illustrates a noteworthy similarity between the Libyan interpretation of the nuclear order and the respective Swiss interpretation in the 1960s. Despite the notable differences between the two cases, Switzerland and Libya share a critical, skeptical view of the NPT and the newly emerging nuclear order; both lament its discriminatory nature. The historiographic reconstruction of the Libyan case reveals, however, that the non-proliferation regime – although it does not figure prominently in the discursive protocols I have analyzed – was indeed significant in curbing the complete unfolding of the Libyan weapons program, since it considerably curtailed Libya's access to relevant materials. In fact, Libya had to rely on obscure, dubious business connections to procure the necessary key components.

Second, the analysis confirms that the threat perception – most notably the threat posed by the US and Israel – plays a significant role within the general Libyan discourse on foreign and security policy as well as within the more specific nuclear discourse. We see, though, that the perceived threat is far from fixed and given, but alters over time. More specifically, the Libyan perception seems to shift from a rather broad but vague apprehension of vulnerability during the first phase (1972–1986) toward a more concrete and specific fear of attack by the US during the second phase (1986–1995). However, three aspects need to be taken into account. First, it appears that the security question was not the crucial factor in the initiation of Libya's nuclear program. While the documents reveal that Libya did feel insecure – because of the unstable situation in the region, its hostilities with Israel and (above all) the US, shifting relations to its neighbors as well as its historical experience of colonial suppression – we do not find evidence of an existential threat in the early years of Libya's nuclear ambitions. As a result, the security rationale does not provide a sufficiently convincing explanation for Libya's initial steps toward a nuclear weapons program. Second, the analysis does not reveal an increased threat perception during the late 1990s or in 2002/2003; instead, the threat climax was reached in around 1986. The claim that Libya's renunciation of its WMD program was triggered by a heightened sense of danger from abroad therefore has to be called into question. More precisely, we do not find sufficient evidence to argue that the Gaddafi administration retracted its efforts because it feared the same fate as Iraq. This does not mean that such fear was absent, just that the perception was more of a constant, and there was no significant increase in fear. Besides, policy change in Libya started in the second half of the 1990s – several years before the Iraqi regime was overthrown. Third, the analysis reveals that even fundamental political categories such as threat, enemy, ally and security were not fixed and settled, but exhibited weaknesses, inconsistencies and openings for the renegotiation of meaning. The consequences for the Libyan case appear to be twofold. The security narrative was not powerful and thus not convincing enough to spur far-reaching, wholesale and sustained efforts toward the acquisition of nuclear weapons. At the same time, it was open and fluid enough to allow for a reconsidering and a reframing of Libya's specific foreign and security policies in the 1990s and thereby to ease the country's rapprochement with the international community.

Both cases thus illustrate the usefulness of the pragmatist lens of inquiry. They reveal that the decision-making processes regarding the (non-)acquisition of nuclear weapons occurred in a multi-layered and non-linear manner. Instead of merely reacting to objectively given exogenous impulses or inputs, the decisions were based on an intersubjective, linguistically mediated exchange of perceptions and key beliefs regarding the countries' identity and their role in the world.

Practical implications: the politics of proliferation

From a pragmatist point of view it would amount to a performative contradiction if we merely restricted our work to the theoretical level. Instead, the pragmatist understanding of professional, social science ethics calls upon us to apply our insights to existing "real world" problems and to offer solutions to the challenges faced by the public. Pragmatism is "oriented to the idea of 'betterment', reconstruction and emancipation,"[22] as Bauer and Brighi remind us. The following paragraphs thus represent an attempt to live up to this call: they will indicate how the findings of the above analyses may be brought to fruition in more practical political terms. There are several underlying questions here. How can we make use of the results of the case studies in tangible political terms? What are the implications for global efforts concerning the mitigation and roll-back of proliferation? Lastly, how can we apply the findings with a view to global non-proliferation efforts?

This study suggests that security considerations do not necessarily play the central role in the rise or dismissal of states' nuclear ambitions – states do not simply react to given security threats. Rather, and more broadly, we can decipher the core *political processes* of interpretation in which actors "make sense of the world." These processes of "sense-making" include, but are not limited to, security perceptions. A government that interprets the country's security situation as deeply threatening *might* seek refuge in the development or acquisition of nuclear weapons. However, a state's foreign and security policy – and hence its nuclear policy – does not merely reflect allegedly straightforward security considerations, but answers to a broader set of questions. This set of questions also encompasses issues such as the perceived role of the state within the international system, socially shared notions of identity or the definition of a defense posture. Likewise, proliferation does not occur as an immediate, straightforward reaction to a given threat: instead, a fundamentally political (and non-linear, co-constitutive) process is interposed between the "definition of the situation" and "action." Consequently, this is where non-proliferation efforts have to come into play. In order to understand security politics in general and the processes of nuclear weapons acquisition in particular, we need to recognize the fundamentally political interpretive processes that take place beneath the more obvious policy decisions. This will eventually allow a broader set of tools to be used to address the "proliferation problem." In this regard, two aspects seem to be of particular significance: (1) the monitoring and "desecuritization" of domestic discourses; and (2) the evolution of a global non-nuclear weapons norm. I will address each of these aspects in turn.

Discursive interventions and desecuritization

First, global nuclear non-proliferation efforts have to be receptive to this very process and to the domestic nuclear discourses of potential "nuclearizers." If the discourses regarding a country's perceived foreign policy role, its security perception and its envisioned nuclear stance are closely monitored, this provides opportunities for early political intervention. More specifically, this monitoring allows the global community to identify those voices within the discourse that contest and oppose calls for nuclearization. In a similar vein, the international community should support those (domestic) participants in the debate who challenge aggressive and hostile narratives and identity conceptions, or who are more willing to compromise. Underlying this is the conviction that opposing groups have the ability to question and perhaps even undermine dominant narratives by instilling counter-narratives, alternative policy logic and "deviant" vocabularies. Certainly, those vocabularies are not free-floating and arbitrary; they cannot easily be shifted from one meaning to another.[23] Yet, as we have seen from the case studies, even central concepts such as "enemy," "ally," "neutrality" or "modernity" are not fixed and permanent. They can shift over time and acquire new meanings or new connotations. The task is thus to offer "de-securitizing" counter-narratives that "move developments from the sphere of existential fear to one where they can be handled by ordinary means, such as politics, economy and culture."[24]

A similar potential for discursive shifts lies in recognizing that the societal discourse is always interwoven with a host of – latent or manifest – identity conceptions and that the construction of "identity can take on different degrees of 'Otherness,' ranging from fundamental difference between Self and Other to constructions of less than 'radical' difference."[25] And while such discursive identity structures are resilient and "sticky," their reproduction and preservation ultimately depends on social practice. This implies that social practice can undermine and question these structures and put forward alternative – less radical, less hostile – interpretations of identity. Obviously, the fluidity of such narratives and frames is not a "one-way street" toward amicability and peace. We must not fall prey to a naive optimism that makes us believe in some kind of irreversible human betterment – identities can become more hostile; relations can deteriorate. From studies in social psychology we know that the concept of enmity and related enemy stereotypes have deep-rooted psychological functions that cannot easily be transformed.[26] Yet, if we agree that intersubjectively shared narratives and frames of self-perception, identity and the political environment enable the foreign and security policy of a state, then it appears sensible to pay more attention to their emergence and potential alteration.

The success of such a strategy of "rhetorical counter-insurgency"[27] or de-securitization depends on the political system as well as on the openness and accessibility of the discourse. However, as has been argued previously, any political system is – to some degree – based on argumentative contestation; in any political system the courses of future action have to be sketched and delineated – they are not naturally given as a matter of fact. The opportunities to influence the political discourse and the ensuing policymaking in a non-democratic system are necessarily smaller, but they should not be discounted.

A global (anti-)nuclear weapons discourse

Second, the case studies suggest that the domestic discourses on nuclear weapons are responsive to discursive developments on the global level – at least under certain conditions. If a global normative discourse resonates well with existing cultural habits or convictions on the domestic level, then the chances are higher that the international norm will become salient within the country's discourse.[28] Switzerland's changing attitude toward the attributes of nuclear weapons seems to exemplify this process: the international negotiation of the Partial Test Ban Treaty in 1963 increased awareness for and recognition of the detrimental effects of atmospheric nuclear weapons tests, thus leading to a strengthening of the nuclear-critical position within the Swiss debate.

Drawing on this insight, one may argue that a consistent and robust – non-discriminatory – global norm against nuclear weapons might proffer additional support for the opponents of nuclearization in today's "states of concern." According to this reasoning, it is conceivable that a "nuclear convention" as discussed most recently at the 2010 NPT Review Conference,[29] while it would most likely not trigger immediate disarmament steps or nuclear reversal by states of concern, could lead to a strengthened non-nuclear movement and an increased opposition to nuclear weapons. In the longer run, a (codified) condemnation of (the possession and use of) nuclear weapons would certainly create a political obligation to act in accordance with the norm. By "calling into question or dele-gitimating alternative choices,"[30] this would raise the burden of defection. For the time being, however, the discriminatory nature of the non-proliferation regime still inhibits the emergence of a strong norm against the possession of nuclear weapons. Libya's and other countries' interpretation and characterization of the non-proliferation regime as unjust and discriminatory exemplify this normative weakness. For many years, the actual discriminatory character of the NPT has provided a welcome "red herring" to divert attention from covert motifs and underlying interests. In the Libyan case the framing of the non-proliferation norm as "unjust" and "inequitable" even provided the ideological legitimacy for a revisionist policy that sought actively to overthrow the existing international (nuclear) order.

In other words, while there may be an international norm – or at least a strong taboo – against the *use* of nuclear weapons,[31] there is in fact no equally compre-hensive and defined norm against the *possession* of these devices.[32] On the con-trary, the privileging of the legitimate nuclear weapons states – while historically explainable and probably militarily preferable – actually opens the way to a sub-versive questioning of the nuclear order. A norm that discriminates between classes of actors is less robust than a universal norm that affects all states in the same way; it is more susceptible to denunciation and opposition.[33] These weak-nesses of the current normative order notwithstanding, the case studies suggest that a comprehensive and consistent international norm can indeed have an impact on the domestic discourse.

In sum, a pragmatist-interactionist approach to proliferation suggests that neither nuclear proliferation nor nuclear reversal result merely from rational cost–benefit analyses based on predetermined interests. Rather, both decisions result from fairly complex, non-linear political processes in which actors envi-sion and outline further courses of action, thereby drawing on those narratives and frames that delineate the actor's identity, its role in the international world, its threat perception and so on. With regard to the design of appropriate non-proliferation measures, this calls for an alternative approach that complements existing tools:

> Arms control experts speak in terms of balance of forces, throw-weights, verification regimes, ratios of warheads to launchers, treaty obligations, and so on. But humans are storytelling animals. We do not live by treaties; we live by narratives. Narratives give us a sense of plot; of characters with fears, hopes, and passions; of events working toward a denouement, no matter how many detours they take on the way.[34]

If we manage to monitor the discourses on a country's perceived foreign policy role, its security perception and on its envisioned nuclear stance, we will have the opportunity to intervene politically – either by "de-securitizing" certain con-flictual issues or by instilling less radical counter-narratives. This is not to argue that we should dispose of our proved set of non-proliferation strategies. On the contrary, traditional arms control and non-proliferation measures such as export controls, test bans, attempts at strengthening the non-proliferation regime, a cut-off of fissile material or sanctions remain useful to enforce compliance with the NPT and to reduce steadily the military significance of nuclear weapons. However, if we want to deal successfully with the challenge of nuclear prolifera-tion we should first of all attempt to achieve a better understanding of the com-plexities and intricacies that shape a state's proliferation process. Looking at cases of weaponization and reversal through a pragmatist-interactionist lens reveals that these processes are rarely straightforward, unilinear and conclusive. On the contrary: processes of proliferation – and the narratives upon which they are based – contain weaknesses, inconsistencies and openings that allow for a renegotiation of meaning and – possibly – a change of course.

The way forward

This analysis has illustrated the potential benefits that a pragmatist approach to the study of nuclear (non-)proliferation can generate. The case studies have revealed insights and arguments that remain outside the scope of more traditional analyses. The findings encourage us to suspend our search for grand theories of nuclear proliferation and instead amplify our efforts to better understand single cases. However, pragmatism is no panacea. It will neither solve all our empirical challenges, nor will it replace existing theoretical disagreements. In directing our attention to different levels of analysis and to different subject matters, it can, however, complement our intellectual repertoire. By increasing theoretical awareness and reflexivity and by providing a bridge between theorists and prac-titioners, pragmatism can, moreover, help to reduce the "ad hoc" character of many of today's non-proliferation initiatives. And yet the success of such a prag-matist "gap-bridging" endeavor is far from certain. Pragmatism's demand that more attention be paid to the intricacies of the social world is likely to encounter skepticism, as Gallagher's observation with regard to the arms control and non-proliferation community indicates:

> [P]roposals based on middle-ground assumptions about mixed motives, mis-perceptions, and security dilemmas are hard to sell to non-experts because they take a long time to explain and are often counter-intuitive. In an age of shrinking soundbites and short attention spans, the "end against the middle" phenomenon will intensify without new strategies to answer criticisms based on less complex conception of international politics.[35]

In a similar vein, the further integration of pragmatism into the scholarly canon of security studies and IR will not come without resistance or at least staunch skepticism from more traditionally oriented gatekeepers. Advocates of positivist forms of inquiry will probably bemoan a lack of scientific rigor in pragmatist studies. They will argue that the absence of parsimony and testable hypotheses makes for bad social science. Perhaps they will also mock pragmatists for their "naiveté" and "relativism" and for their disregard for long-standing principles of IR scholarship. And indeed, if one is looking for straightforward causal explanations and "grand theory" accounts, pragmatist studies will be disappointing. Pragmatist analyses in IR will not – and are not meant to – live up to positivist criteria for "proper" research. Indeed, pragmatism offers us an alternative yet complementary approach to the understanding of social phenomena.

However, their current role as outsiders does not free pragmatist-oriented IR scholars from continuously making their work more amenable and accessible to academics from other schools of thought. So far, pragmatism has rather failed to do this. Even Sil, a known advocate of pragmatist research in IR, concedes:

> [W]hat pragmatists have to say rarely seems intelligible, let alone relevant, to most mainstream IR scholars. For the most part, pragmatists have been attempting to engage the IR field in the same abstract language they use to formulate positions in opposition to analytic philosophy.... Ironically, pragmatist discourse appears either too abstract or too convoluted to be of any practical significance to IR scholars coping with the challenges and requirements of research.[36]

So far, pragmatist authors have merely contributed to theoretical, inter-paradigmatic debates. Yet the utility of pragmatism as a complement to the current IR canon will only become credible once the approach is used as a tool for the study of empirical problems. It is time to demonstrate the benefits and boundaries of pragmatist research through its application to today's global political challenges. This will not only contribute to the widening and diversification of the hitherto fairly narrow thinking about security and (non-)proliferation issues. It will also help to resolve the long-standing idle gridlock between, on the one hand, scholars concerned with metatheory, and advocates of policy relevance on the other. Pragmatism encourages us to confront the complexities and challenges posed by nuclear proliferation in a theoretically mindful manner.

Notes

1 Kratochwil, "Ten Points to Ponder about Pragmatism. Some Critical Reflections on Knowledge Generation in the Social Sciences."
2 Patrick Baert, "A Neopragmatist Agenda for Social Research. Integrating Levinas, Gadamer and Mead," in *Pragmatism in international relations*, ed. Harry Bauer and Elisabetta Brighi (London New York: Routledge, 2009), 50.
3 Thomas and Thomas, *The child in America: behavior problems and programs.*
4 Richard Rorty, *Philosophy as cultural politics. Philosophical papers*, vol. 4 (2007), *passim.*
5 The following contributions mirror this debate: Theda Skocpol, "The Dead End of Matatheory," *Contemporary Sociology* 16, no. 1 (1987); James Rosenau, "Probing

Puzzles Persistently: A Desirable but Improbable Future for IR Theory," in *International theory: positivism and beyond*, ed. Steve Smith, Ken Booth, and Marysia Zalewski (Cambridge: Cambridge University Press, 1996); William Wallace, "Truth and Power, Monks and Technocrats: Theory and Practice in International Relations," *Review of International Studies* 22, no. 3 (1996); Stanley Hoffmann, "International Relations: The Long Road to Theory," *World Politics* 11, no. 3 (1959); Alexander L. George, *Bridging the gap: theory and practice in foreign policy* (Washington, DC: United States Institute of Peace Press, 1993); J.A. Frieden and D.A. Lake, "International Relations as a Social Science: Rigor and Relevance," *Annals of the American Academy of Political and Social Science* 600 (2005); Joseph Lepgold, "Is Anyone Listening? International Relations Theory and the Problem of Policy Relevance," *Political Science Quarterly* 113, no. 1 (1998); Steve Smith, "International Relations and international relations: The Link Between Theory and Practice in World Politics," *Journal of international Relations and Development* 6, no. 3 (2003).

6 Baert, "A Neopragmatist Agenda," 54.

7 Bernstein *et al.*, "God Gave Physics the Easy Problems: Adapting Social Science to an Unpredictable World."

8 King, Keohane, and Verba, *Designing social inquiry: scientific inference in qualitative research*, 43.

9 Rudra Sil, "Simplifying Pragmatism: From Social Theory to Problem-driven Eclecticism," *International Studies Review* 11, no. 3 (2009): 649.

10 Friedrichs and Kratochwil, "On Acting and Knowing," 716.

11 Davis, *Terms of inquiry on the theory and practice of political science*, 175.

12 Robert Jervis, "Models and Cases in the Study of International Conflict," *Journal of International Affairs* 44, no. 1 (1990): 84.

13 Hellmann, "Pragmatismus," 164.

14 Gaddis moreover reminds us that forecasts and predictions based on prevalent IR theories have performed rather poorly, and that they failed to forecast any of the significant political developments and events of the last decades:

> One might as well have relied upon stargazers, readers of entrails, and other 'pre-scientific" methods for all the 'good' our 'scientific' methods did; clearly our theories were not up to the task of anticipating the most significant event in world politics since the end of World War II."
> (John L. Gaddis, "International Relations Theory and the End of the Cold-War," *International Security* 17, no. 3 (1993): 18)

15 Bevir, "How Narratives Explain"; Bernstein *et al.*, "God Gave Physics the Easy Problems: Adapting Social Science to an Unpredictable World."

16 "God Gave Physics the Easy Problems: Adapting Social Science to an Unpredictable World," 54.

17 Sil and Katzenstein, "Analytic Eclecticism in the Study of World Politics"; Katzenstein and Sil, "Eclectic Theorizing in the Study and Practice of International Relations."

18 Sil and Katzenstein, "Analytic Eclecticism in the Study of World Politics," 411.

19 Gunther Hellmann (ed.), "The Forum: Are Dialogue and Synthesis Possible in International Relations?," *International Studies Review* 5, no. 1 (2003): 123–153.

20 Sil and Katzenstein, "Analytic Eclecticism in the Study of World Politics," 419.

21 "Analytic Eclecticism in the Study of World Politics," 421.

22 Bauer and Brighi, "Introducing Pragmatism to International Relations," 2.

23 As Wæver argues, a successful securitizing statement always draws upon

> conditions historically associated with a threat: it is more likely that one can conjure a security threat if there are certain objects to refer to which are generally held to be threatening – be they tanks, hostile sentiments or polluted waters.

In themselves they never make for necessary securitisation, but they are definitely facilitating conditions.

(Ole Wæver, "Securitisation: Taking Stock of a Research Programme in Security Studies" (Copenhagen, 2003), 16)

24 "Securitization and Desecuritization", 55.

25 Hansen, *Security as practice*, 7.

26 See, for example, Stavros Mentzos, *Der Krieg und seine psychosozialen Funktionen* (Göttingen: Vandenhoeck und Ruprecht, 2002).

27 Taylor and Kinsella, "Introduction: Linking Nuclear Legacies and Communication Studies," 5.

28 This finding is very much in line with the large body of literature on norms and norm socialization. See, for example: Cortell and Davis, "Understanding the Domestic Impact of International Norms: A Research Agenda"; Thomas Risse-Kappen, Steve C. Ropp and Kathryn Sikkink, eds, *The power of human rights: international norms and domestic change* (New York: Cambridge University Press, 1999).

29 UN General Assembly, "Model Nuclear Weapons Convention" (2007).

30 Cortell and Davis, "Understanding the Domestic Impact of International Norms: A Research Agenda," 69.

31 Tannenwald, *The nuclear taboo*.

32 Walker describes this dichotomy neatly: "Glory in possession can go hand in hand with shame in its use." William Walker, "The Absence of a Taboo on the Possession of Nuclear Weapons," *Review of International Studies* 36, no. 4 (2010): 870.

33 Krause and Latham argue that underlying this discriminatory nuclear order

is the view that, because the West is pursuing rational and benign NACD [nonproliferation, arms control and disarmament] policies, it can be excused from some of the more onerous restraints that others need to observe if peace and stability are to be maintained. Western states often do not (except in the most abstract way) accept the notion of "equity" in NACD issues that is advanced by China and India.

(Keith Krause and Andrew Latham, "Constructing Non-Proliferation and Arms Control: The Norms of Western Practice," *Contemporary Security Policy* 19, no. 1 (1998): 41)

34 Hugh Gusterson, "Narrating Abolition," *Bulletin of the Atomic Scientists* 65, no. 3 (2009): 13.

35 Nancy W. Gallagher, *Arms control new approaches to theory and policy* (London: Cass, 1998), 13.

36 Sil "Simplifying Pragmatism: From Social Theory to Problem-driven Eclecticism," 648.

Bibliography

Abraham, Itty. "The Ambivalence of Nuclear Histories." *Osiris* 21, no. 1 (2006): 49–65.

Ahmida, Ali Abdullatif. *The making of modern Libya: state formation, colonization, and resistance, 1830–1932.* Albany: State University of New York Press, 1994.

"Al-Bishari Addresses UN General Assembly (JANA)." *Foreign Broadcast Information Service*, October 6, 1992, FBIS-NES-92–195.

"Al-Bishari Interview with AL-HAWADITH." *Foreign Broadcast Information Service*, August 9, 1991, FBIS-NES-91–159.

"Al-Bishari: Interview with AL-AHRAM." *Foreign Broadcast Information Service*, March 22, 1992, FBIS-NES-92–060.

"Al-Fazzani: Interview with Al-Sharq Al Awsat." *Foreign Broadcast Information Service*, April 7, 1997, FBIS-NES-97–067.

"Al-Muntasir: Interview with Al-Sharq Al-Awsat." *Foreign Broadcast Information Service*, April 13, 1996.

"Al-Qadhafi Comments on Spread of Anthrax in USA (JANA)." *BBC Monitoring Middle East*, October 18, 2001.

"Al-Qadhafi: 1 September Revolution Anniversary." *Foreign Broadcast Information Service*, September 1, 1987, V. 3 Sep 87 D 1–15.

"Al-Qadhafi: Evacuation Anniversary Fete." *Foreign Broadcast Information Service*, June 11, 1972, V. 12 Jun 72 T 1–18.

"Al-Qadhafi: Interview with *Le Figaro*." *Foreign Broadcast Information Service*, March 28, 1992, FBIS-NES-92–063 12–14.

"Al-Qadhafi: Interview with CNN." *Lexis Nexis*, April 15, 1996.

"Al-Qadhafi: Interview with *Der Spiegel*." *Foreign Broadcast Information Service*, November 12, 1990, FBIS-NES-90–219.

"Al-Qadhafi: Interview with Indian Magazine." *Foreign Broadcast Information Service*, May 2, 1976, V. 4 May 76 I 8–9.

"Al-Qadhafi: Interview with Jana (Tripoli)." *Foreign Broadcast Information Service*, June 7, 1980, V. 9 Jun 80 I 2–5.

"Al-Qadhafi: Interview with Lebanese Newspaper." *Foreign Broadcast Information Service*, January 13, 1975, V. 14 Jan 75 I 1–6.

"Al-Qadhafi: Interview with NHK Television (Tokyo)." *Foreign Broadcast Information Service*, June 3, 1985, V. 6 Jun 85 Q 1.

"Al-Qadhafi: Interview with Reuters." *Foreign Broadcast Information Service*, January 19, 1975, V. 20 Jan 75 A 1.

"Al-Qadhafi: Interview with *Sunday Telegraph* (London)." *Foreign Broadcast Information Service*, May 2, 1976, V. 4 May 76 I 2–7.

"Al-Qadhafi: Rally at Umm 'Atiqah Airbase." *Foreign Broadcast Information Service*, June 11, 1984, V. 12 Jun 84 Q 2–13.

"Al-Qadhafi: Rally in Benghazi." *Foreign Broadcast Information Service*, May 8, 1986, V. 9 May 86 Q 2–11.

"Al-Qadhafi: Speech at 'Expulsion of US' Anniversary." *Foreign Broadcast Information Service*, June 11, 1986, V. 12 Jun 86 Q 1–12.

"Al-Qadhafi: Speech in Ghadamis." *Foreign Broadcast Information Service*, April 21, 1995, FBIS-NES-95–078.

"Al-Qadhafi: Speech in Sirte (Qadhafi Comments on Trial of Lockerbie Suspects, African Troops for Congo)." *BBC Monitoring Middle East*, October 1, 1998.

"Al-Qadhafi: Students Revolution Anniversary." *Foreign Broadcast Information Service*, April 7, 1987, V. 9 Apr 87 Q 1–9.

"Al-Qadhafi: Youth Conference Address." *Foreign Broadcast Information Service*, May 14, 1973, V 16 May 73 T 1–9.

"Al-Qadhdhafi Ridicules 'Coup Attempt' Reports." *Foreign Broadcast Information Service*, November 2, 1993, FBIS-NES-93–210.

"Al-Qadhdhafi Warns No Leniency for 'Traitors'." *Foreign Broadcast Information Service*, August 4, 1994, FBIS-NES-94–150.

"Al-Shawish Statement to JANA." *BBC Monitoring Middle East*, December 25, 2002.

Al-Qadhafi, Saif Aleslam. "Libyan–American Relations." *Middle East Policy* 10, no. 1 (2003): 35–44.

Albright, David. *Peddling peril: how the secret nuclear trade arms America's enemies.* New York: Free Press, 2010.

Alexander, Nathan. "Libya – The Continuous Revolution." *Middle Eastern Studies* 17, no. 2 (1981): 210–227.

"Ali Abd as-Salam, Speech to the Non-Aligned Meeting in Malta." *BBC Summary of World Broadcasts*, September 11, 1984, ME/7746/A/1.

Altermatt, Urs. "Vom Ende des Zweiten Weltkrieges bis zur Gegenwart (1945–1991)." In *Neues Handbuch der schweizerischen Aussenpolitik*, edited by Hans Haug, Alois Riklin, and Raymond Probst, 61–78. Bern: Haupt, 1992.

Alvesson, Mats. "Beyond Neopositivists, Romantics, and Localists: A Reflexive Approach to Interviews in Organizational Research." *Academy of Management Review* 28, no. 1 (January 1, 2003): 13–33.

Amoretti, B. Scarcia. "Libyan Loneliness in Facing the World: The Challenge of Islam?" In *Islam in foreign policy*, edited by Adeed I. Dawisha, 54–67. Cambridge and New York: Cambridge University Press, 1983.

Anderson, Lisa. *The state and social transformation in Tunisia and Libya, 1830–1980.* Princeton, NJ: Princeton University Press, 1986.

——. "The State in the Middle-East and North-Africa." *Comparative Politics* 20, no. 1 (1987): 1–18.

——. "Tribe and State: Libyan Anomalies." In *Tribes and state formation in the Middle East*, edited by Philip S. Khoury and Joseph Kostiner, 288–302. Berkeley: University of California Press, 1990.

Angermüller, Johannes. "Diskursanalyse: Strömungen, Tendenzen, Perspektiven. Eine Einführung." In *Diskursanalyse: Theorien, Methoden, Anwendungen*, edited by Johannes Angermüller, Katharina Bunzmann, and Martin Nonhoff. Argument-Sonderband, 7–22. Hamburg: Argument Verlag, 2001.

Austin, John L. *How to do things with words.* The William James Lectures. Cambridge: Harvard University Press, 1962.

Baehr, P. and P.C. Salzman. "Tribes and Terror in the Middle East: A Conversation with Philip Carl Salzman." *Society* 46, no. 5 (2009): 394–397.

Baert, Patrick. "A Neopragmatist Agenda for Social Research. Integrating Levinas, Gadamer and Mead." In *Pragmatism in international relations*, edited by Harry Bauer and Elisabetta Brighi, 47–64. London and New York: Routledge, 2009.

Bahgat, Gawdat. "Proliferation of Weapons of Mass Destruction: The Case of Libya." *International Relations* 22, no. 1 (2008): 105–126.

Baldinetti, Anna. *The origins of the Libyan nation: colonial legacy, exile and the emergence of a new nation-state.* Routledge studies in Middle Eastern history. London and New York: Routledge, 2010.

Barakat, Halim Isber. *The Arab world: society, culture, and state.* Berkeley: University of California Press, 1993.

Barnaby, Frank. *How nuclear weapons spread: nuclear-weapon proliferation in the 1990s.* London: Routledge, 1993.

Bauer, Harry and Elisabetta Brighi. "Introducing Pragmatism to International Relations." In *Pragmatism in international relations*, edited by Harry Bauer and Elisabetta Brighi. The new international relations, 1–8. London New York: Routledge, 2009.

——, eds. *Pragmatism in international relations*, The new international relations. London and New York: Routledge, 2009.

Becker, Howard S. and Charles C. Ragin, eds. *What is a case? Exploring the foundations of social inquiry.* Cambridge: Cambridge University Press, 2000.

Berger, Thomas U. "Norms, Identity, and National Security in Germany and Japan." In *The culture of national security: norms and identity in world politics*, edited by Peter J. Katzenstein. New directions in world politics, 317–356. New York: Columbia University Press, 1996.

Bernstein, Richard J. "The Resurgence of Pragmatism." *Social Research* 59, no. 4 (1992): 813–840.

Bernstein, Steven, Richard Ned Lebow, Janice Gross Stein and Steven Weber. "God Gave Physics the Easy Problems: Adapting Social Science to an Unpredictable World." *European Journal of International Relations* 6, no. 1 (March 2000): 43–76.

Bevir, Mark. "How Narratives Explain." In *Interpretation and method: empirical research methods and the interpretive turn*, edited by Dvora Yanow and Peregrine Schwartz-Shea, 281–290. Armonk, NY: M.E. Sharpe, 2006.

Biggar, Nigel. "Christianity and Weapons of Mass Destruction." In *Ethics and weapons of mass destruction: religious and secular perspectives*, edited by Sohail H. Hashmi and Steven P. Lee. The ethikon series in comparative ethics, 168–199. Cambridge: Cambridge University Press, 2004.

Bijker, Wiebe and John Law. "General Introduction." In *Shaping technology, building society: studies in sociotechnical change*, edited by Wiebe E. Bijker and John Law, 1–14. Cambridge, MA: MIT Press, 1992.

Billig, Michael. "Political Rhetoric." In *Oxford handbook of political psychology*, edited by David O. Sears, Leonie Huddy, and Robert Jervis, 222–250. Oxford and New York: Oxford University Press, 2003.

Binder, Interpellation. "Stellungnahme zum geplanten Atomsperrvertrag." *Amtliches Bulletin der Bundesversammlung* 4 (1967): 593–599.

Bindschedler, Rudolf L. *Die Neutralität im modernen Völkerrecht.* Stuttgart: Kohlhammer, 1956.

Bleiker, Roland. "The Aesthetic Turn in International Political Theory." *Millennium* 30, no. 3 (2001): 509–534.

Blumer, Herbert. *Symbolic Interactionism. Perspective and Method.* Englewood Cliffs, NJ: Prentice-Hall, 1969.

Booth, Ken. "Nuclearism, Human Rights and Constructions of Security (Part 1)." *The International Journal of Human Rights* 3, no. 2 (1999): 1–24.

——. "Nuclearism, Human Rights and Constructions of Security (Part 2)." *The International Journal of Human Rights* 3, no. 3 (1999): 44–61.

——. *Theory of world security.* Cambridge: Cambridge University Press, 2007.

Bowen, Wyn Q. *Libya and nuclear proliferation: stepping back from the brink.* Adelphi paper. Abingdon and New York: Routledge, 2006.

Braun, Peter. "Dreaming of the Bomb. The Development of Switzerland's Nuclear Option from the End of World War II to the Non-Proliferation Treaty." Conference Paper: *Uncovering the Sources of Nuclear Behavior. Historical Dimensions of Nuclear Proliferation.* Zurich, 2010.

Braut-Hegghammer, Målfrid. "Libya's Nuclear Turnaround: Perspectives from Tripoli." *Middle East Journal* 62, no. 1 (2008): 55–72.

——. "Nuclear Entrepreneurs: Drivers of Nuclear Proliferation" (dissertation manuscript). London School of Economics, 2009.

Breitenmoser, Christoph. "Strategie ohne Aussenpolitik zur Entwicklung der schweizerischen Sicherheitspolitik im Kalten Krieg" (phil. dissertation). Zürich, 2002.

Brubaker, Rogers and Frederick Cooper. "Beyond 'Identity'." *Theory and Society* 29, no. 1 (2000): 1–47.

Bruce St. John, Ronald. "Redefining the Libyan Revolution: The Changing Ideology of Muammar al-Qaddafi." *The Journal of North African Studies* 13, no. 1 (2008): 91–106.

Bucher, Bernd. "Processual-Relational Thinking and Figurational Sociology in Social Constructivism: The Rogueization of Liberal and Illiberal States" (Ph.D. dissertation). St. Gallen: University of St. Gallen, 2011.

Büger, Christian and Frank Gadinger. "Culture, Terror and Practice in International Relations: An Invitation to Practice Theory." In *The (Re-)turn to Practice: Thinking Practices in International Relations and Security Studies.* Florence: European University Institute, 2007.

Bundesrat. "1513. Schweizerische Studienkommission für Atomenergie, 8. Juni 1946 [Swiss Study Commission for Nuclear Energy, June 8, 1946]." *Diplomatische Dokumente der Schweiz*, June 8, 1946.

——. "5074. Botschaft des Bundesrates an die Bundesversammlung zum Entwurf eines Bundesbeschlusses über die Förderung der Forschung auf dem Gebiete der Atomenergie, 17. Juli 1946 [Report of the Federal Council to the Federal Assembly on the Draft of a Federal Decision Regarding the Funding of Research in the Field of Atomic Energy, July 17, 1946]." *Bundesblatt*, vol. II (1946): 928–935.

——. "7854. Bericht des Bundesrates an die Bundesversammlung über das Volksbegehren für ein Verbot der Atomwaffen, 19. Mai 1959 [Report of the Federal Council to the Federal Assembly Regarding the Referendum on the Prohibition of Nuclear Weapons, May 19, 1959]." *Bundesblatt*, vol. I (1959): 1403–1405.

——. "7987. Botschaft des Bundesrates an die Bundesversammlung betreffend die Organisation des Heeres (Truppenordnung), 30. Juni 1960 [Report of the Federal Council Regarding the Reorganization of the Armed Forces, June 30, 1960]." *Bundesblatt*, vol. II (1960): 321–388.

——. "8153. Botschaft des Bundesrates an die Bundesversammlung über die Beschaffung von Kampfflugzeugen (Mirage III S), 25. April 1961 [Report of the Federal Council to the Federal Assembly Regarding the Acquisition of Combat Aircraft (Mirage III S), April 25, 1961]." *Bundesblatt*, vol. I (1961): 793–825.

———. "8273. Bericht des Bundesrates an die Bundesversammlung über das Volksbegehren für ein Verbot der Atomwaffen, 7. Juli 1961 [Report of the Federal Council to the Federal Assembly Regarding the Referendum on the Prohibition of Nuclear Weapons, July 7, 1961]." *Bundesblatt*, vol. II (1961): 202–223.

———. "8468. Botschaft des Bundesrates an die Bundesversammlung über das Ergebnis der Volksabstimmung betreffend das Volksbegehren für ein Verbot von Atomwaffen, 4. Mai 1962 [Report of the Federal Council to the Federal Assembly on the outcome of the referendum concerning the petition for a ban on nuclear weapons, May 4, 1962]." *Bundesblatt*, vol. I (1962): 913–915.

———. "8509. Bericht des Bundesrates an die Bundesversammlung über das Volksbegehren für das Entscheidungsrecht des Volkes über die Ausrüstung der schweizerischen Armee mit Atomwaffen, 18. Juni 1962 [Report of the Federal Council to the Federal Assembly Regarding the Referendum on the Decision-Making Power of the People Regarding Equipping the Swiss Military with Nuclear Weapons, June 18, 1962]." *Bundesblatt*, vol. II (1962): 18–25.

———. "8509. Ergänzungsbericht des Bundesrates an die Kommission des Nationalrates betreffend das Volksbegehren für das Entscheidungsrecht des Volkes über die Ausrüstung der schweizerischen Armee mit Atomwaffen, 15. November 1962 [Additional Report of the Federal Council to the Commission of the National Council Concerning the Petition for the Decision-Making Power of the People Regarding Equipping the Swiss Military with Nuclear Weapons, November 15, 1962]." *Bundesblatt*, vol. II (1962): 1155–1159.

———. "8816. Bericht des Bundesrates an die Bundesversammlung über das Ergebnis der Volksabstimmung vom 26. Mai 1963 betreffend das Volksbegehren für das Entscheidungsrecht des Volkes über die Ausrüstung der schweizerischen Armee mit Atomwaffen, 19. Juni 1963 [Report of the Federal Council to the Federal Assembly on the Outcome of the Referendum of May 26, 1963 Concerning the Petition for the Decision-Making Power of the People Regarding Equipping the Swiss Military with Nuclear Weapons, June 19, 1963]." *Bundesblatt*, vol. II (1963): 43–45.

———. "8831. Botschaft des Bundesrates an die Bundesversammlung betreffend die Genehmigung des in Moskau geschlossenen Abkommens über das Verbot von Kernwaffenversuchen in der Luft, im Weltraum und unter Wasser, 13. September 1963 [Message of the Federal Council to the Federal Assembly Regarding the Approval of the Agreement Signed in Moscow on the Prohibition of Nuclear Weapons Tests in the Air, in Space, and Underwater, September 13, 1963]." *Bundesblatt*, vol. II (1963): 615–627.

———. "9478. Bericht des Bundesrates an die Bundesversammlung über die Konzeption der militärischen Landesverteidigung, 16. Juni 1966 [Report of the Federal Council to the Federal Assembly on the Concept of Military National Defense, June 16, 1966]." *Bundesblatt*, vol. I (1966): 853–877.

Burgat, François. "Qadhafi's 'Unitary' Doctrine. Theory and Practice." In *The Green and the black: Qadhafi's policies in Africa*, edited by René Lemarchand, 19–28. Bloomington: Indiana University Press, 1988.

Buzan, Barry and Lene Hansen. *The evolution of international security studies*. Cambridge: Cambridge University Press, 2009.

Buzan, Barry, Ole Wæver and Jaap De Wilde. *Security: a new framework for analysis*. Boulder, CO: Lynne Rienner, 1998.

Campbell, David. *Writing security: United States foreign policy and the politics of identity*. Minneapolis: University of Minnesota Press, 1998.

Campbell, Kurt M., Robert J. Einhorn and Mitchell Reiss, eds. *The nuclear tipping point: why states reconsider their nuclear choices*. Washington, DC: Brookings Institution Press, 2004.

Carlsnaes, Walter. "Foreign Policy." In *Handbook of international relations*, edited by Walter Carlsnaes, Thomas Risse-Kappen and Beth A. Simmons, 331–349. London; Thousand Oaks, CA: Sage, 2002.

Cawthra, Gavin and Bjoern Moeller. "Nuclear Africa: Weapons, Power and Proliferation." *African Security Review* 17, no. 4 (2008): 133–153.

Charmaz, Kathy. "Grounded Theory: Objectivist and Constructivist Methods." In *Handbook of qualitative research*, edited by Norman K. Denzin and Yvonna S. Lincoln, 509–535. Thousand Oaks, CA: Sage, 2000.

Checkel, Jeffrey T. *Ideas and international political change: Soviet/Russian behavior and the end of the Cold War*. New Haven, CT: Yale University Press, 1997.

——. "Norms, Institutions, and National Identity in Contemporary Europe." *International Studies Quarterly* 43, no. 1 (1999): 84–114.

Chilton, Paul A. "Introduction." In *Language and the nuclear arms debate: nukespeak today*, edited by Paul A. Chilton, xiii–xxiii. London: F. Pinter, 1985.

——. *Security metaphors: cold war discourse from containment to common house*. Conflict and consciousness, New York: Peter Lang, 1996.

——. *Analysing political discourse: theory and practice*. London and New York: Routledge, 2004.

"Communique from the People's Committee of the People's Bureau for Foreign Liaison to UN General Assembly." *UN General Assembly*, December 31, 1985, A/41/69.

Corbin, Juliet M. and Anselm L. Strauss. *Basics of qualitative research techniques and procedures for developing grounded theory*, 3rd edn. Los Angeles, CA: Sage, 2008.

Cortell, Andrew P. and James W. Davis. "How Do International Institutions Matter? The Domestic Impact of International Rules and Norms" [in English]. *International Studies Quarterly* 40, no. 4 (1996): 451–478.

——. "Understanding the Domestic Impact of International Norms: A Research Agenda." *International Studies Review* 2, no. 1 (2000): 65–87.

Cox, Robert W. "Social Forces, States and World Orders: Beyond International Relations Theory." *Millennium – Journal of International Studies* 10, no. 2 (1981): 126–155.

Crawford, Neta. *Argument and change in world politics: ethics, decolonization, and humanitarian intervention*. Cambridge studies in International Relations. Cambridge and New York: Cambridge University Press, 2002.

Dalby, Simon. "Contesting an Essential Concept: Reading the Dilemmas in Contemporary Security Discourse." In *Critical security studies concepts and cases*, edited by Keith Krause and Michael C. Williams, 3–31. London: Routledge, 1997.

Däniker, Gustav. "Kleinstaatliche Abschreckung." *Allgemeine Schweizerische Militärzeitschrift* 132, no. 9 (1966): 521–524.

Davidson, Donald. "Actions, Reasons, and Causes – Symposium." *Journal of Philosophy* 60, no. 23 (1963): 685–700.

Davies, Matt. "'You Can't Charge Innocent People for Saving Their Lives!' Work in Buffy the Vampire Slayer 1." *International Political Sociology* 4, no. 2 (2010): 178–195.

Davis, James W. *Terms of inquiry on the theory and practice of political science*. Baltimore, MD: Johns Hopkins University Press, 2005.

Davis, Zachary S. "The Realist Nuclear Regime." *Security Studies* 2, nos 3–4 (1993): 79–99.

Deeb, Mary-Jane. "The Primacy of Libya's National Interest." In *The Green and the black: Qadhafi's policies in Africa*, edited by René Lemarchand, 29–38. Bloomington: Indiana University Press, 1988.

Dewey, John. "The Reflex Arc Concept in Psychology." *Psychological Review* 3, no. 4 (1896): 357–370.

———.*The influence of Darwin on philosophy, and other essays in contemporary thought.* Bloomington: Indiana University Press, 1965.

Doty, Roxanne Lynn. "Foreign Policy as Social Construction: A Post-Positivist Analysis of U.S. Counterinsurgency Policy in the Philippines." *International Studies Quarterly* 37, no. 3 (1993): 297–320.

Duffy, Gloria. "Soviet Nuclear Export." *International Security* 3, no. 1 (1978): 83–111.

Dunn, Kevin C. "Examining Historical Representations." *International Studies Review* 8, no. 2 (2006): 370–381.

Dunn, Robert G. "Self, Identity, and Difference." *Sociological Quarterly* 38, no. 4 (1997): 687–705.

Eberhard, Rolf. "Die Abstimmung über die Atominitiative I." *Jahrbuch der Schweizerischen Vereinigung für politische Wissenschaft* 3 (1963): 72–78.

Eckstein, Harry. "Case Study and Theory in Political Science." In *Strategies of inquiry*, edited by Fred I. Greenstein and Nelson W. Polsby, 79–137. Reading, MA: Addison-Wesley, 1975.

Eidgenössisches Militärdepartement. "753.4/63. Möglichkeiten einer eigenen Atomwaffen-Produktion (MAP-Bericht), 15. November 1963 [Possibilities of an Indigenous Nuclear Weapon Production (MAP-Report), November 15, 1963]." *Diplomatische Dokumente der Schweiz* (November 15, 1963 dodis.ch/30592).

———. "1208. Erklärung zur Frage der Beschaffung von Atomwaffen für unsere Armee, 11. Juli 1958 [Statement on the question of nuclear weapon procurement for our military, July 11, 1958]." *Diplomatische Dokumente der Schweiz* (July 11, 1958 dodis.ch/16065).

———. "Richtlinien für die Arbeiten der S.K.A. auf militärischem Gebiet, 5. Februar 1946." In *Diplomatische Dokumente der Schweiz*. Bern, 1997.

Einhorn, Robert J. "Will the Abstainers Reconsider? Focusing on Individual Cases." In *The nuclear tipping point: why states reconsider their nuclear choices*, edited by Kurt M. Campbell, Robert J. Einhorn and Mitchell Reiss, 32–42. Washington, DC: Brookings Institution Press, 2004.

Emirbayer, Mustafa. "Manifesto for a Relational Sociology." *American Journal of Sociology* 103, no. 2 (1997): 281–317.

"Erklärung der 35." *Schweizerische Metall- und Uhrenarbeiter Zeitung*, June 11, 1958.

Eyre, Dana P. and Mark C. Suchman. "Status, Norms, and the Proliferation of Conventional Weapons. An Institutional Theory Approach." In *The culture of national security: norms and identity in world politics*, edited by Peter J. Katzenstein, 79–113. New York: Columbia University Press, 1996.

Fatḥalī, 'Umar Ibrāhīm and Monte Palmer. *Political development and social change in Libya*. Lexington, MA: Lexington Books, 1980.

Fearon, James and Alexander Wendt. "Rationalism v. Constructivism: A Skeptical View." In *Handbook of international relations*, edited by Walter Carlsnaes, Thomas Risse-Kappen, and Beth A. Simmons, 52–72. London, and Thousand Oaks, CA: Sage, 2002.

Finnemore, Martha. *National interests in international society*. Cornell Studies in Political Economy. Ithaca, NY: Cornell University Press, 1996.

——. *The purpose of intervention: changing beliefs about the use of force*. Ithaca, NY: Cornell University Press, 2003.

Flank, Steven. "Exploding the Black Box: The Historical Sociology of Nuclear Proliferation." *Security Studies* 3, no. 2 (1993): 259–294.

Foltz, William J. "Libya's Military Power." In *The Green and the black: Qadhafi's policies in Africa*, edited by René Lemarchand, 52–67. Bloomington: Indiana University Press, 1988.

"Foreign Minister Denies Chemical Weapons Plant (MENA)." *Foreign Broadcast Information Service*, April 11, 1996, FBIS-NES-96–072.

Fragen, Studienkommission für strategische. *Grundlagen einer strategischen Konzeption der Schweiz*. Bern, 1969.

Franke, Ulrich and Ulrich Roos. "Actor, Structure, Process: Transcending the State Personhood Debate by Means of a Pragmatist Ontological Model for International Relations Theory." *Review of International Studies* 36, no. 4 (2010): 1057–1077.

Franke, Ulrich and Ralph Weber. "At the Papini Hotel: On Pragmatism in the Study of International Relations." *European Journal of International Relations* 18, no. 4 (2012): 669–691.

Frankel, Benjamin. "The Brooding Shadow: Systemic Incentives and Nuclear Weapons Proliferation." *Security Studies* 2, nos 3–4 (1993): 37–78.

Freedman, Lawrence. *The evolution of nuclear strategy*. Basingstoke: Palgrave Macmillan, 2003.

Frieden, J.A. and D.A. Lake. "International Relations as a Social Science: Rigor and Relevance." *Annals of the American Academy of Political and Social Science* 600 (July 2005): 136–156.

Friedrichs, Jörg and Friedrichs Kratochwil. "On Acting and Knowing." *Working Papers* MWP 2007/35 (2007).

Friedrichs, Jörg and Friedrich Kratochwil. "On Acting and Knowing: How Pragmatism Can Advance International Relations Research and Methodology." *International Organization* 63, no. 4 (2009): 701–731.

Fuhrmann, Matthew. "Spreading Temptation: Proliferation and Peaceful Nuclear Cooperation Agreements." *International Security* 34, no. 1 (2009): 7–41.

Gaddis, John L. "International Relations Theory and the End of the Cold-War." *International Security* 17, no. 3 (1993): 5–58.

Gallagher, Nancy W. *Arms control new approaches to theory and policy*. London: Cass, 1998.

Gavin, Francis J. "Politics, History and the Ivory Tower-Policy Gap in the Nuclear Proliferation Debate." *Journal of Strategic Studies* 35, no. 4 (2012): 573–600.

Geertz, Clifford James. *Dichte Beschreibung. Beiträge zum Verstehen kultureller Systeme*. Theorie. Frankfurt am Main: Suhrkamp, 1983.

"General People's Congress: Political Communique." *Foreign Broadcast Information Service*, March 10, 1990, FBIS-NES-90–048.

George, Alexander L. "The 'Operational Code': A Neglected Approach to the Study of Political Leaders and Decision-Making." *International Studies Quarterly* 13, no. 2 (1969): 190–222.

——. *Bridging the gap: theory and practice in foreign policy*. Washington, DC: United States Institute of Peace Press, 1993.

George, Alexander L. and Andrew Bennett. *Case studies and theory development in the social sciences*. BCSIA Studies in International Security. Cambridge, MA: MIT Press, 2005.

George, Jim. *Discourses of global politics. A critical (re)introduction to international relations.* Critical Perspectives on World Politics. Boulder, CO: Rienner, 1994.

Gitermann, Interpellation. "7649. Ausrüstung der Armee mit Atomwaffen." *Amtliches Bulletin der Bundesversammlung* 4 (1958): 532–534, 604–607.

Glaser, Barney G. and Anselm L. Strauss. *The discovery of grounded theory: strategies for qualitative research.* New York: de Gruyter, 1967.

——. *The discovery of grounded theory: strategies for qualitative research.* Hawthorne, NY: Aldine de Gruyter, 1999.

Glaser, Charles L. "The Causes and Consequences of Arms Races." *Annual Review of Political Science* 3 (2000): 251–276.

Goetschel, Laurent, Magdalena Bernath, and Daniel Schwarz, eds. *Schweizerische Aussenpolitik Grundlagen und Möglichkeiten.* Zürich: Verlag Neue Zürcher Zeitung, 2002.

Goldgeier, J.M. and P.E. Tetlock. "Psychology and International Relations Theory." *Annual Review of Political Science* 4, no. 1 (2001): 67–92.

Goldstein, Judith and Robert O. Keohane, eds. *Ideas and foreign policy: beliefs, institutions, and political change.* Ithaca, NY: Cornell University Press, 1993.

Golino, Frank R. "Patterns of Libyan National Identity." *Middle East Journal* 24, no. 3 (1970): 338–352.

"GPC Foreign Liaison: Statement to JANA." *BBC Summary of World Broadcasts*, May 9, 2000.

Gross, Neil. "A Pragmatist Theory of Social Mechanisms." *American Sociological Review* 74, no. 3 (2009): 358–379.

Gumbel, Andrew. "Libya Weapons Deal: US Neo-Conservatives Jubilant over WMD Agreement." *Independent*, December 22, 2003.

Gunnell, John G. "Relativism – The Return of the Repressed." *Political Theory* 21, no. 4 (1993): 563–584.

Gusterson, Hugh. "Missing the End of the Cold War in International Security." In *Cultures of insecurity: states, communities, and the production of danger*, edited by Jutta Weldes, Mark Laffey, and Raymond Duvall, 319–345. Minneapolis: University of Minnesota Press, 1999.

——. "Nuclear Weapons and the Other in the Western Imagination." *Cultural Anthropology* 14, no. 1 (1999): 111–143.

——. "Narrating abolition" [in English]. *Bulletin of the Atomic Scientists* 65, no. 3 (2009): 13–18.

Gwertzman, Bernard. "Libyan Expert: Qaddafi, Desperate to End Libya's Isolation, Sends a 'Gift' to President Bush." Interview with Lisa Anderson, Council on Foreign Relations, December 22, 2003, www.cfr.org/libya/libyan-expert-qaddafi-desperate-end-libyas-isolation-sends-gift-president-bush/p6617.

Haas, Peter M. and Ernst B. Haas. "Pragmatic Constructivism and International Institutions." In *Pragmatism in international relations*, edited by Harry Bauer and Elisabetta Brighi, 103–123. London and New York: Routledge, 2009.

Hall, Peter M. "A Symbolic Interactionist Analysis of Politics." *Sociological Inquiry* 42, nos 3–4 (1972): 35–75.

Halliday, Fred. "The Politics of the Umma: States and Community in Islamic Movements." *Mediterranean Politics* 7, no. 3 (2002): 20–41.

Hansen, Lene. *Security as practice: discourse analysis and the Bosnian war.* New York: Routledge, 2006.

Harrison, Carol E. and Ann Johnson. "Introduction: Science and National Identity." *Osiris* 24 (2009): 1–14.

Hart, Gary. "My Secret Talks with Libya, and Why They Went Nowhere." *The Washington Post*, January 18, 2004.

Hart, John and Shannon N. Kile. "Libya's Renunciation of Nuclear, Biological and Chemical Weapons and Ballistic Missiles." In *SIPRI Yearbook 2005*, edited by SIPRI, 629–648. Oxford: Oxford University Press, 2005.

Hashmi, Sohail H. "Islamic Ethics and Weapons of Mass Destruction. An Argument for Nonproliferation." In *Ethics and weapons of mass destruction: religious and secular perspectives*, edited by Sohail H. Hashmi and Steven P. Lee, 321–352.

Hecht, Gabrielle. "Nuclear Ontologies." *Constellations* 13, no. 3 (2006): 320–331.

———."A Cosmogram for Nuclear Things." *Isis* 98, no. 1 (2007): 100–108.

Hellmann, Gunther. "Creative Intelligence. Pragmatism as a Theory of Thought and Action." In *"Millennium" Special Issue Conference on "Pragmatism in International Relations Theory."* London, 2002.

———. "Pragmatismus." In *Handbuch der Internationalen Politik*, edited by Carlo Masala, Frank Sauer, and Andreas Wilhelm, 148–181. VS Verlag für Sozialwissenschaften, 2010.

Hellmann, Gunther, Helena Rytovuori-Apunen, Jörg Friedrichs, Rudra Sil, Markus Kornprobst and Patrick T. Jackson. "Beliefs as Rules for Action: Pragmatism as a Theory of Thought and Action." *International Studies Review* 11, no. 3 (2009): 638–662.

Hellmann, Gunther, Christian Weber, Frank Sauer and Sonja Schirmbeck. "'Selbstbewusst' und 'stolz'. Das außenpolitische Vokabular der Berliner Republik als Fährte einer Neuorientierung." *Politische Vierteljahresschrift* 48, no. 4 (2007): 650–679.

Herrera, Geoffrey L. *Technology and international transformation: the railroad, the atom bomb, and the politics of technological change*. New York: State University of New York Press, 2006.

Herrera, Yoshiko M. and Bear F. Braumöller. "Symposium: Discourse and Content Analysis." *Qualitative Methods* 2, no. 1 (2004): 15–39.

Hewitt, John P. "Symbols, Objects, and Meanings." In *Handbook of symbolic interactionism*, edited by Larry T. Reynolds and Nancy J. Herman-Kinney, 307–325. Lanham, MD: Rowman & Littlefield, 2003.

Hoffmann, Stanley. "International Relations: The Long Road to Theory." *World Politics* 11, no. 03 (1959): 346–377.

Hollis, Martin, and Steve Smith. *Explaining and understanding international relations*. Oxford and New York: Oxford University Press, 1990.

Holsti, K.J. "National Role Conceptions in the Study of Foreign Policy." *International Studies Quarterly* 14, no. 3 (1970): 233–309.

Hopf, Ted. "The Logic of Habit in International Relations." *European Journal of International Relations* 16, no. 4 (2010): 539–561.

House, Freedom. "Worst of the Worst 2010" (2010). www.freedomhouse.org/sites/default/files/inline_images/Worst%20of%20the%20Worst%202010.pdf.

Hubacher, Interpellation. "Atombewaffnung der Armee." *Amtliches Bulletin der Bundesversammlung* 3 (1966): 474–497.

Hudson, Valerie M. and Christopher S. Vore. "Foreign Policy Analysis Yesterday, Today, and Tomorrow." *Mershon International Studies Review* 39 (October 1995): 209–238.

Hymans, Jacques E.C. *The psychology of nuclear proliferation. Identity, emotions and foreign policy*. Cambridge: Cambridge University Press, 2006.

———. "Theories of Nuclear Proliferation." *The Nonproliferation Review* 13, no. 3 (2006): 455–465.

———. "When Does State Become a 'Nuclear Weapons State'? An Exercise in Measurement Validation." In *Forecasting nuclear proliferation in the 21st century*, edited by

William C. Potter and Gaukhar Mukhatzhanova, 102–123. Stanford, CA: Stanford University Press, 2010.

———. "Botching the Bomb: Why Nuclear Weapons Programs Often Fail on Their Own – and Why Iran's Might, Too." *Foreign Affairs* 91, no. 3 (2012): 44–53.

International Atomic Energy Agency (IAEA). "GOV/2004/12. Implementation of the NPT Safeguards Agreement of the Socialist People's Libyan Arab Jamahiriya. Report by the Director General." 2004.

———. "GOV/2004/33. Implementation of the NPT Safeguards Agreement of the Socialist People's Libyan Arab Jamahiriya. Report by the Director General." 2004.

"Interview with Jadallah Azzuz al-Talhi, Secretary of the People's Bureau of the Libyan People's Committee for Foreign Liaison, AL-HAWADITH." *Foreign Broadcast Information Service*, March 16, 1990, FBIS-NES-90-064.

"Interview with Umar Mustafa al-Muntasir, Secretary of the Libyan People's Bureau for Foreign Liaison and International Cooperation, AL-DIYAR." *Foreign Broadcast Information Service*, May 6, 1993, FBIS-NES-93-094.

Jackson, Patrick T. and Daniel H. Nexon. "Relations Before States: Substance, Process and the Study of World Politics." *European Journal of International Relations* 5, no. 3 (1999): 291–332.

James, William and Bruce Kuklick, eds. *Writings, 1902–1910*. New York: Viking, 1987.

"JANA Editorial on Al-Qadhdafi Weapons Remarks." *Foreign Broadcast Information Service*, June 19 1990, FBIS-NES-90-119.

Jasanoff, Sheila. "Ordering Knowledge, Ordering Society." In *States of knowledge. The co-production of science and social order*, edited by Sheila E. Jasanoff, 13–45. London: Routledge, 2006.

———. "Technology as a Site and Object of Politics." In *The Oxford handbook of contextual political analysis*, edited by Robert E. Goodin and Charles Tilly. Oxford Handbooks of Political Science, 745–763. Oxford and New York: Oxford University Press, 2006.

Jentleson, B.W. and C.A. Whytock. "Who 'Won' Libya? The Force–Diplomacy Debate and its Implications for Theory and Policy." *International Security* 30, no. 3 (2005): 47–86.

Jervis, Robert. "Security Regimes." *International Organization* 36, no. 2 (1982): 357–378.

———. "Models and Cases in the Study of International Conflict" [in English]. *Journal of International Affairs* 44, no. 1 (1990): 81–101.

———. *System effects: complexity in political and social life*. Princeton, NJ: Princeton University Press, 1997.

———. "Signaling and Perception." In *Political psychology*, edited by Kristen R. Monroe, 293–312. Mahwah, NJ: L. Erlbaum, 2002.

Joas, Hans. "Praktische Intersubjektivität. Die Entwicklung des Werkes von George Herbert Mead." Frankfurt am Main: Suhrkamp, 1989.

———. *Pragmatismus und Gesellschaftstheorie*. Frankfurt am Main: Suhrkamp, 1999.

Joffé, E.G.H. "The Role of Islam." In *The Green and the black: Qadhafi's policies in Africa*, edited by René Lemarchand, 38–51. Bloomington: Indiana University Press, 1988.

Katzenstein, Peter J. and Rudra Sil. "Eclectic Theorizing in the Study and Practice of International Relations." In *The Oxford handbook of international relations*, edited by Christian Reus-Smit and Duncan Snidal, 109–130. Oxford and New York: Oxford University Press, 2008.

Kelle, Udo. "'Emergence' vs. 'Forcing' of Empirical Data? A Crucial Problem of 'Grounded Theory' Revisited." *Forum Qualitative Social Research* 6, no. 2 (2005). Available at http://nbn-resolving.de/urn:nbn:de:0114-fqs0502275.

Keller, Reiner. "Analysing Discourse. An Approach from the Sociology of Knowledge." *Forum Qualitative Social Research* 6, no. 3 (2005). Available at http://nbn-resolving.de/urn:nbn:de:0114-fqs0503327.

King, Gary, Robert O. Keohane and Sidney Verba. *Designing social inquiry: scientific inference in qualitative research.* Princeton, NJ: Princeton University Press, 1994.

Kowert, Paul and Jeffrey Legro. "Norms, Identity, and their Limits: A Theoretical Reprise." In *The culture of national security: norms and identity in world politics*, edited by Peter J. Katzenstein. New Directions in World Politics, 451–497. New York: Columbia University Press, 1996.

Kramer, Hugo. "Die Schweiz und die Atomwaffen." *Neue Wege* 57, no. 6 (1963): 166–169.

Kratochwil, Friedrich. "Constructing a New Orthodoxy? Wendt's 'Social Theory of International Politics' and the Constructivist Challenge." *Millennium – Journal of International Studies* 29, no. 1 (2000): 73–101.

——. "The Monologue of 'Science'." *International Studies Review* 5, no. 1 (2003): 124–128.

——. "Of False Promises and Good Bets: A Plea for a Pragmatic Approach to Theory Building (the Tartu Lecture)." *Journal of International Relations and Development* 10, no. 1 (2007): 1–15.

——. "Ten Points to Ponder about Pragmatism. Some Critical Reflections on Knowledge Generation in the Social Sciences." In *Pragmatism in international relations*, edited by Harry Bauer and Elisabetta Brighi, 11–25. London and New York: Routledge, 2009.

Krause, Keith and Andrew Latham. "Constructing Non-Proliferation and Arms Control: The Norms of Western Practice." *Contemporary Security Policy* 19, no. 1 (1998): 23–54.

Krause, Keith and Michael C. Williams. "From Strategy to Security: Foundations of Critical Security Studies." In *Critical security studies concepts and cases*, edited by Keith Krause and Michael C. Williams, 33–59. London: Routledge, 1997.

Krieger, Zanvyl and Ariel Ilan Roth. "Nuclear Weapons in Neo-Realist Theory." *International Studies Review* 9, no. 3 (2007): 369–384.

Kriesi, Hanspeter and Alexander H. Trechsel. *The politics of Switzerland. Continuity and change in a consensus democracy.* Cambridge: Cambridge University Press, 2008.

Kroenig, Matthew. "Exporting the Bomb: Why States Provide Sensitive Nuclear Assistance." *American Political Science Review* 103, no. 01 (2009): 113–133.

——. "Importing the Bomb: Sensitive Nuclear Assistance and Nuclear Proliferation." *Journal of Conflict Resolution* 53, no. 2 (2009): 161–180.

Kupper, Patrick. "Sonderfall Atomenergie. Die bundesstaatliche Atompolitik 1945–1970." *Schweizerische Zeitschrift für Geschichte* 53, no. 1 (2003): 87–93.

Kurki, Milja. "Causes of a Divided Discipline: Rethinking the Concept of Cause in International Relations Theory." *Review of International Studies* 32, no. 2 (2006): 189–216.

Laclau, Ernesto and Chantal Mouffe. *Hegemony and socialist strategy: towards a radical democratic politics.* London: Verso, 1985.

Ladner, Andreas. "Das Parteiensystem der Schweiz." In *Die Parteiensysteme Westeuropas*, edited by Oskar Niedermayer, Richard Stöss, and Melanie Haas, 397–420. Wiesbaden: VS Verlag für Sozialwissenschaften, 2006.

Laffey, Mark. "Locating Identity: Performativity, Foreign Policy and State Action." *Review of International Studies* 26, no. 3 (2000): 429–444.

Laffey, Mark and Jutta Weldes. "Beyond Belief: Ideas and Symbolic Technologies in the Study of International Relations." *European Journal of International Relations* 3, no. 2 (1997): 193–237.

Lancaster, John. "Libyan Pilgrimage Flights Challenge Sanctions." *The Washington Post*, April 20, 1995, A34.

Lapid, Yosef. "Culture's Ship: Returns and Departures in International Relations Theory." In *The return of culture and identity in IR theory*, edited by Yosef Lapid and Friedrich Kratochwil, 3–20. Boulder, CO: Lynne Rienner, 1996.

Larsen, Henrik. *Foreign policy and discourse analysis: France, Britain, and Europe*. London and New York: Routledge, 1997.

Latham, Andrew. "Constructing National Security: Culture and Identity in Indian Arms Control and Disarmament Practice." *Contemporary Security Policy* 19, no. 1 (1998): 129–158.

Lebow, Richard Ned. "Social Science as an Ethical Practice." *Journal of International Relations and Development* 10, no. 1 (2007): 16–24.

Leites, Nathan. *A study of Bolshevism*. Glencoe, IL: Free Press, 1953.

Lemarchand, René. "Beyond the Mad Dog Syndrome." In *The Green and the black: Qadhafi's policies in Africa*, edited by René Lemarchand, 1–15. Bloomington: Indiana University Press, 1988.

Lepgold, Joseph. "Is Anyone Listening? International Relations Theory and the Problem of Policy Relevance." *Political Science Quarterly* 113, no. 1 (1998): 43–62.

Levite, Ariel E. "Never Say Never Again: Nuclear Reversal Revisited." *International Security* 27, no. 3 (2002): 59–88.

"Libyan Foreign Ministry: Statement to JANA." *BBC Monitoring Middle East*, March 22, 2002.

"Libyan General People's Congress Resolutions." *Foreign Broadcast Information Service*, March 2, 1985, V. 7 Mar 85 Q 4–11.

"Libyan WMD: Tripoli's Statement in Full." *BBC News*, December 20, 2003.

Ludi, Regula. "Demystification or Restoration of Neutrality? Confronting the History of the Nazi Era in Switzerland." *Holocaust Studies: A Journal of Culture and History* 11, no. 3 (2005): 24–52.

MacKenzie, Donald. "Missile Accuracy: A Case Study in the Social Processes of Technological Change." In *The Social construction of technological systems: new directions in the sociology and history of technology*, edited by Wiebe E. Bijker, Thomas Parke Hughes and T.J. Pinch, 195–222. Cambridge, MA: MIT Press, 1989.

Marquis, Lionel and Pascal Sciarini. "Opinion Formation in Foreign Policy: The Swiss Experience." *Electoral Studies* 18, no. 4 (1999): 453–471.

Martínez, Luis. *The Libyan paradox*. New York and Paris: Columbia University Press, 2007.

McDermott, Rose. *Political psychology in international relations*. Ann Arbor: University of Michigan Press, 2004.

Mead, George H. "The Point of View of Social Behaviorism." In *Mind, Self & Society from the Standpoint of a Social Behaviorist*, edited by George H. Mead and Charles W. Morris, 1–41. Chicago, IL: University of Chicago Press, 1934.

Mearsheimer, John J. "Back to the Future: Instability in Europe after the Cold War." *International Security* 15, no. 1 (1990): 5–56.

——. "The False Promise of International Institutions." *International Security* 19, no. 3 (1994): 5–49.

——. "Nuclear Weapons and Deterrence in Europe." *International Security* 9, no. 3 (1984): 19–46.

Meltzer, Bernard M. "Mind." In *Handbook of symbolic interactionism*, edited by Larry T. Reynolds and Nancy J. Herman-Kinney, 253–266 Lanham, MD: Rowman & Littlefield, 2003.

Mentzos, Stavros. *Der Krieg und seine psychosozialen Funktionen* [in German]. Göttingen: Vandenhoeck und Ruprecht, 2002.

Metzler, Dominique Benjamin. "Die Option einer Nuklearbewaffnung für die Schweizer Armee 1945–1969." *Studien und Quellen* 23 (1997): 121–170.

Meyer, Stephen M. *The dynamics of nuclear proliferation*. Chicago, IL: University of Chicago Press, 1984.

Milivojevic, Marko and Pierre Maurer. *Swiss neutrality and security: armed forces, national defence, and foreign policy* [in English]. New York: St. Martin's Press, 1990.

Miller, Steven E. "The Hegemonic Illusion? Traditional Strategic Studies in Context." *Security Dialogue* 41, no. 6 (2010): 639–648.

Milliken, Jennifer. "The Study of Discourse in International Relations: A Critique of Research and Methods." *European Journal of International Relations* 5, no. 2 (1999): 225–254.

Mills, Jane, Ann Bonner and Karen Francis. "The Development of Constructivist Grounded Theory." *International Journal of Qualitative Methods* 5, no. 1 (2006): 25–35.

Mitzen, Jennifer. "Ontological Security in World Politics: State Identity and the Security Dilemma." *European Journal of International Relations* 12, no. 3 (2006): 341–370.

Möckli, Daniel. *Neutralität, Solidarität, Sonderfall. Die Konzeptionierung der schweizerischen Aussenpolitik der Nachkriegszeit, 1943–1947*. Zürcher Beiträge zur Sicherheitspolitik und Konfliktforschung. edited by Kurt R. Spillmann and Andreas Wenger, vol. 55. Zürich: Forschungsstelle für Sicherheitspolitik und Konfliktanalyse der ETH Zürich, 2000.

Montgomery, Alexander H. and Scott D. Sagan. "The Perils of Predicting Proliferation." *Journal of Conflict Resolution* 53, no. 2 (2009): 302–328.

Moravcsik, Andrew. "Taking Preferences Seriously: A Liberal Theory of International Politics." *International Organization* 51, no. 4 (1997): 513–553.

Morris, Charles W. "Introduction: George H. Mead as a Social Psychologist and Social Philosopher." In *Mind, Self & Society from the Standpoint of a Social Behaviorist*, edited by George H. Mead and Charles W. Morris, ix–xxxv. Chicago, IL: University of Chicago Press, 1934.

Müller, Harald. "Security Cooperation." In *Handbook of international relations*, edited by Walter Carlsnaes, Thomas Risse-Kappen and Beth A. Simmons, 369–391. London, and Thousand Oaks, CA: Sage, 2002.

——. "Libyens Selbstentwaffnung. Ein Modellfall?" *HSFK-Report* 6 (2006).

——. "The Exceptional End to an Extraordinary Libyan Nuclear Quest." In *Nuclear proliferation and international security*, edited by Morten Bremer Mærli and Sverre Lodgaard, 73–95. Abingdon: Routledge, 2007.

Müller, Harald and Andreas Schmidt. "The Little Known Story of Deproliferation. Why States Give Up Nuclear Weapons Activities." In *Forecasting nuclear proliferation in the 21st century*, edited by William C. Potter and Gaukhar Mukhatzhanova, 124–158. Stanford, CA: Stanford University Press, 2010.

Mutimer, David. *The weapons state: proliferation and the framing of security*. Boulder, CO: Lynne Rienner, 2000.

Musolf, Gil R. "The Chicago School." In *Handbook of symbolic interactionism*, edited by Larry T. Reynolds and Nancy J. Herman-Kinney, 91–117. Lanham, MD: Rowman & Littlefield, 2003.

Nationalrat. "5074. Förderung der Atomforschung, 18. Dezember 1946 [Support for Nuclear Research, December 18, 1946]." *Amtliches Bulletin der Bundesversammlung* 5 (1946): 1039–1047.

———. "8509. Ausrüstung der schweizerischen Armee mit Atomwaffen, 17. Dezember 1962 [Equipping the Swiss Army with Nuclear Weapons, December 17, 1962]." *Amtliches Bulletin der Bundesversammlung* 4 (1962): 764–774.

———. "8509. Ausrüstung der schweizerischen Armee mit Atomwaffen, 18. Dezember 1962 [Equipping the Swiss Army with Nuclear Weapons, December 18, 1962]." *Amtliches Bulletin der Bundesversammlung* 4 (1962): 774–792.

Nincic, Miroslav. *Renegade regimes: confronting deviant behavior in world politics.* New York: Columbia University Press, 2005.

Nye, Joseph S. "Maintaining a Nonproliferation Regime." *International Organization* 35, no. 1 (1981): 15–38.

Nye, Joseph S., Jr. and Sean M. Lynn-Jones. "International Security Studies: A Report of a Conference on the State of the Field." *International Security* 12, no. 4 (1988): 5–27.

Oevermann, Ulrich. "Die Struktur sozialer Deutungsmuster." *Sozialer Sinn* 1 (2001): 35–81.

Ogilvie-White, Tanya. "Is There a Theory of Nuclear Proliferation? An Analysis of the Contemporary Debate." *The Nonproliferation Review* 4, no. 1 (1996): 43–60.

"Olmert's Nuclear Slip-up Sparks Outrage in Israel." *Times Online*, December 12, 2006.

Otman, Waniss A. and Erling Karlberg. *The Libyan economy economic diversification and international repositioning.* Berlin: Springer, 2007.

Paul, T.V. *Power versus prudence: why nations forgo nuclear weapons.* Montreal: McGill-Queen's University Press, 2000.

Payne, Rodger A. "Neorealists as Critical Theorists: The Purpose of Foreign Policy Debate." *Perspectives on Politics* 5, no. 3 (2007): 503–514.

Peirce, Charles S. "Some Consequences of Four Incapacities." *The Journal of Speculative Philosophy* 2, no. 3 (1868): 140–157.

———. "The Fixation of Belief." *Popular Science Monthly* 12 (1877).

Pelopidas, Benoît. "The Oracles of Proliferation." *The Nonproliferation Review* 18, no. 1 (2011): 297–314.

"People's Bureau for Foreign Liaison: Statement on US Decision to Close People's Bureau." *BBC Summary of World Broadcasts*, May 7, 1981, ME/6719/A/2.

"Permanent Mission of the Libyan Arab Jamahiriya to the United Nations Addressed to the Secretary-General." *UN Security Council*, June 23, 1993, S/25990.

Petitpierre, Max. "321. Exposé relatif à la Conférence des Ambassadeurs de 1947." *Diplomatische Dokumente der Schweiz* Bd. 17, Nr. 26 (12.9.1947 dodis.ch/321).

Potter, William C. and Gaukhar Mukhatzhanova, eds. *Forecasting nuclear proliferation in the 21st century. The role of theory,* vol. I. Stanford, CA: Stanford University Press, 2010.

Pouliot, Vincent. "The Logic of Practicality: A Theory of Practice of Security Communities" [in English]. *International Organization* 62, no. 2 (2008): 257–288.

Probst, Raymond. "Die "guten Dienste" der Schweiz." *Annuaire de l'Association Suisse de Science Politique = Jahrbuch der Schweizerischen Vereinigung für politische Wissenschaft* 3 (1963): 21–49.

Prus, Robert. "Ancient Forerunners." In *Handbook of symbolic interactionism,* edited by Larry T. Reynolds and Nancy J. Herman-Kinney, 19–38. Lanham, MD: Rowman & Littlefield, 2003.

Qaddafi, Muammar. *The green book: the solution to the problem of democracy, the solution to the economic problem, the social basis of the third universal theory.* Reading, MA: Ithaca Press, 2005.

Randall, Nick. "Imagining the Polity: Cinema and Television Fictions as Vernacular Theories of British Politics." *Parliamentary Affairs* 64, no. 2 (2011): 263–280.

Reckwitz, Andreas. "Toward a Theory of Social Practices: A Development in Culturalist Theorizing." *European Journal of Social Theory* 5, no. 2 (2002 2002): 243–263.

Reiss, Mitchell. *Without the bomb: the politics of nuclear nonproliferation.* New York: Columbia University Press, 1988.

Reynolds, Larry T. "Intellecual Precursors." In *Handbook of symbolic interactionism*, edited by Larry T. Reynolds and Nancy J. Herman-Kinney, 39–58. Lanham, MD: Rowman & Littlefield, 2003.

Rhodes, Edward. "Nuclear Weapons and Credibility: Deterrence Theory Beyond Rationality." *Review of International Studies* 14, no. 1 (1988): 45–62.

Riklin, Alois. "Die Neutralität der Schweiz." In *Schriftenreihe der Schweizerischen Gesellschaft für Aussenpolitik*, edited by Hans Haug, Alois Riklin, and Raymond Probst, 191–209. Bern: Haupt, 1992.

Risse-Kappen, Thomas and Kathryn Sikkink. "The Socialization of International Human Rights Norms into Domestic Practices: Introduction." In *The power of human rights: international norms and domestic change*, edited by Thomas Risse-Kappen, Steve C. Ropp and Kathryn Sikkink, 1–38. New York: Cambridge University Press, 1999.

Risse-Kappen, Thomas, Steve C. Ropp and Kathryn Sikkink, eds. *The power of human rights: international norms and domestic change.* New York: Cambridge University Press, 1999.

Ronen, Yehudit. *Qaddafi's Libya in world politics.* Boulder, CO: Lynne Rienner, 2008.

Roos, Ulrich. *Deutsche Außenpolitik: Eine Rekonstruktion der grundlegenden Handlungsregeln.* Wiesbaden: VS, 2010.

Rorty, Richard. *Consequences of pragmatism: essays 1972–1980.* Minneapolis: University of Minnesota Press, 1982.

——. "Response to Robert Brandom." In *Rorty and His Critics*, edited by Robert B. Brandom, 183–190. Malden, MA: Blackwell, 2000.

——. *Philosophy as cultural politics. Philosophical papers*, vol. 4, 2007.

Rosenau, James. "Probing Puzzles Persistently: A Desirable but Improbable Future for IR Theory." In *International theory: positivism and beyond*, edited by Steve Smith, Ken Booth, and Marysia Zalewski, 309–317. Cambridge: Cambridge University Press, 1996.

Roumani, Jacques. "From Republic to Jamahiriya – Libya Search for Political Community." *Middle East Journal* 37, no. 2 (1983): 151–168.

Rublee, Maria Rost. *Nonproliferation norms. Why states choose nuclear restraint.* Athens: University of Georgia Press, 2009.

Ruggie, John Gerard. "Continuity and Transformation in the World Polity: Toward a Neorealist Synthesis." *World Politics* 35, no. 2 (1983): 261–285.

Russell, Bertrand, and Albert Einstein. "The Russell-Einstein Manifesto." London, 1955.

Sagan, Scott D. "Why Do States Build Nuclear Weapons? Three Models in Search of a Bomb." *International Security* 21, no. 3 (1996): 54–86.

——. "Nuclear Latency and Nuclear Proliferation." In *Forecasting nuclear proliferation in the 21st century*, edited by William C. Potter and Gaukhar Mukhatzhanova, 80–101. Stanford, CA: Stanford University Press, 2010.

——. "The Causes of Nuclear Weapons Proliferation." *Annual Review of Political Science* 14, no. 1 (2011): 225–244.

Sandbothe, Mike. *Die Renaissance des Pragmatismus: aktuelle Verflechtungen zwischen analytischer und kontinentaler Philosophie*. 1. Aufl. ed. Weilerswist: Velbrück Wissenschaft, 2000.

Schneider, Barry R. "Nuclear Proliferation and Counter-Proliferation: Policy Issues and Debates." *Mershon International Studies Review* 38, no. 2 (1994): 209–234.

Schütz, Alfred. *The Phenomenology of the Social World*. Evanston, IL: Northwestern University Press, 1967.

Schweizerische Bewegung gegen die atomare Aufrüstung [Swiss Movement against Atomic Armament]. "Aufruf an das Schweizervolk [Appeal to the Swiss people]." 1958.

——. "Atombulletin Nr. 16." March 1962.

——. "Das Schweizervolk ist gewarnt!," 1962.

——. "Millionen Menschen in allen Ländern der Welt." 1962.

——. "Atombulletin Nr. 23." April 1963.

——. "Noch ist es Zeit!," 1963.

——. "Vertrauen zur Demokratie!," 1963.

Schweizerisches Aktionskomitee gegen die Atominitiative [Swiss Action Committee against the Nuclear Initiative]. "Pressedienst Nr. 3." 1962.

——. "Pressedienst Nr. 4." 1962.

——. "Pressedienst Nr. 5." 1962.

——. "Pressedienst Nr. 6." 1962.

——. "Pressedienst Nr. 7." 1962.

——. "Pressedienst Nr. 9." 1962.

——. "Pressedienst Nr. 10." 1962.

——. "Pressedienst Nr. 11." 1962.

——. "Pressedienst Nr. 12." 1962.

——. "Pressedienst Nr. 1." 1963.

——. "Pressedienst Nr. 9." 1963.

Seibt, Constantin. "Die Macht der PR-Agentur Farner." *Tagesanzeiger*, November 25, 2009.

Shalin, Dimitri N. "The Pragmatic Origins of Symbolic Interactionism and the Crisis of Classical Science." *Studies in Symbolic Interaction* 12, no. 12 (1991): 223–251.

Sil, Rudra. "Simplifying Pragmatism: From Social Theory to Problem-driven Eclecticism." *International Studies Review* 11, no. 3 (2009): 648–652.

Sil, Rudra and Peter J. Katzenstein. "Analytic Eclecticism in the Study of World Politics: Reconfiguring Problems and Mechanisms across Research Traditions." *Perspectives on Politics* 8, no. 2 (2010): 411–431.

Simons, Geoffrey L. *Libya and the West: from independence to Lockerbie*. Oxford: Oxford University Press, 2003.

Skocpol, Theda. "The Dead End of Matatheory." *Contemporary Sociology* 16, no. 1 (1987): 10–12.

Smith, Roger K. "Explaining the Non-Proliferation Regime: Anomalies for Contemporary International Relations Theory." *International Organization* 41, no. 2 (1987): 253–281.

Smith, Steve. "The Discipline of International Relations: Still an American Social Science?" *The British Journal of Politics & International Relations* 2, no. 3 (2000): 374–402.

——. "International Relations and international relations: The Link between Theory and Practice in World Politics." *Journal of International Relations and Development* 6, no. 3 (2003): 233–239.

Snyder, Richard C., H.W. Bruck and Burton M. Sapin. *Decision-making as an approach to the study of international politics*. Princeton, NJ: Princeton University Press, 1954.

Solingen, Etel. *Nuclear logics: contrasting paths in East Asia and the Middle East*. Princeton, NJ: Princeton University Press, 2007.

St. John, Ronald B. "The Libyan Debacle in sub-Saharan Africa 1969–1987." In *The green and the black: Qadhafi's policies in Africa*, edited by René Lemarchand, 125–136. Bloomington: Indiana University Press, 1988.

——. "Libya Is Not Iraq: Preemptive Strikes, WMD and Diplomacy." *The Middle East Journal* 58, no. 3 (2004): 386–402.

Ständerat. "5074. Förderung der Atomforschung, 8. Oktober 1946 [Support for Nuclear Research, October 8, 1946]." *Amtliches Bulletin der Bundesversammlung* 4 (1946): 260–273.

——. "5974. Förderung der Atomforschung, 16. Oktober 1946 [Support for Nuclear Research, October 16, 1946]." *Amtliches Bulletin der Bundesversammlung* 4 (1946): 292–296.

"Statement by Abuzed Omar Dorda to the 2000 NPT Review Conference." *2000 Review Conference of the Parties to the NPT, Final Document*, April 25, 2000, NPT/CONF.2000/28.

Strasser, Bruno J. "The Coproduction of Neutral Science and Neutral State in Cold War Europe: Switzerland and International Scientific Cooperation, 1951–69." *Osiris* 24, no. 1 (2009): 165–187.

Strauss, Anselm L. *Qualitative analysis for social scientists*. Cambridge and New York: Cambridge University Press, 1987.

——. *Mirrors & masks: the search for identity*. New Brunswick, NJ: Transaction Publishers, 1997.

Strauss, Anselm and Juliet Corbin. "Grounded Theory Methodology: An Overview." In *Handbook of qualitative research*, edited by Norman K. Denzin and Yvonna S. Lincoln, 273–285. Thousand Oaks, CA: Sage, 1994.

——. *Basics of qualitative research: techniques and procedures for developing grounded theory*, 2nd edn. Thousand Oaks, CA: Sage, 1998.

Stritzel, Holger. "Towards a Theory of Securitization: Copenhagen and Beyond." *European Journal of International Relations* 13, no. 3 (2007): 357–383.

Strübing, Jörg. *Grounded Theory. Zur sozialtheoretischen und epistemologischen Fundierung des Verfahrens der empirisch begründeten Theoriebildung*. Wiesbaden: VS, 2004.

——. *Pragmatische Wissenschafts- und Technikforschung. Theorie und Methode*. Frankfurt: Campus Verlag, 2005.

Stryker, Sheldon. *Symbolic interactionism. A social structural version*. Menlo Park, CA: Benjamin/Cummings, 1980.

Stüssi-Lauterburg, Jürg. *Historischer Abriss zur Frage einer Schweizer Nuklearbewaffnung*. Bern: Jürg Stüssi-Lauterburg, 1995.

Takeyh, Ray. "The Rogue Who Came In from the Cold." *Foreign Affairs* 80, no. 3 (2001): 62–72.

Tannenwald, Nina. *The nuclear taboo: the United States and the non-use of nuclear weapons since 1945*. Cambridge: Cambridge University Press, 2007.

Tate, Trevor McMorris. "Regime-Building in the Non-Proliferation System." *Journal of Peace Research* 27, no. 4 (1990): 399–414.

Taylor, Bryan C. and William J. Kinsella. "Introduction: Linking Nuclear Legacies and Communication Studies." In *Nuclear legacies: communication, controversy, and the*

U.S. nuclear weapons complex, edited by Bryan C. Taylor, William J. Kinsella, Stephen P. Depoe and Maribeth S. Metzler, 1–37. Lanham, MD: Lexington Books, 2008.

Taylor, Charles. *Philosophy and the human sciences. Philosophical papers.* Cambridge: Cambridge University Press, 1985.

Thomas, William Isaac, and Dorothy Swaine Thomas. *The child in America: behavior problems and programs.* New York: Johnson, 1970.

Tickner, J. Ann. "Feminist Perspectives on International Relations." In *Handbook of international relations*, edited by Walter Carlsnaes, Thomas Risse-Kappen, and Beth A. Simmons, 275–291. London, and Thousand Oaks, CA: Sage, 2002.

Titscher, Stefan, Michael Meyer, Ruth Wodak, Eva Vetter and Bryan Jenner. *Methods of text and discourse analysis.* London: Sage, 2000.

Tuathail, Gearóid Ó. "Review essay: Dissident IR and the identity politics narrative: a sympathetically skeptical perspective." *Political Geography* 15, nos 6–7 (1996): 647–653.

Uhlmann, Ernst. "Die Zielsetzung unserer Landesverteidigung." *Allgemeine schweizerische Militärzeitschrift* 121, no. 4 (1955): 235–241.

UN General Assembly. "Verbatim Record of the 32nd Meeting." A/C.1/41/PV.32, 1986.

———. "Model Nuclear Weapons Convention." 2007.

Vandewalle, Dirk J. *A history of modern Libya.* Cambridge and New York: Cambridge University Press, 2006.

Vatter, Adrian. "Vom Extremtyp zum Normalfall? Die schweizerische Konsensus-demokratie im Wandel: Eine Re-Analyse von Lijpharts Studie für die Schweiz von 1997 bis 2007." *Swiss Political Science Review* 14, no. 1 (2008): 1–47.

Vuori, Juha A. "Illocutionary Logic and Strands of Securitization: Applying the Theory of Securitization to the Study of Non-Democratic Political Orders." *European Journal of International Relations* 14, no. 1 (2008): 65–99.

Wæver, Ole. "Securitization and Desecuritization." In *On security*, edited by Ronnie D. Lipschutz, 46–86. New York: Columbia University Press, 1995.

———. "The Sociology of a Not So International Discipline: American and European Developments in International Relations." *International Organization* 52, no. 4 (1998): 687–727.

———. "Identity, Communities and Foreign Policy." In *European integration and national identity: the challenge of the Nordic states*, edited by Lene Hansen and Ole Waever, 20–50. London: Routledge, 2002.

———. "Securitisation: Taking Stock of a research programme in Security Studies." Copenhagen 2003.

———. "Discursive Approaches." In *European integration theory*, edited by Antje Wiener and Thomas Diez, 197–215. Oxford and New York: Oxford University Press, 2004.

Walker, William. "The Absence of a Taboo on the Possession of Nuclear Weapons." *Review of International Studies* 36, no. 4 (2010): 865–876.

Wallace, William. "Truth and Power, Monks and Technocrats: Theory and Practice in International Relations." *Review of International Studies* 22, no. 3 (1996): 301–321.

Walsh, Jim. "Bombs Unbuilt: Power, Ideas and Institutions in International Politics" (dissertation manuscript). Massachusetts Institute of Technology, 2001.

———. "Learning from Past Success: The NPT and the Future of Non-Proliferation." Edited by Weapons of Mass Destruction Commission. Stockholm, 2005.

Walt, Stephen. "The Renaissance of Security Studies." *International Studies Quarterly* 35, no. 2 (1991): 211–239.

Walton, John. "Making the Theoretical Case." In *What is a case? Exploring the foundations of social inquiry*, edited by Howard S. Becker and Charles C. Ragin, 121–137. Cambridge: Cambridge University Press, 2000.

Waltz, Kenneth N. *The spread of nuclear weapons: more may be better*. Adelphi Papers. London: International Institute for Strategic Studies, 1981.

——. "Nuclear Myths and Political Realities." *The American Political Science Review* 84, no. 3 (1990): 731–745.

——. "The Emerging Structure of International Politics." *International Security* 18, no. 2 (1993): 44–79.

Wehrwissenschaft, Verein zur Förderung des Wehrwillens und der. "Stellungnahme: Aktuelle Militärpolitik." 1962.

Weldes, Jutta. "Constructing National Interests." *European Journal of International Relations* 2, no. 3 (1996): 275–318.

Weldes, Jutta, Mark Laffey, Hugh Gusterson and Raymond Duvall, eds. *Cultures of insecurity: states, communities, and the production of danger*. Minneapolis: University of Minnesota Press, 1999.

Wendt, Alexander. "On Constitution and Causation in International Relations." *Review of International Studies* 24, no. 5 (1998): 101–118.

——. *Social theory of international politics*. Cambridge: Cambridge University Press, 1999.

Wenger, Andreas. "Swiss Security Policy: From Autonomy to Co-operation." In *Swiss foreign policy, 1945–2002*, edited by Jürg Martin Gabriel and Thomas Fischer, 23–46. Basingstoke and New York: Palgrave Macmillan, 2003.

Wiener, Antje. "Enacting Meaning-in-Use: Qualitative Research on Norms and International Relations." *Review of International Studies* 35, no. 1 (2009): 175–193.

Wildi, Tobias. *Der Traum vom eigenen Reaktor die schweizerische Atomtechnologieentwicklung 1945–1969*. Zürich: Chronos, 2003.

Winkler, Theodor. *Kernenergie und Aussenpolitik die internationalen Bemühungen um eine Nichtweiterverbreitung von Kernwaffen und die friedliche Nutzung der Kernenergie in der Schweiz*. Berlin: Berlin Verlag, 1981.

Wohlstetter, Albert J. *Moving Toward Life in a Nuclear Armed Crowd? Final Report Prepared for U.S. Arms Control and Disarmament Agency*. Pan Heuristics, 1976.

Woker, Gertrud "Atomaufrüstung auch in der Schweiz? Zur Erklärung von 35 prominenten Sozialdemokraten und Gewerkschaftern." *Neue Wege* 52, nos 7–8 (1958): 206–211.

Wollenmann, Reto. *Zwischen Atomwaffe und Atomsperrvertrag. Die Schweiz auf dem Weg von der nuklearen Option zum Nonproliferationsvertrag (1958–1969)*. Zürcher Beiträge zur Sicherheitspolitik und Konfliktforschung. Zürich: ETH, 2004.

World Bank. *The economic development of Libya*. Washington, DC, 1960.

Wright, John. *Libya, a modern history*. Baltimore, MD: Johns Hopkins University Press, 1982.

Yanow, Dvora. "Thinking Interpretively: Philosophical Presuppositions and the Human Sciences." In *Interpretation and method: empirical research methods and the interpretive turn*, edited by Dvora Yanow and Peregrine Schwartz-Shea, 5–26. Armonk, NY: M.E. Sharpe, 2006.

Yusuf, Moeed. "Predicting Proliferation: The History of the Future of Nuclear Weapons." *Policy Paper* 11 (2009).

Index

Page numbers in *italics* denote tables, those in **bold** denote figures.